ELEMENTARY SKETCHES

OF

MORAL PHILOSOPHY,

DELIVERED AT

THE ROYAL INSTITUTION,

IN THE YEARS

1804, 1805, AND 1806.

BY THE LATE

REV. SYDNEY SMITH, M.A

NEW YORK:
HARPER & BROTHERS, PUBLISHERS,
329 & 331 PEARL STREET,
FRANKLIN SQUARE.
1855.

INTRODUCTION.

THESE Lectures were privately printed, in the hope that Mr. Sydney Smith's remaining friends would feel some interest in the occupations of his early years. By these partial judges they have been very generally approved. Several eminent men have counseled their publication; but their fragmental and elementary state seemed to forbid it.

The following letter from Lord Jeffrey (written but three days before his sudden illness, which terminated fatally) appears to be *so decisive* of their publication, that, under the shadow of *such* authority, and with the deepest feelings of gratitude to him for the candor and the affectionate approval shown toward their author, they are no longer withheld from the public.

"Edinburgh, January 18th, 1850.

"My ever dear Mrs. Smith,

"I can not tell you how grateful I am to you for having sent me this book; not merely (or chiefly) as a proof of your regard, or as a memorial of its loved and lamented author, but for the great and unexpected pleasure I have already derived, and feel sure I shall continue to derive, from its perusal. Though it came to me in the middle of my judicial avocations, and when my infirm health scarcely admitted of any avoidable application, I have been tempted, in the course of the last two days, to read more than the half of it! and find it so much more original, interesting, and instructive than I had anticipated, that I can not *rest* till I have not merely expressed my thanks to you for the gratification I have received, but made some amends for the rash and I fear somewhat ungracious judgment I passed upon it, after perusing a few passages of the manuscript, some years ago. I have not recognized any of these passages in any part of the print I am now reading, and think I must have been unfortunate in the selection, or chance, by which I was then directed to them. But, however that be, I am now satisfied that in what I then said, *I did great and grievous injustice* to the merit of these Lectures, and was *quite wrong* in dissuading their publication, or concluding that they would add nothing to the reputation of the author; on the contrary, my firm impression is, that, with few exceptions, they will do him as much credit as any thing he ever wrote, and produce, on the whole, a stronger impression of the force and vivacity of his intellect, as well as a *truer* and more engaging view of his character, than most of what the world has yet seen of his writings. The book seems to me to be full of good sense, acuteness, and right feeling —very clearly and pleasingly written—and with such an admirable mixture of logical intrepidity, with the absence of all dogmatism, as is rarely met with in the conduct of such discussions. Some of the conclusions may be questionable; but I do think them generally just, and never propounded with any thing like arrogance or in any tone of assumption, and the whole subject treated with quite as much, either of subtilty or profund ity, as was compatible with *a popular* exposition of it.

"I *retract* therefore, peremptorily and firmly, the advice I formerly gave against the publication of these discourses; and earnestly recommend you to lose no time in letting the public at large have the pleasure and benefit of their perusal. The subject, perhaps, may prevent them from making any great or immediate sensation; but I feel that they will excite considerable interest, and command universal respect; while the previous circulation of your 100 *eleemosynary* copies, among persons who probably include the most authoritative and efficient guides of public taste and opinion now living, must go far to secure its early and favorable notice.

"I write this hurriedly, after finishing my legal preparations for to-morrow, and feel that I shall sleep better for this disburdening of my conscience. I feel, too, as if I was secure of your acceptance of this tardy recantation of my former heresies; and that you will be pleased, and even perhaps a little proud, of your convertite! But if not, I can only say that I shall willingly submit to any penance you can find in your heart to impose on me. I know enough of that heart of old, not to be very apprehensive of its severity; and now good night, and God bless you! I am very old, and have many infirmities; but I am tenacious of old friendships, and find much of my present enjoyments in the recollections of the past.

"With all good and kind wishes,

"Ever very gratefully and affectionately yours,

"F. Jeffrey."

NOTE.

These Elementary Lectures, on Moral (or Mental) Philosophy, were delivered in the Royal Institution in the years 1804–5–6, before a mixed audience of ladies and gentlemen, upon a subject very little considered then in this country.

They are scarcely more than an enumeration of those great men that have originated and treated on this important science, with a short account of their various opinions, and frequent compilations from their works.

Though Mr. Sydney Smith had had the advantage of a close attendance, for five years, upon the beautiful lectures delivered by Mr. Dugald Stewart in the University of Edinburgh, and an almost daily communication with him, and with that remarkable man Dr. Thomas Brown, who succeeded Mr. Stewart in the professor's chair of Moral Philosophy, yet *these* Lectures, from the circumstances under which they were delivered, were *necessarily* very superficial; it being *impossible* to fix the attention of persons wholly unaccustomed to such abstruse and difficult subjects, with any beneficial effect, for the prescribed time of the Lecture.

Some portions of the first course of Lectures were, a few years after, amplified and embodied in the "Edinburgh Review," under the titles of Professional Education,* Female Education, and Public Schools; and as he considered what remained could be of no further use, he destroyed several, and was proceeding to destroy the whole. An earnest entreaty was made that those not yet torn up might be spared, and it was granted.

* These subjects were introduced in the Lectures on Memory, on Imagination, and on Association.

These Lectures then (the first course being rendered very imperfect, though from the ninth they are perfect and consecutive) profess to be nothing more than a *popular colloquial sketch* of a very curious and interesting subject, written to be *spoken.* They are given in clear language, often illustrated by happy allusions, by eloquence, and by a playfulness of fancy that was eminently his own.

Though *very far* from a *learned* book, it may prove perhaps an interesting one; conveying great truths, and much useful knowledge, in a less dry and repulsive shape than in a discussion on Moral Philosophy they are commonly to be found.

CONTENTS.

FRAGMENT OF LECTURE VIII.

LECTURE IX.

LECTURE X.

LECTURE XI.

LECTURE XII.

LECTURE XIII.

LECTURE XIV.

LECTURE XV.

LECTURE XVI.

LECTURE XVII.

LECTURE XVIII.

LECTURE XIX.

LECTURE XX.

LECTURE XXI.

LECTURE XXII.

LECTURE XXIII.

LECTURE XXIV.

LECTURE XXV.

LECTURE XXVI.

LECTURE XXVII.

LECTURES.

INTRODUCTORY LECTURE.

By the term Moral Philosophy, is *popularly* understood ethical philosophy; or that science which teaches the duties of life: but Moral Philosophy, properly speaking, is contrasted to natural philosophy; comprehending every thing spiritual, as that comprehends every thing corporeal, and constituting the most difficult and the most sublime of those two divisions under which all human knowledge must be arranged.

In this sense, Moral Philosophy is used by *Berkeley*, by *Hartley*, by *Hutcheson*, by *Adam Smith*, by *Hume*, by *Reid*, and by *Stewart*. In this sense it is taught in the Scotch Universities, where alone it *is* taught in this island; and in this sense it comprehends all the intellectual, active, and moral faculties of man; the laws by which they are governed; the limits by which they are controlled; and the means by which they may be improved: it aims at discovering, by the accurate analysis of his spiritual part, the system of action most agreeable to the intentions of his Maker, and most conducive to the happiness of man.

There is a word of dire sound and horrible import which I would fain have kept concealed if I possibly could; but as this is not feasible, I shall even meet the danger at once, and get out of it as well as I can. The word to which I allude is that very tremendous one of *Metaphysics;* which, in a lecture on Moral Philosophy, seems likely to produce as much alarm as the cry of fire in a crowded play-house, when Belvidera is left to weep by herself, and every one saves himself in the best manner he can. I must beg my audience, however, to sit quiet, till they hear what can be said in defense of Metaphysics, and in the mean time to make use of the language which the manager would probably adopt on such an occasion,—I can assure ladies and gentlemen, there is not the smallest degree of danger.

The term Metaphysics has no sort of relation to its meaning;—and various attempts have been made to substitute a more appropriate word in its place,—hitherto without success. *Psychology*, and *Pneumatology*, are both candidate expressions for filling this vacancy in our language; but though no objections can be stated to either, they have neither of them fairly got into circulation (even among the few who, by cultivating this science, have acquired a right to adjust the language in which it is taught); but by whatever name the science of the human mind is signified, it has precisely the same foundation in reality that any science conversant with the properties of matter can have. The existence of mind is as much a matter of *fact* as the existence of matter: it is as true that men remember, as that oxygen united to carbon makes carbonic acid. I am as sure that anger, and affection, are principles of the human mind, as I am, that grubs make cockchafers; or of any of those great truths which botanists teach of lettuces and cauliflowers. The same patient observation, and the same caution in inferring, are as necessary for the establishment of truth in this science as in any other: rash hypothesis misleads as much, modest diligence repays as well. Whatever has been done for this philosophy has been done by the inductive method only; and to that alone, it must look for all the improvement of which it is capable. So that those who would cast a ridicule upon Metaphysics, or the intellectual part of Moral Philosophy, as if it were vague and indefinite in its object, must either contend that we have no faculties at all, and that no general facts are to be observed concerning them, or they must allow to this science an equal precision with that which any other can claim.

A great deal of unpopularity has been incurred by this science from the extravagances or absurdities of those who have been engaged in it. When the mass of mankind hear that all thought is explained by vibrations and vibratiuncles of the brain,—that there is no such thing as a material world,—that what mankind consider as their arms, and legs, are not arms and legs, but *ideas* accompanied with the notion of *outness*,—that we have not only no bodies, but no minds;—that we are nothing, in short, but currents of reflection and sensation; all this, I admit, is well calculated to approximate, in the public mind, the ideas of lunacy and intellectual philosophy. But if it be fair to argue against a science, from the bad method in which it is prosecuted, such a mode of reasoning ought to have influenced mankind centuries ago to have abandoned all the branches of physics, as utterly hopeless. I have surely an equal right to rake up the moldy errors of all the other sciences;—to reproach astronomy with its vortices,—chemistry with its philosopher's stone,—history with its fables,—law with its cruelty, and ignorance;—and if I were to open this battery against medicine, I do not know where I should stop. Zinzis Khan, when he was most crimsoned with blood, never slaughtered the human race as they have been slaughtered by rash and erroneous theories of medicine.

If there be a real foundation for this science, if observation can do *any thing*, and has not done all, there is room for *hope*, and reason for *exertion*. The extravagances by which it has been disgraced, ought to warn us of the difficulty, without leading us to despair. To say there is no path, because we have often got into the wrong path, puts an end to all other knowledge as well as to this.

The truth is, it fares worse with this science than with many others, because its errors and extravagances are comprehended by so many. If you tell a man that the ground on which he stamps is not ground, but an idea, he naturally enough thinks you mad. If the same person were told that the planets were rolled about in whirlpools, or that the moon, as Descartes thought, was once a sun,—such a person, who would laugh at the former, might hear these latter opinions advanced, without being struck with their absurdity. Every man is not necessarily an astronomer, but every man has some acquaintance with the operations of his own mind; and you can not deviate *grossly* from the truth on these subjects, without incurring his ridicule, and reprehension. This perhaps is one cause why errors of this nature have been somewhat unduly magnified.

Skepticism, which is commonly laid to the charge of this philosophy, may, in the first place, be fairly said to have done its worst. Bishop Berkeley destroyed this world in one volume octavo; and nothing remained after his time, but mind; which experienced a similar fate from the hand of Mr. Hume in 1737;—so that, with all the tendency to destroy, there remains nothing left for destruction: but I would fain ask if there be any one human being, from the days of Protagoras the Abdērite to this present hour, who was ever for a single instant a convert to these subtile and ingenious follies? Is there any one out of Bedlam who *doubts* of the existence of matter? who doubts of his own personal identity? or of his consciousness? or of the general credibility of memory? Men *talk* on such subjects from ostentation, or because such wire-drawn speculations are an agreeable exercise to them; but they are perpetually recalled by the necessary business and the inevitable feelings of life to sound and sober opinions on these subjects. Errors, to be dangerous, must have a great deal of truth mingled with them; it is only from this alliance that they can ever obtain an extensive circulation: from pure extravagance, and genuine, unmingled falsehood, the world never has, and never can sustain any mischief. It is not in our power to believe all that we please; our belief is modified and restrained by the nature of our faculties, and by the constitution of the objects by which we are surrounded. We may believe any thing for a moment, but we shall soon be lashed out of our impertinence, by hard and stubborn realities. A great philosopher may sit in his study, and deny the existence of matter; but if he take a walk in the streets he must take care to leave his theory behind him. Pyrrho said there was no such thing as pain; and he saw no *proof* that there were such things as carts, and wagons; and he refused to get out of their way: but Pyrrho had, fortunately for him, three or four stout slaves, who followed their master, without following his doctrine; and whenever they saw one of these ideal machines approaching, took him up by the arms and legs, and, without attempting to controvert his arguments, put him down in a place of safety. If you will build an error upon some foundation of truth, you may effect your object; you may divert a little rivulet from the great stream of nature, and train it cautiously, and obliquely, away; but if you place yourself in the very depth of her almighty channel, and combat with her eternal streams, you will be swept off without ruffling the smoothness, or impeding the vigor, of her course.

With respect to skepticism on subjects of natural and revealed religion, I can really see no connection between such species of doubts, and an investigation into the structure of the human mind. Thus much is true, that out of a certain number of men who exercise their understanding vigorously, and the same number who do not exercise it at all, we shall have many more dissentients to any thing established by evidence, among the *first* class, than the *second*. Among a hundred ploughmen, we should not find one skeptic; among the same number of men of very cultivated faculties, we should probably find some who entertained captious and frivolous doubts against religion; but then there is no more probability that *this* science should produce such men, than any *other* science, which compels us to a rigorous exercise of all the powers of the mind: the objection seems to be against exercising the faculties altogether, not against exercising them in this particular manner; but surely it is a sad way to cure the excesses of the human mind, by benumbing it; and a very narrow view of the resources of art, to suppose there is no other remedy for the irregular action of any part, than by its destruction. I might do here what I have done before in speaking of the extravagance of some reasoners upon these subjects,—institute a parallel between the tendency to religious skepticism, produced by *this* science, and *many* others; a much wiser and better man than I, however, shall do it for me. In speaking of the decline of materialism, Mr. Dugald Stewart says:* "There has certainly been, since the time of Descartes, a continual, and, on the whole, a very remarkable approach to the inductive plan of studying human nature. We may trace this in the writings even of those who profess to consider *thought* merely as an agitation of the brain. In the writings of Helvetius and of Hume, both of whom, although they may occasionally have expressed themselves in an unguarded manner concerning the nature of mind, have, in their most useful and practical disquisitions, been prevented, by their own good sense, from blending any theory with respect to the *causes* of the intellectual phenomena with the history of facts, or the investigation of general laws. The authors who form the most conspicuous exceptions to this gradual progress, consist chiefly of men whose errors may be easily accounted for, by the prejudices connected with their circumscribed habits of observation and inquiry;—of physiologists, accustomed to attend to that part alone of the human frame which the knife of the anatomist can lay open;—or of chemists, who enter on the analysis of thought, fresh from the decompositions of the laboratory; carrying into the theory of mind itself (what Bacon expressively calls) the smoke and tarnish of the furnace." But what are we to do? If the enemies of religion derive subtilty and acuteness from this pursuit, ought not their own weapons to be turned against them? and ought not some to study for defense, if others do for the purposes of aggression? When the old anarch Hobbes came out to destroy the foundations of morals, who entered the lists against him? Not a man afraid of metaphysics, not a man who had become skeptical as he had become learned, but Ralph Cudworth, Doctor of Divinity —a man who had learned much from reading the errors of the human mind, and from deep meditation its nature:

* Life of Reid, p. 81. 1802.

who made use of those errors to avoid them, and derived from that meditation principles too broad and too deep to be shaken: such a man was gained to the cause of morality, and religion, by these sciences. These sciences certainly made no infidel of Bishop Warburton, as Chubb, Morgan, Tindal, and half a dozen others found to their cost. Tucker, the author of "The Light of Nature," was no skeptic, Locke was no skeptic, Hartley was no skeptic, nor was Lord Verulam. Malebranche and Arnauld were both of them exceedingly pious men. We none of us can believe that Dr. Paley has exercised his mind upon intellectual philosophy in vain. The fruits of it in him, are sound sense delivered so perspicuously that a man may profit by it, and a child may comprehend it: solid decision, not anticipated by insolence, but earned by fair argument; manly piety, unadulterated by superstition, and never disgraced by cant. The child that is unborn will thank that man for his labors.*

I have already quoted too many names, but I must not omit one which would alone have been sufficient to have shown that there is no necessary connection between skepticism and the philosophy of the human mind; I mean Bishop Butler. To his sermons we are indebted for the complete overthrow of the selfish system; and to his "Analogy," for the most noble and surprising defense of revealed religion, perhaps, which has ever yet been made of any system whatever. But there is no occasion

* Sir James Mackintosh says, in his introductory Law lecture (p. 32):—"The same reason will excuse me for passing over in silence the works of many philosophers and moralists, to whom, in the course of my proposed lectures, I shall owe and confess the greatest obligations; and it might perhaps deliver me from the necessity of speaking of Dr. Paley, if I were not desirous of this public opportunity of professing my gratitude for the instruction and pleasure which I have received from that excellent writer, who possesses, in so eminent a degree, those invaluable qualities of a moralist—good sense, caution, sobriety, and perpetual reference to convenience and practice; and who certainly is thought less original than he really is, merely because his taste and modesty have led him to disdain the ostentation of novelty, and because he generally employs more art to blend his own arguments with the body of received opinions (so as that they are scarce to be distinguished), than other men, in the pursuit of a transient popularity, have exerted to disguise the most miserable commonplaces in the shape of paradox."

to prop this argument up by great names. The school of natural religion is the contemplation of nature; the ancient anatomist who was an atheist, was converted by the study of the human body: he thought it impossible that so many admirable contrivances should exist, without an intelligent cause;—and if men can become religious from looking at an entrail, or a nerve, can they be taught atheism from analyzing the structure of the human mind? Are not the affections and passions which shake the very entrails of man, and the thoughts and feelings which dart along those nerves, more indicative of a God than the vile perishing instruments themselves? Can you remember the nourishment which springs up in the breast of a mother, and forget the *feelings which spring up in her heart?* If God made the blood of man, did he not make that *feeling*, which summons the blood to his face, and makes it the sign of guilt and of shame? You may show me a human hand, expatiate upon the singular contrivance of its sinews, and bones; how admirable, how useful, for all the purposes of grasp, and flexure: *I* will show you, in return, the mind, receiving her tribute from the senses;—*comparing*, *reflecting*, *compounding*, *dividing*, *abstracting*;—the passions *soothing*, *aspiring*, *exciting*, till the whole *world* falls under the dominion of *man;* evincing that in his mind the Creator has reared up the noblest emblem of his wisdom, and his power. The philosophy of the human mind is *no* school for infidelity, but it excites the warmest feelings of piety, and defends them with the soundest reason.

One of the great impediments attendant upon this branch of knowledge is the natural and original difficulty of reflecting upon the operations of our own minds. It is much more easy, for instance, to think of the parts of an intricate machine, than of any act of memory, judgment, or imagination. We may attribute this to the necessity we are under of attending to objects of sense, from our earliest infancy. We are under no necessity of attending with great carefulness and precision to the operations of our minds; but we must examine, over and over again, with extreme care, the ideas of our senses, for the mere purposes of security, and existence: this gives us a familiarity with one set of ideas, that we have had no opportunity of acquiring in the other; and makes this species of study very difficult, and very painful.

Perhaps no habit would ever render it as easy to attend to the manner in which our mind acts, as to attend to those notions we have gathered from the eye, and the ear, and the touch. Providence, intending man for a life of greater activity than contemplation, has placed this impediment to the free exercise of thought, and made use of the pain which generally accompanies profound meditation, as a check and barrier to human power.

Another difficulty which attends this study, is the metaphorical nature of its language. Mankind first give names to the objects of sense which surround them,—to the sun, the wind, the rain, the mountains, woods, and sea; and having established this nomenclature, they call the mind, and its faculties, by the name of some *object* to which they appear to bear a resemblance. For the soul, they have generally taken the name of the most subtile and invisible fluid with which they were acquainted; and, accordingly, in a great variety of languages it is signified by the same word which signifies wind, or breath.*

The misfortune is, that this borrowed language insensibly betrays us into false notions of the human understanding, from which we find it rather difficult to disentangle ourselves. For instance, we talk about recollecting a place as if we had gathered together the

* "It may lead us a little toward the original of all our notions and knowledge, if we remark how great a dependence our words have on *common sensible ideas*, and how those which are made use of to stand for actions and notions quite removed from sense, have their rise from thence, and from obvious, sensible ideas, are transferred to more abstruse significations, and made to stand for ideas, that come not under the cognizance of our senses; v. g., to imagine, apprehend, comprehend, adhere, conceive, instill, disgust, disturbance, tranquillity, &c., are all words taken from the operations of *sensible* things, and applied to certain modes of *thinking*. Spirit, in its *primary* signification, is breath;—angel, a messenger: and I doubt not, but, if we could trace them to their sources, we should find, in all languages, the names, which stand for things that fall under our senses, to have had their first rise from sensible ideas."—*Locke*, book iii. chap. i. paragraph 5, p. 190.

ideas of the parlor, and the drawing-room, and the grass-plot, which lay dispersed in different parts of the brain, and put them into the order in which they really exist. This is what the *word* seems to suggest, and what, I fancy, many people actually suppose to take place in their understandings; whereas the real fact is (as I shall show in some future lecture at full length), that one idea of the whole train first presents itself to our mind, and after we have made every effort to dwell upon, and retain *this*, the others follow of their own accord, without any power of ours, exactly in the order in which they had been previously observed. It would, however, be extremely curious and useful, to collect, in a great variety of languages, all the similitudes which mankind have hit upon, for the operations and divisions of the faculties of the mind. Such a long, extensive, and authentic record of human opinions upon these subjects, might give birth to many interesting speculations, and throw some light upon questions which have long been the opprobrium of this science.

Some very considerable men are accustomed to hold very strong and sanguine language respecting the important discoveries which are to be made in Moral Philosophy, from a close attention to facts; and by that method of induction which has been so invaluably employed in Natural Philosophy: but then this appears to be the difference;—that Natural Philosophy is directed to subjects with which we are little or imperfectly acquainted; Moral Philosophy investigates faculties we have always exercised, and passions we have always felt. Chemistry, for instance, is perpetually bringing to light fresh existences; four or five new metals have been discovered within as many years, of the existence of which no human being could have had any suspicion; but no man, that I know of, pretends to discover four or five new passions, neither can any thing very new be discovered of those passions and faculties with which mankind are already familiar. We are, in natural philosophy, perpetually making discoveries of new properties in bodies, with whose existence we have been acquainted for centuries: Sir James Hall has just discovered that lime can be melted by carbonic acid;—but who hopes that he can discover any new flux for avarice? or any improved method of judging, and comparing? We have have had no occasion to busy ourselves with the chromian or Titanian metal; but we have commonly employed our minds for twenty or thirty years, before we begin to speculate upon them.

There may, indeed, be speculative discoveries made with respect to the human mind; for instance, Mr. Dugald Stewart contends that attention should be classed among our faculties. Now if attention be a faculty, it is certainly a *discovery*, for nobody had ever so classed it before Mr. Stewart: but whether it be so, or only a mode of other faculties, it is of no consequence in practice; for nobody has ever been ignorant of the importance and efficacy of attention, whether it be one thing, or whether it be the other.

So with that notion of the Rev. Mr. Gay's, that all our passions are explicable upon the principle of association; if this opinion be true, it is a *discovery*, and a curious one. But then it affords no practical rule, for mankind are too much acquainted with practical rules to allow of such pure novelty as would constitute discovery.

Of the *uses* of this science of Moral Philosophy one is—the vigor and acuteness, which it is apt to communicate to the faculties. The slow and cautious pace of mathematics is not fit for the rough road of life; it teaches no habits which will be of use to us when we come to march in good earnest: it will not do, when men come to real business, to be calling for axioms, and definitions, and to admit nothing without full proof, and perfect deduction; we must decide sometimes upon the slightest evidence, catch the faintest surmise, and get to the end of an affair before a mathematical head could decide about its commencement. I am not comparing the general value of the two sciences, but merely their value as preparatory exercises for the mind; and there, it appears to me that the science of Moral Philosophy is much better calculated to form intellectual habits, useful in real life. The subtilties about mind and matter, cause and effect, perception and sensation, may be forgotten; but the power of nice discrimination, of arresting and examining the most subtile and evanescent ideas, and of striking rapidly, and boldly, into the faintest track of analogy; to see where it leads, and what it will produce; an emancipation from the *tyranny of words*, an undaunted intrepidity to push opinions up to their first causes;—all these virtues remain, in the dexterous politician, the acute advocate, and the unerring judge.

I have said that no practical discoveries can be made in Moral Philosophy, because I think the word *discovery* implies so much originality, and novelty, that I can hardly suppose they will be met with in a subject with which mankind are so familiar. But then opinions may be discoveries to the individual, which are not discoveries to the world at large. It may be of incalcuable advantage to me, at an early period of life, to guard my understanding from the pernicious effects of association; though those effects can not now be pointed out for the first time; I might have learned something about association *without* the aid of this science, by the mere intercourse of life, but I should not have learned that lesson so early, and so well. I am no longer left to gather this important law of my nature from accidental and disconnected remark, but it is brought fully and luminously before me;—I see that one man differs from another in the rank and nobleness of his understanding, in proportion as he counteracts this intellectual attraction of cohesion; I become permanently, and vigilantly, suspicious of this principle in my own mind; and when called upon, in the great occasions of life, to think, and to act, I separate my judgment from the mere accidents of my life, and decide, not according to the casualties of my fortune, but the unbiased dictates of my reason: without this science, I might have had a general, and faint suspicion—with it, I have a rooted and operative conviction—of the errors to which my understanding is exposed. If it be useful to our talents, and virtues, to turn the mind inwardly upon itself, and to observe attentively the facts relative to our passions and faculties, this is the value, and this the object, of Moral Philosophy.

It teaches, for the conduct of the understanding, a variety of delicate rules which can result only from such sort of meditation; and it gradually subjects the most impetuous feelings to patient examination and wise control: it inures the youthful mind to intellectual difficulty, and to enterprise in thinking; and makes it as keen as an eagle, and as unwearied as the wing of an angel. In looking round the region of spirit, from the mind of the brute and the reptile, to the sublimest exertions of the human understanding, this philosophy lays deep the foundations of a fervent and grateful piety, for those intellectual riches which have been dealt out to us with no scanty measure. With sensation alone, we might have possessed the earth, as it is possessed by the lowest order of beings: but we have talents which bend *all* the laws of nature to our service; memory for the past, providence for the future,—senses which mingle pleasure with intelligence, the surprise of novelty, the boundless energy of imagination, accuracy in comparing, and severity in judging; an original affection, which binds us together in society; a swiftness to pity; a fear of shame; a love of esteem; a detestation of all that is cruel, mean, and unjust. All these things Moral Philosophy observes, and, observing, adores the Being from whence they proceed.

LECTURE II.

HISTORY OF MORAL PHILOSOPHY.

I PURPOSE to give, in this lecture, a succinct history of opinions, both in the intellectual and active divisions of Moral Philosophy; from the formation of the great schools in Greece to the present time.

Of the principles from which the obligations to virtue proceed, most sects have given an account which is at least intelligible, however each particular persuasion may vary from that which precedes it: but the speculations of many of the ancients on the human *understanding*, are so confused, and so purely hypothetical, that their greatest admirers are not agreed upon their meaning; and whenever we can procure a plain statement of their doctrines, all other modes of refuting them appear to be wholly superfluous.

Whoever is fond of picking up little bits of wisdom, in great heaps of folly, and of seeing Moral Philosophy and common sense beaming through the gross darkness of polytheism, and poetical fiction, may sit down and trace this science from Zoroaster the Chaldean, Belus the Assyrian, and Berosus, who taught the Chaldean learning to the Greeks. He will find a very pleasant obscurity in all that we know of the opinions of Zoroaster, of the Persian Magi, Hystaspes, and Hostanes. Of those celebrated men Cadmus, and Sanchoniathon, and poor Moschus the Phœnician, so heartily abused by Dr. Cudworth, he may pick up some acute remarks of *Theut,* or *Thoth,* the founder of Egyptian wisdom, and philosophize with Abaris, Anacharsis, Toxaris, and Zamolxis, the learned Scythians. Passing by all these gallant gentlemen (for whose company I confess I have no very great relish), I shall descend at once upon Athens, where philosophy, as Milton says, came down from heaven to the low-roofed house of Socrates.

> . . . . . "from whose mouth issued forth
> Mellifluous streams that watered all the schools
> Of Academics old and new; with those
> Surnamed Peripatetics, and the sect
> Epicurean, and the Stoic severe."

The morality of Socrates was reared upon the basis of religion. The principles of virtuous conduct which are common to all mankind, are, according to this wise and good man, laws of God; and the argument by which he supports this opinion is, that no man departs from these principles with impunity. "It is frequently possible," says he, "for men to screen themselves from the penalty of human laws, but no man can be unjust or ungrateful without suffering for his crime—hence I conclude that these laws must have proceeded from a more excellent legislator than man." Socrates taught that true felicity is not to be derived from external possessions, but from wisdom; which consists in the knowledge and practice of virtue;—that the cultivation of virtuous manners is necessarily attended with pleasure as well as profit;—that the honest man alone, is happy;—and that it is absurd to attempt to separate things which are in their nature so united as virtue and interest.

Socrates was, in truth, not very fond of subtile and refined speculations; and upon the intellectual part of our nature, little or nothing of his opinions is recorded. If we may infer any thing from the clearness and simplicity of his opinions on moral subjects, and from the bent which his genius had received for the useful and the practical, he would certainly have laid a strong foundation for rational metaphysics. The slight sketch I have given of his moral doctrines contains nothing very new or very brilliant, but comprehends those moral doctrines which every person of education has been accustomed to hear from his childhood;—but two thousand years ago they were great discoveries,—two thousand years since, common sense was not invented. If Orpheus, or Linus, or any of those melodious moralists, sung, in bad verses, such advice as a grand-mamma would now give to a child of six years old, he was thought to be inspired by the gods, and statues and altars were erected to his memory. In Hesiod there is a very grave exhortation to mankind to wash their faces: and I have discovered a very strong analogy between the precepts of Pythagoras and Mrs. Trimmer;—both think that a son ought to obey his father, and both are clear that a good man is better than a bad one. Therefore, to measure aright this extraordinary man, we must remember the period at which he lived; that he was the first who called the attention of mankind from the pernicious subtilties which engaged and perplexed their wandering understandings to the practical rules of life;—he was the great father and inventor of common sense, as Ceres was of the plow, and Bacchus of intoxication. First he taught his cotemporaries that they did not know what they pretended to know; then he showed them that they knew nothing; then he told them what they ought to know. Lastly, to sum up the praise of Socrates, remember that two thousand years ago, while men were worshiping the stones on which they trod, and the insects which crawled beneath their feet;—two thousand years ago, with the bowl of poison in his hand, Socrates said, "I am persuaded that my death, which is now just coming, will conduct me into the presence of the gods, who are the most righteous governors, and into the society of just and good men; and I derive confidence from the hope that something of man remains after death, and that the condition of good men will then be much better than that of the bad." Soon after this he covered himself up with his cloak and expired.

From the Socratic school sprang the Cyrenaic, the Eliac, the Megaric, the Academic, and the Cynic. Of all these I shall notice only the Academic, because all the rest are of very inferior note.

Of all the disciples of Socrates, Plato, though he calls himself the least, was certainly the most celebrated. As long as philosophy continued to be studied among the Greeks and Romans, his doctrines were taught, and his name revered. Even to the present day his writings give a tinge to the language and speculations of philosophy and theology. Of the majestic beauty of Plato's style, it is almost impossible to convey an adequate idea. He keeps the understanding up to a high pitch of enthusiasm longer than any existing writer; and, in reading Plato, zeal and animation seem rather to be the regular feelings than the casual effervescence of the mind. He appears almost disdaining the mutability and imperfection of the earth on which he treads, to be drawing down fire from heaven, and to be seeking among the gods above, for the permanent, the beautiful, and the grand! In contrasting the vigor and the magnitude of his conceptions with the extravagance of his philosophical tenets, it is almost impossible to avoid wishing that he had confined himself to the practice of eloquence; and, in this way giving range and expansion to the mind which was struggling within him, had become one of those famous orators who

> "Wielded at will that fierce democratie,
> Shook th' arsenal, and fulmin'd over Greece
> To Macedon and Artaxerxes' throne."

After having said so much of his language, I am afraid I must proceed to his philosophy; observing always, that, in stating it, I do not always pretend to understand it, and do not even engage to defend it. In comparing the very few marks of sobriety and discretion with the splendor of his genius, I have often exclaimed as Prince Henry did about Falstaff's bill,—"Oh, monstrous! but one halfpennyworth of bread to this intolerable deal of sack!"

His notion was, that the principles out of which the world was composed were three in number,—the subject matter of things, their specific essences, and the sensible objects themselves. These last, he conceived to have no probable or durable existence, but to be always in a state of fluctuation:—but then there were certain everlasting patterns and copies, from which every thing had been made, and which he denominated their specific essences. For instance, the individual rose which I smell at this instant, or a particular pony upon which I cast my eye, are objects of sense which have no durable existence;—the individual idea I have of them this moment is not numerically the same as the idea which I had the moment before; just as the river which I pass now is not the same river which I passed half an hour before, because the individual water in which I trod has glided away: therefore these appearances of the rose, and the pony, are of very little importance; but there is somewhere or other an eternal pony, and an eternal rose, after the pattern of which one and the other have been created. The same with actions as with things. If Plato had seen one person make a bow to another, he would have said that the particular bow was a mere *visible species;* but there was an unchanging bow which had existed from all eternity, and which was the model and archetype and specific essence of all other bows. But, says Plato, all things in this world are individuals. We see *this* man, and *that* man, and the other *man;* but *a* man—the general notion of a man—we do not, and can not gain from our senses: therefore we have existed in some previous state, where we have gained these notions of universal natures. In childhood, where human creatures are governed by the feelings of the body, these general ideas are forgotten: but in proportion as reason assumes the reins of empire, we call to mind these eternal *exemplars,* of which our understanding had before taken notice in a previous state of existence. Thus, to form general ideas was merely an act of memory;—and in this manner Plato attempted to overcome a difficulty which, two thousand years afterward, drove Malebranche to a theory equally extravagant, was too hard for Mr. Locke, and was settled, at last, by the extraordinary acuteness of Bishop Berkeley.

Plato's ideas of virtue were these: he divided the soul into three different natures—*reason,* or the governing power; the passions founded on pride and resentment, or the irascible part of our nature; and the passions which have pleasure for their object, and which we commonly call by the name of appetites. Virtue, according to this system, *then* exhibited herself when each of these three faculties of the mind confined itself to its proper office, without attempting to encroach upon that of any other;—when reason directed, and passion obeyed; and when each passion performed its proper duty easily, and without reluctance. Of this system it may be shortly remarked, that it is generally good as far as it goes, but that it does not go far enough; for if you tell me that prudence and propriety are the test of virtue, I ask you *why* are they the test of virtue? If you can give me no reason, why do you call them so? and if you can, the system does not reach the foundation of morals, or afford me the *ultimate* reason why one action is better than another.

The school of Plato long continued famous, but passed through several changes; on account of which it was distinguished into the old, the middle, and the new Academy. The old Academy consisted of those followers of Plato who taught his doctrine without corruption. It was the doctrine of the new Academy (founded by Carneades) that the senses, the understanding, and the imagination, frequently deceive us, and therefore can not be infallible judges of truth; but that, from the impressions which we perceive to be produced on the mind by means of the senses, we infer appearances of truth, or probabilities: these impressions Carneades called *phantasies* or *images*. He maintained that they do not always correspond to the real nature of things; and that there is no infallible method of determining when they are true or false. Nevertheless, with respect to the conduct of life and the pursuit of happiness, Carneades held, that probable appearances are a sufficient guide, because it is unreasonable not to allow some degree of credit to those witnesses who *commonly* give a true report.

Of probabilities Carneades made the following scale: —The lowest degree was, where the mind, in the casual occurrence of any single image, perceived in it nothing contrary to nature or truth. The second was, when the circumstances by which that image was accompanied afforded no appearance of inconsistency or incongruity which might lead us to suspect the truth of the sensation: as, for instance, if I think I see a horse, the circumstance of his appearing at the same time to be grazing in a meadow is an additional corroboration of the truth of the sensation; but if I think I see a horse upon the top of a house, the circumstances which accompany this idea of the horse, ought to go some way to convince me I am mad, or dreaming. The last point in the scale of probabilities I can really hardly distinguish from the second; it seems only a longer and more serious pause, a more cautious and minute examination of the evidence of the senses;—and thus much of the philosophy of the new Academy (stripped of the magisterial and ostentatious garb in which all the Grecian schools tricked out their theories) seems to be good plain sense. All knowledge founded upon the evidence of the senses is, and can be, *strictly* speaking, nothing more than probable evidence. The mathematics alone afford us *certain* evidence.

The shades of difference between the middle Academy and the new are so slight, and the sketch I am attempting to give must necessarily be so *very* summary, that I shall pass over this first ramification of the Platonic school to the philosophy of Aristotle; humbly imploring the forgiveness of those disciples of Arcesilaus, and favorers of the middle Academy, who may happen to be present this day at the Institution.

Whoever is fond of the biographical art, as a repository of the actions and the fortunes of great men, may enjoy an agreeable specimen of its certainty in the life of Aristotle. Some writers say he was a Jew; others, that he got all his information from a Jew, that he kept an apothecary's shop, and was an atheist; others say, on the contrary, that he did not keep an apothecary's shop, and that he was a Trinitarian. Some say he respected the religion of his country; others that he offered sacrifices to his wife, and made hymns in favor of his father-in-law. Some are of opinion he was poisoned by the priests; others are clear that he died of vexation, because he could not discover the causes of the ebb and flow in the Eurīpus. We now care or know so little about Aristotle, that Mr. Fielding, in one of his novels, says, "Aristotle is not such a fool as many people believe, who never read a syllable of his works."

Before the Reformation, his morals used to be read to the people in some of the churches of Germany, instead of the Scriptures; his philosophy had an exclusive monopoly granted to it by the parliament of Paris, who forbade the use of any other in France; and the President De Thou informs us, that Paul de Foix, one of the most learned and elegant men of his time, in passing through Ferrara, refused to see the famous Patricius, or to meet him at any third house, because he disbelieved in some of the doctrines of Aristotle. Certainly the two human beings who have had the greatest influence upon the understandings of mankind have been Aristotle and Lord Bacon. To Lord Bacon we are indebted for an almost daily extension of our knowledge of the laws of nature in the outward world; and the same modest and cautious spirit of inquiry extended to Moral Philosophy, will probably at last give us clear, intelligible ideas of our spiritual nature. Every succeeding year is an additional confirmation to us that we are traveling in the true path of knowledge; and as it brings in fresh tributes of science for the increase of human happiness, it extorts from us fresh tributes of praise to the guide and father of true philosophy. To the understanding of Aristotle, equally vast, perhaps, and equally original, we are indebted for fifteen hundred years of quibbling and ignorance; in which the earth fell under the tyranny of words, and philosophers quarreled with one another, like drunken men in dark rooms who hate peace without knowing why they fight, or seeing how to take aim. Professors were multiplied without the world becoming wiser; and volumes of Aristotelian philosophy were written which, if piled one upon another, would have equaled the Tower of Babel in height, and far exceeded it in confusion. Such are the obligations we owe to the mighty Stagirite; for that he *was* of very mighty understanding, the broad circumference and the deep root of his philosophy most lamentably evince. His treatises on Government, on Rhetoric, on Poetry, are still highly valued. I have been speaking of him as a natural philosopher, as a metaphysician, and as a logician. I would refer those who are great sticklers for Aristotle's various treatises on morals to Grotius's critique on them in his treatise on Peace and War, and to Barbeyrac's preface to Puffendorf. Of his experiments Lord Bacon says, that, of all the ancient philosophers, Aristotle was the greatest enemy to experimental philosophy; for he first of all laid down a theory in his own mind, and then distorted his experiments to support it. In his treatise on Government, there are some very enormous and atrocious doctrines.

Aristotle held, that all sensible objects were made up of two principles, both of which he calls equally substances,—the matter, and the specific essence. He was not obliged to hold, like Plato, that those principles existed prior in order of time to the objects which they afterward composed. They were prior, he said, in nature, but not in time (according to a distinction which was of use to him upon many other occasions). He distinguished also between actual and potential existence: by the first, understanding what is commonly meant by existence, or reality; by the second, the bare possibility of existence. Neither the material essence of body could, according to him, exist actually without being determined by some specific essence to some particular class of being, nor any specific essence without being embodied in some portion of matter. Each of these two principles, however, could exist potentially in a separate state. *That matter* existed potentially which, being endowed with a particular form, could be brought into actual existence; and *that form* existed potentially which, by being embodied in a particular portion of matter, could in the same manner be called forth into the class of complete realities. What difference there is between the potential existence of Aristotle, and the separate essences of Plato, and what foundation there is in reality either for the one or the other, I confess myself wholly at a loss to comprehend.

Virtue, according to this philosopher, consists in the habit of mediocrity according to right reason. Every particular virtue, according to him, lies in a medium between two opposite vices; of which the one offends from being too much, the other from being too little affected by a particular species of objects. Thus, the virtue of fortitude lies in the middle between the opposite extremes of cowardice and rashness; of which the one offends from being too much, the other too little affected by the objects of fear. And magnanimity, in the same manner, is a sort of medium estimation of our own dignity, equally removed from the extremes of arrogance and pusillanimity.

Aristotle, when he made virtue to consist in practical habits, had it probably in view to oppose the doctrine of Plato, who seems to have been of opinion that just sentiments, and reasonable judgments, concerning what was fit to be done or avoided, were *alone* sufficient to constitute the most perfect virtue. Virtue, according to Plato, might be considered as a sort of science; and no man, he thought, could see clearly what was right and wrong, and not act accordingly. Aristotle, on the contrary, was of opinion, that no conviction of the understanding could get the better of inveterate habits; and that good morals arose not from knowledge, but from action.

Next comes the Stoic sect, whose founder was Zeno.* Zeno was born at Cyprus, and was the son of a merchant, who, having frequent occasion in his mercantile capacity to visit Athens, bought for his son several of the writings of the most eminent Socratic philosophers. These he read with great avidity, and from their perusal laid the foundation of his philosophical fame. In the course of his mercantile pursuits he freighted a ship for Athens, with a very valuable cargo of Phœnician purple, which he completely lost by shipwreck on the coast, near the Piræus. A very acute man, who found himself in a state of sudden and complete poverty at Athens, would naturally enough think of turning philosopher, both as by its doctrines it inspired him with some consolation for the loss of his Phœnician purple, and by its profits

* According to Zeno, the founder of the Stoical doctrine, every animal was by nature recommended to its own care; and was endowed with the principle of self-love, that it might endeavor to preserve, not only its existence, but all the different parts of its nature, in the best and most perfect state of which they were capable.—*Adam Smith's Theory of Moral Sentiments*, vol. ii. part vii. sect. ii.

afforded him some chance of subsistence without it. After attending various masters of the Cynic school, which was then in high reputation, he put forth his own system of opinions, upon which was formed the Stoic school, one of the most considerable in ancient Greece.

The opinions of the Stoics upon the intellectual part of our nature, were either the same as, or very nearly allied to, those of Plato and Aristotle; though they were often disguised in very different langnage. The accounts of the morality of the Stoics I shall read to you from the very beautiful epitome which Dr. Adam Smith has given of their doctrines in the second volume of his "Theory of Moral Sentiments" (p. 186). "The self-love of man embraced, if I may say so, his body and all its different members, his mind and all its different faculties and powers, and desired the preservation and maintenance of them all in their best and most perfect condition. Whatever tended to support this state of existence was, therefore, by nature pointed out to him as fit to be chosen; and whatever tended to destroy it as fit to be rejected. Thus health, strength, agility, and ease of body, as well as the external conveniences which could promote these—wealth, power, honors, the respect and esteem of those we live with—were naturally pointed out to us as things eligible, and of which the possession was preferable to the want. On the other hand, sickness, infirmity, unwieldiness, pain of body, as well as all the external inconveniences which tend to occasion or bring on any of them—poverty, the want of authority, the contempt or hatred of those we live with—were, in the same manner, pointed out to us as things to be shunned and avoided. In each of those two opposite classes of objects, there were some which appeared to be more the objects either of choice or rejection than others in the same class. Thus, in the first class, health appeared evidently preferable to strength, and strength to agility; reputation to power, and power to riches. And thus, too, in the second class, sickness was more to be avoided than unwieldiness of body, ignominy than poverty, and poverty than the loss of power. Virtue, and the propriety of conduct, consisted in choosing and rejecting all different objects and circumstances according as they were by nature rendered more or less the objects of choice or rejection; in selecting always from among the several objects of choice presented to us that which was most to be chosen when we could not obtain them all; in selecting, too, out of the several objects of rejection offered to us, that which was least to be avoided when it was not in our power to avoid them all. By choosing and rejecting with this just and accurate discernment, by thus bestowing upon every object the precise degree of attention it deserved, according to the place which it held in this natural scale of things, we maintained, according to the Stoics, that perfect rectitude of conduct which constituted the essence of virtue. This was what they called to live consistently, to live according to nature, and to obey those laws and directions which nature, or the Author of Nature, had prescribed for our conduct."

From the philosophy of the Stoics I shall proceed to one of a very different complexion, the sect of Epicurus.

Epicurus was the son of a schoolmaster and a woman who gained her livelihood by curing diseases by magic, driving away ghosts, and performing other services equally marvelous. The circumstance which first turned his attention to philosophy is said to have been, that, on reading the works of *Hesiod*, he consulted his master upon the meaning of the word *chaos*. The pedagogue, unable to solve the point, instead of scourging him for asking too difficult a question, as is commonly the custom, referred him to the philosophers for an explanation. To the philosophers, as soon as an opportunity offered, he had recourse for more information than he could gain from schoolmasters, and acquired all he could glean from Pamphilus a Platonist, Nausiphanes a Pythagorean, and Pyrrho the Skeptic. He was at Athens also a student, while Xenocrates taught in the Academy, and Theophrastus in the Lyceum. When Cicero therefore calls him a self-taught philosopher, we are not to understand by that expression that he was never instructed in the tenets of other masters, but that his system of philosophy was the result of his own reflections, after comparing the doctrines of other sects. In the thirty-second year of his age, he opened a school at Mytilene. Not satisfied, however, with the narrow sphere of philosophical fame which this obscure situation afforded him, he repaired to Athens, purchased a pleasant garden, where he took up his residence and taught his philosophy;—and hence his disciples were called the philosophers of the garden. The friendship of the Epicurean sect is described by Cicero, in his treatise "De Finibus," as unexampled in the history of human attachments; and Valerius Maximus relates a memorable example of friendship between Polycrates and Hippoclides, two disciples of this sect. It is impossible, however, to receive these accounts without some sort of mistrust. A set of graminivorous metaphysicians, living together in a garden, and employing their whole time in acts of benevolence toward each other, carries with it such an air of romance, that I am afraid it must be considerably lowered, and rendered more tasteless, before it can be brought down to the standard of credibility and the probabilities of real life. At least we may be tolerably sure, that if half a dozen metaphysicians, such as metaphysicians are in these modern days, were to live in a garden in Battersea or Kew, that their friendship would not be of very long duration; and their learned labors would probably be interrupted by the same reasons which prevented Reaumur's spiders from spinning,—they fabricated a very beautiful and subtile thread, but, unfortunately, they were so extremely fond of fighting, that it was impossible to keep them together in the same place.

There are two totally opposite accounts of the lives and doctrines of the Epicureans:—the one, that they only recommended and pursued such sort of pleasures as they deemed not inconsistent with that virtuous tranquillity which was the chief end of their philosophy; the opposite opinion goes to fix upon them the charge of shameless and unlimited debauchery. Unfortunately, all the writings of Epicurus (by far the most prolific writer among the Grecian philosophers) have perished, with the exception of a very few fragments dispersed among ancient authors. It is probable, however, that both accounts are true; for it must be observed, that the philosophy of Epicurus, in its most favorable garb, contains within itself a principle of rapid corruption: it is precisely that which may inhabit a great and vigorous mind with safety, but which, dispersed abroad among all the medley of human minds and dispositions, would shoot up into rank licentiousness.

Epicurus held that there are three instruments of judgment—*sense, preconception,* and *passion.* Sense, he was of opinion, could never be deceived; though the judgment founded upon the representations of the senses might be either true or false. For instance, if a person of imperfect sight were to mistake the head of a post for the head of a cow, Epicurus would contend that the eye conveyed to the mind a notice of every ray of light that acted upon it in this instance, and that the mind had determined hastily upon the evidence presented to it. Every opinion he thought to be true which was attested, or not contradicted, by the senses. Lastly, opinions might be received as true, which were established by some immediate inference from the senses: as, if I see any thing move, it is a plain proof there must be a vacuum in nature, to admit of the motion of any body whatever; and the contrary opinion, that there is no vacuum, can not be true, because it contradicts the evidence of the senses. By preconceptions he appears to have meant what we denominate general ideas, which are formed, he contends, either by the repeated impression of the senses; by enlarging or diminishing a sensation, as in the instances of a giant or of a dwarf; by resemblance, as of an unknown city to one which has been seen; or by composition, as in the instance of a centaur. Preconception is necessary to enable us to inquire, reason, or judge of any thing. Truths not self-evident, are to be deduced from some manifest preconception; or, where the relation of ideas is obscure, it is to be made manifest by the intermediate use of some acknowledged principle.

This philosopher considered the pleasures and pains of the body to be the *sole* objects of desire and aversion

That they were *always* the object of desire and aversion he considered to be a matter of fact too notorious to require proof; but he contended that they were also the *sole* original object. The pains and pleasures of the mind, he contended, were all, in the first instance, derived from those of the body, though they afterward became incomparably more powerful and important, because the body feels but for the present moment,—the mind joys and grieves, by anticipation and by recollection; therefore to keep the mind easy was at all times the most important object. The virtues he thought of no importance for themselves, but for their *consequences.* For example, to save a guinea, when you may spend it agreeably, is not in itself desirable, for it is rather painful at the moment; but it is *important* only in its consequences. To be temperate, and abstain from a particular food, is a virtue not agreeable *while* it is exercised, but by the consequences it produces *after* it is exercised. Thus with justice: if one boy abstain from taking away another boy's pie, it is not because he receives any pleasure from *not* taking away the pie, but because he wishes to avoid certain *consequences* which would follow the seizure. Such was the idea Epicurus had of virtue; and before I conclude I shall offer a very few remarks on his system.

In the first place, the plan of solving all the phenomena of the passions by the dread of bodily pain, and the love of bodily pleasure, is very simple and beautiful; and I have no doubt that several of the passions commonly supposed to be original, may be proved to be put in motion by these springs of the machine: but it will not do for *all;*—for how shall we explain compassion by it? I learn what pain is in *another man* by knowing what it is in *myself;* but I might know this without feeling the pity. I might have been so constituted as to rejoice that another man was in agony: how can you prove that my own aversion to pain must necessarily make me feel for the pain of another? I have a great horror of breaking my own leg, and I will avoid it by all means in my power; but it does not *necessarily* follow from thence that I should be struck with horror because you have broken yours. The reason why we *do* feel horror, is, that nature has superadded to these two principles of Epicurus the principle of pity; which, unless it can be shown by stronger arguments to be derived from any other feeling, must stand as an ultimate fact in our nature. Did Epicurus mean to say that all the pleasures of the mind, as they were originally derived from the body, still kept the body in view? and that, as we only began to value respect from the advantages we gained by it, so we only continue to regard it for the same reason? If this be the doctrine of Epicurus, it betrays an extraordinary ignorance of our nature; because we all know there are innumerable objects which we began to value for their advantages, which we learn to value for themselves; and for respect, men commonly value the thing itself so much more than its beneficial consequences, that they every day are found casting away all that fame can give, in order to preserve fame itself. I might say a great deal more upon the philosophy of Epicurus; but I must not forget one of his habits in philosophizing, which I dare say will meet with the hearty approbation of every body here present; and that was, never to extend any single lecture to an unreasonable period; in imitation of which Epicurean practice, I shall conclude, and finish the history of moral philosophy at our next meeting.

LECTURE III.

HISTORY OF MORAL PHILOSOPHY.—PART II.

[IMPERFECT.]

If the *very* confined plan of these Lectures would allow of such an extended review of the history of moral philosophy, the proper method of resuming the subject from the concluding period of the schools purely Grecian would be, to trace the introduction of Grecian philosophy into the East, from the expedition of Alexander, and the effects it produced upon the mythology of the oriental theology. The same philosophy was introduced, by the same conquest, into Egypt; and the greatest encouragement given to learning and learned men by the successors of Alexander in that government. When the remains of the Pythagorean school fled from Italy into Egypt, an alliance took place between the Egyptian, Platonic, and Pythagorean systems; and from this heterogeneous compound, philosophy and theology assumed a new form.

When the philosophers, under Ptolemy Physcon, were driven from Egypt into Asia, upon their return the oriental philosophy was added to the mass, and the confusion of opinions was completed in the Eclectic sect.

Into Rome, the Grecian philosophy was not introduced without considerable difficulty. For when Carneades, Diogenes, and Critolaus were sent to Rome on an embassy from the Athenians, and the Roman youths of distinction flocked together to hear the philosophers, it was thought necessary, after dismissing the ambassadors honorably, to pass a decree that no philosopher should reside at Rome. Soon after, however, when Scipio

Africanus, Lælius, and Furius visited Athens in a military capacity, they frequented the schools of the philosophers, and became acquainted with their doctrines. The example of these noble Romans was soon followed by many others. Lucullus, who was instructed in philosophy by Antiochus the Ascalonite, erected a magnificent library at his house, which he opened for the use of the learned; and, by that means, allured many philosophers of every different sect to settle at Rome. Sylla, after the siege of Athens, first brought to light the writings of Aristotle, and conveyed them to Rome. From the period of Lucullus and Sylla, every one of the Grecian sects had its patrons and followers among the Romans; but, so far as I know, no original sect of philosophy ever sprang up among that people.

The philosophy which, a little before the Christian era, emanated from the remains of the doctrine of Zoroaster, had many followers in various parts of Asia. Of these, not a few passed over into Egypt, and contaminated not only the Pagan, but the Christian and Jewish schools; producing among the Jews the Cabalistic mysteries, and among the Christians the Gnostic heresies. Among the Jews, the Samaritans embraced a mixed system of religion, partly Jewish and partly Pagan; and, adding to these certain doctrines of the oriental school, produced the heresy of *Simon Magus*. The interpretation of the law called Cabala was brought over from Egypt to Palestine by Simeon Shettach. After this, there were learned men among the Jews who studied Pagan philosophy, such as Josephus the historian. Of the origin of the sects which existed before the destruction of Jerusalem—the Sadducees, Pharisees, Essenes, and Therapeutics—we know little or nothing.

After the destruction of Jerusalem, their learned men who escaped the general ruin erected schools at Jamnia, Tiberias, and Lydda; and among the Jewish schools erected at Babylon, the Babylonian Talmud was compiled. The traditionary mystical wisdom, so called by special indulgence, was studied by the learned Jews till near the tenth century. At this time, the Jews persecuted by the Saracens, fled into Spain; where they paid considerable attention to Pagan learning, and translated, among other things, the writings of Aristotle, from the Arabic into the Hebrew language.

When Mohammed first appeared among the Arabians, philosophy could hardly be said to exist among them. At the beginning of the dynasty of the Abbassides they first began to show a disposition for science; and under Al Mammon, in the ninth century, learning and philosophy of every kind flourished among them. These were greatly aided by the numerous Christian libraries which fell into their possession. Public schools were instituted and long flourished at Bagdad, Bassora, and Bochara; and, as the empire of the Saracens extended over the West, they carried with them their zeal for the promotion of knowledge.

The dark ages of Europe may be divided into four periods—from Alcuin, who was the cause of the renewal of public instruction; 2dly, the period of Roscelin, who gave rise to the celebrated controversy between the Nominalists and Realists. The third period, in which Aristotelian metaphysics, obscured by passing through the Arabian channel, were applied, with wonderful subtilty, to the elucidation of Christianity, begins with Albert and ends with Durand. The fourth period is the arrival of the learned Greeks who were expelled from Constantinople. This was the period in which the Genius of Science rose up from the dust and ashes, and, mindful of his past glory, began to resume his ancient dominion over the human mind.

"Behold! each Muse, in Leo's golden days,
Starts from her trance, and trims her wither'd bays.
Rome's ancient Genius, o'er its ruins spread,
Shakes off the dust, and rears his rev'rend head.
With sweeter notes each rising temple rung;
A Raphael painted, and a Vida sung."

The first great name after this period of the restoration of learning was that of Lord Bacon; to whom, however, we are more indebted for the opportunity of applying those rules of philosophizing which he laid down for the pursuit of physical science, than for any thing he did directly for morals. It is supposed that Descartes never read any of Bacon's writings; though there is good reason to believe that we are indebted to them for the original idea of Grotius's work on natural law, which he afterward carried into execution at the earnest solicitation of the famous Nicholas Paresi. "We must consider Grotius," says Barbeyrac (in his preface to Puffendorf), "we must consider Grotius as the first who broke the ice: nor can we, without the blackest envy, or the grossest ignorance, deny to him an extraordinary clearness of understanding, exquisite discernment, profound meditation, universal erudition, a prodigious extent of reading, a sincere love of truth, and a laborious application to study, among various interruptions, and the vast variety of duties imposed upon him by situations of the highest trust and importance."

"The wonder of Grotius," says Barbeyrac, "is, that his good sense has been able, in so astonishing a manner, to remedy the darkness and deficiencies of his times;" and this is certainly the real and proper defense of, and the just style of criticism for, every writer.

Two very eminent men, Mr. Hume and Mr. Horne Tooke, have spoken with a great spirit of depreciation, and even of contempt, of John Locke. I confess there is a sort of ingratitude of science in this, which it is very difficult to bear with patience. It is truly painful to see the great teachers of mankind insulted and disdained by those, whose very talents and sagacity have been fostered by their labors. It would be as uncandid and as unjust that those who are now cultivating the earth with so much skill and science, should sneer at the coarse but necessary labors of their ancestors, who cleared the impenetrable woods, drained the stagnant marshes, banked out the encroachments of the sea, and, by the sweat and the struggles of industry, left the earth ready for the refinements of science. To whatever height we may carry all human knowledge, I hope we shall never forget those energetic and enterprising men who met the difficulty in its rudest shape. That Grotius will never be forgotten, as the† * * * * *

† [The conclusion of this sentence has been on the outside cover of the MS. book. and torn off.]

After this period, the schools of Moral Philosophy may be divided into those of Locke, Descartes, and Leibnitz, originating in England, France, and Germany.

Descartes was, at an early period of life, so disgusted with the uncertainty which appeared to him to hang over every science which he attempted to cultivate, that he quitted a life of study altogether, and turned soldier and man of pleasure. So strong, however, is the original bent and direction of men's minds, that the first instance of his prowess recorded in the Dutch army is, an attack upon an eminent mathematician at Breda, for some erroneous doctrines which Descartes conceived him to entertain respecting that science. From the Dutch service, Descartes entered into the Bavarian army; and there, instead of attending to any subjects connected with his profession, be busied himself in endeavoring to comprehend the Rosicrucian mysteries. At last, Descartes quitted the military profession, retired to Holland, and published there his system of philosophy, which soon engaged the attention of learned men in every quarter of Europe. In this country the Cartesian system obtained such a degree of credit, that Sir Charles Cavendish, brother to the Duke of Newcastle, gave him an invitation to settle here; and Charles the First gave him reason to expect a very liberal appointment. Descartes would certainly have accepted the offer if the civil wars had not immediately afterward banished all consideration for learning and learned men. He afterward accepted an invitation from Christina, Queen of Sweden, and, in four months after his arrival, fell a sacrifice to the rigor of the climate.

The account of Descartes's philosophy I shall read to you from Dr. Reid's "Intellectual Powers,"* where it is stated with admirable precision, and commented on with great good sense. "Descartes, about the middle of the last century, dissatisfied with the *materia prima*, the *substantial forms*, and the *occult qualities* of the Peripatetics, conjectured boldly that the heavenly bodies of our system are carried round by a vortex or whirlpool of subtile matter, just as straws and chaff are carried

* Vol. i. p. 147.

round in a tub of water. He conjectured, that the soul is seated in a small gland in the brain, called the *pineal gland:* that there, as in her chamber of presence, she receives intelligence of every thing that affects the senses, by means of a subtile fluid contained in the nerves, called the animal spirits; and that she dispatches these animal spirits, as her messengers, to put in motion the several muscles of the body, as there is occasion. By such conjectures as these, Descartes could account for every phenomenon in nature, in such a plausible manner, as gave satisfaction to a great part of the learned world for more than half a century.

"Such conjectures in philosophical matters have commonly got the name of *hypotheses* or *theories;* and the invention of an hypothesis, founded on some slight probabilities, which accounts for many appearances in nature, has been considered as the highest attainment of a philosopher. If the hypothesis hang well together, is embellished by a lively imagination, and serve to account for common appearances, it is considered by many as having all the qualities that should recommend it to our belief, and all that ought to be required in a philosophical system.

"There is such proneness in men of genius to invent hypotheses, and in others to acquiesce in them as the utmost which the human faculties can attain in philosophy, that it is of the last consequence to the progress of real knowledge, that men should have a clear and distinct understanding of the nature of hypotheses in philosophy, and of the regard that is due to them.

"Although some conjectures may have a considerable degree of probability, yet it is evidently in the nature of conjecture to be uncertain. In every case, the assent ought to be proportioned to the evidence; for to believe firmly what has but a small degree of probability, is a manifest abuse of our understanding. Now, though we may, in many cases, form very probable conjectures concerning the works of men, every conjecture we can form with regard to the works of God, has as little probability as the conjectures of a child with regard to the works of a man."

The merits of Descartes are briefly these:—that he revolted against the Aristotelian tyranny, and overthrew it; that he was the first philosopher who drew a fixed and definite line between matter and spirit; that he was the first philosopher who taught mankind that the only source of this sort of knowledge was an accurate contemplation of the human mind. Malebranche, Locke, Berkeley, were all taught this lesson by Descartes; he, as well as Lord Bacon, laid this foundation, and led us into that tract which all wise men now allow to be the *only* one in which we can expect success.

The most illustrious of his disciples were Bossuet, Fenelon, and Malebranche; and the extraordinary system of Spinosa has, I fancy, some connection with Cartesianism. Malebranche was clearly the forerunner of Berkeley: so much so, indeed, that there is not a single argument of the bishop's but what may be found stated with equal force in Malebranche. His system briefly was, that there is no material world, and that all our ideas of a material world we gain from the intimate presence of the Deity in our own minds. The system of Malebranche was adopted by an English clergyman of the name of *Norris,* in an essay which he calls the "*Theory of the Intellectual World,*" and which he published in 2 vols., in the year **1701.**

In England, the Cartesian philosophy, though his name was held in high estimation, never took any root: in fact, the English, for the first half-century of the Cartesian philosophy, were so occupied with civil war, hypocrisy, and profligacy, that they had no leisure to attend to systems of philosophy. In France, its native country, the Cartesian moral philosophy has entirely yielded to the philosophy of Locke; and his natural philosophy to that of Newton: and Germany is at present entirely divided between the old schools of Wolfe and Leibnitz, and the modern system of the celebrated Professor Kant.

M. Degerando, in the true French style, endeavors to show that Locke was preceded in many of his discoveries by Gassendi, a Frenchman, whose philosophy was made known to this country by Walter Charleton, thirty-six years before the first publication of Locke's Essay. I am wholly incapable of answering this charge, as I am entirely ignorant of Gassendi's writings; but I should strongly suspect, from the simplicity and honesty of Mr. Locke's character, he would not have borrowed from any other writer any material part of his doctrines, without the most scrupulous avowal of the source from whence it was derived.

Locke agreed with Descartes in thinking that we perceive by means of some intermediate agent between the object and the mind; he disagreed with him as to the origin of our ideas,—Descartes being of opinion that some were innate, and Locke conceiving that they were all derived either from our senses or from the power we possess of reflecting on the operations of our understandings. They differed with regard to the essence of matter and mind. Descartes believed that the essence of mind consisted in thought, and had a very singular idea that the essence of matter consisted in extension. Locke very properly determined that the word *essence* has no meaning; and that we know nothing about the *essence* of either one or the other, and never can know any thing at all about essences.

With respect to innate ideas, it has been objected to Mr. Locke that he has not sufficiently explained the meaning of the word. Does he mean connate ideas, that develop themselves as soon as we are born? if so, the dispute is quite insignificant. If Mr. Locke mean by the word idea (as I believe he may be shown to do) any impression or passion of our nature, does it not seem very strange to deny that self-love, anger, and pity are innate, though some of these do not develop themselves at the immediate period of our birth? In his account of the formation of abstract general ideas, Mr. Locke has been, as is generally thought, completely confuted by Bishop Berkeley; in that notion which he held, in common with all his predecessors, of an intermediate agent between the mind and the outer world, he has been refuted by Dr. Reid. His book upon the Use and Abuse of Language is generally considered as one of the most valuable in his Essay. The wonder is, that so few important errors should be discovered in a work which takes up the science of the human mind at so barbarous a period, and which has stood for a century the critical inquisition of the ablest men in the keenest and most inquisitive of all the branches of knowledge.

One of the most extraordinary men who appeared after Locke was Berkeley, Bishop of Cloyne in Ireland; of whom Pope says, that there was given

"*To Berkeley every virtue under Heaven;*"

and of whom Bishop Atterbury said, that, "before he saw that gentleman, he did not think that so much understanding, so much knowledge, so much innocence, and so much humility, had been the portion of any but angels." To give a clear notion of the bishop's theory, we must, for a moment, advert to Mr. Locke's doctrines on the same subject. He thought, for instance, that there were outward objects; some intermediate agents coming from that outward agent, which excited the idea in the mind: and, lastly, that there was the mind itself. For instance, that there was a moon, an image coming from the moon, an idea excited by that image, and a mind in which that image existed. Now, says Bishop Berkeley, you allow that you do not see the objects themselves, but only certain representatives of those objects; therefore, as you never see the objects themselves, what proof have you of their existence? You have none; and all your notions on these subjects are fallacious. There is no sun, no moon, no stars, nor earth, nor sea,—they are all notions of the mind. Such was the system of one of the most pious men that ever lived; and a system by which he hoped to put an end forever to all skepticism and irreligion.

In this sketch the name of Arthur Collier must not be omitted. He was Rector of Langford Magna, near Salisbury, and published a book, in 1713, which he calls "The Universal Key, or a New Inquiry after Truth; being a Demonstration of the Non-existence or Impossibility of an External World." He is a very acute man, but a very bad writer; and, what is singular enough, he had never read Berkeley's theory (which had then been published three years), or Locke's Essay (which had been published twenty-four years). That two writers, Berkeley and Collier, should meet together at such a conclusion, without the smallest knowledge of each other's intentions, is certainly a very extraordinary fact in the history of philosophy.

The outward world being thus annihilated, Mr. Hume determined to cure men of the absurdity of supposing they had any minds; and turned the same sort of argument to their destruction. As thought is only a representative of mind, and as you never see the original, how do you know there *is* any original? And so, in this manner, the rash and extraordinary hypothesis, that man is a being made up of body and mind, was detected, exposed, and ridiculed.

In answer to these metaphysical lunacies, Dr. Reid has contended, that, for all reasoning, there must be some first principles from whence such reasoning originates, and which must *necessarily* be incapable of proof or they would not be *first principles;* and that facts so irresistibly ingrafted upon human belief as the existence of mind and matter, must be assumed for truths, and reasoned upon as such. All that these skeptics have said of the outer and the inner world may, with equal justice, be applied to every other radical truth. Who can prove his own personal identity? A man may think himself a clergyman, and believe he has preached for these ten years last past; but I defy him to offer any sort of *proof* that he has not been a fishmonger all the time.† * * * * * *
* * * * * * * *

ever doubt that all reasoning *must* end in arbitrary belief;—that we must, at last, come to that point where the only reply can be, "*I am so*,—this belief is the constitution of my nature,—God willed it." I grant that this reasoning is a ready asylum for ignorance and imbecility, and that it affords too easy a relief from the pain of rendering a reason: but the most unwearied vigor of human talents must at last end there; the wisdom of ages can

† [Two pages of manuscript are here wanting.]

get no further; here, after all, the porch, the garden, the Academy, the Lyceum, must close their labors.

Much as we are indebted to Dr. Reid for preaching up this doctrine, he has certainly executed it very badly; and nothing can be more imperfect than the table of first principles which he has given us,—an enumeration of which is still a desideratum of the highest importance. The skeptics may then call the philosophy of the human mind merely hypothetical; but if it be so, all other knowledge must of course be hypothetical also; and if it be so, and all is erroneous, it will do quite as well as reality, if we keep up a certain proportion in our errors: for there *may* be no such things as lunar tables, no sea, and no ships; but, by falling into one of these errors after the other, we avoid shipwreck, or, what is the same thing, as it gives the same pain, the idea of shipwreck. So with the philosophy of the human mind: I may have no memory, and no imagination,—they may be mistakes; but if I cultivate them both, I derive honor and respect from my fellow-creatures, which may be mistakes also; but they harmonize so well together, that they are quite as good as realities. The only evil of errors is, that they are never supported by consequences; if they were, they would be as good as realities. Great merit is given to Dr. Reid for his destruction of what is called the ideal system, but I confess I can not see the important consequences to which it has yet led.

Oswald, Beattie, and a few more Scotch writers, who are very little known or read, have supported that appeal to the common sense of mankind in favor of first principles which, in my very humble opinion, was so wisely and philosophically instituted by Dr. Reid, and which hereafter promises to rear up the strongest bulwark against the skeptical school.

About the year 1730, the Rev. Mr. Gay published a dissertation on the fundamental principle of virtue. It was not published in a separate form, but prefixed to Archdeacon Law's translation of Archbishop King's "Origin of Evil." In this dissertation Mr. Gay asserted the possibility, and explained the mode, of deducing all our intellectual pleasures and pains, from the principle of association. It was this publication of Mr. Gay which first induced Dr. Hartley to turn his thoughts to the subject; and the result of his studies, was a conviction that not only all our intellectual pleasures and pains, but that all the phenomena of memory, imagination, volition, and reasoning, may be referred to this principle: so that nothing more is requisite to make a man what he is, but a sentient principle, with this single property, and the influence of such circumstances as he has been actually exposed to. As Dr. Hartley was excited to this part of his system by Mr. Gay's dissertation, he was led to the next and more reprehensible part of it by a query of Sir Isaac Newton's, at the end of his Optics." "Do not the rays of light," says Sir Isaac, "in falling upon the bottom of the eye, excite vibrations in the tunica retinæ? and do not these vibrations, propagated along the solid fibers of the optic nerves into the brain, cause the sense of seeing?"[1] This was enough for Dr. Hartley's system, which contends that the mind receives its notices of things by means of a vibration excited in the nerve and brain. When the excitement is considerable, he calls it a vibration; when less, it is a vibratiuncle. I need not add, that all this is a mere hypothesis, without a shadow of proof; and that if it were true it would leave the connection between body and mind just as unintelligible as it was before. This part, however, of Dr. Hartley's system has nothing to do with the other, and if it were entirely brushed away would leave his doctrines of association untouched. These doctrines have certainly made no great fortune on the Continent; and none in Scotland, where every man is a metaphysician. Their most able defender here has been Dr. Priestley, who has left out Hartley's vibrations, ameliorated his language, and (to use an expression which will be very well understood at the Royal Institution) has completely "*Rumfordized*" his system. I have read his book, and, in spite of the disgust which the style excites even in this renovated state, it appeared to me impossible not to allow that the principle of association is a much more extensive key to the great phenomena of our nature than any previous writer had considered it to be. At the same time (I say it with deference) I could not help thinking that he failed considerably in the universal and systematic application of this principle; and that the entire building he wished to display to the eye was erected with great inequalities in strength and skill. I shall barely mention the names of Price and Priestley, without offering any comment upon their writings; and having so done, I believe I have nearly completed the list of all the very considerable writers who have appeared since the time of Locke in this country.

May I be allowed to add to this splendid list the names of two gentlemen now living,—to one of whom the world may fairly look for no common improvement of this science, and from the other of whom it has already received it: I mean Sir James Mackintosh and Mr. Dugald Stewart. In my expectations from the first of these gentlemen, those will not think I am too sanguine who have witnessed the circumference, the order, and the connection of his knowledge, his zeal in prosecuting it, his perspicuity in detailing it, and that extraordinary mixture of enterprise and judgment which makes him as new and original as he is judicious and safe. Of the latter gentleman, if I am not misled by the suavity of his manners, the spotless integrity of his life, and the marvelous effects of that eloquence to which many others here can bear witness as well as myself,—if all these circumstances do not mislead me, I think I may say that never any man has taken up this science of the human mind with such striking and comprehensive views of man's nature. You begin with thinking you are taking up a curious, yet barren, speculation; and you find it, under the masterly hand of this writer, gradually unfolding itself into a wide survey of passions, motives, and faculties, made in chaste language, watched over with correct taste, and adorned with beautiful illustrations. He is ever drawing from those discussions which, in the hands of common men, are mere scholastic subtilties, principles useful in the conduct of life, and valuable for the improvement of the understanding. He is the *first* writer who ever carried a feeling heart and a creative fancy into the depth of these abstract sciences, without rendering them a mass of declamatory confusion. He has not rendered his metaphysics dry and disgusting, like Reid; he has not involved them in lofty obscurity, like Plato; nor has he poisoned them with impiety, like Hume. Above all, he has that invaluable talent of inspiring the young with the love of knowledge, the love of virtue, and that feeling of modest independence which has ever been the ornament of his conduct. I have been his pupil, and have received kindness at his hands. Perhaps I am overrating his merit; but I am truly sincere when I say, that I know no reason why he is not ranked among the first writers of the English language, except that he is still alive; and my most earnest and hearty wish is, that *that* cause of his depreciation may operate for many, many years to come!

I ought, in point of time, to have mentioned Hobbes before; but as I could not connect him with the school of Locke, I was forced to put him out of his proper place. Hobbes lived in the reign of Charles the First, and was, at one period of his life, very much connected with Descartes. He offered to that philosopher some comments on one of his publications, which Descartes treated with great contempt; and they separated. Though he incurred the contempt of Descartes, he excited the astonishment of Leibnitz by his profundity, who always used to speak of him as one of the deepest thinkers that ever existed. For the origin of our ideas he referred entirely to sensation; and divided all human faculties into conception and imagination. Thinking, according to Hobbes, is the succession of one imagination after another,—which may be either irregular, or regulated with a view to some end. Truth and falsehood are attributes, not of things, but of language. The intellect, peculiar to man, is a faculty arising from speech; and the use of reason is the deduction of remote consequences from the definitions of terms. Science is the knowledge of these consequences.

There are in animals two kinds of motion, one vital and involuntary, the other animal and voluntary. The latter, if it tend toward an object, is appetite; if it recede from it, is aversion: and the object in the former case is said to be good; in the latter, evil. Appetite is attended with pleasure, aversion with pain. In deliberation, the last impulse is *will;* success in obtaining its object, *enjoyment.* His notion of virtue was, that the law of the civil magistrate was the sole standard of right and wrong; that there was no natural distinction between them antecedent to the institution of positive law. This last part of his system was answered and refuted by Dr. Cudworth, in his "Immutable Morality." Hobbes, though a man of the highest order of faculties, is a most pernicious and paradoxical writer upon almost all subjects. As a mathematician he is generally accused of ignorance; his morality is subversive of all morals, as his policy is of all free government. His works produced, at the time, the most prodigious effect; they are now read by a few speculative men, and he is entirely passed away from common notice,—as every writer always *will* pass away, whatever be his talents, who thinks himself mightier than nature, and would expunge from the hearts of men their primordial and irresistible feelings.

Having said all I have to say of English moral philosophers, it may not be unacceptable to give some short account of the progress of Mr. Locke's doctrine in France. *Pere Buffier*, after *Gassendi* (whom I have already mentioned), was the first person in France who developed any philosophical views analogous to those of Mr. Locke. He was the first person who attempted an enumeration of first principles to serve as a basis for all moral reasoning; but though he has the merit of being the first to enforce this method of philosophizing, he has, in the execution of it, been still more unfortunate than his disciple Dr. Reid, and has multiplied his catalogue of fundamental truths beyond all bounds of good sense and discretion. The Essay upon Abstraction by Dumarsais, is an admirable abridgment of Locke's Essay. The reputation of Locke was very widely disseminated by Voltaire. Vauvenargues, whose maxims are so little read in this country, appears to have studied him; but Condillac is the person who has almost naturalized Locke in France. He has expanded and exemplified Locke's doctrines of sensation. Locke only perceived a very little chapter of the law of association, and treated it as a mere disease of the mind; Condillac has shown its effects upon the entire system of our knowledge. Locke showed that language registers our ideas; Condillac points out to us that it analyzes them, and is an indispensable instrument in reasoning. In short, we must unquestionably consider Condillac as the most valuable disciple and commentator that Locke has yet had. The effect of his book in disseminating the philosophy of Locke among the French, has been prodigious. D'Alembert undoubtedly, in his intellectual philosophy, is a pupil of the Locke school; and to his name may be added those of Condorcet, Charles Bonnet, and Dege rando,—who wrote his Essay upon Natural Signs, when a common soldier in the army of General Moreau.

Germany had principally received its tone of moral philosophy from Leibnitz and Wolfe, before this last revolution effected by Professor Kant. Perhaps no man that ever lived combined in so eminent a degree as Leibnitz, the faculty of invention with the habit of labor. His theories abound with boldness and originality, as any one who has cast a glance upon them may easily perceive; and he had acquired more knowledge, taking it in extent and accuracy, than any man, perhaps, that ever existed. His habits of labor were so intense, that he sometimes was known to sit in his study for forty-eight hours together; and for whole months confined himself to his books, without any other interruptions than those which hunger and sleep rendered absolutely necessary. His system was, that Nature, in granting organs to animals, had made them capable of distinct perception, memory, and imagination. Man is distinguished from inferior animals by the power of knowing necessary and eternal truths: it is from this power, that we are capable of those reflex acts by which we are conscious of our own existence, and form the ideas of being, substance, and God. Our reasonings are raised upon two great principles: the one, that of consistency, by means of which we judge that to be false which involves a contradiction, and that to be true which is the reverse of the false; the second, is that of *sufficient reason*, which admits nothing to exist without a sufficient reason for its existence, though that reason may not be known to us. In the united state of soul and body, each follows its own laws; but they agree together by means of a *pre-established harmony* between all substances, which renders each a representation of the universe. The soul, he says, acts according to the law of final causes, or by motives; the body, according to efficient causes, or by motion: and between these two kingdoms of nature there is a harmony, originally established, and continually preserved, by the power of God. Such is a very summary view of the theory of the great Leibnitz, whom both Locke and Molyneux evidently consider as a very overrated man, and whose system Voltaire calls "*une bonne plaisanterie.*"

To Leibnitz, and his successor Wolfe, succeeded an endless list of German metaphysicians, whose systems I am so far from being acquainted with, that I am too ignorant to pronounce their authors' names—Baumgarten, Meyer, Crousaz, Plouquet, Mendelsohn (the antagonist of Hume), and Eberhard, Platner, and names without any vowels or any end.

This superb list is terminated by Professor Kant, the explanation of whose philosophy I really can not attempt: first, from some very faint doubts whether it is explicable; next, from a pretty strong conviction that this good company would not be much pleased to sit for another half-hour and hear me commenting on his twelve categories; his distinctions between empirical, rational, and transcendental philosophy; his absolute unity, absolute totality, and absolute causation; his four reflective conceptions, his objective nonmenal reality, his subjective elements, and his pure cognition. I am very far from saying that these terms are without their share of relish and allurement; I must only decline, myself, the interpretation of them, and refer those whose curiosity they may excite, to the exposition of Villiers and Degerando, in their lately-published history of philosophy.

I can not conclude this lecture without remarking the high destiny and splendid fortune of this country, in giving to the world its great masters of philosophy. We will allow to other countries the most splendid efforts of genius directed to this object; but they have passed away, and are now no more than beautiful and stupendous errors. We will give up to them the mastery in all that class of men who can diffuse over bad and unsocial principles, the charms of eloquence and wit; but the great teachers of mankind, big with better hopes than their own days could supply,—who have looked backward to the errors, and forward to the progress of mankind,—who have searched for knowledge only from experience, and applied it only to the promotion of human happiness,—who have disdained paradox and impiety, and coveted no other fame than that which was founded upon the modest investigation of truth,—such men have sprung from this country, and have shed upon it the everlasting luster of their names. Descartes has perished, Leibnitz is fading away; but Bacon, and Locke, and Newton remain, as the Danube and the Alps remain:—the learned examine them, and the ignorant, who forget lesser streams and humbler hills, remember them as the glories and prominences of the world. And let us never, in thinking of perpetuity and duration, confine that notion to the physical works of nature, and forget the eternity of fame! God has shown his power in the stars and the firmament, in the aged hills and in the perpetual streams; but he has shown it as much, in the minds of the greatest of human beings! Homer and Virgil and Milton, and Locke and Bacon and Newton, are as great as the hills and the streams; and will endure till heaven and earth shall pass away, and the whole fabric of nature is shaken into dissolution and eternal ashes.

LECTURE IV.

ON THE POWERS OF EXTERNAL PERCEPTION.

[IMPERFECT.]

I PROMISED, in the beginning of these lectures, to be very dull and unamusing; and I am of opinion that I have hitherto acted up to the spirit of my contract; but if there should perchance exist in any man's mind the slightest suspicion of my good faith, I think this day's lecture will entirely remove that suspicion, and that I shall turn out to be a man of unsullied veracity!

A list of great and splendid names, such as I gave in my last lecture, of itself was *some* obstacle to the completion of my promise. I have no doubt, however, but that I overcame that obstacle with sufficient success; and, of course, that aided as I am by the subject to-day, it will be still more perfect, and my fortune more complete. It is some encouragement to me, however, in the execution of my plan, to perceive the extreme patience with which subjects are listened to, upon other occasions, which in their nature are not capable of eloquence, and in which all ornament would be impertinent and misplaced. I think I have observed, that the ornaments called for here are established facts and fair reasonings; and that the object for which both sexes pass an hour in this place is, to hear the investigation of some important subject, made with some care, and conducted without any pretense. Without offering, therefore, any other apology in future, for the dryness and barrenness of the subject, but trusting to the candor and good sense of those who hear me, I shall at once proceed upon my subject.

Every one knows that the senses are five number, Smell, Taste, Hearing, Feeling, and Seeing. The nostril, the eye, and the ear, are affected by objects at a distance through the instrumentality of light, air, or the thin element which emanates from odorous bodies. The senses of taste and feeling are commonly, if not always, affected by actual contact with the bodies themselves.

In the dissection of the human body, there are found thin, white, minute filaments penetrating every part of it in every direction. Every one of these, let its ramifications be ever so extensive, can at last be distinctly traced either to the brain, or to the spinal marrow, which proceeds immediately from the brain, and is of course connected with it. The use of these nerves is, to convey notions or ideas from exterior objects to the brain; and if this communication between the various parts of the body and the brain be intercepted by any injury done to the nerve which keeps up the communication, no intelligence can reach the understanding from that part of the body. For instance, at present I feel perfectly well with my hand; but if the great nerve that runs down my arm were divided, I should have no sort of feeling in that part of my arm below which the separation took place. I might pierce my hand with a knife, or burn it with fire, without having the smallest sense of pain, or being in the least degree conscious that my hand was even touched. In the same manner, if the spinal marrow be injured, all the parts of the body whose nerves fall into that great channel of intelligence below the part injured become absolutely devoid of all feeling; and though in this case the lower extremities do not mortify, they are dead branches, without the privilege of sensibility, or the enjoyment of any of the functions of their healthy condition; and as the extremities can not convey, in the case of an injured nerve, any intelligence to the understanding, it can not exercise any sort of power over the diseased limb. For when my arm (to put the case I before cited) is injured, and can not feel, it can not obey the will; for, however I may *wish* to move it, its motion is utterly impossible. Therefore a nerve not only conveys the knowledge of outward objects to the mind, but it conveys the decisions of the will to the various parts of the body. In short, to use a very trite and obvious simile, the brain is the metropolis, the nerves are paths and roads to it from every part of the animal frame, the greatest of which is the spinal marrow, absorbing a vast number of lesser communications before it is terminated in the grand emporium of thought. To carry on this threadbare simile a little further, we may say, that the information thus brought to the brain, is rapid and telegraphic beyond all conception; the obedience rendered to its commands, dispersed over the body, instant and profound; and the effects of a very short interruption of correspondence so fatal, that the importance of the region thus separated is forever destroyed.

Now, then, this is a short history of the connection between mind and body. We know that the notion must enter by one of the senses, we know it must be conveyed by a nerve to the brain, and there our knowledge ends! All beyond this is mere fiction and hypothesis. Whether there be a fluid passing through the nerve, as was long supposed,—whether the nerve excite vibrations and vibratiuncles in the brain, as Newton queried, and Hartley thought,—whether the pineal gland be the seat of the soul, according to Descartes; or whether it lodge in the oval center of the brain, according to Vieussens; or whether, as Willis contends, common sense is lodged in the *corpora striata,* and imagination in the *corpus callosum,*—all these are the opinions of rash or ingenious men, without any foundation. What additions may hereafter be made to these discoveries it is impossible to say, but at present our knowledge is stopped exactly where I have stated. We know the *entrance,* the *path,* and the place of *destination; the mode* of proceeding, and the effects after it has reached its goal, we do *not* know.

There are two common errors respecting our sensations which those who have been in any degree accustomed to these sorts of speculations will hardly remember, and those who have not, will find, perhaps, some trifling difficulty in correcting,—I mean, the reference of our sensations to the objects which cause them, and to the senses which convey them. I say that I feel with my hand, and that I see with my eye; but what *are* seeing and feeling? They are affections of the *mind, not* of the body. My eye conveys to me the notion that this paper is white, and my hand is an instrument to inform me this table is hard; but the notions themselves exist only in my mind, and can not exist in my eye or my hand, which are mere brute matter, and quite incapable of intelligence. There are many things which we can only see through a microscope, but it would be very absurd to suppose that the microscope sees;—put away the microscope, and it is just as absurd to suppose the eye sees. The eye is a mere machine, like the other, to convey knowledge to the mind; the only difference is, when we use a microscope we use two optical machines, when we use the eye alone we employ only one. If we suppose the thought itself to exist in the mere instrument of thinking, we must, in the case of feeling, suppose mind to be spread over all the body. There is a mind in each foot and in every finger, and we kneel upon mind and sit down upon it; and the old proverb, "many men, many minds," may with equal propriety be asserted of a single individual. The second popular mistake which I specified is, that of attributing our own sensations to the bodies which occasion them. If I speak of the smell of a rose, I mean that that flower affects my mind through the organs of smelling in that particular manner;—the smell is not in the rose, it is in my mind; there is an unknown cause in the rose which excites this feeling of the mind called smell. There is an organ through which that effect is produced; but the effect *itself* is in my mind. Just so, the color is not in the table, for the word color means nothing more than an affection of my mind; but there is an unknown cause in this wood which produces that effect upon my mind through the medium of my eye. And, in general, we must always carry it in our recollection, that in speaking of *sensation*, we are speaking of what exists in our minds; and that when we refer these to the objects *by* which, or the instruments *through* which, they are excited, it is a mere fashion of speaking, and not an accurate statement of the fact.

I decline to discuss the question of the difference between the primary and secondary qualities of bodies; and I assume, with Dr. Reid, the existence of matter as *a first principle* not proved by reason, and not *provable* by reason.

Almost all the senses are possessed by some one animal or another, in greater perfection than by man, though perhaps there is none that inherits such excellence in all the five senses. We are not to judge of the degree of sensation with which nature has endowed us from the blunted condition of these organs in a state of society. An American Indian has such an acute sight, that he can discover the prints of his enemies' feet, can ascertain their number with the greatest exactness, and the length of time which has elapsed since their passage; he can discover the fires, and hear the noises of his enemies, when no sign of the contiguity of any human being can be discovered by the most vigilant European. Nothing can be plainer than that a life of society is unfavorable to all the animal powers of man. Such a minute and scrupulous exercise of his senses is not necessary to his safety or his support, and he gradually subsides into that mediocrity of organs, which is sufficient for his altered condition. One of the immediate effects of civilization is to render such excessive bodily perfection entirely useless. A Choctaw could run from here to Oxford without stopping: I go in the mail coach; and the time that the savage has been employed in learning to run so far, I have employed in something else. It would not only be useless in me to run like a Choctaw, but foolish and disgraceful.

An irresistible proof of the vast improvement of which the senses are capable, is the education of the deaf and dumb, and the blind; which proceeds upon the principle that, after one sense is taken away, the others may be made much more acute in their exercise, and much more extensive in their employment. The sense of touch became so acute in Professor Saunderson, who had been blind from one year old, that he could discover with the greatest exactness the slightest inequality of surface, and could distinguish, in the most finished works, the slightest oversight in the polish. In the cabinet of medals at Cambridge he could single out the Roman medals with the utmost exactness. When any object passed before his face, though at some distance, he discovered it, and eould guess its size with considerable accuracy. When he walked, he knew when he passed by a tree, a wall, or a house. His ear had become so accurate from habit, that he could not only recognize those with whom he was acquainted, by the sound of their voices, but could judge with the utmost accuracy of the size of any room into which he was conducted.

The most singular instance of this substitution of one sense for another, and the degree of perfection to which particular senses can be carried, is recorded in the Transactions of the Manchester Society, from whence I have taken it. "John Metcalf, a native of the neighborhood of Manchester, became blind," says Dr. Bew, "at a very early age, so as to be quite unconscious of light and its various effects. This man passed the younger part of his life as a wagoner, and occasionally as a guide during the night in intricate roads, when the tracks were covered with snow. Strange as this may appear to those who can see, the employment he has since undertaken is still more extraordinary; it is one of the last to which we should ever suppose a blind man would turn his attention;—his present occupation is that of a projector and surveyor of highways in difficult and mountainous parts. With the assistance only of a long staff, I have several times met this man traversing the roads, ascending precipices, exploring valleys, and investigating their several extents, forms, and situations, so as to answer his design in the best manner. The plans which he designs, and the estimates which he makes, are done in a manner peculiar to himself, and of which he can not well convey the meaning to others. His abilities, nevertheless, in this way are so great, that he finds constant employment. Most of the roads over the Peak in Derbyshire have been altered by his direction, particularly those in the vicinity of Buxton; and he is at this time constructing a new one between Wilmslow and Congleton, with a view to open a communication with the great London road, without being obliged to pass over the mountains."

To these very remarkable cases, may be added that of Stanley the organist; the blind at Paris, who are taught to read, write, and print; and the equally extraordinary Institution for the Deaf and Dumb, which I dare say many persons here present have visited. All these valuable and useful institutions, which do honor to the ingenuity and humanity of man, merely avail themselves of that superfluity of senses (if I may use the expression) which nature has given us, and make those which survive, do the duties of that which is deceased. It seems, at first sight, very singular that a blind child should be taught to read; but observe what the common process is with every child: a child sees certain marks upon a plain piece of paper, which he is taught to call A, B, C; but if you were to raise certain marks in relief upon pasteboard, as you may of course do, and teach a blind child to call these marks which he felt A, B, C, a blind child would as easily learn his alphabet by his fingers as another would do by his eyes, and might go on feeling through Homer or Virgil as we do by persevering in looking at the book. Just in the same manner, I should not be surprised if the alphabet could be taught by a series of well-contrived flavors; and we may even live to see the day when men may be taught to smell out their learning, and when a fine scenting day shall be (which it certainly is not at present) considered as a day peculiarly favorable to study.

A curious question may be agitated as to the resemblance of the senses to each other. All the ideas of seeing bear a resemblance to each other, and all of hearing, and so forth; or do we only conceive them to resemble each other because they enter the mind by the same channel? Is there any more resemblance in the taste of vinegar and the taste of a peach, than there is between the taste of vinegar and the sound of an Æolian harp? I am very much inclined to think there is not; and that the only reason of supposing a resemblance is, that they affect the same organ. I believe there is a much greater analogy between those ideas of every sense which produce a similar tone of mind, whether of excitement, or soothing, or dislike, or horror, than there is between ideas of the same sense which stand in very different degrees of favor with the mind. The resemblance seems to be much more intimate between soft sounds, fragrant smells, smooth surfaces, pleasant tastes, and refreshing colors, than between soft sounds and horrible crashes, smooth surfaces and lacerating inequalities, pleasant tastes and caustic bitterness, refreshing color and sable gloom.

In mere sensation, the mind appears to be very nearly passive: when the organ is in a free and healthy state, it is impressed by outward objects without any choice of ours. Whoever walks out into the country, can not avoid seeing the color of the grass and the shape of the trees to which his eyes are directed. He has not sensations because he chooses to have them, but they come upon him till he removes the organ, and for a time deprives it of its powers.† * * * *
* * * * * * * *

One of the most important branches of this subject of sensation is, the distinction between those sensations which are really derived from the sense itself, and those which are connected with them by mere association. We say we hear a bell ring when in fact it is utterly impossible we should do so, for a bell is an object of sight and touch; and we might as well say that we heard a color, or heard a thick substance. The fact is, we hear only a sound, which constant experience has led us to refer to a bell as its *cause*. We smell that something is burning, in the same manner. *Burning* is an object of sight, and can not be smelt; but that odor can be smelt which experience has taught us to connect with the phenomena of burning. So that what we are at first apt to 'consider and to call simple sensations are in fact accompanied by, and involved with, numberless *other* sensations, which experience has combined together. Our senses would be comparatively of small

† [Four pages of manuscript are here wanting.]

importance to us but for these rapid, compound, and indissoluble associations; so that a man becomes to have a sort of sixth sense, compounded of all the others, and exercising, in a single act, their aggregate perfections. A child can hear, and see, and feel, as well as a man; but he exercises these senses without connecting them with all that their intelligences imply. The case is precisely the same with men skilled in any art or profession, and others ignorant of it;—the difference between them is in those intimate associations of sensation which one has formed and the other not. I can see out at sea as well as a sailor; but he pronounces that object to be a three-decked ship in which I can neither distinguish mast, or deck, or any thing else. We both *see* precisely the same thing,—a brown mass of a certain magnitude. It was to him, when first he went to sea, a brown lump also; long experience has taught him, that this is the appearance of a man-of-war. I have had no experience, and it is to me only a simple sensation. *I* see only the object; *he* sees the thing signified. There are, in the case of vision, a prodigious variety of sensations which we suppose ourselves to derive from the eye, and which are, in fact, derived from the touch. It will appear very singular to those who have never reflected on these subjects, when I say, that we can neither see the distance of any objects, nor their size, nor their figure; and yet there is nothing which science has more clearly proved. The eye originally sees nothing but color and surface. A man born blind and suddenly restored to sight would not have the least conception of the distance of objects; all objects, whether far or near, would appear to be near to his eye. This was long *imagined* to be the fact, and was afterward proved to be so, in the memorable case of the young man who was couched by Cheselden. He actually *made* this mistake, and conceived the pictures on the opposite wall to be quite close to his eye. If the eye can see nothing but color and surface, why should the alteration of color and surface give the idea of distance? A color half as bright, and a surface half as great, do not *necessarily* imply a distance proportionally greater. We might have been so constituted as that an object should have become fainter the nearer it approached. The fact is, we have determined by experience that these signs to the eye, of fainter color and diminished surface, are inseparably connected with *distance*, and that bodies are nearer to the touch when they are brighter to the eye: therefore the moment we see brightness we think of proximity, and so *imagine* we see that a thing is near; and the moment the color becomes confused we think of remoteness, and so *imagine* we see that a thing is remote. It is by rendering color more languid and confused, that painters can represent objects at a very different distance upon the same flat canvas. The mere diminution of the magnitude of an object would not have the effect of making it appear at a greater distance. For if, in a cattle piece, the artist were to make one cow ten times as little as all the rest, the animal would by no means appear ten times as distant from the eye, but would be taken for a calf in the foreground instead of a cow in the distant scenery.

Dr. Reid quotes a very curious observation made by Bishop Berkeley in his travels through Italy and Sicily, which, by the by, I rather believe he performed on foot. He observed that, in those countries, cities and palaces seen at a great distance appeared to him nearer by several miles than they really were; and he very judiciously imputed it to this cause,—that the purity of that air gave to very distant objects a degree of brightness and distinctness which, in the grosser air of his own country, belonged only to those which are near. It would be curious to know whether Italians are apt to make the reverse of the bishop's observation in this country, and to ascertain what the apparent distance is, according to their estimation, from London to Kensington, during a thick fog in this pleasant month of December. This mode of discovering distance by the distinctness or indistinctness of color, is the reason why we mistake the size of objects in a fog. A little gentleman who understands optics, may always be sure to enjoy a temporary elevation in a fog; and by walking out in that state of the weather, will be quite certain of being taken for a man six feet high; for the indistinctness of color first makes us consider him to be at a much greater distance than he really is, and then a man who appears so big at the supposed distance of 300 yards, we can not but judge to be one of the tallest and most robust of men. Secondly, another mode in which we determine the distance of objects, is by changing the form of the eye. Nature has given us the power of adapting this organ to certain distances by contracting one set of muscles, and to other distances by contracting another set. As to the manner in which this is done, anatomists are not agreed; but whatever be the manner, it is certain that young people have commonly the power of adapting their eyes to all distances of the object, from six or seven inches to fifteen or sixteen feet, so as to have perfect and distinct vision at any distance within these limits. Now, place an object at the distance of six inches from the eye, and gradually remove it to sixteen or seventeen feet, you will find that all the muscles of the eye are employed all that time in altering the shape of the eye, and accommodating it to different distances; so that, by long experience, the efforts I am compelled to make in order to see at these different distances become themselves the signs of these distances; and if any person were wounded in these muscles about the eye, so as to disturb his usual efforts to obtain distinct vision, he would lose his guide of distance, and become unable to see as well as before, though precisely the same appearances would be presented to his eye.

A third mode by which we acquire the notion of distance is, the inclination of the eyes toward each other. A line drawn through the center of the eye to the retina, and produced beyond it, is called the axis of the eye; and it is plain that the inclination of these lines toward each other must vary as the distance of the objects varies toward which they are directed. Of this inclination we are not conscious; but we are conscious of the effort employed in making it; and this effort, as well as the others of which I have been last speaking, becomes the sign of the distance of objects. It is for this reason that those who have lost the sight of one eye are apt, even within arm's length, to make mistakes in the distance of objects which are easily avoided by those who see with two eyes; though, after some time, in persons blind of one eye, this inclination of the axes ceases to be a criterion of distance, and these mistakes are avoided. This inclination of the optic axes is the principal obstacle to complete deception in the art of painting. The coloring (one mode by which we determine distance) may be perfect, and may give us the notion of an object being at the distance of many miles; but, unfortunately, the figure of the eye, and the inclination of the axes, are set for the distance of two or three yards (the real space between the eye and the picture), so that the mind, wanting one of its signs of distance, is far from being completely deceived. In order to remove this defect, connoisseurs in painting look at a picture with one eye, through a tube, which excludes the view of all other objects. By this means, the inclination of the eyes toward each other (one method by which we judge of the deception) is prevented. Dr. Reid proposes, as an improvement, this method,—that the aperture of the tube next the eye should be as small as a pin-hole; because then the other mode of judging of distances, the conformation of the eye, is avoided, and we have no means left of judging of the distances but the light and the color, which are in the power of the painter. When the optic axes are, on account of the great distance of objects, nearly parallel, so that to look at an object still more distant requires no fresh effort, our power of judging of distances entirely ceases. This is the reason why the sun, moon, planets, and fixed stars appear to be all at the same distance, as if they touched the concave surface of a great sphere. The sphere itself is at that distance beyond which all objects affect the eye in the same manner.

Another mode in which we determine the distance of objects is by referring them to those intervening objects whose distance is known. We are so much accustomed to measure with our eye the ground which we travel, and to compare the judgments of distance formed by sight with our experience or information, that we learn by degrees in this manner to form a more accurate judgment of the distance of terrestrial objects than we could do by any of the means above mentioned. It is for want of some intervening objects that it is so difficult to measure distances by the eye up in the air, out at sea, or on extensive plains. This mode of estimating distance accounts for the superior apparent magnitude of the moon in the horizon: for, first, its distance seems greater on account of the known distance of the terrestrial objects that intervene; and where the visible magnitude is the same, the real magnitude of objects is always determined to be in proportion to the distance.

The proof of this being the real solution of the difficulty is, that if the horizontal moon be viewed through a tube which excludes all terrestrial objects, its appearance is precisely the same as at any other time.

The last method by which we determine the distance of objects is by their visible magnitude. By experience, I know what figure a man or any other known object makes to my eye at the distance of ten feet; I perceive the gradual diminution of this visible figure at the distance of twenty, forty, one hundred feet, till it vanish altogether: hence a certain visible magnitude of a known object becomes the sign of a certain determinate distance, and carries along with it the conception and belief of that distance.

I shall say nothing here of the *moral* method of measuring distances;—the distance from home to school, in the days of our youth, being generally double the distance from school to home; and so forth with all other passions which quicken or retard the feeling of time.

It is just the same with the cubical magnitudes of bodies. We think we see that a body is thick and round; it is quite certain that we see neither the one nor the other, for the eye can see nothing but plain surfaces; but then we learn from experience that certain different appearances of light or shade upon plain surfaces are constantly connected with those feelings of bodies which we *call* round and thick. Just in the same manner it is probable that the notions which the ear has of distance and position are entirely the result of experience; and that a person deaf from his birth, and suddenly cured would be quite ignorant from what quarter, and from what distance, sound originated. Thus we see that the senses soon learn to lay aside their own homely and barren language, and to speak in a more elegant and universal dialect; and we see that man, endowed with the senses he now is, and deprived of the power of connecting their notices together by indissoluble associations, would have risen very little above the rank of the lower animals. All the labors of the human mind point and tend toward the same process which has been carried on in our early infancy with respect to associated sensation,—so to connect together, by copious induction, the *sign* with the *thing* signified, that the one may suggest the other with the certainty and velocity of sensation.

The phenomena of double vision and inverted images I must, for fear of protracting my lecture too long, entirely pass over; referring those whose curiosity may be excited on these subjects to Bishop Berkeley's Essay on Vision, Dr. Porterfield on the Eye, Dr. Wells's Essay on Vision, and Dr. Reid's admirable first work on the Human Mind. To prove, in some measure, how much of our sight is original, and how much acquired, and to illustrate therefore a great deal of what I have said throughout this lecture, I shall read to you the famous case of a young man born blind, and suddenly restored to his sight by undergoing the operation of couching.

A young gentleman, who was born with two cataracts upon each of his eyes, was, in 1728, couched by Mr. Cheselden, and by that means for the first time made to see distinctly. "At first," says the operator, "he could bear but very little light, and the things he saw he thought extremely large; but upon seeing things larger, those first seen he conceived less, never being able to imagine any lines beyond the bounds he saw. The room he was in, he said, he knew to be but part of the house, yet he could not conceive that the whole house would look bigger.

"Though we say of this gentleman that he was blind, as we do of all people who have ripe cataracts, yet they are never so blind from that cause but that they can discern day from night, and, for the most part, in a strong light, distinguish black, white, and scarlet: but they can not perceive the shape of any thing; for the light by which these perceptions are made, being let in obliquely through the aqueous humor, or the anterior surface of the crystaline humor, by which the rays can not be brought into a focus upon the retina, they can discern in no other manner than a sound eye can through a glass of broken jelly, where a great variety of surfaces so differently refract the light, that the several distinct pencils of rays can not be collected by the eye into their proper foci; wherefore the shape of an object in such a case can not be discerned at all, though the color may: and thus it was with this young gentleman, who, though he knew those colors asunder, in a good light, yet, when he saw them after he was couched, the faint ideas he had of them before, were not sufficient for him to know them by afterward; and therefore he did not think them the same which he had before known by those names.

"When he first saw, he was so far from making any judgment about distances, that he thought all objects whatever touched his eyes (as he expressed it), as what he felt did his skin; and thought no objects so agreeable as those which were smooth and regular, though he could form no judgment of their shape, or guess what it was in any object that was pleasing to him. He knew not the shape of any thing, nor any one thing from another, however different in shape or magnitude; but upon being told what things were whose form he before knew from feeling, he would carefully observe that he might know them again; but having too many objects to learn at once, he forgot many of them, and (as he said) at first learned to know, and again forget, a thousand things in a day. One particular only, though it may appear trifling, I will relate. Having often forgot which was the cat and which the dog, he was ashamed to ask; but catching the cat (which he knew by feeling), he was observed to look at her steadfastly, and then, setting her down, said, 'So, Puss! I shall know you another time.'

"We thought he soon knew what pictures represented

which were shown him; but we found afterward we were mistaken, for, about two months after he was couched, he discovered at once they represented solid bodies, when to that time he considered them only as party-colored planes, or surfaces diversified with variety of paints: but even then, he was no less surprised,—expecting the pictures would feel like the things they represented; and was amazed when he found those parts which, by their light and shadow, appeared now round and uneven, felt only flat like the rest,—and asked which was the lying sense, feeling or seeing.

"In a year after seeing, the young gentleman being carried upon Epsom Downs, and observing a large prospect, he was exceedingly delighted with it, and called it a new kind of seeing."

FRAGMENT OF LECTURE V.

ON CONCEPTION.

* * * * * * *
* * * * * before the mind can gaze upon the scene with any portion of tranquillity and composure. This mistake of conception for sensation is also the best key to the phenomena observed in madness. A madman has the conception of all the pageantry of a court, and so may any man in his senses; the difference is, the one knows it to be only a creation of his mind, the other really believes he sees dukes, and marquises, and all the splendor of a real court. If he is not very far gone, he pays some attention to the objects of sense about him, and tells you that he is confined in this sorry situation by the perfidy and rebellion of his subjects. As the disease further advances, he totally neglects the objects of his senses;—does not see that he sleeps on straw and is chained down, but abandons himself wholly to the creations of his mind, and riots in every extravagance of thought. This, though by far the most common species of insanity, is not the only one. There are some persons quite rational in their perceptions, who are considered as deranged only from a morbid association of ideas; as in the instance of the patient mentioned in Mr. Haslam's book, who persevered in a vegetable diet because, he said, roast and boiled meat felt the most exquisite pain while any person was devouring them.

The mistaking of conceptions for sensations appears also to be the proper explanation of what passes in our minds during sleep. To consider sleep aright, we must divide it into stages. In profound sleep, there is no evidence that we think at all. When we have been exhausted with great fatigue or acute pain, we often lie motionless for hours, without the smallest recollection that a single idea has passed through our minds: the periods of sleeping and waking appear to be consecutive instants of time. In this state of sleep it seems as if every operation of the mind were entirely suspended; and in the instance of those who have taken quantities of opium, or become drowsy from long journeys over snow, it seems to have a great tendency to death. We frequently dream in our sleep without recollecting the slightest feature of our dreams when we wake. It would appear at first, that processes of thought which have made such faint impressions on the memory must have been the slightest and most disconnected of all dreams; and yet the most rational and systematic dreamers—those who walk in their sleep—have seldom or ever the most distant recollection that they have been dreaming at all.

In the common state of sleep, where we dream without stirring, or, at least, without walking about, there seems to be, first, a great diminution of the power of the will over the body, but by no means a total suspension of that power: for a person much agitated in his dreams can cry out, and therefore subject the organs of speech to his will; or he can toss about his hands and feet, and so subject *those* parts of his body to his will; but, however, the influence of the will upon the body, though not wholly suspended, is certainly considerably weakened. In this sort of sleep it is still less suspended over the mind, for a man makes a bargain in his dreams, and examines the terms of the bargain, and dwells upon one part of it with some accuracy; he argues in his sleep, not merely repeating, as has been said, arguments which have occurred to him in his waking hours, but inventing new ones, with some pains and attention. I mention these circumstances in opposition to those who have contended that the influence of the will is entirely suspended in sleep. I should think *diminished* would be a better word,—for suspended it certainly is not in the body, and still less so in the mind; though its power is incomparably less than in our waking hours. But the most striking phenomenon in our sleep is that which I have shown to take place in madness—the confusion between our *sensations* and *conceptions*. I may think when I am awake of a chariot drawn by tigers; but I know *then*, it is merely a thought. When I am in a revery, I am in a confused state between doubt and belief of its existence. When I am asleep, I take this thought for a reality; and as our sensations follow one another in a regular and established order, and our conceptions are very loosely connected together, this is the reason of all the absurdity and incongruity of our dreams. Indeed, sense and nonsense, congruity and incongruity, are only determined by the outer world; and we consider our conceptions to be wild or rational only as they correspond with it.

According as sleep is more or less perfect, sensations do or do not produce an effect upon the mind, exactly the same as in revery or in madness. A person may, in some cases, sleep so soundly, that the firing a pistol close to his ear will not rouse him;—at other times the slightest sensation of light or noise will rouse him. A sort of intermediate state between these two is that where the sensation comes to the mind in so imperfect a state, that it produces some effect upon the current of conceptions without correcting them. If there is a window left open, and the cold air blows in, the sufferer may think himself on the top of Mount Caucasus, buried in the snow; or the cat making a noise shall immediately transport him in imagination to the Opera.

The most singular phenomenon respecting sleep is somnambulism, or walking in the sleep. The instances are innumerable of men who have walked along the ridges of houses in their sleep; have got up, dressed themselves, taken pen, ink, and paper, have written very rationally and connectedly, and acted precisely as they would have done had they been awake. Out of this mass of histories I shall make a short extract from a well-authenticated one, reported by a Physical Society at Lausanne. It is the case of Devaux, a lad about thirteen years of age, who lived in the town of Vevay.

He did not walk in his sleep every nignt, but passed sometimes six or seven weeks, without a fit of somnambulism. Before the fit begins he utters broken words, sits up in his bed, abruptly begins to talk with more coherence, then rises, and goes wherever the nature of his dream prompts him. Having risen one night with the intention of eating grapes, he left the house, went through the town, and passed on to a vineyard, where he expected good cheer. He was followed by several persons, who kept at a distance from him, one of whom fired a pistol, the noise of which immediately awoke him, and he fell down in a fit. Once he was observed dressing himself in the dark. His clothes were on a large table mixed with those of some other persons. At last a light was brought: he separated the clothes and dressed himself with sufficient precision. Another time he got out of bed and finished a piece of writing, in order, as he said, to please his master. It consisted of three kinds of writing, text, half-text, and small writing, each of them performed with the proper pen. He drew, in the corner of the same paper, the figure of a hat. He then asked for a penknife, to take out a blot of ink which he had made between two letters; and he erased it without injuring either. Lastly, he made some calculations with great accuracy.

Now, in this case of Devaux's, and in all such cases of somnambulism, there is an approach to the awaking state of the mind: they afford an intermediate step between sleep and vigilance, and differ only from madness in the time of their duration. For in somnambulism the will has recovered great part of its dominion over the body and mind which it had lost in perfect sleep; for we see that a somnambulist walks about, and thinks, and reasons, and acts, with a great share of precision. The difference between a somnambulist and a man awake, is, that the first distinguishes between his sensations and perceptions only *in part*, the latter *entirely*. Devaux got up and wrote a copy for his master, —he saw the pen and ink, and the writing, and various other things, as plainly as if he had been awake; but he did not attend to the appearance of the room, the beds, and the faces about him; he most probably thought he was in school, with his school-fellows about him, and so far he was under the influence of his conceptions. This is just the case with innumerable madmen we see in Bedlam. Somnambulism continued would, so far as I can see, differ nothing from madness. Dreaming differs from madness only in the diminution of the power of the will; excepting that there are very few madmen in Bedlam so mad as a dreamer. There seems also to be a certain connection between the augmented power of conception and the diminished power of will; so that a man becomes, in sleeping, motionless, exactly as he becomes mad, and regains his power of moving as he regains his power of moving for a rational purpose. This happens, luckily enough for dreamers, who would otherwise infallibly break their limbs every time they dreamed; and for the somnambulist, who, when he can move about, has acquired a considerable share of reason: so that we may perceive, if these observations be true, the following phenomena to take place, exactly in proportion as the outward senses lose their power, and the conceptions acquire a greater vigor than is natural to them:—revery, absence, somnambulism, madness, and sleep; and by reversing the scale, the conceptions gradually lose their force, and the sensations gain it.

A similar mistake is often seen to take place between the ideas of memory and those of conception; they are in many instances confounded together. Children are often detected in falsehoods which evidently originate from this cause: they have not learned to distinguish between their memory and their conception, and therefore believe they have seen and heard things which they have only fancied. In the same manner, very old men, approaching to their second infancy, are apt to confound what they have only conceived, with what they have remembered; and for this cause to become somewhat unintelligible to those who converse with them.

Nature has *probably* made a strong original difference between our sensations and conceptions; but whatever the *original* difference may be, it is considerably strengthened by habit. Every year we live, till our faculties decline, the difference becomes more and more considerable, and is, of course, much less remarkable in infancy than in manhood. This I take to be the reason why children can amuse themselves so well and so long with dolls, and talk to them as if they were alive: not that I suppose the deception is ever perfect, but that their conceptions approaching much nearer to their sensations, communicate more of the interest of real life. As the child gets older, and the difference between these two classes of ideas more wide, the wooden darling is tossed aside, because the conception has become a more languid and uninteresting representative of reality. There seems to be a regular process carried on in the mind throughout its whole existence, by which ideas of memory are converted into ideas of conception. If a poet writes two or three hundred verses, very many of the combinations of words, perhaps whole verses, will be faithful copies of what he has once remembered, and which, divested of all the marks of their origin, have reappeared to the writer as productions of his own brain. In the same manner, in a fancy landscape, or in grounds laid out by a man of taste, many of the combinations are in all probability copies of real scenes, which the person who introduced them could once have referred to some particular spot, but have now become his own property, from an inability to discover their former master,—like domestic animals which run away into the woods, and belong to whoever can catch them.

I shall mention only one more fact respecting conception, and it is a curious one, for which no reason can be given but that such is the constitution of our nature;—I mean, the great facility we all exhibit of conceiving the impressions of one sense better than those of another. It is, for instance, much easier to conceive any sight, than to conceive a taste, or a smell, or a feeling, or a sound. Sight is indeed so much the favorite and impressive sense, that almost the whole language of metaphysics is borrowed from it. Let any person attempt to conceive the smell or the taste of a melon,—they will find their conceptions of those sensations extremely faint;

but they will without difficulty form a clear conception of its figure and color.

To epitomize then the tedious account I have given of this class of ideas, we must remember the threefold division of ideas with which I began—ideas of the outward senses, ideas we conceive in our mind, and ideas we remember. We must recollect that when ideas of the senses are little heeded, and the conceptions of the mind acquire the force of realities, then we are said to be absent, or to be in a revery, or we are under the influence of great passions, or asleep, or somnambulists, or madmen. There is less difference between ideas of sense and conceptions in our infancy than in our mature age, when the difference is widened by experience; and this difference again becomes less, when the effects of experience are lost in extreme old age. We conceive some objects of sense better than others.

Men differ in their power of lively conception, but more in their habits of attention; but conception is in all men much strengthened by habit. Lastly, ideas of memory fade away, and appear in a renovated shape, as the mere creatures of the brain. These are the faint and imperfect notices of the great operations which are passing within us: the practical inference from them is, while we give vigor, extent, and variety to our conceptions, by cultivating an ardent curiosity for knowledge, to repress their dangerous vivacity by a cool and steady appeal to the realities of life; to cherish this reproductive faculty, as the source of eloquence, poetry, and wit; but so to cherish it that we will govern it, and even exact from it a ready obedience to the natural majesty of truth. He who can thus manage his mind has two worlds before him instead of one: he can contemplate and act; and, dispelling the vision of a rich and creative mind, can come down into the world of realities to observe with steadfastness, and to act with consistency.

FRAGMENT OF LECTURE VI.

ON MEMORY.

* * * * * * *
* * * * * He obtains all the convenience which he does obtain by the reference of individual transactions to certain general heads; and thus, by knowing only the nature of any transaction he wishes to refer to, and by seeking for it under its appropriate division, it is found with facility and dispatch.

Mr. Stewart conceives (and, as it appears to me, with great justice) that the decay of memory observable in old men, proceeds as frequently from the very little interest they take in what is passing around them, as in any bodily decay by which their powers of mind are weakened:—"In so far as this decay of memory which old age brings along with it, is a necessary consequence of a physical change in the constitution, or a necessary consequence of a diminution of sensibility, it is the part of a wise man to submit cheerfully to the lot of his nature. But it is not unreasonable to think, that something may be done by our own efforts, to obviate the inconveniences which commonly result from it.

"If individuals who, in the early part of life, have weak memories, are sometimes able to remedy this defect by a greater attention to arrangement in their transactions, and to classification among their ideas, than is necessary to the bulk of mankind, might it not be possible, in the same way, to ward off, at least to a certain degree, the encroachments which time makes on this faculty? The few old men who continue in the active scenes of life to the last moment, it has often been remarked, complain, in general, much less of a want of recollection than their cotemporaries. This is undoubtedly owing, partly, to the effect which the pursuits of business must necessarily have in keeping alive the power of attention. But it is probably owing also to new habits of arrangement, which the mind gradually and insensibly forms from the experience of its growing infirmities. The apparent revival of memory in old men, after a temporary decline (which is a case that happens not unfrequently) seems to favor this supposition.

"One old man I have, myself, had the good fortune to know, who, after a long, an active, and an honorable life, having begun to feel some of the usual effects of advanced years, has been able to find resources in his own sagacity, against most of the inconveniences with which they are commonly attended; and who, by watching his gradual decline with the cool eye of an indifferent observer, and employing his ingenuity to retard its progress, has converted even the infirmities of age into a source of philosophical amusement."*

I believe that this old gentleman was Dr. Reid; and he certainly is a memorable instance of a victory gained over the infirmities of age. I have heard, from a friend of his, that at the age of seventy he was as keen and eager about the then new discoveries of chemistry as if he had been just beginning his career of science. Such facts appear to me to be of the greatest importance, as they evince what may be done by a noble effort of resolution. A modern writer, who at one time made some noise, says, that it is men's own faults if they die; that dying is a mere trick, which may be avoided with a little resolution. I can not quite go so far as this, but I am convinced, that it is for a long time in every man's power to determine whether he will be old or not. The *outward* marks of age we are all of us very willing to defer; forgetting that we may wear the inward bloom of youth with true dignity and grace, and be ready to learn, and eager to give pleasure to others, to the latest moment of our existence.

In the same manner, memory may be wonderfully

* Stewart's Elements of Philosophy, chap. vi. p. 416.

strengthened by referring single facts and observations to one simple principle; and by these means we can either remember the principle by remembering the fact, or the fact by remembering the principle.

It is very common to hear people complain that they can not remember what they read; and the reason is very obvious,—that they are perpetually admitting into their minds a string of insulated events without arranging them with any method, which may be instrumental to their reproduction. Let us take a few instances of this. The first shall be in history, and in the history of religion. I believe the rule which all wise and moderate men adopt, with respect to toleration, at present, is this—that no man ought to undergo persecution for his religious opinions, if they have not a tendency to disturb the public peace: that point secured, the rest is left to discussion only; and every man must adjust his faith as his understanding enlightens, and his conscience governs him, without the fear of human punishment. An ignorance of this wise and simple rule, and of the proper limits of human interference, is a key to all the bloody and atrocious persecutions which for three hundred years desolated Europe. Again, nobody now thinks that Providence *perpetually* and *immediately* interferes to punish vice—that if any man, for instance, commits a murder this night, Providence will work a miracle to discover it; but the rude idea of religion in all barbarous ages is, that Divine justice is like human justice, and that guilt is immediately overtaken by punishment. This mistake may be traced in the legal institutions of almost all barbarous people, and is the principle to which innumerable separate facts may be referred at all periods of the world. It is, of course, the origin of the corsenet, of the ordeal, of the μύδρος among the Greeks, the judicial tournament in the days of chivalry, and of the trial by red water on the coast of Africa. France has fallen under the dominion of a single man, so did Rome, so have innumerable free countries. The cause, in many instances, has been precisely the same—that anarchy which has been produced by the licentiousness of the people, and which has rendered them an easy prey to the first ambitious man who could ingratiate himself with the army. Such examples are very trite, and what might occur to any one; I only mention them to illustrate the importance of philosophical arrangement to memory, and to show how much more likely facts are to reappear when we want them, if we have clustered numbers of them together as illustrative of a simple principle, than if they are promiscuously scattered through the understanding without any such connecting tie. The most striking instance of it is botany. What but the most precise and rigorous classification could possibly enable a botanist to remember one thousandth part of the plants which at present he can remember with unerring certainty?

A considerable degree of importance has been attached by some writers on education to the scheme of artificial memory; the general intention of which is, not to impress the thing to be remembered *directly* upon the memory, but to impress something easier than the original matter, which, by arbitrary association, shall recall it to the mind. Thus, the Battle of Hastings in the year *life*. What is the meaning of the year life? Why, *l* stands for 1, *i* for 0, *f* for 6, and *e* for 6; and so we have the year 1066: and by extending this idea we may put numbers into whole lines, and convey a system of chronology in a sort of poem. Another plan is, to keep in mind a house, with the apartments of which we are minutely acquainted, and, in speaking, to arrange our subject according to a preconcerted association, between the division of the matter and the house. This was a very common custom among the speakers of antiquity, though at present it seems to be quite disused I confess, myself, I have no very high opinion of these inventions: the expression of facts in verse, as is done in those doggerel rhymes by which we remember the days of the month, appears to be the best of them; but, in general, the remedy is much worse than the disease, and the difficulty less difficult than the assistance which is to overcome it. They accustom the mind to light and foolish associations, which have no foundation in nature; they convey an exaggerated notion of the difficulty of remembering, when such inventions are resorted to to effect it,—increase the disgust which such difficulties are apt to inspire,—weaken that confidence in the strength of memory, and the intense habits of labor founded upon that confidence, which breed up a race of great scholars, and carry men through the most intricate and extended inquiries.

Upon nearly the same principles there can, I should think, be very little doubt, of the bad effects of habitually writing down those facts and events which we wish to remember ;—they are taken down for future consideration, and consequently receive very little *present* consideration. From a conviction that our knowledge can be thus easily recalled, it is never systematically arranged or deeply engraved; we atone for the passive indolence of the mind by the mechanical labor of the hands, and write a volume without remembering a line. The desirable and the useful thing is, that we should carry our knowledge about with us, as we carry our health about with us ; that the one should be exhibited in the alacrity of our actions, and the other proved by the vigor of our thoughts. I would as soon call a man healthy who had a physician's prescription in his pocket, which he could take and recover from, as I would say that a man had knowledge who had no other proof of it to afford, than a pile of closely-written commonplace books.

Every body knows the importance of exercising the memory ; and it seems to be very useful to carry it to the extent of getting select passages by heart ;—it insensibly adds to the riches and the copiousness of fancy, and communicates, perhaps, a habit of attentive reading. This practice is carried to a prodigious extent in our public schools, and furnishes men with materials for wit and imagination through the whole of their lives. At the same time this practice is not without its danger, and that a very considerable one. He who trusts to what he *can* produce of other men's imagination is apt to lose the flower and freshness of his own, and gradually to sacrifice the vigor and originality of his mind. There is a homely old English proverb, that an ounce of mother is worth a pound of clergy ; and I confess, from my own feelings, I like better a very common production which seems to be the natural growth of the soil, than that exotic luxuriance which art has cherished, and which harmonizes so badly with every thing which surrounds it.

But the great secret above all others for remembering, is, to work the mind up to a certain pitch of enthusiasm

* * * * * * *

* * * * * * *

FRAGMENT OF LECTURE VII.

ON IMAGINATION.

*   *   *   *   *   *   *

*   *   * These are conceptions. If I gather together in my mind various implements of war, and create out of them the picture of that armor in which I clothe the hero of my poem, this is an act of imagination; so that imagination involves conception, though it is not involved by it.   *   *   *   *

*   *   *   *   * their respective arts to any high degree of excellence without a considerable share of the faculty of imagination, and to them have the efforts of this faculty commonly been confined; but there appear to be various exertions of mind perfectly similar to these, and to which we never think of applying the same word. For instance, in mechanical invention, no one would ever think of saying that Mr. Bramah had displayed a great deal of imagination in his patent locks, or that there was any poetry in a steam engine; and yet the process in one and the other composition does not seem to be very dissimilar. Mr. Gray, in speaking of Mars, gives to his lance the epithet of *thirsty*,—

> " On Thracia's hill the Lord of War
> Shall curb the fury of his car,
> And drop his *thirsty* lance at thy command."

Now let us see how this epithet of thirsty got into the mind of Mr. Gray. Perhaps he stole it (I believe he did); but if he did, we have only to reflect how it got into the mind of the person whose original property it was. But let us *suppose* it to have been Mr. Gray's own. By what process did he acquire it? He began thinking about lances, and all the common notions attached to that of a lance rushed into his mind,—bloody, fierce, cruel, thick, thin, murderous, rapid, brazen, iron, &c. &c. At last came, all of a sudden, the epithet of *thirsty;* and the poet, perceiving its relation to his original substantive, and its aptitude to excite poetical feelings in the mind, immediately made it a part of his poem. If we follow out any long and complicated description in a poem, the same process will be found constantly to have taken place. Now is there any thing very different from this which takes place with respect to mechanical invention? You want to work the rod of a pump by means of a horizontal axis which revolves above it. In considering how it is to be effected, innumerable ideas connected with machinery crowd into the mind. A thousand projects are proposed, examined, and rejected, till at last the idea of a crank is hit upon. Its relation to the other parts is immediately perceived, and it becomes a part of the machine. Now in these two processes of mind, which have received such different names, I am not able to discover any difference; —association brings together in each, a great number of connected ideas, and judgment discovers some relation between them which was not at first obvious: the only difference is in the ultimate objects which they have in view. The imagination of a poet proposes to itself to give pleasure by the sublime and beautiful; that of a mechanical inventor has in view to promote some purpose of utility. It is precisely the same with every sort of invention. Pythagoras, in inventing his media of proof for the forty-seventh proposition, went to work very much as a poet goes to work,—first raising a multitude of images by dint of association, and then selecting and applying them from the perception of their relations. In the same manner with wit: the object differs, and the rapidity differs; but the process of the understanding is the same as that we designate by the word *imagination*,—ideas are gathered together, connected by the lighter sort of association, and then that particular relation which constitutes wit is discovered. Indeed all the processes I have specified have received the common name of invention, though they have not been called by that of imagination: we speak of poetical, mechanical, geometrical invention, and of the invention of wit; though we use the word *imagination* in a much more restricted sense.

Imagination of all sorts, though originally dealt out with very different degrees of profusion to different men, is capable of great improvement from habit. As great part of imagination depends upon association, and the power of association always increases with practice, men acquire extraordinary command over particular classes of ideas, and are supplied with copiousness of materials for their collection, to which inexperienced and unpracticed minds can never attain. What a prodigious command, for instance, over all those associations which are productive of wit, must the head wit of such a city as this or Paris have acquired in twenty years of facetiousness,—having been accustomed, for that space of time, to view all the characters and events which have fallen under his notice with a reference to these relations! What an enormous power of versification must Pope have gained, after his translations of the Iliad and the Odyssey! so that no combination of words or inflection of sounds, could possibly have been new to him; and he must have almost meditated in hexameters, and conversed in rhyme. What a powerful human being must that man become who, beginning with original talents, has been accustomed, for half his life, to the eloquence of the bar or the senate! No combination of circumstances can come before him for which he is unprepared; he is always ready for every purpose of defense and attack; and trusts, with the most implicit confidence, to that host of words and images which he knows from long experience will rise up at any moment of exigence for his ornament and support.

Imagination is improved by imitation; as in living with men who are eminent for that faculty, or by reading those works in which its greatest efforts are to be found. It was the practice of some notorious man (I believe Bossuet) to read a hundred lines of Homer before he sat down to compose; and I have no doubt but that he might have derived from such a practice unusual energy and elevation,—that it must have filled his mind full of great images, and diffused heat and light over all that he thought and wrote.

The imagination (which delights to be fed by the eye) is cherished and inflamed by great sights. Nothing can be more striking and solemn than the first sight of a mountainous country to a person who has been only accustomed to the sleepy flatness of an alluvial district. The abruptness and audacity of the scene, the swelling and magnitude of nature, the universal appearances of convulsion, the magnificent disorder and ruin, astonish a feeling mind, and not only fill it with grand images at present, but awaken its dormant life, rouse slumbering irritability, and tell those whom nature has made orators and poets that it is time to fulfil the noble purposes for which they were born.

Mere magnitude—any thing vast—affects the imagination and sets it to work. A first-rate ship of war, or a Gothic cathedral, the waters of an immense river discharging itself into the sea, the boundless prospect of the earth below, that we gain from the top of a high mountain, an expanse of stormy sea, the concave of heaven in a serene night,—all these examples of immensity are ever found to have a powerful effect upon this faculty of imagination. The imagination is stimulated by novelty; and so much so, that whatever other cause affects it, it must be joined * * * * *
* * * * * * *

FRAGMENT OF LECTURE VIII.

ON REASON AND JUDGMENT.

* * * * * * *
* * * * * we connect together two ideas in early life, which we find it absolutely impossible to separate in advanced age;—we reason from them as from intuitive truths, and upon such topics are utterly impregnable to every attempt at conviction. These are the principal obstacles to the progress of the reasoning faculty; and they are disorders of the mind so common, and so detrimental, that I shall speak of them more at large in my next and concluding lecture. When they happen not to exist, or when they have been guarded against by a good understanding or a superior education, the conclusions we draw upon most subjects are sound and just: for if a question be discussed coolly, if the parties have no other interest in its termination but that of truth, if they thoroughly understand the *terms* they employ, if they are well informed upon the related facts, and if they are, both, in the habit of guarding against accidental associations, the conclusions in which they terminate will probably be the same: there is hardly any difference of opinion not resolvable into one or the other of these causes. Here, then, we have an outline of that manly and high-prized reason, which, under the blessing and direction of God, arranges the affairs of this world; which cools passion, unravels sophism, enlightens ignorance, and detects mistake; which wit can not disconcert, nor eloquence bear down; which appeals always to realities, and ever follows truth without insolence and without fear. For it is disgraceful to the immortal un-

derstanding of man to be governed by *sounds,* and to be the slave of that speech which was given to do him service. It is beneath the loftiness of his faculties to take his notions of truth from the little hamlet in which he was bred, or from the fashions of thought which prevail in his hour of life: for truth dwells not on the Danube, or the Seine, or the Thames; she is not this thing to-day, and to-morrow another; but she is of all places, and all times the same, in every change and in every chance,—as firm as the pillars of the earth, and as beautiful as its fabric. Add to the power of discovering truth, the desire of using it for the promotion of human happiness, and you have the great end and object of our existence. This is the immaculate model of excellence that every human being should fix in the chambers of his heart; which he should place before his mind's eye from the rising to the setting of the sun,—to strengthen his understanding that he may direct his benevolence, and to exhibit to the world the most beautiful spectacle the world *can* behold, of consummate virtue guided by consummate talents. "For some men," says Lord Bacon, "think that the gratification of curiosity is the end of knowledge; some, the love of fame; some, the pleasure of dispute; some, the necessity of supporting themselves by their knowledge: but the real use of *all* knowledge is this,—that we should dedicate that reason which was given us by God to the use and advantage of man."

LECTURE IX.

ON THE CONDUCT OF THE UNDERSTANDING.

It appeared to me rather singular when I sat down to consider this subject, that one man should get up in the midst of six hundred others, and tell them how they were to conduct their understandings. One man may very fairly be supposed to have made greater attainments in botany or in chemistry than others, because he may have dedicated to those sciences a greater portion of his time and attention than others have done; but he who speaks of the conduct of the understanding, speaks of a science to which *every one* who hears him has been apprenticed as well as himself, and therefore his right of instructing can not rest upon the same clear and indisputable grounds.

Having reared up this edifice of modesty, and stopped a little while to admire it, I immediately proceed to demolish it by the following reflections:—that to advance opinions is not to prescribe laws; that knowledge is only extended and confirmed by this contribution of individual sentiments, which every one is free to reject or to adopt; and that nothing would ever *be* done if every person were to enter into a nice calculation of his own deficiencies, and the talents and acquisitions of others, to which they were contrasted; that the only practical way was, to say what you have to say at once, leaving it to time and chance whether your present opinions will be strengthened or refuted by further observation. I beg leave to renew an observation which I made in my first lecture,—that in saying any thing *is* so, I only mean to say *I think it is so.* I have a rational conviction of the difficulty of such subjects; but to express that sense of the difficulty on *all* occasions would be tiresome, and inconsistent with the energy of public speaking.

As the general object of my lecture will be to guard against the most ordinary and flagrant errors committed in the conduct of the understanding, and as I see no use in preserving any order in their enumeration, I shall put them down only in the order in which they happen to occur to me.

The first thing to be done in conducting the understanding is precisely the same as in conducting the body,—to give it regular and copious supplies of food, to prevent that atrophy and marasmus of mind, which comes on from giving it no new ideas. It is a mistake equally fatal to the memory, the imagination, the powers of reasoning, and to every faculty of the mind, to think too early that we can live upon our stock of understanding,—that it is time to leave off business, and make use of the acquisitions we have already made, without troubling ourselves any further to add to them. It is no more possible for an idle man to keep together a certain stock of knowledge, than it is possible to keep together a stock of ice exposed to the meridian sun. Every day destroys a fact, a relation, or an inference; and the only method of preserving the bulk and value of the pile is by constantly adding to it.

The prevailing idea with young people has been, the incompatibility of labor and genius; and therefore, from the fear of being thought dull, they have thought it necessary to remain ignorant. I have seen, at school and at college, a great many young men completely destroyed by having been so *un*fortunate as to produce an excellent copy of verses. Their genius being now established, all that remained for them to do was, to act up to the dignity of the character; and as this dignity consisted in reading nothing new, in forgetting what they had already read, and in pretending to be acquainted with all subjects by a sort of off-hand exertion of talents, they soon collapsed into the most frivolous and insignificant of men. "When we have had continually before us," says Sir Joshua Reynolds, "the great works of art, to impregnate our minds with kindred ideas, we are then, and not till then, fit to produce something of the same species. We behold all about us with the eyes of those penetrating observers whose works we contemplate; and our minds, accustomed to *think* the thoughts of the noblest and brightest intellects, are prepared for the discovery and selection of all that is great and noble in nature. The greatest natural genius can not subsist on its own stock: he who resolves never to ransack any mind but his own, will be soon reduced from mere barrenness to the poorest of all imitations;—he will be obliged to imitate himself, and to repeat what he has before repeated. When we know the subject designed by such men, it will never be difficult to guess what kind of work is to be produced." There is but one method, and that is hard labor; and a man who will not pay that price for distinction, had better at once dedicate himself to the pursuits of the fox,—or sport with the tangles of Neæra's hair,—or talk of bullocks, and glory in the goad! There are many modes of being frivolous, and not a few of being useful; there is but one mode of being intellectually great.

It would be an extremely profitable thing to draw up a short and well-authenticated account of the habits of study of the most celebrated writers with whose style of literary industry we happen to be most acquainted. It would go very far to destroy the absurd and pernicious association of genius and idleness, by showing them that the greatest poets, orators, statesmen, and historians,—men of the most brilliant and imposing talents,—have actually labored as hard as the makers of dictionaries and the arrangers of indexes; and that the most obvious reason why they have been superior to other men is, that they have taken more pains than other men. Gibbon was in his study every morning, winter and summer, at 6 o'clock; Mr. Burke was the most laborious and indefatigable of human beings; Leibnitz was never out of his library; Pascal killed himself by study; Cicero narrowly escaped death by the same cause; Milton was at his books with as much regularity as a merchant or an attorney,—he had mastered all the knowledge of his time; so had Homer. Raffaelle lived but thirty-seven years; and in that short space carried the art so far beyond what it had before reached, that he appears to stand alone as a model to his successors. There are instances to the contrary; but, generally speaking, the life of all truly great men has been a life of intense and incessant labor. They have commonly passed the first half of life in the gross darkness of indigent humility, —overlooked, mistaken, contemned, by weaker men,— thinking while others slept, reading while others rioted, feeling something within them that told them they should not always be kept down among the dregs of the world; and then, when their time was come, and some little accident has given them their first occasion, they have burst out into the light and glory of public life, rich with the spoils of time, and mighty in all the labors and struggles of the mind. Then do the multitude cry out "a miracle of genius!" Yes, he *is* a miracle of genius, because he is a miracle of labor; because instead of trusting to the resources of his own single mind, he has ransacked a thousand minds; because he makes use of the accumulated wisdom of ages, and takes as his point of departure the very last line and boundary to which science has advanced; because it has ever been the object of his life to assist every intellectual gift of nature, however munificent, and however splendid, with every resource that art could suggest, and every attention diligence could bestow.

If we are to read, it is a very important rule in the conduct of the understanding, that we should accustom the mind to keep the best company, by introducing it only to the best books. But there is a sort of vanity some men have, of talking of, and reading, obscure half-forgotten authors, because it passes as a matter of course, that he who quotes authors which are so little read, must be completely and thoroughly acquainted with those authors which are in every man's mouth. For instance, it is very common to quote Shakspeare; but it makes a sort of stare to quote Massinger. I have very little credit for being well acquainted with Virgil; but if I quote Silius Italicus, I may stand some chance of being reckoned a great scholar. In short, whoever wishes to strike out of the great road, and to make a short cut to fame, let him neglect Homer, and Virgil, and Horace, and Ariosto, and Milton, and, instead of these, read and talk of Fracastorius, Sannazarius, Lorenzini, Pastorini, and the thirty-six primary sonneteers of Bettinelli;—let him neglect every thing which the suffrage of ages has made venerable and grand, and dig out of their graves a set of decayed scribblers, whom the silent verdict of the public has fairly condemned to everlasting oblivion. If he complain of the injustice with which they have been treated, and call for a new trial with loud and importunate clamor, though I am afraid he will not make much progress in the estimation of men of sense, he will be sure to make some noise in the crowd, and to be dubbed a man of very curious and extraordinary erudition.

Then there is another piece of foppery which is to be cautiously guarded against—the foppery of *universality*,—of knowing all sciences and excelling in all arts,—chemistry, mathematics, algebra, dancing, history, reasoning, riding, fencing, Low Dutch, High Dutch, natural philosophy, and enough Spanish to talk about Lope de Vega: in short, the modern precept of education very often is, "Take the Admirable Crichton for your model; I would have you ignorant of nothing!" Now *my* advice, on the contrary, is, to have the *courage* to be ignorant of a great number of things, in order to avoid the calamity of being ignorant of every thing. I would exact of a young man a pledge that he would never read Lope de Vega; he should pawn to me his honor to abstain from Bettinelli, and his thirty-five original sonneteers; and I would exact from him the most rigid securities that I was never to hear any thing about that race of penny poets who lived in the reigns of Cosmo and Lorenzo di Medici.

I know a gentleman of the law who has a thorough knowledge of fortifications, and whose acquaintance with bastions, and counterscarps, and parallels, is perfectly astonishing. How impossible it is for any man not professionally engaged in such pursuits to evince a thorough acquaintance with them, without lowering himself in the estimation of every man of understanding who hears him! How thoroughly aware must all such men be, that the time dedicated to such idle knowledge has been lost to the perfection of those mental habits, any one of which is better than the most enormous load of ill-arranged facts!

It is not only necessary that a man should choose the best books, to whatever department of knowledge he desires to dedicate himself, but it is expedient he should aim at the highest departments of knowledge,—that he should not content himself, as some men are apt to do, throughout the whole of his life, with his school habits of acquiring languages and cultivating imagination, but that he should attend to the principles of civil policy,—the practices by which nations become rich, the rules by which their relations with other countries should be arranged; the intellectual nature of man,—of what his understanding consists, and what are the great facts observable of his active and moral powers. I venerate the ancient languages, and our English universities where they are preserved, as much as man can do; but I really do not see why at least a co-ordinate importance might not be given to subjects of such value as those of which I have been speaking.

In looking to the effects of education upon after-life (which is the only mode of determining whether education is good or bad), I do allow it to be of great consequence that a young man should be a good scholar; but I also beg leave humbly to contend, that it is not without its beneficial consequences, that the minds of our young men may be early awakened to such subjects as the philosophy of law, the philosophy of commerce, the philosophy of the human mind, and the philosophy of political government. If an equal chance be given to these subjects and to the classics, if they are all equally honored and rewarded, the original diversities and caprices of nature will determine a sufficient number of minds to each channel; on the contrary, if a young man, from his earliest days, hears nothing held in honor and estimation but classical reading,—if we have no other idea of ignorance than false quantities, and no other idea of excellence than mellifluous longs and shorts, the bias of his mind is fixed,—his line of distinction is taken; he either despises these sciences because he knows them not, or, if he have the ability to discover his deficiencies, and the candor to own them, he feels the want of that early determination, that instinctive zeal, which no circumstance in after-life can ever divert or extinguish.

We do not want readers, for the number of readers seems to be very much upon the increase, and mere readers are very often the most idle of human beings. There is a sort of feeling of getting through a book,—of getting enough out of it, perhaps, for the purpose of conversation,—which is the great cause of this imperfect reading, and the forgetfulness which is the consequence of it: whereas the ambition of a man of parts should be, not to know *books*, but *things;* not to show other men that he has read Locke, and Montesquieu, and Beccaria, and Dumont, but to show them that he knows the subjects on which Locke and Beccaria and Dumont have written. It is no more necessary that a man should remember the different dinners and suppers which have made him healthy, than the different books which have made him wise. Let us see the result of good food in a strong body, and the result of great reading in a full and powerful mind.

If you measure the value of study by the insight you get into subjects, not by the power of saying you have read many books, you will soon perceive that no time is so badly saved, as that which is saved by getting through a book in a hurry. For if, to the time you have given, you had added a little more, the subject would have been fixed on your mind, and the whole time profitably employed; whereas, upon your present arrangement, because you would not give a little more, you have lost all. Besides, this is overlooked by rapid and superficial readers, —that the best way of reading books with rapidity is, to acquire that habit of severe attention to what they contain, that perpetually confines the mind to the single object it has in view. When you have read enough to have acquired the habit of reading without suffering your mind to wander, and when you can bring to bear upon your subject a great share of previous knowledge, you may then read with rapidity: before that, as you have taken the wrong road, the faster you proceed the more you will be sure to err. Upon this subject of the wandering of the mind, I shall read a passage from Mr. Locke. "That there is constant succession and flux of ideas in our minds, I have observed in the former part of this Essay, and every one may take notice of it himself. This, I suppose, may deserve some part of our care, in the conduct of our understandings; and I think it may be of great advantage, if we can, by use, get that power over our minds as to be able to direct that train of ideas, that so, since there will no new ones perpetually come into our thoughts by a constant succession, we may be able, by choice, so to direct them, that none may come in view but such as are pertinent to our present inquiry, and in such order as may be most useful to the discovery we are upon; or, at least, if some foreign and unsought ideas will offer themselves, that yet we might be able to reject them, and keep them from taking off our minds from its present pursuit, and hinder them from running away with our thoughts quite from the subject in hand."*

A sincere attachment to truth, moral and scientific, is a habit which cures a thousand little infirmities of mind, and is as honorable to a man who possesses it, in point of character, as it is profitable in point of improvement. There is nothing more beautiful in science than to hear any man candidly owning his ignorance. It is *so* little the habit of men who cultivate knowledge to do so,—they so often have recourse to subterfuge, nonsense, or hypothesis, rather than to a plain manly declaration, either that they themselves do not understand the subject, or that the subject is not understood,—that it is really quite refreshing to witness such instances of philosophical candor, and it creates an *immediate* prepossession in favor of the person in whom it is observed.

Next to this we have the abuse of words, and the fal-

* Vol. iii. p. 410.

lacy of associations; compared with which, all other modes of misconducting the understanding are insignificant and trivial. What do you *mean* by what you say? Are you prepared to give a clear account of words which you use so positively, and by the help of which you form opinions that you seem resolved to maintain at all hazards? Perhaps I should astonish many persons by putting to them such sort of questions:—Do you know what is meant by the word *nature?* Have you definite notions of justice? How do you explain the word chance? What is virtue? Men are every day framing the rashest propositions on such sort of subjects, and prepared to kill and to die in their defense. They never, for a single instant, doubt of the meaning of that, which was embarrassing to Locke, and in which Leibnitz and Descartes were never able to agree. Ten thousand people have been burned before now, or hanged, for one proposition. The proposition has no meaning. Looked into and examined in these days, it is absolute nonsense. A man quits his country in disgust at some supposed violation of its liberties, sells his estates, and settles in America. Twenty years afterward, it occurs to him, that he had never reflected upon the meaning of the word,—that he has packed up his goods and changed his country for a sound.

Fortitude, justice, and candor, are very necessary instruments of happiness; but they require time and exertion. The instruments I am now proposing to you you must not despise—*grammar*, *definition*, and *interpretation*—instruments which overturn the horrible tyranny of adjectives and substantives, and free the mind from the chains of that *logocracy* in which it is so frequently enslaved, Now have the goodness to observe what I mean. If you choose to quarrel with your eldest son, do it; if you are determined to be disgusted with the world, and to go and live in Westmoreland, do so; if you are resolved to quit your country and settle in America, go!—only, when you have settled the reasons upon which you take one or the other of these steps, have the goodness to examine whether the *words* in which those reasons are contained have really any distinct meaning;

and if you find they have not, embrace your first-born, forget America, unloose your packages, and remain where you are!

There are men who suffer certain barren generalities to get the better of their understandings, by which they try all their opinions, and make them their perpetual standards of right and wrong: as thus—Let us beware of *novelty;* The excesses of the people are *always* to be feared: or these contrary maxims—that there is a natural tendency in all governments to encroach upon the liberties of the people; or, that every thing modern is probably an improvement of antiquity. Now what can the use be of sawing about a set of maxims to which there are a complete set of antagonist maxims? For of what use is it to tell me that governors have a tendency to encroach upon the liberties of the people? and is that a reason why you should throw yourself systematically in opposition to the government? What you *say* is very true; what you *do* is very foolish. For is there not another maxim quite as true, that the excesses of the people are to be guarded against? and does not one evil *à priori* require your attention as well as another? The business is, to determine, at any one particular period of affairs, which is in danger of being weakened, and to act accordingly, like an honest and courageous man; not to lie like a dead weight at one end of the beam, without the smallest recollection there is any other, and that the equilibrium will be violated alike whichever extreme shall preponderate. In the same manner, a thing is not good because it is new, or good because it is old;—there is no end of retorting such equally true principles: but it is good because it is fit for the purpose for which it was intended, and bad because it is not.

A great deal of talent is lost to the world for the want of a little courage. Every day sends to their graves a number of obscure men who have only remained obscure because their timidity has prevented them from making a first effort; and who, if they could only have been induced to begin, would in all probability have gone great lengths in the career of fame. The fact is, that in order to do any thing in this world worth doing, we must not stand shivering on the bank, and thinking of the cold and the danger, but jump in and scramble through as well as we can. It will not do to be perpetually calculating risks, and adjusting nice chances: it did all very well before the Flood, when a man could consult his friends upon an intended publication for a hundred and fifty years, and then live to see its success for six or seven centuries afterward; but at present a man waits, and doubts, and hesitates, and consults his brother, and his uncle, and his first cousins, and his particular friends, till one fine day he finds that he is sixty-five years of age,—that he has lost so much time in consulting first cousins and particular friends, that he has no more time left to follow their advice. There is such little time for over-squeamishness at present, the opportunity so easily slips away, the very period of life at which a man chooses to venture, *if ever*, is so confined, that it is no bad rule to preach up the necessity, in such instances, of a little violence done to the feelings, and of efforts made in defiance of strict and sober calculation.

With respect to that fastidiousness which disturbs the right conduct of the understanding, it must be observed that there are two modes of judging of any thing: one, by the test of what has actually been done in the same way before; the other, by what we can conceive *may* be done in that way. Now this latter method of mere imaginary excellence can hardly be a just criterion, because it may be in fact impossible to reduce to practice what it is perfectly easy to conceive: no man, before he has tried, can tell how difficult it is to manage prejudice, jealousy, and delicacy, and to overcome all that friction which the world opposes to speculation. Therefore, the fair practical rule seems to be, to compare any exertion, by all similar exertions which have preceded it, and to allow merit to any one who has improved, or, at least, who has not deteriorated the standard of excellence, in his own department of knowledge. Fastidious men are always judging by the other standard; and, as the rest of the understanding can not fill up in a century what the imagination can sketch out in a moment, they are always in a state of perpetual disappointment, and their conversation one uniform tenor of blame. At the same time that I say this, I beg leave to lift up both my hands against that pernicious facility of temper, in the estimation of which every thing is charming and delightful. Among the smaller duties of life I hardly know any one more important than that of not praising where praise is not due. Reputation is one of the prizes for which men contend: it is, as Mr. Burke calls it, "the cheap defense and ornament of nations, and the nurse of manly exertions;" it produces more labor and more talent than twice the wealth of a country could ever rear up. It is the coin of genius; and it is the imperious duty of every man to bestow it with the most scrupulous justice and the wisest economy.

I am about to recommend a practice in the conduct of the understanding which I dare say will be strongly objected to, by many men of the world who may overhear it, and that is, the practice of arguing, or, if that be a word in bad repute, of *discussing*. But then I have many limitations to add to such recommendation. It is as unfair to compel a man to discuss with you, who can not play the game, or does not like it, as it would be to compel a person to play at chess with you under similar circumstances: neither is such a sort of exercise of the mind suitable to the rapidity and equal division of general conversation. Such sort of practices are, of course, as ill-bred and as absurd as it would be to pull out a grammar and dictionary in a general society, and to prosecute the study of a language. But when two men meet together who love truth, and discuss any difficult point with good nature and a respect for each other's understandings, it always imparts a high degree of steadiness and certainty to our knowledge; or, what is nearly of equal value, and certainly of greater difficulty, it convinces us of our ignorance. It is an exercise grossly abused by those who have recourse to it, and is very apt to degenerate into a habit of perpetual contradiction, which is the most tiresome and most *disgusting* in all the catalogue of imbecilities. It is an exercise which timid men dread,—from which irritable men ought to abstain; but which, in my humble opinion, advances a man, who is calm enough for it, and strong enough for it, far beyond any other method of employing the mind. Indeed, a promptitude to discuss, is so far a proof of a sound mind, that, whenever we feel pain and alarm at our opinions being called in question, it is almost a certain sign that they have been taken up without examination, or that the reasons which once determined our judgment have vanished away.

I direct these observations only to those who are capable of discussing; for there are many who have not the quickness and the presence of mind necessary for it, and who, in consequence, must be compelled to yield their opinions to the last speaker. And there is no question, that it is far preferable to remain under the influence of moderate errors, than to be bandied about for the whole of life from one opinion to another, at the pleasure, and for the sport of superior intelligence.

But other men's understandings are to be made use of, in the conduct of your own, in many other methods than in that of discussion. Lord Bacon says, that to enter into the kingdom of knowledge, we must put on the spirit of little children; and if he means that we are to submit to be taught by whoever can, or will teach us, it is a habit of mind which leads to very rapid improvement; because a person who possesses it is always putting himself in a train to correct his prejudices, and dissolve his unphilosophical associations. The truth is, that most men want knowledge, not for itself, but for the superiority which knowledge confers; and the means they employ to secure this superiority, are as wrong as the ultimate object, for no man can ever end with being superior, who will not begin with being inferior. The readiest way of founding that empire of talent and knowledge which is the mistaken end such men propose to themselves of knowledge, is, patiently to gather from every understanding that will impart them, the materials of your future power and importance. There are some sayings in our language about merit being always united with modesty, &c. (I suppose because they both begin with an *m*, for alliteration has a great power over proverbs, and proverbs over public opinion); but I fancy that in the majority of instances, the fact is directly the reverse,—that talents and arrogance are commonly united, and that most clever young men of eighteen or nineteen believe themselves to be about the level of Demosthenes, or Virgil, or the Admirable Crichton, or John Duke of Marlborough: but whatever the fact be with respect to modesty, and omitting all the popularity and policy of modesty, I am sure modesty *is* a part of talent; that a certain tendency to hear what others have to say, and to give it its due weight and importance, is quite as valuable as it is amiable; that it is a vast promoter of knowledge; and that the contrary habit of general contempt, is a very dangerous practice in the conduct of the understanding. It exists, I am afraid, commonly in the minds of able men, but they would be much better without it.

As for general skepticism, the only way to avoid it is, to seize on some first principles arbitrarily, and not to quit them. Take as few as you can help,—about a tenth part of what Dr. Reid has taken will suffice,—but take some, and proceed to build upon them. As I have before mentioned, the leading principle of Descartes' philosophy was, *Cogito, ergo sum*—"I think, therefore I exist;" and having laid this foundation stone, he built an enormous building, the ruins of which lie scattered up and down among the sciences in disordered glory and venerable confusion. Some of his disciples, however, could never get a single step further;—they admitted their own existence, but could never deduce any one single truth from it. One might almost wish that these gentlemen had disencumbered themselves of this their only idea, by running down steep places, or walking very far into profound ponds, rather than that they should exhibit such a spectacle of stupidity and perversion.

Such sort of questions as the credibility of memory, and personal identity, are not merely innocent subtilties. I admit it is quite impossible in practice to disbelieve either the one or the other: but they excite a suspicion of the perfect uncertainty of all knowledge; and they often keep young men hesitating and quibbling about the rudiments of all knowledge, instead of pushing on their inquiries with cheerfulness and vigor. I am sure I am not stating an ideal evil; but I know from actual experience, that many understandings have been retarded for years in their prosecution of solid and valuable knowledge, because they could see no evidence for first principles, and were unable to prove that which, by the very meaning of the expression, must be incapable of *all* proof. They considered the whole as an unstable and unphilosophical fabric, and contracted either an indifference to, or contempt for, truth. And if you choose to call all knowledge hypothetical, because first principles are arbitrarily assumed, you certainly *may* call it so, if you please; but then I only contend that it does quite as well as if it were not hypothetical, because all the various errors agree perfectly well together, and produce that happiness which is the end of knowledge.

It is a very wise rule in the conduct of the understanding, to acquire early a correct notion of your own peculiar constitution of mind, and to become well acquainted, as a physician would say, with your *idiosyncrasy*. Are you an acute man, and see sharply for small distances? or are you a comprehensive man, and able to take in wide and extensive views into your mind? Does your mind turn its ideas into wit? or are you apt to take a common-sense view of the objects presented to you? Have you an exuberant imagination, or a correct judgment? Are you quick, or slow? accurate, or hasty? a great reader, or a great thinker? It is a prodigious point gained if any man can find out where his powers lie, and what are his deficiencies,—if he can contrive to ascertain what Nature intended him for: and such are the changes and chances of the world, and so difficult is it to ascertain our own understandings, or those of others, that most things are done by persons who could have done something else better. If you choose to represent the various parts in life by holes upon a table, of different shapes,—some circular, some triangular, some square, some oblong,—and the persons acting these parts by bits of wood of similar shapes, we shall generall·

find that the triangular person has got into the square hole, the oblong into the triangular, and a square person has squeezed himself into the round hole. The officer and the office, the doer and the thing done, seldom fit so exactly, that we can say they were almost made for each other.

But while I am descanting so minutely upon the conduct of the understanding, and the best modes of acquiring knowledge, some men may be disposed to ask, "Why conduct my understanding with such endless care? and what is the use of so much knowledge?" What is the use of so much knowledge?—what is the use of so much life!—what are we to do with the seventy years of existence allotted to us?—and how are we to live them out to the last? I solemnly declare that, but for the love of knowledge, I should consider the life of the meanest hedger and ditcher, as preferable to that of the greatest and richest man here present: for the fire of our minds is like the fire which the Persians burn in the mountains,—it flames night and day, and is immortal, and not to be quenched! Upon something it *must* act and feed,—upon the pure spirit of knowledge, or upon the foul dregs of polluting passions. Therefore, when I say, in conducting your understanding, love knowledge with a great love, with a vehement love, with a love coeval with life, what do I say, but love innocence,—love virtue,—love purity of conduct,—love that which, if you are rich and great, will sanctify the blind fortune which has made you so, and make men call it justice,—love that which, if you are poor, will render your poverty respectable, and make the proudest feel it unjust to laugh at the meanness of your fortunes,—love that which will comfort you, adorn you, and never quit you,—which will open to you the kingdom of thought, and all the boundless regions of conception, as an asylum against the cruelty, the injustice, and the pain that may be your lot in the outer world,—that which will make your motives habitually great and honorable, and light up in an instant a thousand noble disdains at the very thought of meanness and of fraud! Therefore, if any young man here have embarked his life in pursuit of knowledge, let him go on without doubting or fearing the event;—let him not be intimidated by the cheerless beginnings of knowledge, by the darkness from which she springs, by the difficulties which hover around her, by the wretched habitations in which she dwells, by the want and sorrow which sometimes journey in her train; but let him ever follow her as the Angel that guards him, and as the Genius of his life. She will bring him out at last into the light of day, and exhibit him to the world comprehensive in acquirements, fertile in resources, rich in imagination, strong in reasoning, prudent and powerful above his fellows, in all the relations and in all the offices of life.

LECTURE X.

ON WIT AND HUMOR.

The question I have very often had asked me respecting the present subject of my lecture is, what has *Wit* to do with Moral Philosophy? Little or nothing, certainly, if Moral Philosophy is merely understood *practical* Moral Philosophy, or *Ethics;* but if the term be taken as it universally is wherever Moral Philosophy is taught,—as in contradistinction to Physical Philosophy, or the philosophy which concerns itself with the laws of the material world,—then Moral Philosophy will include every thing which relates to the human mind—of which mind these phenomena of wit and humor are very striking peculiarities. But if, though allowed to appertain to Moral Philosophy because they appertain to the human mind, they should be considered as very *frivolous* parts of that science, this must not, on any account, be allowed to pass for truth. The feeling of the ridiculous produces an immense effect upon human affairs. It is so far from being powerless or unimportant, that it has a strong tendency to overpower even truth, justice, and all those high-born qualities which have the lawful mastery of the human mind.

Such sort of subjects are no less difficult than they are important. I may not always speak on them with the forms of modesty, but no man *can* be more thoroughly convinced that I am, of the difficulty with which such investigations are attended, and of the folly of dogmatizing upon topics where the best understandings may arrive, and *have* arrived, at very opposite conclusions. In addition to this plea for indulgence, it so happens this year that I am extremely ill prepared for what I have undertaken. To read lectures upon Moral Philosophy is not a very easy thing under *any* circumstances;—to read them before a *mixed audience of both sexes*, and *for the first time*, are accidents which do not come in diminution of that difficulty. These difficulties are best overcome by a little practice. The same indulgence should be extended to young lecturers and young professors that is extended to the young of all other animals,—who can not reasonably be supposed to have arrived at the top of their cunning, or to have reached the perfection of their strength. I shall only advertise my hearers, that when I have finished this lecture I have not finished this subject;—I shall have a great deal more to say upon it in my next lecture, and the two must be taken together, in order to analyze the ridiculous, and, perhaps, as some evil-disposed persons may say, to *exemplify it*.

"Wit," says Dr. Barrow, "is a thing so subtile, so versatile, and so multiform,—appearing in so many shapes, so many postures, and so many garbs,—so variously apprehended by several eyes and judgments, that it seemeth no less hard to settle a clear and certain notion thereof than to make a portrait of Proteus, or to define the figure of the fleeting air. Sometime it lieth in pat allusion to a known story, or in seasonable application of a trivial saying, or in forging an apposite tale;—sometimes it playeth in words and phrases, taking advantage of the ambiguity of their sense, or the affinity of their sound;—sometimes it is wrapped in a dress of humorous expression;—sometimes it lurketh under an odd similitude;—sometimes it is lodged in a sly question, in a smart answer, in a quirkish reason, in a shrewd intimation, in cunningly diverting, or cleverly retorting an objection; sometimes it is couched in a bold scheme of speech, in a tart irony, a lusty hyperbole, a startling metaphor, a plausible reconciling of contradictions, or in acute nonsense;—sometimes a scenical representation of persons or things, a counterfeit speech, a mimical look or gesture, passeth for it;—sometimes an affected simplicity, sometimes a presumptuous bluntness, giveth it being;—sometimes it ariseth only from a lucky hitting upon what is strange ;—often it consisteth in one knows not what, and ariseth one knows not how : its ways are unaccountable and inexplicable, being answerable to the numberless rovings of fancy and windings of language. It is, in short, a manner of speaking out of the plain way, which, by an uncouthness in conceit or expression, doth amuse the fancy, stirring in it some wonder, and breeding some delight. It raiseth admiration, as signifying a nimble sagacity of apprehension, a special felicity of invention, a vivacity of spirit, and reach of wit more than vulgar. It seemeth to argue a rare quickness of parts that can produce such applicable conceits, a notable skill that can dexterously accommodate them to the purpose before him, together with a lively briskness of humor, not apt to damp those sportful flashes of imagination. It procures delight, by gratifying curiosity with its rarity, by diverting the mind from its road of serious thoughts, by instilling gayety and airiness of spirit, and by seasoning matters, otherwise distasteful and insipid, with an unusual and a grateful twang." This is Dr. Barrow's famous definition of wit,—which is very witty, and nothing else ! and in which the author has managed as a man would do, who should take a degree in music by singing a song, or in medicine by healing a surfeit. He has exemplified his subject instead of explaining it ; and given you a specimen, instead of a solution, of wit. It is surprising what very little has been written in the English language upon this curious subject. Congreve has written upon it in the same witty manner as Barrow, without throwing the smallest light upon the nature of wit. Cowley says,

"Tell me, oh tell, what kind of thing is wit,
Thou who master art of it?
A thousand different shapes it bears,
Comely in thousand shapes appears.
Yonder we see it plain ; and here 'tis now,
Like spirits, in a place, we know not how."

And so he goes on, with a string of witty allusions, for twenty stanzas, in an ode which Johnson calls inimitable, and which, as a mere piece of poetry of the school of the metaphysical poets, certainly *is* so; but has nothing to do with a serious explanation of the subject. Dryden says of wit, that it is a propriety of thoughts and words, or thoughts and words elegantly adapted to the subject; but there is a propriety of thoughts and words in one of Blair's Sermons, which I never yet heard praised for their wit. And the thoughts and words are elegantly adapted to the subject in Campbell's "Pleasures of Hope," which is something much *better* than a witty poem. Pope says of wit,

> "True wit is nature to advantage drest,
> Oft thought before, but ne'er so well exprest."

Then the Philippics of Cicero, the Orations of Demosthenes, are witty; Cæsar's Commentaries are witty; Massillon is one of the greatest wits that ever lived; the Oraisons funèbres of Bossuet are prodigies of facetiousness. Sir Richard Blackmore's notion of wit is, that it is a series of high and exalted ferments. It very possibly *may* be; but, not exactly comprehending what is meant by "a series of high and exalted ferments," I do not think myself bound to waste much time in criticizing the metaphysics of this learned physician.

The first definition of wit worth noticing is that of Mr. Locke, which I shall read to you. "How much the imperfection of accurately discriminating ideas one from another, lies either in the dullness or faults of the organs of sense,—or want of acuteness, exercise, or attention in the understanding,—or hastiness and precipitancy, natural to some tempers,—I will not here examine: it sufficeth to take notice, that this is one of the operations that the mind may reflect on and observe in itself. It is of that consequence to its other knowledge, that, so far as this faculty is in itself dull, or not rightly made use of, for the distinguishing one thing from another, so far our notions are confused, and our reason and judgment disturbed or misled. If, in having our ideas in the memory ready at hand, consists quickness of parts,—in this of having them unconfused, and being able nicely to distinguish one thing from another, where there is but the least difference, consists, in a great measure, the exactness of judgment and clearness of reason, which is to be observed in one man above another. And hence, perhaps, may be given some reason for that common observation, that men who have a great deal of wit, and prompt memories, have not always the clearest judgment or deepest reason: for wit lying mostly in the assemblage of ideas, and putting those together with quickness and variety wherein can be found any resemblance or congruity, whereby to make up pleasant pictures and agreeable visions in the fancy; judgment, on the contrary, lies quite on the other side, in separating carefully, one from another, ideas wherein can be found the least difference,—thereby to avoid being misled by similitude, and by affinity to take one thing for another. This is a way of proceeding quite contrary to metaphor and allusion, wherein, for the most part, lies that entertainment and pleasantry of wit which strikes so lively on the fancy, and therefore is so acceptable to all people,—because its beauty appears at first sight, and there is required no labor of thought to examine what truth or reason there is in it. The mind, without looking any further, rests satisfied with the agreeableness of the picture, and the gayety of the fancy; and it is a kind of an affront to go about to examine it by the severe rules of truth and good reason, whereby it appears that it consists in something that is not perfectly conformable to them."* Now this notion of wit,—that it consists in putting those ideas together with quickness and variety wherein can be found any resemblance or congruity, in order to excite pleasure in the mind,—is a little too comprehensive, for it comprehends both eloquence and poetry. In the first place, we must exclude the idea of their being put together *quickly*, as this part of the definition applies only to *colloquial* wit. The "Avare" and the "Tartuffe" of Molière, would be witty even though we knew each of those plays had taken the author a year to compose. But as for the resemblance and congruity, there is a resemblance and congruity in the well-known picture Mr.

* Works, vol. i. p. 60.

Burke has drawn of the Queen of France; but nobody can with any propriety call it *witty* without degrading it. The fact is, that the combinations of ideas in which there is resemblance and congruity, will as often produce the sublime and the beautiful, as well as the witty;—a circumstance to which Mr. Locke does not appear to have attended, in the very short and cursory notice he has taken of wit. Addison's papers in the "Spectator" on this subject are more dedicated to the establishment of a good *taste* in wit, than to an analysis of its nature. He adds to this definition, by way of explanation, that it must be such a resemblance as excites delight and surprise in the reader; but this still leaves the account of wit as it found it, without discriminating the witty from the sublime and the beautiful, for many sublime and beautiful passages in poetry entirely correspond with this definition of wit.

> "He scarce had ceas'd, when the superior Fiend
> Was moving toward the shore: his ponderous shield,
> Ethereal temper, massy, large, and round,
> Behind him cast; the broad circumference
> Hung on his shoulders like the moon, whose orb
> Through optic glass the Tuscan artist views
> At evening from the top of Fesolé,
> Or in Valdarno, to descry new lands,
> Rivers, or mountains, in her spotty globe.
> His spear—to equal which the tallest pine
> Hewn on Norwegian hills, to be the mast
> Of some great ammiral, were but a wand—
> He walk'd with to support uneasy steps
> Over the burning marle."

In this picture there certainly is an assemblage of very grand and very beautiful images, exciting delight and surprise, and gathered together expressly for their resemblance; yet no effect can be more distinct from the feeling of *wit* than the effect produced by these lines. "Wit," says Johnson, "may be more rigorously and philosophically considered as a kind of *concordia discors*—a combination of dissimilar images, or discovery of occult resemblances in things apparently unlike;" but if this be true, then the discovery of the resemblance between diamond and charcoal, between acidification and combustion, are pure pieces of wit, and full of the most ingenious and exalted pleasantry.

It is very little worth while to stop to examine what Lord Kames has said upon the subject of wit and humor: he has said so very little, and that little in so very hasty a manner, that there is no occasion to delay the progress of the investigation by dwelling on his opinions.

The best account in our language of wit and humor (as far as I know) is to be found in the first volume of Campbell's Philosophy of Rhetoric. I say the *best*, though I must take the liberty of saying that there appears to me to be very material defects in it. In the first place he seems to make precisely the same mistake which all the other definers and describers of wit have done. "Wit," he says, "is that which excites agreeable surprise in the mind, by the strange assemblage of related images presented to it." Now, this account of wit, as I have before remarked more than once, is too extensive, and includes the sublime and the beautiful. He then adds, that "wit effects its objects three ways: first, in debasing things pompous; next in aggrandizing things mean; thirdly, by setting ordinary objects (by means not only remote, but apparently contrary) in a particular and uncommon point of view." If this threefold division be meant as a distinguishing criterion of the operations of wit, it fails; for eloquence effects all these three objects as well as wit: and if it be meant as an exhaustive analysis of modes of wit, it is extremely incomplete; for wit may find similitudes for, and relations between, *great objects* without debasing them, and do the same with *little* objects without exalting them. I may find a hundred ingenious points of resemblance between a black beetle and a birchen broom, without adding much dignity either to the insect or the instrument. I mention these objections to Dr. Campbell's Essay because it is my duty to discriminate, though I repeat again, that, as far as I know, and upon the whole, it is the best account of these subjects extant in the English language.

Now to begin at the beginning of this discussion, it is plain that wit concerns itself with the relations which subsist between our ideas: and the first observation which occurs to any man turning his attention to this subject is, that it can not, of course, concern itself with *all* the relations which subsist between all our ideas; for then every proposition would be witty;—The rain wets me through,—Butter is spread upon bread,—would be propositions replete with mirth; and the moment the mind observed the plastic and diffusible nature of butter, and the excellence of bread as a substratum, it would become enchanted with this flash of facetiousness. Therefore, the first limit to be affixed to that observation of relations, which produces the feeling of wit, is, that they must be relations which excite *surprise*. If you tell me that all men must die, I am very little struck with what you say, because it is not an assertion very remarkable for its novelty; but if you were to say that man was like a time-glass,—that both must run out, and both render up their dust, I should listen to you with more attention, because I should feel something like surprise at the sudden relation you had struck out between two such apparently dissimilar ideas as a man and a time-glass.

Surprise is so essential an ingredient of wit, that no wit will bear repetition;—at least the original electrical feeling produced by any piece of wit can never be renewed. There is a sober sort of approbation succeeds at hearing it the second time, which is as different from its original rapid, pungent volatility, as a bottle of champagne that has been open three days is, from one that has at that very instant emerged from the darkness of the cellar. To hear that the top of Mont Blanc is like an umbrella, though the relation be new to me, is not sufficient to excite surprise; the idea is so very obvious, it is so much within the reach of the most ordinary understandings, that I can derive no sort of pleasure from the comparison. The relation discovered, must be something remote from all the common tracks and sheep-walks made in the mind; it must not be a comparison of color with color, and figure with figure, or any comparison which, though individually new, is specifically stale, and to which the mind has been in the habit of making many similar; but it must be something removed from common apprehension, distant from the ordinary haunts of thought,—things which are never brought together in the common events of life, and in which the mind has discovered relations by its own subtilty and quickness.

Now, then, the point we have arrived at, at present, in building up our definition of wit, is, that it is the discovery of those relations in ideas which are calculated to excite surprise. But a great deal must be taken away from this account of wit before it is sufficiently accurate; for, in the first place, there must be no feeling or conviction of the *utility* of the relation so discovered. If you go to see a large cotton-mill, the manner in which the large water-wheel below, works the little parts of the machinery seven stories high, the relation which one bears to another, is extremely surprising to a person unaccustomed to mechanics; but, instead of feeling as you feel at a piece of wit, you are absorbed in the contemplation of the *utility* and *importance* of such relations,—there is a sort of rational approbation mingled with your surprise, which makes the *whole* feeling very different from that of wit. At the same time, if we attend very accurately to our feelings, we shall perceive that the discovery of any surprising relation whatever, produces some slight sensation of wit. When first the manner in which a steam-engine opens and shuts its own valves is explained to me, or when I at first perceive the ingenious and complicated contrivances of any piece of machinery, the surprise that I feel at the discovery of these connections has always something in it which resembles the feeling of wit, though that is very soon extinguished by others of a very different nature. Children, who view the different parts of a machine not so much with any notions of its utility, feel something still more like the sensation of wit when first they perceive the effect which one part produces upon another. Show a child of six years old, that, by moving the treadle of a knife-grinder's machine, you make the large wheel turn round, or that by pressing the spring of a repeating watch you make the watch strike, and you probably raise up a feeling in the child's mind precisely similar to that of wit. There is a mode of teaching children geography by disjointed parts of a wooden map, which they fit together. I have no doubt that the child, in finding the kingdom or republic which fits into a great hole in the wooden sea, feels exactly the sensation of wit. Every one must remember that fitting the inviting projection of Crim Tartary into the Black Sea was one of the greatest delights of their childhood; and almost all children are sure to scream with pleasure at the discovery.

The relation between ideas which excite surprise, in order to be witty, must not excite any feeling of the beautiful. "The good man," says a Hindoo epigram, "goes not upon enmity, but rewards with kindness the very being who injures him. So the sandal-wood, while it is felling, imparts to the edge of the axe its aromatic flavor." Now here is a relation which would be witty if it were not beautiful: the relation discovered betwixt the falling sandal-wood, and the returning good for evil, is a new relation which excites surprise; but the *mere* surprise at the relation, is swallowed up by the contemplation of the moral beauty of the thought, which throws the mind into a more solemn and elevated mood than is compatible with the feeling of wit.

It would not be a difficult thing to do (and if the limits of my lecture allowed I would do it) to select from Cowley and Waller a suite of passages, in order to show the effect of the beautiful in destroying the feeling of wit, and *vice versâ*. First, I would take a passage purely witty, in which the mind merely contemplated the singular and surprising relation of the ideas; next, a passage where the admixture of some beautiful sentiment,—the excitation of some slight moral feeling,—arrested the mind from the contemplation of the relation between the ideas; then, a passage in which the beautiful overpowered still more the facetious, till, at last, it was totally destroyed.

If the relation between the ideas, to produce wit, must not be mingled with the beautiful, still less must they be so with the sublime. In that beautiful passage in Mr. Campbell's poem of "Lochiel," the wizard repeats these verses,—which were in every one's mouth when first the poem was written:—

> "Lochiel! Lochiel! though my eyes I should seal,
> Man can not keep secret what God would reveal.
> 'Tis the sunset of life gives *me* mystical lore,
> And *the coming events cast their shadows before.*"

Now this comparison of the dark uncertain sort of prescience of future events implied by the gift of second sight, and the notice of an approaching solid body by the previous approach of its shadow, contains a new and striking relation; but it is not *witty*, nor would it ever have been considered as witty, if expressed in a more concise manner, and with the rapidity of conversation, because it inspires feelings of a much higher cast than those of wit, and, instead of suffering the mind to dwell upon the mere relation of ideas, fills it with a sort of mysterious awe, and gives an air of sublimity to the fabulous power of prediction. Every one knows the Latin line on the miracle at the marriage-supper in Cana of Galilee,—on the conversion of water into wine. The poet says,

> "*The modest water saw its God, and blush'd!*"

Now, in my mind, that sublimity which some persons discover in this passage is destroyed by its wit; it appears to me witty, and *not* sublime. I have no *great* feelings excited by it, and can perfectly well stop to consider the mere relation of ideas. I hope I need not add, that the line, *if it produce the effect of a witty conceit, and not of a sublime image*, is *perfectly misplaced* and *irreverent:* the *intent*, however, of the poet, was *undoubtedly* to be *serious*. In the same manner, whenever the mind is not left to the mere surprise excited by the relation of ideas, but when that relation excites any powerful emotion—as those of the sublime and beautiful, or any high passion—as anger or pity, or any train of reflections upon the *utility* of the relations, the feeling of wit is always diminished or destroyed. It seems to be occasioned by those relations of ideas which excite surprise, and surprise *alone*. Whenever relations excite any other strong feeling as well as surprise, the wit is either destroyed, diminished, or the two co-existent feelings of wit and the other emotion may, by careful reflection, be distinguished from each other. I may be very wrong (for these subjects are extremely difficult), but I know no single passage in any author which is at once beautiful and witty, or sublime and witty. I know innumerable passages which are intended to be beautiful or sublime, and which are merely witty; and I know many passages in which the relation of ideas is very new and surprising, and which are *not* witty because they are beautiful and sublime. Lastly, when the effect of wit is heightened by strong sense and useful truth, we may perceive in the mind what part of the pleasure arises from the mere relation of ideas, what from the utility of the precept; and many instances might be produced, where the importance and utility of the thing said, prevents the mind from contemplating the mere relation, and considering it as wit. For example: in that apophthegm of Rochefoucault, that hypocrisy is a homage which vice renders to virtue, the image is witty, but all attention to the *mere wit* is swallowed up in the justness and value of the observation. So that I think I have some color for saying, that wit is produced by those relations between ideas which excite surprise, and surprise only. Observe, I am only defining the *causes* of a certain feeling in the mind called wit;—I can no more define the feeling itself, than I can define the flavor of venison. We all seem to partake of one and the other, with a very great degree of satisfaction; but why each feeling *is* what it is, and nothing else, I am sure I can not pretend to determine.

Louis XIV. was exceedingly molested by the solicitations of a general officer at the levée, and cried out, loud enough to be overheard, "That gentleman is the most troublesome officer in the whole army." "Your Majesty's enemies have said the same thing more than once," was the answer. The wit of this answer consists in the sudden relation discovered in his assent to the King's invective and his own defense. By admitting the King's observation, he seems, at first sight, to be subscribing to the imputation against him; whereas, in reality, he effaces it by this very means. A sudden relation is discovered where none was suspected. Voltaire, in speaking of the effect of epithets in weakening style, said, that the adjectives were the greatest enemies of the substantives, though they agreed in gender, number, and in cases. Here, again, it is very obvious that a relation is discovered which, upon first observation, does not appear to exist. These instances may be multiplied to any extent. A gentleman at Paris, who lived very unhappily with his wife, used, for twenty years together, to pass his evenings at the house of another lady, who was very agreeable, and drew together a pleasant society. His wife died; and his friends all advised him to marry the lady in whose society he had found so much pleasure. He said, no, he certainly should not, for that if he married her, he should not know where to spend his evenings. Here we are suddenly surprised with the idea that the method proposed of securing his comfort may possibly prove the most effectual method of destroying it. At least, to enjoy the pleasantry of the reply, we view it through *his* mode of thinking, who had not been very fortunate in the connection established by his first marriage. I have, in consequence of the definition I have printed of wit in the cards of the Institution, passed one of the most polemical weeks that ever I remember to have spent in my life. I think, however, that if my words are understood in their fair sense, I am not wrong. I have said, surprising relation between *ideas*,—not between *facts*. The difference is very great. A man may tell me he sees a fiery meteor on the surface of the sea: he has no merit in the discovery,—it is no extraordinary act of mind in him,—any one who has eyes can ascertain this relation of facts as well, if it really exist; but to discover a surprising relation in *ideas*, is an act of power in the discoverer, in which, if his wit be good, he exceeds the greater part of mankind: so that the very terms I have adopted, imply comparison and superiority of mind. The discovery of any relation of ideas exciting pure surprise involves the notion of such superiority, and enhances the surprise. To discover relations between facts exciting pure surprise, involves the notion of no such superiority; for any man could ascertain that a calf had two heads if it had two heads: therefore, I again repeat, let any man show me that which is an acknowledged proof of wit, and I believe I could analyze the pleasure experienced from it into surprise, partly occasioned by the unexpected relation established, partly by the display of talent in discovering it; and, putting this position synthetically, I would say, whenever there is a superior act of intelligence in discovering a relation between ideas, which relation excites surprise and no other high emotion, the mind will have the feeling of wit. Why is it not witty to find a gold watch and seals hanging upon a hedge? Because it is a mere relation of facts discovered without any effort of mind, and not (as I have said in my definition) a relation of ideas. Why is it not witty to discover the relation between the moon and the tides? Because it raises other notions than those of mere surprise. Why are not all the extravagant relations in Garagantua witty? Because they are merely odd and extravagant; and mere oddity and extravagance is too easy to excite surprise. Why is it witty, in one of Addison's plays, where the undertaker reproves one of his mourners for laughing at a funeral, and says to him, "You rascal, you! I have been raising your wages for these two years past upon condition that you should appear more sorrowful, and the higher wages you receive the happier you look!" Here is a relation between ideas the discovery of which implies superior intelligence, and excites no other emotion than surprise.

It is imagined that wit is a sort of inexplicable visitation, that it comes and goes with the rapidity of lightning, and that it is quite as unattainable as beauty or just proportion. I am so much of a contrary way of thinking, that I am convinced a man might sit down as systematically, and as successfully, to the study of wit, as he might to the study of mathematics: and I would answer for it, that, by giving up only six hours a day to being witty, he should come on prodigiously before midsummer, so that his friends should hardly know him again. For what is there to hinder the mind from gradually acquiring a habit of attending to the lighter relations of ideas in which wit consists? Punning grows upon every body, and punning is the wit of words. I do not mean to say that it is so easy to acquire a habit of discovering new relations in *ideas* as in *words*, but the difficulty is not so much greater as to render it insuperable to habit. One man is unquestionably much better calculated for it by nature than another: but association, which gradually makes a bad speaker a good one, might give a man wit who had it not, if any man chose to be so absurd as to sit down to acquire it.

I have mentioned puns. They are, I believe, what I have denominated them—the wit of words. They are exactly the same to words which wit is to ideas, and consist in the sudden discovery of relations in language. A pun, to be perfect in its kind, should contain two distinct meanings; the one common and obvious; the other, more remote: and in the notice which the mind takes of the relation between these two sets of words, and in the surprise which that relation excites, the pleasure of a pun consists. Miss Hamilton, in her book on Education, mentions the instance of a boy so very neglectful, that he could never be brought to read the word *patriarchs;* but whenever he met with it he always pronounced it *partridges.* A friend of the writer observed to her, that it could hardly be considered as a mere piece of negligence, for it appeared to him that the boy, in calling them partridges, was *making game* of the patriarchs. Now here are two distinct meanings contained in the same phrase: for to make game of the patriarchs is to laugh at them; or to make game of them is, by a very extravagant and laughable sort of ignorance of words, to rank them among pheasants, partridges, and other such delicacies, which the law takes under its protection and calls *game:* and the whole pleasure derived from this pun consists in the sudden discovery that two such different meanings are referable to one form of expression. I have very little to say about puns; they are in very bad repute, and so they *ought* to be. The wit of language is so miserably inferior to the wit of ideas, that it is very deservedly driven out of good company. Sometimes, indeed, a pun makes its appearance which seems for a moment to redeem its species; but we must not be deceived by them: it is a radically bad race of wit. By unremitting persecution, it has been at last got under, and driven into cloisters,—from whence it must never again be suffered to emerge into the light of the world. One invaluable blessing produced by the banishment of punning is, an immediate reduction of the number of wits. It is a wit of so low an order, and in which some sort of progress is so easily made, that the number of those endowed with the gift of wit would be nearly equal to those endowed with the gift of speech. The condition of putting together ideas in order to be witty operates much in the same salutary manner as the condition of finding rhymes in poetry;—it reduces the number of performers to those who have vigor enough to overcome incipient difficulties, and makes a sort of provision that that which need not be done at all, should be done *well* whenever it *is* done. For we may observe, that mankind are always more fastidious about that which is pleasing, than they are about that which is useful. A commonplace piece of morality is much more easily pardoned than a commonplace piece of poetry or of wit; because it is absolutely necessary for the well-being of society that the rules of morality should be frequently repeated and enforced; and though in any individual instance the thing may be badly done, the sacred necessity of the practice itself, atones in some degree for the individual failure: but as there is no absolute necessity that men should be either wits or poets, we are less inclined to tolerate their mediocrity in superfluities. If a man have ordinary chairs and tables, no one notices it; but if he stick vulgar, gaudy pictures on his walls, which he need not have at all, every one laughs at him for his folly.

The wit of irony consists in the surprise excited by the discovery of that relation wich exists between the apparent praise and the real blame; or, if it be good natured irony, between the apparent blame and the real praise. I shall quote a noble specimen of irony from the preface of "Killing no Murder:"—

"TO HIS HIGHNESS OLIVER CROMWELL.

"May it please your Highness,

"How I have spent some hours of the leisure your Highness has been pleased to give me, this following paper will give your Highness an account. How you will please to interpret it, I can not tell; but I can with confidence say, my intention in it is, to procure your Highness that justice nobody yet does you, and to let the people see, the longer they defer it, the greater injury they do both themselves and you. To your Highness justly belongs the honor of dying for the people: and it can not choose but be an unspeakable consolation to you in the last moments of your life, to consider, with how much benefit to the world you are like to leave it. It is then only, my Lord, the titles you now usurp will be truly yours. You will then be indeed the deliverer of your country, and free it from a bondage little inferior to that from which Moses delivered his. You will then be that true reformer which you would now be thought; religion shall be then restored, liberty asserted, and parliaments have those privileges they have sought for. We shall then hope that other laws will have place beside those of the sword, and that justice shall be otherwise defined than the will and pleasure of the strongest; and we shall then hope men will keep oaths again, and not have the necessity of being false and perfidious to preserve themselves, and be like their ruler. All this we hope from your Highness's happy expiration, who *are the true father* of your country; for while *you* live, we can call nothing ours, and it is from your death that we hope for our inheritances. Let this consideration arm and fortify your Highness's mind against the fears of death, and the terrors of your evil conscience,—that the good you will do by your death, will somewhat balance the evils of your life. And if, in the black catalogue of high malefactors, few can be found that have lived more to the affliction and disturbance of mankind, than your Highness has done; yet your greatest enemies will not deny, that there are likewise as few that have expired more to the universal benefit of mankind, than your Highness is like to do. To hasten this great good, is the chief end of my writing this paper; and if it have the effects I hope it will, your Highness will quickly be out of the reach of men's malice, and your enemies will only be able to wound you in your memory, which strokes you will not feel. That your Highness may be speedily in this security, is the universal wish of your grateful country; this is the desire and prayers of the good and of the bad, and, it may be, is the only thing wherein all sects and factions do agree in their devotion, and it is our only common prayer! But among all that put in their request and supplication for your Highness's speedy deliverance from all earthly troubles, none is more assiduous nor more fervent than he, that, with the rest of the nation, hath the honor to be (may it please your Highness),

"Your Highness's present slave and vassal."

Now, through the whole of this passage, there is an apparent praise of the person to whom it is addressed, and a real censure of that person. The surprise excited by this union of visible eulogium and real satire constitutes the pleasure we receive from the passage.

A sarcasm (which is another species of wit) generally consists in the obliquity of the invective. It must not be direct assertion, but something established by inference and analogy;—something which the mind does not at first perceive, but in the discovery of which it experiences the pleasure of surprise. A true sarcasm is like a sword-stick,—it appears, at first sight, to be much more innocent than it really is, till, all of a sudden, there leaps something out of it—sharp, and deadly, and incisive—which makes you tremble and recoil.

I have insisted, in the beginning of my lecture, on the great power of the ridiculous over the opinions of mankind; including in that term wit, humor, and every other feeling which has laughter for its distinguishing characteristic.

I know of no principle which it is of more importance to fix in the minds of young people than that of the most determined resistance to the encroachments of ridicule. Give up to the world, and to the ridicule with which the world enforces its dominion, every trifling question of manner and appearance: it is to toss courage and firmness to the winds, to combat with the mass upon such subjects as these. But learn from the earliest days to inure your principles against the perils of ridicule: you can no more exercise your reason, if you live in the constant dread of laughter, than you can enjoy your life, if you are in the constant terror of death. If you think it right to differ from the times, and to make a stand for any valuable point of morals, do it, however rustic, however antiquated, however pedantic it may appear;—do it, not for insolence, but *seriously* and *grandly*,—as a man who wore a soul of his own in his bosom, and did not wait till it was breathed into him by the breath of fashion. Let men call you mean, if you know you are just; hypocritical, if you are honestly religious; pusillanimous, if you feel that you are firm: resistance soon converts unprincipled wit into sincere respect; and no after time can tear from those feelings which every man carries within him who has made a noble and successful exertion in a virtuous cause.

LECTURE XI.

ON WIT AND HUMOR.—PART II.

HOBBES defines laughter to be "a sudden glory, arising from a sudden conception of some eminency in ourselves, by comparison with infirmity of others, or our own former infirmity." By *infirmity* he must mean, I presume, marked and decided inferiority, whether accidental and momentary, or natural and permanent. He can not, of course, mean by it, what we usually denominate infirmity of body or mind; for it must be obvious, at the first moment, that humor has a much wider range than this. If we were to see a little man walking in the streets with a hat half as big as an umbrella, we should laugh; and that laughter certainly could not be ascribed to the infirmities either of his body or mind: for his diminutive figure, without his disproportionate hat, I shall suppose by hypothesis, to be such as would excite no laughter at all;—and, indeed, an extraordinary large man, with a hat such as is worn by boys of twelve years old, would be an object quite as ludicrous.

Taking, therefore, the language of Hobbes to mean the sudden discovery of any inferiority, it will be very easy to show that such is *not* the explanation of that laughter excited by humor: for I may discover suddenly that a person has lost half-a-crown,—or, that his tooth aches,—or, that his house is not so well built, or his coat not so well made, as mine; and yet none of these discoveries give me the slightest sensation of the humorous. If it be suggested that these proofs of inferiority are very slight, the theory of Hobbes is still more weakened, by recurring to greater instances of inferiority: for the sudden information that any one of my acquaintance has broken his leg, or is completely ruined in his fortunes, has decidedly very little of humor in it;—at least it is not very customary to be thrown into paroxysms of laughter by such sort of intelligence. It is clear, then, that there are many instances of the sudden discovery of inferiorities and infirmities in others, which excite no laughter; and, therefore, pride is not the explanation of laughter excited by the humorous. It is true, the object of laughter is always inferior to us; but then the converse is *not* true,—that every one who is inferior to us is an object of laughter: therefore, as some inferiority is ridiculous, and other inferiority *not* ridiculous, we must, in order to explain the nature of the humorous, endeavor to discover the discriminating cause.

This discriminating cause is *incongruity*, or the conjunction of objects and circumstances not usually combined,—and the conjunction of which is either useless, or what in the common estimation of men would be considered as rather troublesome, and not to be desired. To see a young officer of eighteen years of age come into company in full uniform, and with such a wig as is worn by grave and respectable clergymen advanced in years, would make every body laugh, because it certainly is a very unusual combination of objects, and such as would not atone for its novelty by any particular purpose of utility to which it was subservient. It is a complete instance of incongruity. Add ten years to the age of this incongruous officer, the incongruity would be very faintly diminished;—make him eighty years of age, and a celebrated military character of the last reign, and the incongruity almost entirely vanishes: I am not sure that we should not be rather more disposed to *respect* the peculiarity than to laugh at it. As you increase the incongruity, you increase the humor; as you diminish it, you diminish the humor. If a tradesman of a corpulent and respectable appearance, with habiliments somewhat ostentatious, were to slide down gently into the mud, and dedecorate a pea-green coat, I am afraid we should all have the barbarity to laugh. If his hat and wig, like treacherous servants, were to desert their falling master, it certainly would not diminish our propensity to laugh;

but if he were to fall into a violent passion, and abuse every body about him, nobody could possibly resist the incongruity of a pea-green tradesman, very respectable, sitting in the mud, and threatening all the passers-by with the effects of his wrath. Here, every incident heightens the humor of the scene:—the gayety of his tunic, the general respectability of his appearance, the rills of muddy water which trickle down his cheeks, and the harmless violence of his rage! But if, instead of this, we were to observe a dustman falling into the mud, it would hardly attract any attention, because the opposition of ideas is so trifling, and the incongruity so slight.

Surprise is as essential to humor as it is to wit. In going into a foreign country for the first time, we are exceedingly struck with the absurd appearance of some of the ordinary characters we meet with: a very short time, however, completely reconciles us to the phenomena of French abbés and French postilions, and all the variety of figures so remote from those we are accustomed to, and which surprise us so much at our first acquaintance with that country. I do not mean to say, either of one class of the ridiculous or of the other, that perfect novelty is *absolutely* a necessary ingredient to the production of any degree of pleasure, but that the pleasure arising from humor diminishes, as the surprise diminishes;—it is less at the second exhibition of any piece of humor than at the first, less at the third than the second, till at last it becomes trite and disgusting. A piece of humor will, however, always bear repetition much better than a piece of wit; because, as humor depends in some degree on manner, there will probably always be in that manner, something sufficiently different from what it was before, to prevent the disagreeable effects of complete sameness. If I say a good thing to-day, and repeat it again to-morrow in another company, the flash of to-day is as much like the flash of to-morrow as the flash of one musket is like the flash of another; but if I tell a humorous story, there are a thousand little diversities in my voice, manner, language, and gestures, which make it rather a different thing from what it was before, and infuse a tinge of novelty into the repeated narrative.

It is by no means, however, sufficient, to say of humor, that it is incongruity which excites surprise;—the same limits are necessary here which I have before affixed to wit,—it must excite surprise, and nothing *but* surprise; for the moment it calls into action any other high and impetuous emotion, all sense of the humorous is immediately at an end. For, to return again to our friend dressed in green, whom we left in the mud,—suppose, instead of a common, innocent tumble, he had experienced a very severe fall, and we discovered that he had broken a limb; our laughter is immediately extinguished, and converted into a lively feeling of compassion. The *incongruity* is precisely as great as it was before; but as it has excited another feeling not compatible with the ridiculous, all mixture of the humorous is at end.

The sense of the humorous is as incompatible with tenderness and respect as with compassion. No man would laugh to see a little child fall; and he would be shocked to see such an accident happen to an old man, or a woman, or to his father! It is an odd case to put, but I should like to know if any man living could have laughed if he had seen Sir Isaac Newton rolling in the mud? I believe that not only Senior Wranglers and Senior Optimi would have run to his assistance, but that dustmen, and carmen, and coal-heavers would have run and picked him up, and set him to rights. It is a beautiful thing to observe the boundaries which nature has affixed to the ridiculous, and to notice how soon it is swallowed up by the more illustrious feelings of our minds. Where is the heart so hard that could bear to see the awkward resources and contrivances of the poor turned into ridicule? Who could laugh at the fractured, ruined body of a soldier? Who is so *wicked* as to amuse himself with the infirmities of extreme old age? or to find subject for humor in the weakness of a perishing, dissolving body? Who is there that does not feel himself disposed to overlook the little peculiarities of the truly great and wise, and to throw a veil over that ridicule which they have redeemed by the magnitude of their talents, and the splendor of their virtues? Who ever thinks of turning into ridicule our great and ardent hope of a world to come? Whenever the man of humor meddles with these things, he is astonished to find, that in all the great feelings of their nature the mass of mankind always think and act aright;—that they are ready enough to laugh,—but that they are quite as ready to drive away with indignation and contempt, the light fool who comes with the feather of wit to crumble the bulwarks of truth, and to beat down the Temples of God!

So, then, this turns out to be the nature of humor: that it is incongruity which creates surprise, and *only* surprise. Try the most notorious and classical instances of humor by this rule, and you will find it succeed. If you find incongruities which create surprise and are not humorous, it is always, I believe, because they are accompanied with some *other* feeling,—emotion, or an interesting train of thought, beside surprise. Find an incongruity which creates surprise, and surprise *only*, and, if it be not humorous, I am, what I very often am, completely wrong; and this theory is, what theories very often are, unfounded in fact.

Most men, I observe, are of opinion that humor is entirely confined to character;—and if you choose to confine the word humor to those instances of the ridiculous which are excited by character, you may do so if you please,—this is not worth contending. All that I wish to show is, that this species of feeling is produced by something beside character; and if you allow it to be the same feeling, I am satisfied, and you may call it by what name you please. One of the most laughable scenes I ever saw in my life was, the complete overturning of a very large table, with all the dinner upon it,—which I believe one or two gentlemen in this room remember as well as myself. What of character is there in seeing a roasted turkey sprawling on the floor? or ducks lying in different parts of the room, covered with trembling fragments of jelly? It is impossible to avoid laughing at such absurdities, because the incongruities they involve are so very great; though they have no more to do with character than they have with chemistry.

A thousand little circumstances happen every day which excite violent laughter, but have no sort of reference to character. The laughter is excited by throwing inanimate objects into strange and incongruous positions. Now, I am quite unable, by attending to what passes in my own mind, to say, that these classes of sensations are not alike: they may differ in degree, for the incongruous observed of things living, is always more striking than the incongruous observed in things inanimate; but there *is* an incongruous not observable in character, which produces the feeling of humor.

Having thus endeavored to ascertain the nature of humor, I come next to the various classes and divisions of the ridiculous which have no affinity with humor.

Buffoonery is voluntary incongruity. To play the buffoon, is to counterfeit some peculiarity incongruous enough to excite laughter: not incongruities of *mind*, for this is a humor of a higher class, and constitutes comic acting; but incongruities of body,—imitating a drunken man, or a clown, or a person with a hunched back, or puffing out the cheeks as the lower sort of comic actors do upon the stage. Buffoonery is general in its imitations; mimicry is particular, and seizes on the incongruous in *individual* characters. I think we must say, that mimicry is always employed upon defects: a good voice, a gentleman-like appearance, and rational, agreeable manners, can never be the subject of mimicry;—they may be exactly represented and imitated, but nobody would call this mimicry, as the word always means the representation of defects. Parody is the adaptation of the same thoughts to other subjects. Burlesque is that species of parody, or adaptation of thoughts to other subjects, which is intended to make the original ridiculous. Pope has parodied several Odes of Horace; Johnson has parodied Juvenal; Cervantes has burlesqued the old romances.

A bull,—which must by no means be passed over in this recapitulation of the family of wit and humor,—a bull is exactly the counterpart of a witticism: for as wit discovers real relations that are not apparent, bulls admit apparent relations that are not real. The pleasure arising from bulls, proceeds from our surprise at suddenly discovering two things to be dissimilar in which a resemblance might have been suspected. The same doctrine will apply to wit and bulls in action. Practical wit discovers connection or relation between actions, in which duller understandings discover none; and practical bulls originate from an apparent relation between two actions which more correct understandings immediately perceive to have none at all. In the late rebellion in Ireland, the rebels, who had conceived a high degree of indignation against some great banker, passed a resolution that they would burn his notes;—which they accordingly did, with great assiduity; forgetting, that in burning his notes they were destroying his debts, and that for every note which went into the flames, a correspondent value went into the banker's pocket. A gentleman, in speaking of a nobleman's wife, of great rank and fortune, lamented very much that she had no children. A medical gentleman who was present observed, that to have no children was a great misfortune, but he thought he had remarked it was *hereditary* in some families. Take any instance of this branch of the ridiculous, and you will always find an apparent relation of ideas leading to a complete inconsistency.

I hardly know whether quaintness belongs to this subject, and the word is now used so loosely that it is no very easy matter to determine at what it points. I think it means an attention to petty excellences in style, an over-scrupulous and affected delicacy of expression; and that *quaint* humor, is humor in this peculiar garb.

Good caricature is the humorous addressed to the eye. It represents you as doing something which it would be extremely incongruous and absurd in you to do; but it *adds* the effects of mimicry to those of humor, laying hold of personal defects and peculiarities, and aggravating them in a very high degree.

I shall say nothing of charades, and such sorts of unpardonable trumpery: if charades are made at all, they should be made without benefit of clergy, the offender should instantly be hurried off to execution, and be cut off in the middle of his dullness, without being allowed to explain to the executioner why his first is like his second, or what is the resemblance between his fourth and his ninth.

Incongruities, which excite laughter, generally produce a feeling of contempt for the person at whom we laugh. I do not know that I can state an instance of the humorous in persons, where the person laughing does not feel himself superior to the person laughed at,—whether that sense of the humorous be excited by an accidental incongruity of situation, or by a permanent incongruity interwoven in the character. Remember, I am not speaking of persons laughed *with*, but of persons laughed *at:* and in all such cases the laugher is, in his own estimation, the superior man; the person laughed at, the inferior: at the same time, contempt accompanied by laughter, is always mitigated by laughter, which seems to diminish hatred, as perspiration diminishes heat.

Laughing contempt is by no means the strongest contempt; whenever contempt increases to a very high degree, it becomes serious, and all laughter ceases. Contempt verges upon anger, and the humorous is at an end. A very foolish, insignificant man, may give himself airs of great importance in society, and provoke laughter; but the laughter by no means goes on increasing with the incongruity, for at last a degree of contempt ensues, which is rather painful than agreeable; and *so* painful, as to put an end to laughter, and chase away the humorous.

The ridiculous is not so much opposed to the proper and the decent, as to that which is *very* proper and *very* decent. There is a propriety so unusual, that it obtains positive praise whenever it is observed; there is a fainter sense of propriety, just sufficient to guard a man from observation, but for which he obtains neither blame nor praise. There is a deficiency of propriety so great, that it is universally ridiculous. Take it in language:—my mode of expressing myself may be so happy and so accurate, I may throw my ideas into such agreeable combinations of words, that I may derive a considerable share of reputation from my style, either in talking or in writing; or my language may be just so mediocre, as to escape all attention; or so bad, and so full of incongruities, that it may be laughed at. Now the last of these, which is so bad as to excite the powerful emotion of laughter, is to be opposed and contrasted, in all speculations upon this subject, to that which is so excellent as to excite a strong feeling of approbation. I mention this, in order to show that nature acts as much by rewards as by punishments; and that men are as much allured to do that which is fit and decent, by the love of each other's approbation, as they are by the fear of each other's laughter and disapprobation. Laughter is, to many men, worse than death. Innumerable duels have been fought to prevent the pangs of ridicule, and to revenge them; and there are very few who would not rather be hated than be laughed at. The effects of this feeling, entertained in a rational and moderate degree, are, to render men dependent upon each other's judgment, and to lay the basis of that propriety and decorum upon which the pleasure and happiness of our intercourse are founded.

In Bedlam (where there is no fear of the ridiculous), within ten yards one man is singing, another reciting, and another sleeping; a young man is dressed like an old one, and an old one as if he were young; there is that universal selfishness, which of course must predominate where every human being is utterly indifferent to the censure or praise of the other. In polished society, the dread of being ridiculous, models every word and gesture into propriety, and produces an exquisite attention to the feelings and opinions of others; it is the great cure of extravagance, folly, and impertinence; it curbs the sallies of eccentricity, it recalls the attention of mankind to the one uniform standard of reason and common sense.

It has often been remarked, that wit never excites laughter, and that humor does. This is putting the matter in rather too strong a light. The laughter is not so long and so loud in wit as it is in humor, but there is certainly a faint approach to the same bodily affection. Nature seems to have intended that we should have been affected by both, in a similar manner, but not in the *same degree.* I do not pretend to give any *reason* for this fact; except, perhaps, it be this, that humor is in general longer than wit: in a piece of wit there is but a single flash of surprise and pleasure; in a piece of humor, as in Don Quixote's battle with the mills, one impression follows quick upon another, the mind is thrown into an attitude of pleasing surprise by the first occurrence of the idea, and then all the other touches of humor act one on another with a compound force and accumulated impression, till at last the convulsion of laughter ensues;—and it is a confirmation of this idea, that the tranquil smile with which wit is received, is soon disturbed and roused into something more disorderly, when there is much reduplication of wit; when it comes out, as it does in some men, flash after flash, with a brisk multiplication of surprises, a continued irritability,—where one nerve no sooner ceases to vibrate than another is struck, and the mind is kept in a constant agitation of pleasure. In cases like this, I have very often seen wit produce loud and convulsive laughter; and am inclined to believe, that the different effects of humor and wit, in this respect, are a good deal to be attributed to the continuity of one, and the brevity of the other; to which, perhaps, may be added, that wit excites more admiration than humor,—a feeling by no means favorable to laughter.

Wit and humor, though the first consists in discovering connection, the latter in discovering incongruity, are closely and nearly related to each other. The respective feelings both depend upon surprise, are both incompatible with serious and important ideas, and both communicate the same sort of pleasure to the understanding. A man who gives the reins to his wit, may repress his humor as undignified; the one may be rooted out by design and attention; but they seem, where no pains of this kind have been taken, to spring up naturally in the same soil, and to be plants of the same tribe and family. The ingenious and philosophical Dr. Millar, of Glasgow, has a very interesting speculation of the different effects of civilization on wit and humor, the progress of which he conceives to have a direct tendency to encourage wit, and to diminish humor. It is so very well done, and so clever, that I shall, I am sure, be excused for reading it:—

"The higher advances of civilization and refinement, contributed not only to explode the ludicrous pastimes which had been the delight of a former age, but even to weaken the propensity to every species of humorous exhibition. Although humor be commonly productive of more merriment than wit, it seldom procures to the possessor the same degree of respect. To show in a strong light the follies, the defects, and the improprieties of mankind, they must be exhibited with peculiar coloring. To excite strong ridicule, the picture must be changed, and the features, though like, must be exaggerated. The man who, in conversation, aims at the display of his talents, must endeavor to represent with peculiar heightening the tone, the aspect, the gesture, the deportment of the person whom he ridicules. To paint folly, he must, for the time, appear foolish. To exhibit oddity and absurdity, he must himself become odd and absurd. There is, in this attempt, something low and buffoonish; and a degree of that meanness which appeared in the person thus exposed, is likely, by a natural association, to remain with his representative. The latter is beheld in the light of a player, who degrades himself for our entertainment, and whom nothing but the highest excellence in his profession can save from our contempt.

"But though the circumstances and manners of a polished nation are *adverse* to the cultivation of humor, they are peculiarly calculated to promote the circulation and improvement of wit. The entertainment arising from the latter, has no connection with those humiliating circumstances which are inseparable from the former; but is derived from such occasional exertions of the fancy, as may be consistent with the utmost elegance and correctness. The man of wit has no occasion to personate folly, or to become the temporary butt of that ridicule which he means to excite. He assumes no grotesque attitude, he employs no buffoonish expression, nor appears in any character but his own. Unlike the man of humor, he is never prolix or tedious, but, passing with rapidity from one object to another, selects from the group whatever suits his purpose. He sees with quickness those happy assemblages, those unexpected oppositions and resemblances, with which the imagination is delighted and surprised, and by a sudden glance he directs the attention to that electrical point of contact by which the enlivening stroke is communicated."*

I admire this very much, for, whether true or not, it is very interesting and ingenious; but I confess I am not *quite* convinced by it, nor can I easily concede that the effect of civilization is to diminish and check the humorous. There are many circumstances in a civilized country, which, on the contrary, go directly to the encouragement of humor. Dr. Millar himself, mentions one of very considerable importance. To this cause may be added, that there are a greater number of minds in a civilized state, capable of seizing the finer inconsistencies in character, and relishing that humor which they excite; there are a thousand little traits of the humorous, which a man of fine and cultivated understanding perceives, which are utterly lost upon grosser faculties; but an age of civilization is an age in which the number of fine and cultivated understandings is the greatest, and in which, therefore, for these reasons, the field of humor is enlarged.

It is unfair to take the stage as a proof, and to ask why we have not Molières and Shakspeares starting up at every period! The preceding age has gleaned all the twenty or thirty characters of strong and extravagant humor which lie upon the surface of society; not because it had greater talents for humor, but merely because it *was* the preceding age. The blustering captain,—the inebriated and witty rake,—the obese alderman,—the squire in London,—slaving poets, homicide physicians, chambermaids, valets, and duennas,—are all gone; employed by dramatic writers who had the first of the market. These characters can not be reintroduced on the stage; they are worn out there; but they exist in real life, and of course *must* exist, while men are what they ever have been.

* Millar's Historical View of the English Government, iv. 357.

Another reason which would induce me to suspect that Professor Millar is wrong in supposing that humor decays in a civilized age, is, that in a civilized age the number of idle people is so immensely augmented, and, of course, the demand for every thing amusing considerably increased. There are several meanings included under the term civilization; it means, having better cups and saucers than we had a century or two centuries ago; better laws, better manners; and it means, also, having nothing to do,—and those who have nothing to do, must either be amused, or expire with gaping. For this reason an amusing and entertaining man, who has humor, appears to me to be in high request in a civilized country. I allow that his humor, to be well received, must be of a very different complexion from what would pass current in more barbarous times; it must be the humor of the mind, not the humor of the body. It must be devoid of every shade of buffoonery and grimace, and managed with a great degree of delicacy and skill. Civilization improves the humor, but I can hardly allow that it *diminishes* it: in spite of all Professor Millar has said, I am strongly inclined to think there will be more humor, more agreeable raillery, and more facetious remark, displayed between seven and ten o'clock this evening, in the innumerable dinners which are to be eaten by civilized people in this vast city, than ten months could have produced in the reigns of Queen Elizabeth or Henry the Seventh.

On the very face of the proposition there is indeed something which it is difficult to digest. The effect of civilization is, to avert mankind from the contemplation of a great part of their own nature: they observe incongruities better in a state of barbarism, or *half* barbarism; and in proportion as they are elegant, acute, and learned, they become dull and careless observers of some of the most stiking phenomena of the human mind.

I wish, after all I have said about wit and humor, I could satisfy myself of their good effects upon the character and disposition; but I am convinced the probable tendency of both is, to corrupt the understanding and the heart. I am not speaking of wit where it is kept down by more serious qualities of mind, and thrown into the background of the picture; but where it stands out boldly and emphatically, and is evidently the master quality in any particular mind. Professed wits, though they are generally courted for the amusement they afford, are seldom respected for the qualities they possess. The habit of seeing things in a witty point of view, increases, and makes incursions from its own proper regions, upon principles and opinions which are ever held sacred by the wise and good. A witty man is a dramatic performer; in process of time, he can no more exist without applause, than he can exist without air; if his audience be small, or if they are inattentive, or if a new wit defrauds him of any portion of his admiration, it is all over with him,—he sickens, and is extinguished. The applauses of the theater on which he performs are so essential to him that he must obtain them at the expense of decency, friendship, and good feeling. It must always be *probable*, too, that a *mere* wit is a person of light and frivolous understanding. His business is not to discover relations of ideas that are *useful*, and have a real influence upon life, but to discover the more trifling relations which are only amusing; he never looks at things with the naked eye of common sense, but is always gazing at the world through a Claude Lorraine glass,—discovering a thousand appearances which are created only by the instrument of inspection, and covering every object with factitious and unnatural colors. In short, the character of a *mere* wit it is impossible to consider as very amiable, very respectable, or very safe. So far the world, in judging of wit where it has swallowed up all other qualities, judge aright; but I doubt if they are sufficiently indulgent to this faculty where it exists in a lesser degree, and as one out of many other ingredients of the understanding. There is an association in men's minds between dullness and wisdom, amusement and folly, which has a very powerful influence in decision upon character, and is not overcome without considerable difficulty. The reason is, that the *outward* signs of a dull man and a wise man are the same, and so are the outward signs of a frivolous man and a witty man; and we are not to expect that the majority will be disposed to look to much *more* than the outward sign. I believe the fact to be, that wit is very seldom the *only* eminent quality which resides in the mind of any man; it is commonly accompanied by many other talents of every description, and ought to be considered as a strong evidence of a fertile and superior understanding. Almost all the great poets, orators, and statesmen of all times, have been witty. Cæsar, Alexander, Aristotle, Descartes, and Lord Bacon, were witty men; so were Cicero, Shakspeare, Demosthenes, Boileau, Pope, Dryden, Fontenelle, Jonson, Waller, Cowley, Solon, Socrates, Dr. Johnson, and almost every man who has made a distinguished figure in the House of Commons. I have talked of the *danger* of wit: I do not mean by that to enter into commonplace declamation against faculties because they *are* dangerous;—wit is dangerous, eloquence is dangerous, a talent for observation is dangerous, *every* thing is dangerous that has efficacy and vigor for its characteristics; nothing is safe but mediocrity. The business is, in conducting the understanding well, to risk something; to aim at uniting things that are commonly incompatible. The meaning of an extraordinary man is, that he is *eight* men, not one man; that he has as much wit as if he had no sense, and as much sense as if he had no wit; that his conduct is as judicious as if he were the dullest of human beings, and his imagination as brilliant as if he were irretrievably ruined. But when wit is combined with sense and information; when it is softened by benevolence, and restrained by strong principle; when it is in the hands of a man who can use it and despise it, who can be witty and something much *better* than witty, who loves honor, justice, decency, good nature, morality, and religion, ten thousand times better than wit;—wit is *then* a beautiful and delightful part of our nature. There is no more interesting spectacle than to see the effects of wit upon the different characters of men; than to observe it expanding caution, relaxing dignity, unfreezing coldness,—teaching age, and care, and pain, to smile,—extorting reluctant gleams of pleasure from melancholy, and charming even the pangs of grief. It is pleasant to observe how it penetrates through the coldness and awkwardness of society, gradually bringing men nearer together, and, like the combined force of wine and oil, giving every man a glad heart and a shining countenance. Genuine and innocent wit like this, is surely the *flavor of the mind!* Man could direct his ways by plain reason, and support his life by tasteless food; but God has given us wit, and flavor, and brightness, and laughter, and perfumes, to enliven the days of man's pilgrimage, and to "charm his pained steps over the burning marle."

LECTURE XII.

ON TASTE.

All language which concerns the mind is borrowed from language which respects material objects.

The mind itself is called breath, wind, air, in almost all the languages of the world. Apprehension, comprehension, understanding, perception, are all *metaphors* taken from the human body, or from substance of some sort or another. The reason is plain: the attention of man is first called powerfully to outer objects; they are the first observed and the first named, they make the basis of all languages; and then, when men can turn their attention inwardly upon themselves, and want words for new ideas, they naturally borrow them from already existing language, and are determined in their choice by some fanciful analogy between the object of *mind*, and the object of *body*. This is exactly the case with taste. There are certain feelings of the mind which take place upon the perception of certain objects, or the contemplation of certain actions, which men have chosen to compare to the sensations of the palate upon the application of certain flavors. There is no *reason*, that I know of, why they should compare them to sensations excited by taste, rather than by smell or by touch. The feeling of beauty, excited by the view of a pleasant landscape, no more resembles any flavor which the palate can taste, than it resembles a soft and smooth object which the hand can touch: one metaphor has established itself, the other has not. We have begun, though of late years, to use the word *tact;* we say of such a man that he has a good tact in manners, that he has a fine tact, exactly as we would say he has a good taste. We might, in familiar style, extend the metaphor to the sense of smelling, and say of a man that he had a good nose for the ridiculous.

Taste, then, is a metaphorical expression; and it is a mere word of classification, including several distinct feelings of the mind, exactly as the primary taste includes several distinct feelings of the body. It includes the feeling of beauty in all its very numerous meanings, the feeling of novelty, the feeling of grandeur, the feeling of sublimity, the feeling of propriety, and perhaps many others, which, in a subsequent part of my lecture, I shall take pains to enumerate.

Precisely in the same manner, the natural taste includes the taste of sweet, sour, hot, cold, moist, savory, and many others, which are so pleasantly exemplified every day in this great town; so that, when we use the word *taste,* we must recollect that there is no single feeling of the mind which has obtained that name, but that it is a *classifying, comprehensive word,* embracing a great number of distinct feelings. But why have we called all these feelings by the name of taste? and why have we denied the appellation of taste to other feelings of the mind? This is a very important question in the discussion, and I will endeavor to answer it hereafter; at present I pass it by for the sake of order and arrangement. It is very clear why we call all the various feelings of the palate by the name of taste,—simply because they originate from the same bodily organ, the palate: and this analogy has given rise to a very strange sort of language,—of the *organ of taste;*—as if there were any separate quarter of the mind set apart for the generation of these feelings. All that we know about the matter, is this: men have chosen to take a metaphor from the body, and apply it to the mind; they have chosen, for reasons hereafter to be conjectured, and from some remote resemblance, to class some feelings under the appellation of taste, others not. This is the plain history of the fact; further than this, is all metaphorical fallacy; and as for any separate *organ of taste,* there is either no meaning to the expression, or, if there be, it is impossible to ascertain the fact which the expression implies.

I shall now endeavor to state the various feelings which have been classed under this appellation, and the extent to which practice has extended and applied the metaphor of taste. It matters not which of the feelings I state first, and I do not think I shall give much offence by beginning with that of beauty.

I do not mean to analyze the feeling of the beautiful (that I reserve for a separate lecture), but merely to state it as one of those feelings of the mind to which the metaphor of taste is applied. To talk first of the simplest and most uncompounded kinds of beauty. We say that gay colors are beautiful; that all children, or those muscular and robust children called savages, have a taste for beautiful colors, for smooth surfaces, for harmonious sounds, and for regular figures. We say of such a man, meaning to pay him a high compliment, that he has a good taste in the beauty of the person; of another, that he has a fine taste in architecture, meaning by the expression, that he feels the beauties of architecture: in short, wherever we use the word beauty with any degree of strictness, we *almost* always refer it to the general class of taste. There is a lax usage of the word beautiful, which implies any thing that is agreeable or convenient. I have heard country gentlemen talk of a beautiful scenting-day; and Mrs. Glasse talks of a beautiful receipt for curing a ham; but this is evidently an analogical, and even a violent, usage of the word.

It is used to the sublime. We say of such a man, "He has not *taste* enough to *relish* the sublimity of the description;" or, "Such sublime scenery is quite to his *taste.*"

The metaphor of taste has never been much extended to novelty, though there are forms of language in which it would not be improper to apply it. "Such continued novelty is not to my *taste*;"—"I go into different societies, because I have a strong *relish* for novelty." However, the word does not seem so well placed here, and does not satisfy the ear so cleverly as in the preceding instances; and perhaps for this reason the word taste is most *frequently* and *emphatically* applied, both in its original, and in its figurative sense, in cases of some difficulty. If a man were to discover that vinegar was sour, we should give him no great credit for his natural taste. If any man were to discover the true language of nature and of feeling in this little poem of Mrs. Opie's, he would gain no credit for his metaphorical taste, because the beauties of it are *too* striking for a moment's hesitation :

"Go, youth beloved ! in distant glades,
New friends, new hopes, new joys to find !
Yet sometimes deign, midst fairer maids,
To think on her thou leav'st behind.
Thy love, thy fate, dear youth, to share,
Must never be my happy lot ;
But thou may'st grant this humble prayer,—
Forget me not, forget me not !

"Yet should the thought of my distress
Too painful to thy feelings be,
Heed not the wish I now express,
Nor ever deign to think of me.
But oh ! if grief thy steps attend,
If want, if sickness, be thy lot,
And thou require a soothing friend,
Forget me not, forget me not !"*

For this very reason, the word taste has not been applied so often to novelty; because whether a thing be novel or not, is no question of critical inquiry, but of plain fact, which one man can answer to with as much satisfaction as another.

It is certainly applied to ridicule.

Dr. Gerard classes the pleasures of imitation under the head of taste, for it must be remembered there is a pleasure arising from mere imitation, whether the original be agreeable or not. We should be much pleased to see an accurate picture of the greatest beauty now living; and we should not be displeased to see the picture of a rat or a weasel: the mere imitation itself, abstracted from all other considerations, gives pleasure; but though this pleasure very much resembles those which are said to be pleasures of taste, and though it ought, perhaps, from such resemblance, to be so classed, yet I doubt very much if it ever has been, or if custom has extended the

* Edinburgh Review, i. 116

metaphor to this sensation. Could we say of a man, who from frequently gazing on portraits had become a good judge of their resemblance to the original, that he had a good taste in imitation? We might say he had a good taste in portraits; meaning by that, that he could judge of their spirit, their grace, and their beauty: but I much question if we should refer his accuracy, in judging of the mere *resemblance*, to the class of tastes; though, as I have before said, I can see no sort of reason why we do not.

Harmony, which Dr. Gerard enumerates as a separate object of taste, appears to me to rank under the two preceding heads of sublimity and beauty. Propriety, the same author has omitted, though it clearly is one of the feelings referred to taste. A person observant of proprieties, is said to have a good taste in manners; and any impropriety in any character of a play, or a poem, is imputed to bad taste,—the discovery of it, to critical taste.

In the lighter parts of morals, we may, perhaps, use the metaphor of taste; but in the greater virtues and vices, certainly not. If a man were to kill the minister and church-wardens of his parish, nobody would accuse him of want of taste. The Scythians always ate their grandfathers; they behaved very respectfully to them for a long time, but as soon as their grandfathers became old and troublesome, and began to tell long stories, they immediately eat them: nothing could be more improper, and even disrespectful, than dining off such near and venerable relations; yet we could not with any propriety accuse them of bad taste in morals. Neither is the word taste used in subjects of pure reasoning. We could not say, that he who discovered an error in a mathematical problem had a good taste for reasoning; that he who made the error had a bad taste;—to find that 12 times 12 is 144, is not a business of taste. Neither can we use the word taste with respect to very useful inventions. We could not say that Bolton and Watt exhibited a great deal of taste in the improvements they made upon the steam-engine; nor could we say that Archimedes exhibited a fine taste in the machines he invented for dashing to pieces the Roman galleys, and knocking out the brains of the Roman soldiers. Some of these things appear too important for the application of that word; others, too certain. It seems to have been intended that the metaphor should apply to feelings connected with pleasure and pain, not with duties and crimes; with the superfluous, the lighter, and more luxurious sensations of the mind, not with those which become the subjects of approbation and disapprobation; not with those parts of knowledge which are reducible to proof and demonstration, but in those which are shaded with doubt, and rest only on the basis of opinion. In order to see the tendency and spirit of the metaphor, try to misapply it in one or two instances, and observe what sort of feelings and objections the misapplication suggests. Suppose any body were to talk to you of the bad taste of a mother who had murdered her child, what would your answer be? "Do you call that by the light name of taste, on which the dearest interests of mankind depend? Is the feeling which a mother has for her child to be classed with the love of splendid colors, accurate imitation, and judicious description? Is there the same doubt which hangs upon both? Are the great rules of morals referable to no other and more certain proofs than those which decide upon the novel, the beautiful, and the sublime?" These are the feelings and objections which naturally pass through every man's mind, and evince the conceptions he has gradually formed of the limits and province of taste.

There is another consideration, perhaps, which has contributed to affix the limits of this metaphor. When we ascribe good or bad taste to any one, it is most commonly for doing or feeling something, where he was at full liberty to have done or said the contrary. We are not apt to impute the excellence, or the defect, where there is no fair exertion of the will. We may say of a lady that she walks in good taste, but not that she tumbles down in good taste. We could not say that a lady fainted away in good taste, though I think we might speak of a good and bad taste in blushing. For the same reason, we can not talk of the bad taste of deep melancholy or despair, or the bad taste of being very short and very ugly; because it is presumed that all men and women would be cheerful, tall, and beautiful, if they could.

Natural tastes are sometimes so plain and strong, that they are immediately pronounced upon by every body. The most determined skeptic, if you catch him in a moment of candor, would allow that a good ripe peach was sweet. We say that a man recognizes this plain, indisputable fact by his taste, though he exercises no reasoning powers, and employs no reflection in arriving at the determination. So in the plainest and most undoubted examples of intellectual taste. If he were struck with some of the sublimest traits of Mrs. Siddons' acting, or if he was enchanted with the first view of Juan Fernandez, we should still refer these impressions to the class of tastes, even though they had cost him no effort in the acquisition, and though the feelings followed in all human beings as directly as any one fact can follow another in the various works of nature. We should call the detection of good or bad flavor, made by repeated efforts and close attention, an act of taste; and in the same manner the detection of beauty or deformity in intellectual taste, with whatever degree of labor and reflection effected. If, from natural superiority of that organ, any man could discover flavor, insensible to common palates, we of course should refer his power, however extraordinary, to taste. Or if, by long practice, he had acquired the same rapid precision, we should still refer it to the same bodily organ. So in the intellectual taste, whether the feeling follow immediately upon the perception, whether it be preceded by critical investigation, whether it be unusually delicate and true, either from natural talents or long habit, the feeling is always referred to taste, which is a general word for that affection of the mind existing in any degree, and proceeding from any cause. I lay the greater stress upon this observation, because I perceive in many persons who speculate upon these subjects, a disposition only to allow the use of the word in cases where there is a critical, active exertion of the mind, and an effort to discriminate; whereas it is undoubtedly used also, in those cases where the mind is merely passive, and where the feeling of beauty would be strongly excited in any human being, without the smallest effort to judge between conflicting sensations.

The subject of taste has given rise to a very curious controversy;—whether every feeling of taste depends upon accidental association, or whether, by the original constitution of nature, it is connected with any particular object of sense, it is admitted on all hands that the feeling of beauty and sublimity very frequently, and even in a great majority of instances, depends upon mere association. For one instance:—in the estimation of Europeans, part of the beauty of a face is the color of the cheek; not that there is something in that particular position of red color, which, I believe, is of itself beautiful,—but habit has connected it also with the idea of health. An Indian requires that his wife's face should be of the color of good marketable sea-coal; another tribe is enamored of deep orange; and a cheek of copper is irresistible to a fourth. Every color is agreeable, in each of these instances, which is connected with the idea of youth and beauty; the beauty is not in the color itself, but in the notions which the color summons up. Instances of this source of our ideas of the beautiful are innumerable, and universally admitted. The question is, Is there any object which originally, and of *itself*, excites that feeling? The very newest and the most fashionable philosophy says, No. The Rev. Mr. Alison, in his very beautiful work on Taste, says no,—and says no, as he says every thing, with great modesty, and great ingenuity; but though he is a very agreeable writer, and one of the best of men, I have very great doubts if he is right in his system. "In the first place," says Mr. Alison, "every feeling of beauty and sublimity is an emotion. Now mere matter is unfitted to produce *any* kind of emotion." If this be true, it settles the question; it is only upon the supposition that mere matter *can* produce emotion, that the opposite opinion has ever been advanced: it is precisely the thing to be proved. It appears to me very singular to say, that mere matter can never produce emotion upon the senses, and that we can only apply to it the expressions of sensation and perception. The theory of this school is, that Providence has created a great number of objects which it intends you should see, hear, feel, taste, and smell, without caring a single breath whether you exercised your senses upon them or not; that all the primary impulses of the mind must be mere intelligences, unaccompanied by any emotion of pleasure; that pleasure might be added to them afterward, by pure accident, but that originally, and according to the scheme of nature, the senses were the channels of intelligence, never the sources of gratification. This doctrine was certainly never conceived in a land of luxury. I should like to try a Scotch gentleman, upon his first arrival in this country, with the taste of ripe fruit, and leave him to judge after that, whether nature had confined the senses to such dry and ungracious occupations, as whether mere matter could produce emotion. Such doctrines may do very well in the chambers of a northern metaphysician, but they are untenable in the light of the world; they are refuted, nobly refuted, twenty times in a year, at Fishmongers' Hall. If you deny that matter can produce emotion, judge on these civic occasions, of the power of gusts, and relishes, and flavors! Look at men when (as Bishop Taylor says) they are "gathered round the eels of Syene, and the oysters of Lucrinus, and when the Lesbian and Chian wines descend through the limbec of the tongue and larynx; when they receive the juice of fishes, and the marrow of the laborious ox, and the tender lard of Apulian swine, and the condited stomach of the scarus:"—is this nothing but mere sensation? is there no emotion, no panting, no wheezing, no deglutition? is this the calm acquisition of intelligence, and the quiet office ascribed to the senses?—or is it a proof that Nature has infused into her original creations, the power of gratifying that sense which distinguishes them, and to every atom of matter has added an atom of joy?

That there are some tastes originally agreeable, I think can hardly be denied; and that Nature has originally, and independently of all associations, made some sounds more agreeable than others, seems to me, I confess, equally clear. I can never believe that any man could sit in a pensive mood listening to the sharpening of a saw, and think it as naturally agreeable, and as plaintive, as the song of a linnet; and I should very much suspect that philosophy, which teaches that the odor of superannuated Cheshire cheese, is, by the constitution of nature, and antecedent to all connection of other ideas, as agreeable as that smell with which the flowers of the field thank Heaven for the gentle rains, or as the fragrance of the spring when we inhale from afar "the milk-white thorn that scents the evening gale."

One circumstance, which appears to have led to these conclusions, is the example of those same sensations which are sometimes ludicrous, sometimes sublime, sometimes fearful, according to the ideas with which they are associated. For instance, the sound of a trumpet suggests the dreadful idea of a battle, and of the approach of armed men; but to all men brought up at Queen's College, Oxford, it must be associated with eating and drinking, for they are always called to dinner by sound of trumpet: and I have a little daughter at home, who, if she heard the sound of a trumpet, would run to the window, expecting to see the puppet-show of Punch, which is carried about the streets. So with a hiss: a hiss is either foolish, or tremendous, or sublime. The hissing of a pancake is absurd: the first faint hiss that arises from the extremity of the pit on the evening of a new play, sinks the soul of the author within him, and makes him curse himself and his Thalia; the hissing of a cobra di capello is sublime,—it is the whisper of death! But all these instances prove nothing; for we are not denying that there are many sounds, tastes, and sights, which nature has made so indifferent, that association may make them any thing. It is very true what Mr. Alison says, "that there are many sensations universally called sublime, which association may make otherwise."* This is true enough, but it is not to the purpose. I admit readily, that a fortuitous connection

* Alison on Taste, p. 139.

of thought can make it otherwise than sublime; but the question is, Did it receive from nature the character of sublime? does *any* thing receive from nature the character of sublime, or the character of beautiful? and would any thing perpetually display, and constantly preserve, such character, if no accident intervened to raise up a contrary association? Certainty on such subjects can not be attained; but I, for one, strongly believe in the affirmative of the question,—that Nature speaks to the mind of man *immediately* in beautiful and sublime language; that she astonishes him with magnitude, appals him with darkness, cheers him with splendor, soothes him with harmony, captivates him with emotion, enchants him with fame; she never intended man should walk among her flowers, and her fields, and her streams, unmoved; nor did she rear the strength of the hills in vain, or mean that we should look with a stupid heart on the wild glory of the torrent, bursting from the darkness of the forest, and dashing over the crumbling rock. I would as soon deny hardness, or softness, or figure, to be qualities of matter, as I would deny beauty or sublimity to belong to its qualities.

Every man is as good a judge of a question like this, as the ablest metaphysician. Walk in the fields in one of the mornings of May, and if you carry with you a mind unpolluted with harm, watch how it is impressed. You are delighted with the beauty of colors; are not those colors beautiful? You breathe vegetable fragrance; is not that fragrance grateful? You see the sun rising from behind a mountain, and the heavens painted with light; is not that renewal of the light of the morning sublime? You reject all obvious reasons, and say that these things are beautiful and sublime because the accidents of life have made them so;—I say they are beautiful and sublime, BECAUSE GOD HAS MADE THEM SO! that it is the original, indelible character impressed upon them by Him, who has opened these sources of simple pleasure, to calm, perhaps, the perturbations of sense, and to make us love that joy which is purchased without giving pain to another man's heart, and without entailing reproach upon our own.

There is one other question, before I conclude this subject, on which I wish to say something; a question like a German chancery suit, which is handed down from father to son as a matter of course, and the decision of which no man ever dreams of as a possible event. Some late traveler in Germany speaks of a suit in the imperial chamber of Wetzlar, which had been pending 170 years. The cause came on for a first hearing as he passed through the country; the result he did not hear, as the Teutonic Master of the Rolls took time to consider. In the same manner, the world is always taking time to consider about the standard of taste. Is there *any* standard of taste, and what is it? This is the question that has been discussed and re-discussed from time immemorial, and in which question I suppose I have little to add to those who have so often handled it before me. As I have before said, taste is a *general* term for a great number of distinct feelings: if there be no standard for approbation and disapprobation in these feelings, which are the constituent elements of taste, there is no standard for taste; but if a good and a bad can be asserted of these feelings with any degree of certainty, then there *is* a standard of taste. Let us try it in one of the departments of taste, the beautiful; and then the question will be, is there any standard of the beautiful? Now, if a delirious virtuoso were to purchase one of those sign-paintings in which King Charles the Second, seated on the oak-tree, announces the dispensation of beer and other uncourtly refreshments, and if he were to pronounce it more beautiful than Mr. Troward's noble picture by Leonardo da Vinci,*—so long as he *thinks* it is so, it unquestionably *is* so to *him*. There can be no doubt but that he is the standard of taste to *himself*, because, when he calls the thing beautiful, he only means to say that it excites in him that emotion, of the real existence of which he of course can be the only judge. But will this same sign-post appear beautiful to others? and to whom? and to

* This picture of the Logos was in the possession of Mr. Troward when this lecture was delivered: it is now in the collection of Mr. Miles, of Leigh Court, near Bristol.

how many must it appear to be so, before you call it absolutely beautiful? To the mob, to all human beings, or only to the enlightened few? I answer to this, that the judges differ just according to the difficulty of the subject: there are some questions of the beautiful so very simple, for the decision of which such very little understanding is required, and where the experience of all men is so much upon a level, that in those, the mass of mankind are certainly the proper referees. Are splendid colors more beautiful than dull colors? Is a soft surface more agreeable than a hard surface? In such simple questions of beauty as this, the most ordinary understanding is as good as the best. But when you come to the complicated meaning of the word beauty, adopted in the phrase of "a beautiful poem," or "a beautiful picture,"—when the subject is to be understood, the selection decided on, comparison with other rival efforts made,—a laborer from the streets can be no judge of such excellences as these, and therefore his opinion can form no part of that standard to which I refer the decision in this species of beauty; for we must take along with us, that as the word *taste* is merely a general expression for several distinct feelings, so the term *beauty*, itself involves no small number of distinct feelings which have received this common appellation. If, then, the species of beauty be stated, and a standard required for its excellences and defects, I determine it by voting, by no means admitting universal suffrage, but requiring that a man shall have forty shillings a year in common sense, and have paid the usual taxes of labor, attention, observation, and so on. But, to drop the metaphor, these are the ingredients which must enter into the composition of any mind which can be allowed to decide upon any species of beauty. In the first place there must be an absence of all prejudice and party spirit, because, though this may inspire the feeling of beauty, as well as any other cause, still it is a very ephemeral cause of that feeling; and in speaking of the standard of beauty, we do not mean only that which will be judged beautiful to-day, but that which will be judged beautiful for ages to come. Then we must re member, that the word *beautiful* always implies some comparison. The prose of Bunyan is agreeable to me till I have read that of Dryden; Dryden's, till I am familiarized to the works of Addison. The arrantest daub in painting may appear agreeable to me, till I have seen the masters in the Flemish school; and I cease to admire these latter when I am become acquainted with the great Italian pictures. The very term *beautiful* implies something superior to common effects; and therefore we require in a judge of the beautiful, that from experience he should have ascertained what *is* a common effect, what *not*. A man who has seen very few pictures, is a bad judge of any single picture, because, though he can tell whether he is pleased or not, he can not tell whether he is pleased more or less than he should be by pictures in general. Therefore, in addition to candor, a judge of the beautiful must have experience;—and he must also have delicacy of feeling: a man may reason himself out of this feeling of beauty, or reason himself into it; but, after all, the thing *is* a matter of *feeling*, and there are some men of such metallic nerves, and blunt entrails, that Milton could never have written them into sublimity, or Michael Angelo painted them into emotion: of course they can be no judges of the beautiful, any more than the blind can determine upon the diversity of colors. Wherever, then, the standard of any species of beauty is required, we may safely say it rests in the opinion of candid men, of men who have had experience in that department of beauty, who have feeling for it, and who have competent understandings to judge of the design and reasoning, which are always the highest and most excellent of all beauties. Such men, where they are to be found, form the standard in every department of beauty, and in every ingredient of taste. How such critics are to be found, is another question: that they exist, no man doubts; and their joint influence ultimately prevails, and gives the law to public opinion. But I hear some men asking where they are to be found? and who they are? with a sort of exultation, as if there were any wit, or talent, or importance, in the question. They are to be found in Dover Street, Albemarle Street, Berkeley Square, the Temple; anywhere wherever reading, thinking men, who have seen a great deal of the world, are to be found. I myself could mention the names of twenty persons, whose opinions influence the public taste in this town; and then, when opinions are settled here, those opinions go down by the mail-coach, to regulate all matters of taste for the provinces.

The progress of good taste, however, though it is certain and irresistible, is slow. Mistaken pleasantry, false ornament, and affected conceit, perish by the discriminating hand of time, that lifts up from the dust of oblivion, the grand and simple efforts of genius. Title, rank, prejudice, party, artifice, and a thousand disturbing forces, are always at work to confer unmerited fame; but every recurring year contributes its remedy to these infringements on justice and good sense. The breath of living acclamation can not reach the ages which are to come: the judges and the judged are no more; passion is extinguished; party is forgotten: and the mild yet inflexible decisions of taste, will receive nothing, as the price of praise, but the solid exertions of superior talent. Justice is pleasant, even when she destroys. It is a grateful homage to common sense, to see those productions hastening to that oblivion, in their progress to which they should never have been retarded. But it is much *more* pleasant to witness the power of taste in the work of preservation and lasting praise;—to think that, in these fleeting and evanescent feelings of the beautiful and the sublime, men have discovered something as fixed and as positive, as if they were measuring the flow of the tides, or weighing the stones on which they tread;—to think that there lives not, in the civilized world, a being who knows he has a mind, and who knows not that Virgil and Homer have written, that Raffaelle has painted, and that Tully has spoken. Intrenched in these everlasting bulwarks against barbarism, Taste points out to the races of men, as they spring up in the order of time, on what path they shall guide the labors of the human spirit. Here she is safe; hence she never *can* be driven, while one atom of matter clings to another, and till man, with all his wonderful system of feeling and thought, is called away to Him who is the great Author of all that is beautiful, and all that is sublime, and all that is good!

LECTURE XIII.

ON THE BEAUTIFUL.

THE three next lectures which I propose to deliver in this place, will be on the same subject as that with which I am at present engaged (*the Beautiful*). I have found it quite impossible to compress this very ample subject into a less space; and even with such limits I have been compelled to pass over many topics of discussion with a brevity very ill suited to their importance, and little favorable to perspicuity. I mention the length to which I intend to carry this discussion, lest any one should conceive, after I had finished this lecture, that I had done with the subject, and consequently had treated it very jejunely and imperfectly: that I *shall* treat it imperfectly enough at last, I can easily believe; but still I prefer to be judged after I am heard, rather than before.

The best evidence we can procure of the resemblance of our feelings, is by language. When men give one common name to very dissimilar objects, it is most probable that they give it because these objects, though apparently dissimilar, produce effects upon the mind which materially resemble each other: therefore, the mode in which I propose to examine the nature of the beautiful, is, first, to state the fact with respect to language, the various classes of objects and occasions where a person understanding his own language thoroughly, and applying it properly, would use the expression of *beautiful*.

In the first place, it is applied to the simplest sensations of sight, as color, figure, and so forth; it is applied to sounds, either simple or compound; but, I believe, neither to touch, taste, nor smell. We should not say that the feeling of velvet, or the taste of sugar, or the smell of a rose, was beautiful: the latter instance, however, is rather doubtful; if the expression be not already legitimated, I think we may say it will be so very soon. We apply the expression to the face of nature, to landscape, to personal appearance, to animals, to poetry, painting, sculpture, and all the fine arts which are called mimetic, and represent animate or inanimate nature. We apply it to several moral feelings of the mind, to architecture, and to invention in machinery. These are, I fancy, the principal subjects which justify the application of the word.

There is one usage of the word to which I shall not refer in the subsequent discussion, because it is evidently used in a figurative sense; as when we say that any thing which is good, is beautiful; and in this sense we should say that Milton's description of the falling angels was beautiful, though in strictness it is *sublime*, and *not* beautiful:—

"Him the Almighty Power
Hurl'd headlong flaming from the ethereal sky,
With hideous ruin and combustion, down
To bottomless perdition; there to dwell
In adamantine chains and penal fire,
Who durst defy the Omnipotent to arms.
Nine times the space that measures day and night
To mortal men, he with his horrid crew
Lay vanquish'd, rolling in the fiery gulf,
Confounded, though immortal: But his doom
Reserv'd him to more wrath; for now the thought
Both of lost happiness, and lasting pain,
Torments him; round he throws his baleful eyes,
That witness'd huge affliction and dismay
Mixt with obdurate pride and steadfast hate
At once, as far as angels, ken, he views
The dismal situation waste and wild:
A dungeon horrible on all sides round,
As one great furnace flam'd; yet from those flames
No light; but rather darkness visible
Serv'd only to discover sights of woe,
Regions of sorrow, doleful shades, where peace
And rest can never dwell; hope never comes
That comes to all; but torture without end
Still urges, and a fiery deluge, fed
With ever-burning sulphur unconsum'd."

But the word *beautiful*, as a general word for excellence, is a part of that practice in language, which, where there are many qualities, or many things, puts one of the most conspicuous, to stand for the whole. Thus, virtue, which originally signifies personal courage, has become a general name for all good qualities. England is the general name for all the three branches of the empire; and *the beautiful* has become a general term for all the various excellences in poetry.

Having, then, ascertained the facts respecting the application of the term *beauty*, there are two things which remain to be done,—to ascertain the causes, in each respective instance, which excite the feeling of the beautiful in my mind; and next, to discover whether these various examples of this feeling, which are called by a common name, do, in fact, possess a common nature: for if I can point out the cause or causes of this emotion, or class of emotions, and ascertain its nature, or their natures, I see nothing else which I have to do.

A very great ambiguity has arisen in all language, from the confusion which has been made between the causes which act upon the mind, and the affections of the mind itself. In hardness or softness, there ought to be one word to signify that cause, which impresses the mind in that particular manner, and another for the impression itself. So in beauty, the same word expresses the emotion of the mind, and the *cause* of that emotion: it is absolutely necessary, in order to arrive at any definite opinions on this subject, to specify to ourselves and others, in which of these two senses we are making use of the term; and, to follow my own advice, I use the term beauty always as a feeling of the *mind.* When I say that such an object is beautiful, I mean that it has in itself the power of exciting in my mind that particular feeling. It does all very well in popular language, where no great precision is wanted, to say that a landscape is beautiful; or the expression may stand where men know how to translate it into common sense: but in strictness the *feeling* only can be in my mind;—the *causes* which excite that feeling, whatever they be, are in the landscape; all the effects which these causes can produce, are in me. Emotion can not reside upon the banks of rivers, or be green with the grass, flexible with the boughs, and pearly with the dew: the *causes* of this particular emotion may be in matter; the thing itself can not.

I hear some men contend that beauty, in strictness, only means personal beauty, or beauty of landscape; and that when applied to such objects as an ox, or an invention, as in a steam-engine, it is merely a metaphor. Now a metaphor is nothing but a short simile, and a simile is a resemblance; and why, I should be glad to know, is one feeling of the mind, by general consent, said to resemble another feeling of the mind, if, in fact, there is no resemblance between them? If it be used metaphorically, it is the clearest proof that mankind have *felt* a resemblance, which has guided them in the application of the metaphor. When you compare an object of sense, to a feeling of mind, as pity to a balsam, or the feeling of anger to a storm, it is very obvious that such metaphors are derived from those faint analogies which are convenient enough for poetry, but utterly unsuitable to philosophy. But where mankind, or great numbers of mankind, have agreed to call two mere feelings by the same name, or, as other persons would say, to use one metaphorically for the other, it is a pretty clear proof that these two feelings do very strongly resemble each other.

First, it is necessary to observe that the term *beauty*, to whatever object it is applied, is applied *only* to that which is very superior to other objects of the same species. Suppose an average appearance in human countenances, the term *beauty* is applied *only* where that average is very far exceeded; it is as emphatical on one side of the middle point, as *ugly* is on the other,—both point at extremes. So in poetry; a beautiful poem is one very superior to the common merit of poetry: a beautiful invention in mechanics is one in which much more than ordinary ingenuity is displayed. It is always a term of the superlative degree, implying comparison, and an opinion of pre-eminence, the result of that comparison.

I shall set out, after these premises, with reasserting my opinion, advanced in the last lecture, that beauty is an original quality of matter: not that all matter has it, any more than all matter has hardness; but that some matter has it, as some matter has hardness. As I said a great deal about it in my last lecture, I shall not expatiate further on this subject at present, but assume the principle, and reason upon it.

Though I contend that there is an original beauty of matter, I do not by any means lay much stress upon it, or compare it with that feeling of the beautiful which matter excites when associated with some agreeable quality of mind. I believe a clear red, passing through a beautiful white color, is of itself beautiful; but it is certainly more beautiful when it becomes the sign of health, and we learn habitually to consider it as such. The lively green that the herbage assumes after rain, is of itself agreeable to the eye, but it is infinitely *more* agreeable when that color becomes the sign of plenty, of freshness, of liberty, of boundless range, and innocent enjoyment, and all the pleasures of *mind* we associate with the idea of the country.

> "For what are all
> The forms which brute, unconscious matter wears,—
> Greatness of bulk, or symmetry of parts?
> Not reaching to the heart, soon feeble grows
> The superficial impulse; dull their charms,
> And satiate soon, and pall the languid eye.
> Not so the moral species, nor the powers
> Of genius and design; the ambitious mind
> There sees herself: by these congenial forms
> Touch'd and awaken'd, with intenser act
> She bends each nerve, and meditates well pleas'd
> Her features in the mirror. For, of all
> The inhabitants of earth, to man alone
> Creative Wisdom gave to lift his eye
> To Truth's eternal measures; thence to frame
> The sacred laws of action and of will,
> Discerning justice from unequal deeds,
> And temperance from folly."*

I shall begin the analysis of the beautiful with music, a subject which I can not pass over, but in which I must beg for great indulgence, because it is impossible for any one to be more completely ignorant of that art than I am. Let us take the plainest instance, simple melody, or

* Akenside's "Pleasures of Imagination," line 526.

an air sung by the human voice; why do we call this combination of sounds beautiful, and what is the cause of the striking and beautiful emotion we derive from it? In the first place, because each single sound of which the air is composed is beautiful,—that is, it is beautiful if the voice be good; for I should suppose that any air sung by a wretched voice, or performed upon such an instrument as the bagpipe, could not with any propriety be denominated beautiful; it may become so from association, but it requires the *aid* of association to make it so. We may say this air, sung by a good voice, or performed upon a good instrument, would be beautiful; but this is only describing what other sounds would be, not saying what these are. Therefore, a simple air, sung by a good voice, is beautiful for one reason, because each particular sound of which it is composed is beautiful; and the pleasure is of course immensely increased, from the variation and contrast of these sounds.

> "And ever, against eating cares,
> Lap me in soft Lydian airs,
> * * * * *
> In notes, with many a winding bout
> Of linked sweetness long draw out,
> With wanton heed and giddy cunning;
> The melting voice through mazes running,
> Untwisting all the chains that tie
> The hidden soul of harmony."

Melody is not only beautiful from its variety of originally beautiful sounds, but from its originally beautiful combinations. Some two notes joined together are naturally agreeable, others naturally disagreeable: at least, it is the commonly received opinion that concords are pleasant, discords unpleasant, from the constitution of our organs of hearing. Whether this be the fact, and whether concords here are concords the world through, I can not take upon me to determine; but, however this be, the fact is indisputable, that very unpracticed ears are delighted with some combinations of sounds, and that this pleasure must be considered as another additional cause of the beauty of music. Rhythm, or number in music, is a copious source of variety and uniformity;

every piece of regular music is, as every one knows, supposed to be divided into small portions, separated in writing by a cross line, called a bar, which, whether they contain more or fewer sounds, are all equal in respect of time. In this way the rhythm is a source of uniformity, which pleases by suggesting the agreeable ideas of regularity, and, still more, by rendering the music intelligible. But the principal cause of the beauty of music is, that it can be translated into feelings of the mind. Let a simple air be sung by a pleasing voice, not in words, but in articulate sounds,—as it is quick, or as it is solemn, as it is high or low, we immediately connect it with some feeling; because experience has taught us that some of our passions are expressed in a solemn measure and low tone, others in quick measure and with an elevation of voice. If any one were for the first time to hear the tune of "*Farewell to Lochaber,*" without words, there could, I should think, be little doubt but that he would associate it with some calm, melancholy emotion: nor could any person imagine that such a tune as that of "*Dainty Davy,*" was intended to express profound and inconsolable grief. In these airs, we immediately associate with them some feeling of mind, and from this association their beauty is principally derived. "The objects, therefore, which produce such sensations, though in themselves not the immediate signs of such interesting or affecting qualities, yet, in consequence of this resemblance, become gradually expressive of them; and, if not always, yet at those times, at least, when we are under the dominion of any emotion, serve to bring to our minds the images of all those affecting or interesting qualities, which we have been accustomed to suppose they resemble. How extensive this source of association is, may easily be observed in the extent of such kinds of figurative expression in every language."*

Nothing can be more just and philosophical than these opinions of Mr. Alison and Dr. Beattie. Music itself can express only classes of feelings; it can express only melancholy, not any *particular* instance or action of melancholy. The tune of "Lochaber," which I have

* Alison, p. 185.

before alluded to, expresses the pathetic in general; language only can tell us that it is that *particular* instance of the pathetic, where a poor soldier takes leave of his native land, Lochaber, and his wife Jean, with a feeling that he shall see them no more:—

"Borne on rough seas to a far distant shore,
I'll maybe return to Lochaber no more!"

Therefore, the principal cause of the beauty of melody is, that as we hear the air, we not only translate it into human feelings, but, remembering the words connected with it, we summon up the particular exemplification of that feeling; we think of the poor soldier who is never to see again his wife and his children in Lochaber; we love his affection for that spot where he has spent many blithesome days, and we are touched with his misery. Whenever we hear an air to which we know no words, it can inspire only *general* emotion, and the comparative effect is feeble; when poetry applies the general emotion to particular instances, musical expression has attained its maximum of effect. It is said that the "Pastorale" of Corelli was intended for an imitation of the song of angels hovering above the fields of Bethlehem, and gradually soaring up to heaven; it is impossible, however, that the music *itself* can convey any such expression,—it can convey only the feelings of solemnity, of rapture, of enthusiasm; imagination must do the rest. If another name were given to this piece of music, and it were supposed to relate to a much less awful event, its effects, though still powerful, would be very considerably diminished.

Such appear to me to be the causes of that feeling of the beautiful excited by simple melody. The more complicated beauty of harmony is easiest explained by denying that it has any beauty; the music often praised by professors and connoisseurs has often no other merit than that of difficulty overcome, which excites the feeling of wonder, *not* of beauty: the mass of hearers, who can not estimate the difficulty, can not participatein the admiration; they can derive no other gratification from it than the mere animal pleasure of beautiful sounds, which, when they are devoid of moral expression, soon fatigue and disgust: and the parts of a long concerto which give universal pleasure are precisely those which do excite some feeling, which express either what is gay, or the strong passions, or a pleasing melancholy. See the effects of a long piece of music at a public concert. The orchestra are breathless with attention, jumping into major and minor keys, executing figures, and fiddling with the most ecstatic precision. In the midst of all this wonderful science, the audience are gaping, lolling, talking, staring about, and half devoured with ennui. On a sudden there springs up a lively little air, expressive of some natural feeling, though in point of science not worth a halfpenny: the audience all spring up, every head nods, every foot beats time, and every heart also; an universal smile breaks out on every face; the carriage is not ordered; and every one agrees that music is the most delightful rational entertainment that the human mind can possibly enjoy. In the same manner the astonishing execution of some great singers has in it very little of the beautiful; it is mere difficulty overcome, like rope-dancing and tumbling; and such difficulties overcome (as I have before said) do *not* excite the feeling of the beautiful, but of the wonderful.

Independently of these causes of pleasure in music, it may be aided by innumerable associations. It may be national music; it may record some great exploit of my countrymen, as the "Belleisle March;" it may be the "Ranz des Vaches;" and innumerable other causes may aid its effects. In very loud music, as the organ, or in the assemblage of many instruments, an immediate physical effect is produced upon the body, independent of any feeling of the mind. I have seen one or two people so nervous, that they could not hear an organ without crying; and every body remembers the innumerable instances of fainting and weeping at the commemoration in the Abbey, merely from the effect produced upon the nerves by sound. So that, to sum up all the causes I have alledged of the beautiful in music, we may say it proceeds from an original power in sound to create that feeling, either in its simplest state, or in those instances of its combinations which we call concords; that that feeling of beautiful may be aided by our admiration of the skill displayed in harmony, as one agreeable feeling always aids and increases another;—but that the principal cause of beauty in music, is the facility with which it is associated with feeling, from its resemblance to the tones in which feelings are expressed; and that these feelings are made specific by the ministration of poetry, from the combination of which with music, great part of the power of the latter is derived.

Passing from the beauty judged of by the ear, to that which falls under the province of sight, I can not (as I have before said) agree with those who would consider all colors as originally equally pleasing to the eye. I admit, association can make any color agreeable, or any disagreeable: but I contend, that, antecedent to all association, the eye delights in one color more than another; that it passes over some with indifference, and receives exquisite delight from others. Fling among some common pebbles a Bristol stone, or some bits of colored glass; present them to a child of two years old, which will he seize upon first? When Captain Cook first broached his cargo of beads among the savages, and bought a large hog for a couple of beads, which were not worth the decimal of a farthing,—what association can it be imagined the savages had formed with the various colors which proved so alluring to their eyes? The association, philosophers would tell us, that they liked blue, because it was the color of the sky; white, because it was the color of the day. But why did they like faint yellow? why orange color? why deep purple? and why would they have rejected unglazed beads, as dull as this green baize, or of a color as insipid as that of a common stone? It seems so very strange to me, that men should doubt any more of the gluttony of the *eye* than of the gluttony of the mouth. As the palate feasts upon savory and sweet, the ear feasts upon melody, and the eye gorges upon light and color till it aches with pleasure.

With respect to the beauty of forms, I am much more inclined to agree that there is no original beauty of form; but that it entirely depends on association. For the superior pleasure I receive from bright and transparent colors, to that of which I am conscious in looking at those which are dull and opaque, I can give *no* reason. It appears to me an original fact, that the perception of this color should be followed by the emotion of beauty. But I can not say the same of forms: I certainly prefer one form to another, but then I *think* I can always give some reason for the preference.

We must divide forms into those which are simple, and those which are compounded of many other forms; and it appears to me the following causes may be stated of that feeling of the beautiful, excited by the *forms* of objects.

Any form which excites the idea of smoothness, or faint resistance to the touch, is beautiful; except where such notion of smoothness is accidentally united with any unpleasing notion.

"On the whole," says Mr. Burke, "if such parts in human bodies as are found proportioned, were likewise constantly found beautiful,—as they certainly are not; or if they were so situated, as that a pleasure might flow from the comparison,—which they seldom are; or if any assignable proportions were found, either in plants or animals, which were always attended with beauty,—which never was the case; or if, where parts were well adapted to their purposes, they were constantly beautiful, and when no use appeared, there was no beauty,—which is contrary to all experience; we might conclude that beauty consisted in proportion or utility. But since, in all respects, the case is quite otherwise, we may be satisfied that beauty does not depend on these, let it owe its origin to what else it will."*

The form of a solid globe of glass would be much more beautiful than if its surface were broken into inequalities, because it would be much more agreeable to the touch. Is, then, the smoothness of trees cut into a round form, more beautiful than their natural irregularity and roughness? No, certainly not; it gives an idea of restraint and injury to the tree, which is painful. Is the smoothness of a swelled face beautiful? No, it gives the idea

* Burke, p. 230.

of disease. Here are disagreeable associations connected with the appearance of smoothness; but any single object, considered by itself, is considered as more beautiful when smooth than when rough, except where (as I have said before) the roughness is the sign of a pleasant, or the smoothness of an unpleasant, quality.

The forms of regular figures are agreeable, from the relations observed between the parts. The mind takes some pleasure in noticing that one side of a square is precisely like the other; that one angle is exactly of the same magnitude as its diagonal. All forms which are regular are much more distinctly comprehended, and easily retained, than any irregular form; because the accurate observation of one or two parts often leads to the knowledge of the whole. Thus, from a side, and solid angle, we have the whole regular solid; the measure of one side gives the whole square, one radius the whole circle, two diameters an oval, one ordinate and abscissa the parabola; and so on in more complex figures, which have any regularity, they can easily be determined and known in every part from a few data: whereas it might cost a man half his life to remember the form of the first pebble he picked up in the streets, so as to reproduce it at pleasure. Is, then, that form always agreeable in single objects which is regular? Is a square nose agreeable? or a head tapering off to a cone beautiful? No; they are both monstrous. Is a square tree upon espaliers more beautiful than a tree left to itself? No; it gives you an idea of restraint and confinement. Does, then, a square house give you an idea of restraint and confinement? No, by no means; you do not expect wildness in walls, and luxuriancy in buttresses: no man is so fond of the picturesque that he raises part of his drawing-room floor into hillocks, and depresses the rest into glens and valleys: the approach from the door to the table is not by any spiral and circuitous progress, but the servant enters, and, with the most unpicturesque straightness, deposits what he has to leave. The regularity of the figures, instead of the notion of restraint, conveys the notion of comfort in the use, and of skill and economy in the building. Walls have no natural disposition to assume one form more than another: trees have.

Those forms are beautiful which are associated with agreeable ends; as strength, and health, and activity. Strength, however, is a quality in animals, which may be so easily turned to our destruction, that it requires to be joined with the notion of utility, to legitimate the usage of the word *beautiful.* The form of a rhinoceros indicates that he is as strong as a village, yet no one calls him beautiful. The form of an ox, or a cart-horse, which indicates strength supereminently above other animals of the same sort, is called beautiful—not by him whose mind has not been impressed with a strong association between the form and the useful quality; but as breeders, and men curious in cattle, do not scruple to apply to forms indicative of useful qualities the appellation of *beauty.* However, I will discuss this more at length, when I come to consider the question synthetically, and to show (what I believe to be true), that any surprising adaptation of means to ends, immediately excites the feeling of the beautiful, except where association intervenes to prevent it.

Forms which excite the notion of swiftness, are commonly beautiful; or of a mixture of swiftness and strength. The greater part of our associations respecting beautiful forms, are taken from our own species. We find magnitude and strength of form, united with good qualities, which excite respect rather than affection; and with bad ones, which excite fear rather than pity: with courage, perseverance, and intrepidity; with violence, harshness, and oppression. Experience, on the contrary, teaches us that delicacy of form is united with gentleness and benevolence, which are the objects of affection; and with indecision, timidity, and fluctuation, which are the objects of compassion. This, if I mistake not, is the origin of that association in favor of delicacy of form, and of the application to it of the term *beautiful:* and of course, when the association is once established, it is extended to those inanimate objects from whence it would never have originated; for I can not conceive that the delicacy of a flower, by which is principally meant its fragility, the facility with which any exterior violence can destroy it, can of *itself* be any cause of our deeming it beautiful,—unless our experience of moral beings had previously taught us to associate with the emblem of outward weakness, a thousand beautiful feelings of pity, gratitude, kindness, and other the best and fairest emotions of the mind.

LECTURE XIV.

ON THE BEAUTIFUL.—PART II.

"ALL the objects which are exhibited to our view by Nature," says Sir Joshua Reynolds, "upon close examination will be found to have their blemishes and defects. The most beautiful forms have something about them like weakness, minuteness, or imperfection. But it is not every eye that perceives these blemishes; it must be an eye long used to the contemplation and comparison of these forms, and which, by a long habit of observing what any set of objects of the same kind have in common, has acquired the power of discerning what each wants in particular. This long, laborious comparison, should be the first study of the painter who aims at the greatest style. By this means he acquires a just idea of beautiful forms; he corrects Nature by herself, her imperfect state by her more perfect. His eye being enabled to distinguish the accidental deficiencies, excrescences, and deformities of things, from their general figures, he makes out an abstract idea of their forms, more perfect than any one original: and, what may seem a paradox, he learns to design naturally, by drawing his figures unlike to any one object. This idea of the perfect state of nature, which the artist calls the ideal beauty, is the great leading principle by which works of genius are conducted. By this, Phidias acquired his fame; he wrought upon a sober principle what has so much excited the enthusiasm of the world; and by this method you who have courage to tread the same path, may acquire equal reputation.

"This is the idea which has acquired, and which seems to have a right to, the epithet of *divine;* as it may be said to preside, like a supreme judge, over all the productions of nature, appearing to be possessed of the will and intention of the Creator, as far as they regard the external form of living beings. When a man once possesses this idea in its perfection, there is no danger but that he will be sufficiently warmed by it himself, and be able to warm and ravish every one else.

"Thus it is from a reiterated experience, and a close comparison of the objects of nature, that an artist becomes possessed of the idea of that *central* form, if I may so express it, from which every deviation is deformity. But the investigation of this form, I grant, is painful; and I know but of one method of shortening the road;—that is, by a careful study of the works of the ancient sculptors, who, being indefatigable in the school of nature, have left models of that perfect form behind them, which an artist would prefer as supremely beautiful, who had spent his whole life in that single contemplation. But if industry carried them thus far, may not you also hope for the same reward from the same labor? We have the same school opened to us that was opened to them, for Nature denies her instructions to none who desire to become her pupils."

Every body must perceive that in this opinion of Sir Joshua's there is a great deal of ingenuity as well as justice: and, in order to ascertain the effect of custom on the beauty of forms, I begin with stating, that where the customary figure of animals is very materially deviated from, there we have always a sense of deformity and disgust. I carefully avoid mentioning those parts of animals where a deviation from the customary figure would imply disease and weakness, and prevent the animal from acting as Nature intended it should. A crooked spine gives us the very opposite notions to the beautiful, not merely because it is contrary to the customary figure of the animal, but because experience has taught us to associate it with the notions of disease and imbecility of body. But, in order to show the effect of custom upon the beautiful, take a chin, which is of no use at all. A chin ending in a very sharp angle would be perfect deformity. A man whose chin terminated in a point, would be under the immediate necessity of retiring to America; he would be a perfect horror: and for no other reason that I can possibly see, but that Nature has shown no intention of making such a chin,—we have never been accustomed to see such chins. Nature, we are quite certain, did not intend that the chin should be brought to a perfect angle, nor that it should be perfectly circular, and therefore either of these extremes is a deformity. Now, something considerably removed from the perfect circle and the perfect angle, is the chin we have been most accustomed to see, and which, for that reason, we most approve of. Within certain limits, one chin is as common as another, and as handsome as another: there are degrees of tendency to the circle and the angle, which we can at once pronounce to be ugly; but there is a middle region of some extent, where all approximations to these two figures are equally common and equally handsome. The only objection to this doctrine of the central form, is, that it has been pushed too far; it has been urged that there is an exact middle point between the two extremes, which is the perfection of beauty, and to which nature is perpetually tending. This attempt at such very precise and minute discovery in the subject of beauty, appears to me to give a fanciful air to the whole doctrine, and to do injustice to the real truth it contains. In the construction of every form, Nature takes a certain range: to ascertain the ordinary limits of her range, is practical, rational, and useful; to aim at greater precision, and to speak as if you knew the very prototype at which Nature was always aiming, and from which she was always deviating on one side or the other, is to cheat yourself with your own metaphors, and to substitute illusion for plain fact. Within certain limits, every tendency to the circle or the angle, are equally removed from deformity, because they are equally common, and they are (all other things being equal) equally beautiful. Of course I mean this only to apply where the expression is equal, and where mere historical association does not interfere to disturb the justice of the conclusions. The Grecian face is not common: I hardly know what a Grecian face is, but I am told by those who have studied these matters, that there are some parts of it,—the length, I fancy, between the nose and the lip,—which are extremely uncommon, and very rarely to be met with in Europe. This is very probable; but it is mere association. If the elegant arts had been transmitted to us from the Chinese instead of the Greeks, that singular piece of deformity, a Chinese nose, would very probably have been held in high estimation. Now what I have said about forms amounts to this:—Forms are beautiful which are associated with the notion of smoothness of touch, which are regular, which give the notion of delicacy, or recall any of a particular class of feelings of mind. What that particular class is, I shall attempt hereafter to specify.

So far I have attempted to show, that the contrary to that, which is the customary form of any species, is deformity. But is the customary form itself beautiful? does it create the opposite to disgust? I am strongly inclined to think it does not; that the mere commonness of any form does not give the notion of beauty;—it prevents the notion of deformity, but does not give the notion of beauty, for beauty itself is always uncommon.

Mr. Burke says, "If I am not mistaken, a great deal of the prejudice in favor of proportion has arisen, not so much from the observations of any certain measures found in beautiful bodies, as from a wrong idea of the relation which deformity bears to beauty, to which it has been considered as the opposite: on this principle it was concluded, that where the causes of deformity were removed, beauty must naturally and necessarily be introduced. This, I believe, is a mistake; for *deformity* is opposed, not to beauty, but to the *complete common form*. If one of the legs of a man be found shorter than the other, the man is deformed, because there is something wanting to complete the whole idea we form of a man: and this has the same effect in natural faults, as maiming and mutilation produce from accidents. So if the back be humped, the man is deformed, because his back has an unusual figure, and what carries with it the idea of some misfortune: so if a man's neck be considerably longer or shorter than usual, we say he is deformed in that part, because men are not commonly made in that manner. But surely every hour's experience may convince us, that a man may have his legs of an equal length, and resembling each other in all respects, and his neck of a just size, and his back quite straight, without having at the same time the least perceivable beauty. Indeed, beauty is so far from belonging to the idea of custom, that, in reality, what affects us in that manner, is extremely rare and uncommon. The beautiful strikes us as much by its novelty, as the deformed itself."*

Custom has precisely the same effect upon our ideas of relative magnitude or proportion, as on our ideas of figure. There is a certain breadth of the mouth, in proportion to the breadth of the whole face, which is monstrous; another opposite proportion equally monstrous. There is a certain middle limit, within which all proportions are equally removed from deformity. Mr. Burke contends, and in my humble opinion with great success, that proportion is never of *itself* the original cause of beauty. It is the cause of beauty, as it is an indication of strength and utility in buildings, of swiftness in animals, of any feeling morally beautiful; and it is agreeable, as it is customary in animals, or the proof of the absence of deformity; but no proportion of itself, and without one of these reasons, ever pleases. No man would contend Nature ever intended that 6 to 2, or 9 to 14, are perfection: that the moment a monkey could be discovered and brought to light, the length of whose ear was precisely the cube root of the length of his tail, that he ought to be set up as a model of perfect conformation to the whole simious tribe. Certain proportions are beautiful, as they indicate skill, swiftness, convenience, strength, or historical association; and then philosophers copy these proportions, and determine that they must be originally and abstractedly beautiful,—applying that to the sign, which is only true of the thing indicated by the sign.

Custom has also the same effect upon magnitudes. *Tall* and *short* mean only *unusual.* The excellence of

* Burke, p, 221.

stature would lie within those limits where one height was equally common with another, were it not for the idea of utility which intervenes and overcomes the slight deviation from that which is most common. For instance: I believe there are many more Englishmen between 5 feet 6 and 5 feet 9, than there are between 5 feet 9 and 6 feet; but I believe Mr. Flaxman, in making a statue of a beautiful young man, would rather choose between the last proportion than the first,—because, though the deviation from custom would be greater, it would be compensated for by the superior notions of strength and energy it would convey. But every sculptor would undoubtedly take the commonest proportion between the nose and the chin he could discover, because no superior pleasure would be gained by deviating from that proportion. Mr. Burke has a notion that things, to be beautiful, must be small,—that smallness is one cause of beauty. This, I confess, I can not agree to. *Little* is a term of affection, but not a term of beauty: where the stature is small, we are rather inclined to use some less powerful word than beautiful, as *pretty.* There is a certain feeling of admiration, a faint tinge of awe, connected with personal beauty, which, if not diminished, is certainly not assisted, by smallness. If smallness were one cause of beauty, we should have remarked it in the great mass of amatory poetry, which has been accumulating since the beginning of the world: the lover would have told his mistress, from time immemorial, that she was so short that she could walk under his arm; that she weighed less by 20 or 30 pounds than any other beauty in the neighborhood; that he solemnly believed her only to be five feet; and he would have diminished her down by elegant adulation, to think as lowly of herself as possible. I think if the poetical gentlemen who attend the Institution will recollect, they will rather find, when they speak of stature at all, that their adulation runs in an opposite channel; and that, though they may speak of grand stately figures, they never allude to those remarkable only for weighing very little, and being shorter and thinner than the average of the human race.

Having now gone through the various effects of magnitude, proportion, and figure, on beauty, I think I have said enough to explain the causes of the most remarkable sort of beauty, the beauty of the human face. I shall first take a very beautiful female face, entirely without expression,—why do we call that face beautiful? Take twenty other faces, all devoid of expression; why do we denominate the one beautiful, the others not? The beautiful face is a most uncommon assemblage of common figures, common proportions, common magnitudes, and common relations. Take all the other twenty,—the first has features too large, that is, larger than is *common;* the second violates proportion, that is, the customary proportion between the length of the forehead and the length of the chin is violated; in a third, the figure of the mouth is extraordinary, it is not the average *customary* figure of mouths. In the beautiful face alone, there is not a single deviation from custom: the figure of every feature is the average figure; the magnitude the average magnitude; the proportion each part bears to the other, the *customary* proportion. The only thing which is not average, and not customary, is the extraordinary *assemblage of averages and common standards in one single face:* that whereas all human faces deviate from the custom of Nature in some of their magnitudes, figures, and proportions, she has assembled, in this single face, one and all her models for every separate feature; and indulged the eye of man, unused to excellence, with the spectacle of that which is without spot, blemish, or objection. Now mind what we have to add to this bare assemblage of proportions, figures, and magnitudes: in the first place we add to it smoothness, a great cause of beauty; then beautiful colors, which are also the signs of health, youth, and delicacy of feeling. It shall also express goodness, compassion, gentleness, an obliging spirit, and a mild wisdom; and, putting all these powerful causes together, I think I have said enough to explain the effects which personal beauty produces on the destinies of man.

"These, when the Spartan queen approach'd the tower,
In secret own'd resistless beauty's power:

> They cried, 'No wonder such celestial charms
> 'For nine long years had set the world in arms;
> What winning graces, what majestic mien!
> She looks a goddess, and she moves a queen!'"

These are the causes which made all the old senators of Troy exclaim, at the sight of Helen, that the Trojans and the well-booted Greeks were by no means to blame for having endured such griefs so long a time for such a beautiful lady.

All the beauty of motion I should suspect to be the result of association. Motion is either quick or slow, direct or circuitous, uniform or irregular. Sometimes quick motion is *not* beautiful, from the association it excites of violent resistance to the touch; in other instances there is a want of variety, both in direct motion and in slow motion, which is tiresome. All motion which gives us the notion of ease, is beautiful; of restraint, is painful. All movements in human creatures, which express any feeling of mind which itself would be called beautiful, is as beautiful as the thing it signifies. The motion of a rivulet is beautiful from its variety; of a balloon, from its ease; and the apparent absence of effort of a sailing kite, from the same reason; of a man of war moving slowly, for the same reason.

Grace is either the beauty of motion, or the beauty of posture. Graceful motion is motion without difficulty or embarrassment; or that which, from experience, we know to be connected with ingenious modesty, a desire to increase the happiness of others, or any beautiful moral feeling. A person walks up a long room, observed by a great number of individuals, and pays his respects as a gentleman ought to do;—why is he graceful? Because every movement of his body inspires you with some pleasing feeling; he has the free and unembarrassed use of his limbs; his motions do not indicate forward boldness, or irrational timidity;—the outward signs perpetually indicate agreeable qualities. The same explanation applies to grace of posture and attitude: that is a graceful attitude which indicates an absence of restraint; and facility, which is the sign of agreeable qualities of mind: apart from such indications, one attitude I should conceive to be quite as graceful as another.

Mr. Burke has a long dissertation respecting the effect of utility or fitness, as a cause of beauty: he determines that it is not a cause of beauty, but I can not think this decision conformable with matter of fact. I took occasion to observe, in my last lecture, that the term *beauty* implied comparison, and that it was a term of the superlative degree. Now certainly, mere utility, unaccompanied by surprise, does never excite the feeling of beauty. There is nothing more useful than a plow, an axe, or a hammer, but nobody calls them beautiful; but whenever utility is promoted by a surprising adaptation of means to ends, there the feeling of the beautiful is always excited, unless counteracted by some accidental association. "Why," says Mr. Burke, "upon this principle of utility, the wedge-like snout of a sow, with its tough cartilage at the end, the little sunk eyes, and the whole make of the head, so well adapted to its offices of digging and rooting, would be extremely beautiful." The great bag hanging to the bill of a pelican, a thing highly useful to this animal, would be likewise as beautiful in our eyes. In the first place, the pig is an animal degraded by all sorts of dirty associations, and therefore the instance is rather unfair: the bag of the pelican raises up, also, some association of disease; and this is the notion both the one and the other excites in common minds. But the anatomist, who has examined the structure of these parts carefully, and knows how they are composed, how moved, how connected with the rest of the body, is immediately struck with the feeling of the beautiful, and does not hesitate to denominate both the one and the other a beautiful provision of nature. In the same manner all the instances Mr. Burke quotes are easy to be answered,—porcupines and hedgehogs are well provided by nature with means of defense; but any thing associated with the idea of pain, wounds, and contention, is disagreeable. For the same reason, all the inventions of war, bombs, mines, cannon,—though they are useful, and excite surprise if they have not been often seen,—are never considered as beautiful, from the dreadful ideas with which they are connected. But I think it would be difficult to find any thing useful, done by a surprising adaptation of means to end, which would not be called beautiful. How beautiful is the adaptation of the condensible nature of steam, to overcome the greatest obstacles in mechanics! or that adaptation of the elastic power of air, to produce a continued stream in the engines employed for fires! What is more useful than a saucepan? nothing,—but the adaptation of means to the end excites no surprise. But what if a man were to invent a new and better kind of snuffers, effecting his object by a very striking method,—would that be beautiful? Probably not; the end proposed is so trifling, that we should rather feel a sort of contempt for the man who had lavished his talent upon such an object; though it is very possible that the great ingenuity of the means may sanctify an object otherwise unimportant. Argand's lamp certainly deserves the appellation of a beautiful invention. Go to the Duke of Bedford's piggery at Woburn, and you will see a breed of pigs with legs so short, that their stomachs trail upon the ground: a breed of animals entombed in their own fat, overwhelmed with prosperity, success, and farina. No animal could possibly be so disgusting if it were not useful; but a breeder, who has accurately attended to the small quantity of food it requires to swell this pig out to such extraordinary dimensions,—the astonishing genius it displays for obesity,—and the laudable propensity of the flesh to desert the cheap regions of the body, and to agglomerate on those parts which are worth ninepence a pound,—such an observer of its utility does not scruple to call these otherwise hideous quadrupeds, a beautiful race of pigs. It is asked if perfection is the cause of beauty? Before the question is asked, it may be as well to determine what is meant by perfection? It often means the superlative of any thing. Perfect strength must mean the greatest strength that that species, or any other species, is accustomed to exhibit. Such strength would give no notion of beauty, nor would perfect swiftness; but rather of the sublime: less perfect swiftness would be much more likely to inspire us with the notion of the beautiful.

What notion of beauty could perfect justice impart, or perfect courage?

Perfect symmetry is the symmetry which is the most beautiful, which I have before referred to custom; I see no reason whatever for considering perfection as a cause of beauty.

Variety is another very strong cause of beauty; and this is the reason why we are so fond of natural objects, and is the cause of the great bustle made about nature. I have no doubt but that (all other things being equal) a regular figure is more beautiful than an irregular figure, and that the principal reason why we are like the strange figures presented to us in a forest, among the boughs of the trees, or in a field by the irregular lay of the ground, is the perpetual gratification of this passion for variety which it affords. I went for the first time in my life, some years ago, to stay at a very grand and beautiful place in the country, where the grounds are said to be laid out with consummate taste. For the first three or four days I was perfectly enchanted; it seemed something so much better than nature, that I really began to wish the earth had been laid out according to the latest principles of improvement, and that the whole face of nature wore a little more the appearance of a park. In three days' time I was tired to death; a thistle, a nettle, a heap of dead bushes, any thing that wore the appearance of accident and want of intention, was quite a relief. I used to escape from the made grounds, and walk upon an adjacent goose-common, where the cart-ruts, gravel-pits, bumps, irregularities, coarse ungentlemanlike grass, and all the varieties produced by neglect, were a thousand times more gratifying than the monotony of beauties the result of design, and crowded into narrow confines with a luxuriance and abundance utterly unknown to nature.

When we speak of a beautiful landscape, we include under that term a vast variety of sensations,—the beauty of colors, of smells, and of sounds. It would be difficult to look at milch cattle without thinking of the fragrance of their milk,—or at hay in the haymaking season, without enjoying in imagination its delightful smell.

"As one who long in populous city pent,
Where houses thick and sewers annoy the air,
Forth issuing on a summer's morn to breathe
Among the pleasant villages and farms
Adjoin'd, from each thing met conceives delight;
The smell of grain, or tedded grass, or kine,
Or dairy, each rural sight, each rural sound;
If chance, with nymph-like step, fair virgin pass,
What pleasing seem'd, for her now pleases more;
She most, and in her look sums all delight."

To the beauty of sounds, smells, and colors, is to be added the beauty of variety, the notion of liberty, of health, of innocence, the association of a childhood passed in the country, of the happy days every man has spent there,—all that Virgil has written, and Claude painted, of the country,—the beautiful exertions of the highest minds to make that fairer which God has made so fair, —all these feelings go to make up the beauty of landscape, and give birth, by their united force, to that calm pleasure which has been felt in every age by those who have raised their minds above the struggles of passion, and the emotions of sense. Then every man, in looking at a landscape, paints to himself that scene of imaginary felicity he likes best; a merchant looks at an asylum from the toils of business; a mother marks out a healthy and sheltered spot for her children; an improver plants; a poet feels; an old man builds himself a retired cottage, and gradually wears away his remaining days amid the health and quiet of the fields. A landscape is every thing to every body; it is one person's property as well as another's; it gratifies every man's desire, and fills up every man's heart.

The beauties of architecture I should conceive to be referable to the beauties of utility, of regularity, of delicacy, and of association. Why is the west window of the cathedral at York beautiful? Let us endeavor to follow what passes in the mind, in looking at this celebrated piece of architecture. It is, in the first place, Gothic, and there is an association in favor of Gothic architecture; we have heard it is beautiful, and are prepared to admire it. The stone-work is very light, and therefore does not obstruct the passage of the sun's rays; nor does it give us the idea of labor uselessly employed, but, on the contrary, the idea of delicacy, which I have before stated to be a cause of beauty. It is full of regular figures, neatly cut, which it is not easy to make of stone. The whole is a regular figure, and bears a just proportion to the size of the building. As to the different orders of architecture, it is quite impossible to assent to the observations of those who would contend that their proportions are absolutely beautiful,—that nature has made these proportions originally a cause of that feeling, independent of any utility to which those proportions may be subservient, and of any association with which they may be connected. The common sense of the business appears to me to be this:—I see a pillar; I conceive it, as erected, to support *something*. I know the nature of stone, and its strength. If the proportions are so managed that I conceive the thing to *be* supported, will fall, it gives me the idea of weakness and frailty, which is unpleasant: if they are such as to indicate a much greater degree of strength than is wanted, then I am equally disgusted. Between these two extremes, all proportions are naturally of equal beauty; the rest is done by Pericles, Miltiades, the battle of Thermopylæ, and all the military and literary glory of the Greeks. There is an excellent chapter in Mr. Alison's book, upon the orders of architecture, in which he, to my mind, sets this matter in the clearest point of view, and shows that in this instance, as well as in all others, the pleasure arising from the proportions of the orders, is to be referred to the utility of those proportions, or to the associations which they excite.

"The proportions of these orders," says Mr. Alison, "it is to be remembered, are distinct subjects of beauty from the ornaments with which they are embellished, from the magnificence with which they are executed, from the purposes of elegance they are intended to serve, or the scenes of grandeur they are destined to adorn. It is in such scenes, however, and with such additions, that we are accustomed to observe them: and while we feel the *effect* of all these accidental associations, we are seldom willing to examine what are the *causes* of the complex emotions we feel; and readily attribute to the nature of the architecture itself, the whole pleasure which we enjoy.

"But, beside these, there are other associations we have with these forms, that still more powerfully serve to command our admiration, for they are the Grecian orders: they derive their origin from those times, and were the ornaments of those countries, which are most hallowed in our imaginations; and it is difficult for us to see them, even in their modern copies, without feeling them operate upon our minds as relics of those polished nations where they first arose, and of that greater people by whom they were afterward borrowed.

"While this species of architecture is attended with so many and so pleasing associations, it is difficult, even for a man of reflection, to distinguish between the different sources of his emotion; or, in the moments in which this delight is felt, to ascertain what is the exact portion of his pleasure which is to be attributed to these proportions *alone*. And two different causes combine to lead us to attribute to the style of architecture itself, the beauty which arises from many other associations.

"In the first place, while it is under our eye, this architecture itself is the great object of our regard, and the central object of all these associations. It is the material sign, in fact, of all the various affecting qualities which are connected with it; and it disposes us in this, as in every other case, to attribute to the sign, the effect which is produced by the qualities signified.

"When we reflect, upon the other hand, in our calmer moments, upon the source of our emotion, another motive arises to induce us to consider these proportions as the sole, or the principal, cause of our pleasure; for these proportions are the only qualities of the object which are perfectly or accurately ascertained. They have received the assent of all ages since their discovery; they are the acknowledged objects of beauty; and, having thus got possession of one undoubted principle, our natural love of system induces us to ascribe the whole of the effect to this principle *alone*, and easily satisfies our minds, by saving us the trouble of a long and tedious investigation.

"That this cause has had its full effect in this case, will, I believe, appear very evident to those who attend to the enthusiasm with which, in general, the writers on architecture speak of the beauty of proportion, and compare it with the common sentiments of men, upon the subject of this beauty. Both these causes conspire to mislead our judgment in this point, and to induce us to attribute to one quality, in such objects, that beauty which, in truth, results from many united qualities."*

In my next lecture I shall conclude this subject of the beautiful, and sum up all that I have said upon it. If any man feel himself inclined to think that I have pushed this subject of the beautiful too far, and that its importance does not merit such long discussion, I would desire him to reflect upon the immense effect which it produces on human life. What are half the crimes in the world committed for? What brings into action the best virtues? The desire of possessing. Of possessing what?—not mere money, but every species of the beautiful which money can purchase. A man lies hid in a little, dirty, smoky room for twenty years of his life, and sums up as many columns of figures as would reach round half the earth, if they were laid at length;—he gets rich; what does he do with his riches? He buys a large, well-proportioned house: in the arrangement of his furniture, he gratifies himself with all the beauty which splendid colors, regular figures, and smooth surfaces, can convey; he has the beauties of variety and association in his grounds; the cup out of which he drinks his tea is adorned with beautiful figures; the chair in which he sits is covered with smooth, shining leather; his table-cloth is of the most beautiful damask; mirrors reflect the lights from every quarter of the room; pictures of the best masters feed his eye with all the beauties of imitation. A million of human creatures are employed in this country in ministering to this feeling of the beautiful. It is only a barbarous, ignorant people that can ever be occupied by the necessaries of life *alone*.

* Alison, pp. 367–369.

If to eat, and to drink, and to be warm, were the only passions of our minds, we should all be what the lowest of us all are at this day. The love of the beautiful calls man to fresh exertions, and awakens him to a more noble life; and the glory of it is, that as painters imitate, and poets sing, and statuaries carve, and architects rear up the gorgeous trophies of their skill,—as every thing becomes beautiful, and orderly, and magnificent,—the activity of the mind rises to still greater, and to better objects. The principles of justice are sought out; the powers of the ruler, and the rights of the subject, are fixed; man advances to the enjoyment of rational liberty, and to the establishment of those great moral laws, which God has written in our hearts, to regulate the destinies of the world.

LECTURE XV.

ON THE BEAUTIFUL.—PART III.

I WISH, for the completion of the subject on which I have been engaged, to consider what causes produce the feeling of the beautiful in poetry. I must observe here, as I observed before, that there is a lax and general usage of the word *beautiful,* to which I am not now referring. We might say of Milton's Paradise Lost, that it is a beautiful poem, though its characteristic is rather grandeur and sublimity, than beauty. It is a general term, standing for every species of excellence; but I am speaking now of that which is properly beautiful, as distinguished from what is sublime or excellent in any other kind.

The first reason, then, why poetry is beautiful, is, because it describes natural objects, or moral feelings, which are themselves beautiful. For an example, I will read to you a beautiful sonnet of Dr. Leyden's upon the Sabbath morning, which has never been printed:—

"With silent awe I hail the sacred morn,
Which slowly wakes while all the fields are still;
A soothing calm on every breeze is borne,
A graver murmur gurgles from the rill,
And Echo answers softer from the hill,
And softer sings the linnet from the thorn,
The skylark warbles in a tone less shrill.
Hail, light serene! hail, sacred Sabbath morn!
The rooks float silent by, in airy drove;
The sun, a placid yellow luster shows;
The gales, that lately sigh'd along the grove,
Have hush'd their downy wings in dead repose;
The hov'ring rack of clouds forget to move:—
So smiled the day when the first morn arose!"

Now, there is not a single image introduced into this very beautiful sonnet, which is not of itself beautiful; the soothing calm of the breeze, the noise of the rill, the song of the linnet, the hovering rack of clouds, and the airy drove of rooks floating by, are all objects that would be beautiful in nature, and of course are so in poetry. The notion that the whole appearance of the world is more calm and composed on the Sabbath, and that its sanctity is felt in the whole creation, is *unusually* beautiful and poetical. There is a pleasure in imitation,—this is exactly a picture of what a beautiful placid morning is, and we are delighted to see it so well represented.

There is also a certain degree of pleasure from the measure of the poetry,—from the recurrence of certain cadences at certain intervals;—this makes the distinction between the language of prose and poetry. Now, in which of these two passages are the sounds most agreeably arranged:—"The master saw the madness rising, took notice of his glowing cheeks and his ardent eyes, and, while he defied heaven and earth, changed his own hand, and checked the pride of Alexander. He chose a mournful song, in order to infuse into him soft pity; he sung of Darius, a very great and good man,"—and so on.

"The master saw the madness rise;
His glowing cheeks, his ardent eyes;
And, while he Heaven and Earth defied,
Changed his hand, and check'd his pride.
He chose a mournful muse
Soft pity to infuse:
He sung Darius great and good,
By too severe a fate,
Fallen, fallen, fallen, fallen,
Fallen from his high estate,
And welt'ring in his blood;
Deserted, at his utmost need,
By those his former bounty fed:
On the bare earth exposed he lies,
With not a friend to close his eyes.
With downcast looks the joyless victor sate,
Revolving in his alter'd soul
The various turns of Chance below;
And, now and then, a sigh he stole;
And tears began to flow."

Now, the ideas are precisely the same in the two arrangements of sounds; but I think no one can doubt of the superior pleasure of that order of sounds, in which there appears to be arrangement and design.

Part of the pleasure proceeds also from the rhymes. Children will go on for ten minutes together, repeating a rhyme, merely delighted with the sameness of the sound: so will mad people. I have seen laborers and common people in the country, quite delighted with the accidental discovery of a rhyme; it has appeared to have very much the same effect upon them as wit. I mention these things very cursorily, because they are connected with my subject of the beautiful, though they are facts of great curiosity, and which may lead to very interesting speculations, which I have no doubt they will do, in the very able hands in which they are at present placed by the managers of this Institution.

To these causes may be added a strong admiration of the skill of the poet, whether exemplified in his selection of words, or his choice of the most striking objects and incidents in description. These, I apprehend to be the causes which excite the feeling of the beautiful in poetry, where the subject itself is beautiful. But what is the reason that poetry is called beautiful, where the subject is quite the reverse? There might be a very beautiful description of the flat, dreary fens of Holland, which are themselves as far from being beautiful as any natural scenery can be. Now, here is a passage out of Thomson, in which there is not a single image naturally beautiful, and yet the whole passage certainly must be so called:—

"When o'er this world, by equinoctial rains
Flooded immense, looks out the joyless sun,
And draws the copious stream; from swampy fens,
Where putrefaction into life ferments,
And breathes destructive myriads; or from woods,
Impenetrable shades, recesses foul,
In vapors rank and blue corruption wrapt,
Whose gloomy horrors yet no desperate foot,
Has ever dared to pierce—then, wasteful, forth
Walks the dire power of pestilent disease.
A thousand hideous fiends her course attend,
Sick nature blasting, and to heartless woe,

And feeble desolation, casting down
The towering hopes and all the pride of man.
Such as, of late, at Cartagena quench'd
The British fire. You, gallant Vernon, saw
The miserable scene; you, pitying, saw
To infant weakness sunk the warrior's arm;
Saw the deep racking pang, the ghastly form,
The lip pale quivering, and the beamless eye
No more with ardor bright; you heard the groans
Of agoni ing ships, from shore to shore;
Heard, nightly plung'd amid the sullen waves,
The frequent corse—while on each other fix'd,
In sad presage, the blank assistants seem'd
Silent, to ask, whom fate would next demand."*

The question is, why is such an extraordinary assemblage of unbeautiful images beautiful? In the first place, the mention or description of putrefaction, stagnation of air, and consequent plague, is of course not so disgusting or horrible as the reality: the obstacles to the feeling of the beautiful are immensely overcome, in comparison to that degree of force which they would possess if these things were seen and felt instead of read. Then there is a certain pleasure of security in reading the description of danger, or of comfort in reading the description of disgust. I think we should all be conscious of the feeling of security, in reading Thomson's celebrated description of a snow-storm, and of the father perishing while his children are looking out for him and demanding their sire. Add to all this, the same causes of the beautiful which exist in beautiful subjects,—the meter, the cadence, choice of language, and admiration of skill,—and their united force will explain the reason why poetry is beautiful, when the subject, in nature, would be much otherwise; though, I suppose (all other things being equal), the more beautiful the subject, the more beautiful the poem.

This also is to be said, that some passions, though painful when very strong, are agreeable when weaker. It would be horrible to be staying at a house on a snowy night, where there was every reason to believe that the husband would perish on his road home over a bleak common; and nothing could be more dreadful than to

* Summer, ver. 1026–1051.

see the agony of the mother and the children. But poetical snow is so much less dangerous than real snow, and poetical wives and children always excite our compassion so much less than wives and children devoid of all rhyme and meter, and composed of prosaic flesh and blood, that the degree of compassion excited is rather pleasing than painful.

The beautiful in painting seems to be quite referable to the same causes,—the pleasures of imitation, the reflex pleasure of natural beauty, the pleasure of skill; and where the subject itself is not beautiful, there, reflected horror is less intense than real or original horror, and a certain pleasure is enjoyed from the consciousness that we are exempt from the evil we behold.

Throughout the whole of my lectures on the beautiful, in my explanation of the beauty of exterior objects, I have thought it sufficient to trace their connection with feelings of the mind, which have received that appellation. It therefore becomes necessary I should state what those feelings are. To class feelings with the same precision with which it is possible to arrange earths, and stone, and minerals, is a degree of order in these matters, which the most ardent metaphysician, unassisted by lunacy, will of course never attempt to attain. The similarity of feelings is not a truth which it is possible to prove; it must be left to every man's inward reflection to determine, and to his candor to confess; and, after all, opinions upon such subjects must always fall far short of that clearness of conviction, which is easily obtained upon physical subjects.

The emotions of the mind may be divided into painful and pleasing, and the pleasing into calm emotions and tumultuous emotions; and the beautiful, I believe, comprehends almost every calm emotion of pleasure. I am using old and well-established phrases, when I speak of calm and tumultuous emotions, and (which is rather a bold thing to say in the language adopted for the phenomena of mind) I really believe they have *some meaning*. The names have evidently been derived from the outward bodily signs of the two kinds of emotion; and no one can doubt, but that what passes in the mind on such occasions, is just as different as what appears in the face and actions, which are the indications of the mind. The joy of a washerwoman who has just got the £20,000 prize in the lottery, and the joy of a sensible, worthy man, who has just succeeded in rescuing a family from distress, are both feelings of pleasure; but while the one is dancing in frantic rapture round her tubs, the signs by which the other indicates his satisfaction are characteristic of nothing but tranquillity and peace.

If, then, the beautiful in feeling includes every calm emotion of pleasure, it must of course comprehend content,—health leading to serenity of body and mind; not when it breaks out into violence of action (the absence of restraint). It must include innocence, affection, and even esteem, as well as benevolence: it also includes ingenuity mingled with utility, or the surprising adaptation of means to useful ends; and a long catalogue of feelings, which are pleasing as well as calm. These seem to be the characteristics which have governed men in their usage of this term. No feeling which excites pain can be beautiful. There is nothing beautiful in envy, hatred, or malice, in cruelty and oppression; but when we see a man bearing testimony to the merit of his rival, *that* is beautiful; when real injuries are rapidly forgiven, *that* is beautiful. When any human being, who has power and influence to defend his oppressions, is as just and considerate to the feelings of others, as if he were poor and defenseless, *that* is eminently beautiful, and gives to every human being who beholds it, the purest emotion of joy. I have said a great deal about prospect and landscape; I will mention an action or two, which appear to me to convey as distinct a feeling of the beautiful, as any landscape whatever. A London merchant, who, I believe, is still alive, while he was staying in the country with a friend, happened to mention that he intended, the next year, to buy a ticket in the lottery; his friend desired he would buy one for him at the same time, which of course was very willingly agreed to. The conversation dropped, the ticket never arrived, and the whole affair was entirely forgotten, when the country gentleman received information that the ticket purchased for him by his friend, had come up a prize of £20,000. Upon his arrival in London, he inquired of his friend where he had put the ticket, and why he had not informed him that it was purchased. "I bought them both the same day, mine and your ticket, and I flung them both into a drawer of my bureau, and I never thought of them afterward." "But how do you distinguish one ticket from the other? and why am I the holder of the fortunate ticket, more than you?" "Why, at the time I put them into the drawer, I put a little mark in ink upon the ticket which I resolved should be yours; and upon re-opening the drawer, I found that the one so marked was the fortunate ticket." Now this action appears to me perfectly beautiful; it is *le beau ideal* in morals, and gives that calm, yet deep emotion of pleasure, which every one so easily receives from the beauty of the exterior world.

There is a very pretty story which I shall read to you, and which, to my mind, is a complete instance of the beautiful in morals.

"At the siege of Namur by the Allies, there were in the ranks of the company commanded by Captain Pinsent, in Colonel Frederick Hamilton's regiment, one Unnion, a corporal, and one Valentine, a private sentinel. There happened between these two men a dispute about a matter of love, which, upon some aggravations, grew to an irreconcilable hatred. Unnion, being the officer of Valentine, took all opportunities even to strike his rival, and profess his spite and revenge which moved him to it; the sentinel bore it without resistance, but frequently said he would die to be revenged of that tyrant. They had spent whole months thus, one injuring, the other complaining; when, in the midst of this rage toward each other, they were commanded upon the attack of the castle, where the corporal received a shot in the thigh and fell. The French pressing on, and he expecting to be trampled to death, called out to his enemy, 'Ah, Valentine, can you leave me here?' Valentine immediately ran back, and, in the midst of a thick fire of the French, took the corporal upon his back, and brought him through all that danger as far as the Abbey of Salsine, where a cannon-ball took off his head: his body fell under his enemy whom he was carrying off. Unnion immediately forgot his wound, rose up, tearing his hair, and then threw himself upon the bleeding carcass, crying, 'Ah, Valentine! was it for me, who have so barbarously used thee, that thou hast died! I will not live after thee.' He was not by any means to be forced from the body, but was removed with it bleeding in his arms, and attended with tears by all their comrades who knew their enmity. When he was brought to a tent, his wounds were dressed by force; but the next day, still calling upon Valentine, and lamenting his cruelties to him, he died in the pangs of remorse and despair.

"It may be a question among men of noble sentiment, whether of these unfortunate persons had the greater soul—he that was so generous as to venture his life for his enemy, or he who could not survive the man who died in laying upon him such an obligation?"*

These are the beautiful feelings which lie hidden in every man's heart, which alone make life worth having, and prevent us from looking upon the world as a den of wild beasts, thirsting for each other's blood.

There are some feelings that are always beautiful, such as content and benevolence; there are others that appear to be beautiful, exactly according to the degree in which they are felt, or to the other feelings with which they are mingled. We compassionate a man who has broken both his legs, but the feeling is accompanied with too much pain, and is far too tumultuous, to be called beautiful.

I should compassionate two young people who were just married, and who, after their marriage, had experienced a loss of fortune that reduced them to embarrassments; but this feeling of compassion, being much less violent and tumultuous, approaches much nearer to the beautiful. All description in poetry, or imitation in painting, of any degree of compassion, would be so much less powerful than the real observation of it in nature, that it might convey the feeling of the beautiful. The

* Tatler, No. V. p. 18.

real compassion we should have felt for Lady Randolph deploring the loss of her son, if there had been a real Lady Randolph, would have been a feeling much too violent for the beautiful; but, lowered and diminished by the imperfect deception of imitation, or the refrigerating medium of description, it is brought to the standard which renders it compatible with that feeling. It appears also, that those feelings which are the reverse of beautiful may, in poetry and in painting, be rendered compatible with it, by being softened and lowered from that intense effect they produce in real nature,—by being joined with harmonious sounds, conveyed in metrical language,—by exciting admiration of skill, and gratifying that pleasure which results from accurate imitation.

I consider mere imitation, rather as an auxiliary to the feeling of the beautiful, than as sufficient to produce it of itself. Mere imitation is agreeable, but I question if it ever excites, *alone*, the feeling of the beautiful. Could the most accurate drawing of a rat, or a weasel, ever be beautiful?—or, if it be contended that these are animals which excite disgusting associations, could the accurate drawing of a block of Portland stone, or of mahogany, ever be beautiful? If mere imitation can excite the feeling of beauty, these subjects, well imitated, ought to come up to that character, which I hardly think they ever could.

Thus, then, I have, with some pains to myself (and I am afraid with much more to my audience), gone through this subject of the beautiful; a subject certainly of great difficulty, and on which probable opinion must be expected, rather than certain conviction. To silence opposition on such a subject, is of course impossible: every man, in discussing it, must fling himself upon the candor of his audience, and, instead of defying their objections, request them to assist him in overcoming them.

One method of trying the justice of what I have said respecting the beautiful, will be, to see what is meant by the opposite expression of *ugliness*. An ugly face is a face which is not smooth, nor of a clear, transparent color; which expresses unpleasant passions, and where the magnitudes, proportions, and figures, are very uncustomary. An ugly landscape is one devoid of variety, of beautiful color; and which excites feelings of dreariness, coldness, and disease, rather than of warmth, health, and enjoyment. An ugly animal is one, in the conformation of which, the custom of nature is violated, or which excites the associations of sloth, gluttony, inutility, and malice, rather than the opposite of all these qualities. If pigs did not make such excellent hams, they would be the most detestable of all animals on the face of the earth; and, accordingly, all nations that do not eat them, hate them: they are only restored to favor upon condition of being dressed for dinner.

Ugly buildings, are buildings in which the figures are not regular, nor the divisions convenient, nor the proportions such as are associated with durability, or elegance, or any pleasant impression. In ugly music, if I may use the expression, the sound is not in itself pleasing, and it conveys no pleasing association. In short, we shall always find, that in using this word, which is the exact contrary to *beauty*, we shall always be influenced by the absence of those causes, from which I, and many others before me, have stated the feeling of the beautiful to proceed. The sum, then, of what I have said on these subjects is, that there is a mere beauty of matter,—or rather I should say a feeling of the mind, occasioned by certain qualities of matter, to which we have given the name of the beautiful; and other feelings of the mind, not occasioned by the intervention of any thing material, which are found to resemble the first class, and have received the same name. How it comes about that large masses of green or blue light should produce any effects similar to those which are produced by benevolence,—that there should be such an analogy between content and smoothness, between any material and any moral beauty—I can not take upon me to determine; but that consent among mankind so to consider them, evinced by the language of many countries, is an evidence that there is some real foundation in nature for the resemblance. The emotion produced by both, is calm and gentle: both are pleasing: both lose their character of the beautiful, the moment that they hurry the mind into any tumultuous sensation, or afflict it with any degree of pain. What was the intention of Providence, in creating this affinity between our minds and the planet on which we dwell, it would be rash, perhaps, to conjecture. The effects of it, however, I can not help thinking, are often very perceptible. The mind, composed by the beauty of natural objects, is brought into that state, in which the beautiful in morals spontaneously rises up to its notice, and, amid the fragrance and verdure of the earth, is still more refreshed by the feeling of the mild and amiable virtues. In the stillness of an evening in the summer, when every sense is gratified by the beauties of the creation, we have all felt the kindred beauties of the mind; we have all felt disposed to forgiveness on such moments, to pity, to kindness, to be gracious and merciful to every created being; we have felt ourselves drawn toward virtue by some invisible power, and betrayed into the gentlest and happiest tenor of mind. If the very form and color of things have a tendency to guide the mind of man to rectitude of thought, and propriety of action, it is a new proof of the goodness of Providence, and gives fresh dignity to that class of feelings which have hitherto been considered to exist for pleasure alone.

> "For as old Memnon's image, long renown'd
> By fabling Nilus, to the quivering touch
> Of Titan's ray, with each repulsive string
> Consenting, sounded through the warbling air
> Unbidden strains; even so did Nature's hand
> To certain species of external things,
> Attune the finer organs of the mind:
> So the glad impulse of congenial powers,
> Or of sweet sounds, or fair-proportion'd form,
> The grace of motion, or the bloom of light,
> Thrills through Imagination's tender frame,
> From nerve to nerve: all naked and alive
> They catch the spreading rays; till now the soul
> At length discloses every tuneful spring,
> To that harmonious movement from without
> Responsive. Then the inexpressive strain
> Diffuses its enchantment: Fancy dreams
> Of sacred fountains and Elysian groves,
> And vales of bliss: the intellectual power
> Bends from his awful throne a wondering ear

And smiles: the passions, gently sooth'd away,
Sinks to divine repose, and love and joy
Alone are waking; love and joy, serene
As airs that fan the summer."*

There is another class of objects—the picturesque—which have given rise to various controversies between some very ingenious gentlemen; and which have, from the elegance of the subject, and the very pleasing manner in which it has been discussed, attracted a considerable share of attention.

Mr. Gilpin defines picturesque objects to be those which please from some quality capable of being illustrated in painting, or such objects as are *proper* for painting. Mr. Price attempts to show that the picturesque has a character no less separate and distinct, than either the sublime, or the beautiful; and quite as much independent of the art of painting. The characteristics of the beautiful, are smoothness and gradual variation; those of the picturesque, directly the reverse,—roughness, and sudden variation. A temple of Grecian architecture in its smooth state, is beautiful; in its ruin, is picturesque. Symmetry, which, in works of art, accords with the beautiful, is in the same degree adverse to the picturesque. Many old buildings, such as hovels, cottages, mills, ragged insides of old barns and stables, whenever they have any peculiar effect of light, form, tint, or shadow, are eminently picturesque; though they have not a pretension to be called either grand or beautiful. Smooth water is beautiful, rough water picturesque. The smooth young ash, the fresh tender beech, are beautiful; the rugged old oak, and knotty whych-elm, picturesque. In animals, the same distinction prevails. The ass is more picturesque than the horse. Of horses, the wild forester, with his rough coat, his mane, and tail, ragged and uneven, or the worn-out cart-horse, with his staring bones, are the most picturesque. The picturesque abhors sleekness, plumpness, smoothness, and convexity, in animals. Among our own species, beggars, gipsys, and all such rough, tattered figures as are merely picturesque, bear a close analogy, in all the qualities

* Akenside's Pleasures of Imagination book 1.

that make them so, to old hovels and mills, to the wild forest horse, and other objects of the same kind. "If we ascend," adds Mr. Price, "to the highest order of created beings, as painted by the grandest of our poets, they, in their state of glory and happiness, raise no ideas but those of beauty and sublimity. The picturesque (as in earthly objects) only shows itself when they are in a state of ruin; when shadows have obscured their original brightness, and that uniform, though angelic, expression of pure love and joy, has been destroyed by a variety of warring passions.

> 'Darken'd so, yet shone
> Above them all the Archangel; but his face
> Deep scars of thunder had entrench'd, and care
> Sat on his faded cheek, and under brows
> Of dauntless courage and considerate pride
> Waiting revenge; cruel his eye, but cast
> Signs of remorse and passion.'"*

Mr. Price then goes on to show, that these two characters of the picturesque and beautiful, are perfectly distinguishable in painting and in grounds. He traces it in color; and maintains that there is a picturesque in taste and in smell. One principal effect of smoothness, according to Mr. Burke and Mr. Price, the essential characteristic of beauty, is, that it gives an appearance of quiet and repose to all objects; roughness, on the contrary, a spirit and animation. Hence, where there is a want of smoothness, there will be a want of repose; and where there is no roughness, there is a want of spirit and stimulus. Picturesqueness, therefore, appears in this theory to hold a station between beauty and sublimity; and, on that account, to be more frequently and happily blended with them both, than they are with each other; it is, however, distinct from either. It is not the beautiful, because it is founded on qualities totally opposite to the beautiful—on roughness, and sudden variation; on that of age, and even of decay. It is not the sublime, because it has nothing to do with greatness of dimensions, and is found in the smallest as well as the largest objects; it inspires no feelings of

* Price on the Picturesque, p. 71.

awe and terror, like the sublime: the picturesque loves boundaries,—infinity is one of the efficient causes of the sublime. Lastly: uniformity, which is so great an enemy to the picturesque, is not only compatible with the sublime, but often the cause of it. Concerning the elegance with which this dissertation on the picturesque is expressed, and the ingenuity with which it is conceived, there can, I should think, be but one opinion; it is not often, in such difficult investigations, that perspicuity, acuteness, good taste, and admirable writing, are so eminently united. But, however, it is not quite so easy to determine upon the real truth and justice which the system contains. One thing seems quite clear, that Mr. Price has chosen a very bad word for the class of feelings which he conceives himself to have discovered; nor does he, in my humble opinion, at all justify it, by what he says of its etymology. The word will naturally be taken by every body for that which is fit to make a good picture; and so, according to the genius of our language, it ought to be taken; and one of the most considerable difficulties Mr. Price's theory will have to encounter, will be that of affixing any *other* meaning to this expression of the picturesque. With respect to the theory itself, the first question seems to be, Is there any class of objects, to be distinguished by any assignable circumstances, which inspire the mind with a common feeling? This, Mr. Price has, I think, proved clearly enough. All the objects he has mentioned—the old horse, the jackass, the mill, the beggar—do arrest the attention, and arrest it in a similar manner; and not merely with a reference to the art of painting, for a person wholly unacquainted with pictures, but who had leisure to contemplate the appearances of natural objects, would probably notice these, which I have mentioned, and refer them to one class, from the similar manner in which they affected his mind. They all rouse the mind agreeably, and provoke instant attention. After the first sensation is over, the different objects lead the mind into a different set of feelings, according to the particular nature of each object; but there is I think one common sensation they excite at first, which establishes a common nature, and justifies the classification of Mr. Price. These are very difficult subjects to speculate upon, and not quite as important as they are difficult; but I should rather think it might be the very faintest feeling of grandeur or sublimity which Mr. Price distinguishes under the appellation of *picturesque*. Sudden variation, for instance, in a great scale, is most commonly either grand or sublime; it sets all the faculties up in arms, and communicates that feeling of faint danger, which is so necessary an ingredient to the sublime. To come upon a sudden on a yawning abyss, unless the danger be imminent, is sublime. The sudden variation from the hill country of Gloucestershire to the Vale of Severn, as observed from Birdlip, or Frowcester Hill, is strikingly sublime. You travel for twenty or five-and-twenty miles over one of the most unfortunate, desolate countries under heaven, divided by stone walls, and abandoned to screaming kites and larcenous crows; after traveling really twenty, and to appearance ninety miles, over this region of stone and sorrow, life begins to be a burden, and you wish to perish. At the very moment when you are taking this melancholy view of human affairs, and hating the postilion, and blaming the horses, there bursts upon your view, with all its towers, forests, and streams, the deep and shaded Vale of Severn. Sterility and nakedness are thrown in the background: as far as the eye can reach, all is comfort, opulence, product, and beauty; now it is an ancient city, or a fair castle rising out of the forests, and now the beautiful Severn is noticed winding among the cultivated fields, and the cheerful habitations of men. The train of mournful impressions is quite effaced, and you descend rapidly into a vale of plenty, with a heart full of wonder and delight. Now the effect produced by sudden variation on a great scale, impresses itself, perhaps, on the mind, and is not forgotten on lesser occasions; and what Mr. Price calls the picturesque may be the faintest state of this feeling, which requires nothing but greater dimensions to exalt itself into the real sublime. I only mention this as a very frivolous conjecture, upon a very unimportant subject, which I bring forward without reflection, and part with without difficulty.

LECTURE XVI.

ON THE SUBLIME.

I MEAN by the sublime, as I meant by the beautiful, a feeling of mind; though, of course, a very different feeling. It is a feeling of pleasure, but of exalted tremulous pleasure, bordering on the very confines of pain; and driving before it every calm thought, and every regulated feeling. It is the feeling which men experience when they behold marvelous scenes of nature; or when they see great actions performed. Such feelings as come on the top of exceeding high mountains; or the hour before a battle; or when a man of great power, and of an unyielding spirit, is pleading before some august tribunal against the accusations of his enemies. These are the hours of sublimity, when all low and little passions are swallowed up by an overwhelming feeling; when the mind towers and springs above its common limits, breaks out into larger dimensions, and swells into a nobler and grander nature. It is necessary here to notice the opinions of Dr. Reid and Mr. Alison, upon the subject of the sublime, which I think may be very fairly expressed by this short quotation from the former of these gentlemen:—"When we consider matter as an inert, extended, divisible, and movable substance, there seems to be nothing in these qualities which we can call *grand;* and when we ascribe grandeur to any portion of matter, however modified, may it not borrow this quality from something intellectual, of which it is the effect, or sign, or instrument, or to which it bears some analogy; or, perhaps, because it produces in the mind an emotion that has some resemblance to that admiration, which truly grand objects raise?

* * * * * * *

"Upon the whole, I humbly apprehend, that true grandeur is such a degree of excellence as is fit to raise an enthusiastic admiration; that this grandeur is found originally and properly in qualities of the mind; that it is discerned in objects of sense, only by reflection, as the light we perceive in the moon and planets is, truly, the light of the sun; and that those who look for grandeur in mere matter, seek the living among the dead.

"If this be a mistake, it ought at least to be granted, that the grandeur which we perceive in qualities of mind, ought to have a different name from that which belongs properly to the objects of sense, as they are very different in their nature, and produce very different emotions in the mind of the spectator."*

Upon the justice of these observations every one must determine for themselves. When I look upon a forest, I confess I am quite unconscious of any qualities of mind, which excite in me the feelings by which I am then possessed; nor can I, upon mature reflection, find that any other feelings are excited in me but wonder and terror: nor can I admit that the sublimity excited by matter, or by qualities of mind, should have different names, because I firmly believe that the two feelings do very much resemble each other; and if that be the case, their similarity of name indicates their affinity, and introduces something like classification into such a dark and mysterious subject as the feelings of the mind. I have said so much in my Lectures on the Beautiful, against referring *that* feeling to moral qualities *alone*, and the arguments would be so precisely the same for this feeling of the sublime, that I forbear going over them again. "The first cause of this feeling," says Mr. Burke, "is obscurity. 'In thoughts from the visions of the night, when deep sleep falleth upon men, fear came upon me, and trembling; which made all my bones to shake: then, a spirit passed before my eyes; the hair of my flesh stood up! it stood still, but I could not discern the form thereof: an image was before mine eyes! there was silence, and I heard a voice! Shall mortal man be more

* Reid's Essays on the Powers of the Mind.

just than God?'" Now, throughout the whole of this description, as Mr. Burke very justly observes, there is an obscurity which fills the mind with terror (such terror, I mean, as is excited by description;) every thing is half obscure; it takes place in a dream. The apparition is half seen,—it has no determinate form. There is space and verge enough for every horror that the most fruitful imagination can suggest; there are no limits to the conception of the dreadful: no man's fancy could paint any thing positive, so terrific, as every man's *fancy*, in this instance, is left to paint for itself.

Obscurity here seems to operate in the production of the sublime, as it is a medium of terror; for whatever else be added to it, terror seems in one shape or another, or in some degree or another, to be essential to the sublime. The degree that each individual can bear of terror, without destroying the feeling of the sublime, must of course depend upon the force of every man's blood, and the strength of his nerves. I have heard of a clergyman so extremely fond of the sublime, that he procured admission into the foremost parallels at the siege of Valenciennes, in order to contemplate the firing from the batteries of the town the more distinctly: such a situation, I should have thought, would have been a little too sublime for Longinus himself, and evinces certainly a disregard for personal danger, with which the generality of the world, in their enjoyment of this high feeling, can not keep pace.

Mere terror, even in that moderated degree of which I am speaking, does not produce the sublime by *itself;* for if an angry man flourishes a loaded pistol near me, in all directions, and exhibits a very careless management of that interesting machine, I have fear in a certain degree, without a particle of sublimity. If a cow shows some slight disposition to run at me as I am crossing a field, I am frightened, but my mind experiences nothing of the sublime. If I am attended by a bad apothecary in an illness, I am excessively frightened, but he never appears to me in the light of a sublime apothecary. Fear, therefore, commonly enters into the feeling of the sublime as an ingredient; or rather, I should say, *is* an ingredient of the cause of that feeling; though it can not excite it by itself. But some men tell you it is not fear which is the ingredient, but awe; but is not fear an ingredient of awe?—for what is awe, but fear and admiration mingled together; both existing, perhaps, in a less degree, than they are to be met with in the sublime? But if the feeling of awe be not of the family of fear, I am quite ignorant both of its genealogy and nature.

A mixture of wonder and terror almost always excites the feeling of the sublime. Extraordinary power generally excites the feeling of the sublime by these means,—by mixing wonder with terror. A person who has never seen any thing of the kind but a little boat, would think a sloop of eighty tons a goodly and somewhat of a grand object, if all her sails were set, and she were going gallantly before the wind; but a first-rate man-of-war would sail over such a sloop, and send her to the bottom, without any person on board the man-of-war perceiving that they had encountered any obstacle. Such power is wonderful and terrible,—therefore, sublime. Every body possessed of power is an object either of awe or sublimity, from a justice of peace up to the Emperor Aurungzebe—an object quite as stupendous as the Alps. He had thirty-five millions of revenue, in a country where the products of the earth are, at least, six times as cheap as in England: his empire extended over twenty-five degrees of latitude, and as many of longitude: he had put to death above twenty millions of people. I should like to know the man who could have looked at Aurungzebe without feeling him to the end of his limbs, and in every hair of his head! Such emperors are more sublime than cataracts. I think any man would have shivered more at the sight of Aurungzebe, than at the sight of the two rivers which meet at the Blue Mountains, in America, and, bursting through the whole breadth of the rocks, roll their victorious and united waters to the Eastern Sea.

Homer represents the horses of Juno as leaping at one bound across the horizon:

"For as a shepherd, from some point on high,
O'er the wide main extends his boundless eye,—

> Through such a space of air, with thund'ring sound,
> At one long leap, the immortal coursers bound!"

Power is here the cause of the sublime; and Longinus observes of this thought, that if the steeds of the deity were to take a second leap, the world itself would want room for it. I must beg leave to mention here, that wonder is not always mingled with fear; and that fear is by no means the necessary consequence of wonder. I may be living in Portuguese America, and find a diamond as big as a hen's egg;—here is wonder, but nothing like fear. Count Borrilowski excites a sufficient degree of wonder, but a feeling as distinct from fear as any feeling can be.

Magnitude is a cause of the sublime, as it excites a mixture of wonder and terror. The great horse, now to be seen for a shilling, is not sublime, because it is so exceedingly tame, and even stupid, that it does not excite the smallest degree of danger. A bull of the size of this animal would be an object of sublimity, because it would excite feelings both of wonder and fear.

Magnitudes may be considered either as relative to the species of the thing itself, or relative to all other things. Any object of unusual magnitude for its species, accompanied by danger, would have a strong tendency to excite some feeling of the sublime. The largest snake ever seen in this country, might have some chance of exciting the feeling of sublimity, though a middling-sized one certainly would not. We call this object large, because it is large for its *own species;* though, going through all the chain of magnitudes, from a mountain to a grain of dust, we could hardly call such a snake a large object. Magnitude in height—as a very lofty mountain—would excite the sublime, from mingling wonder with terror. In looking down from a lofty place, every one is aware of the terror mingled with the wonder. In looking up to a lofty place, the terror is more faint, but still it may be distinctly recognized. The word we commonly use to express our feelings on such occasions, is *awe;* but such awe is most probably nothing but a distant conception of the personal danger we should experience if we were upon the height at which we are looking, if we were to slip from it, and be precipitated to the bottom. Silence is sublime to those who are unaccustomed to it, after a long residence in London. The profound silence of the country is quite affecting and impressive :—

——*" all the air a solemn stillness holds !"*

The solitude of a Gothic cathedral, or that which reigns throughout an extensive ruin—as at Tintern and Fountain's Abbey,—are very sublime. That such scenes of solitude and silence excite wonder in those little accustomed to them, there can be no doubt ; but that faint tinge of danger is also discoverable in them which is so common an ingredient of the sublime : they remind us, however distantly, of our weak and unprotected state, and bring with them a faint and obscure image of death and danger.

" Tis as the general pulse
Of life stood still, and nature made a pause—
An awful pause ! prophetic of her end."

Infinity, perhaps, raises the idea of the sublime, by mixing the wonderful with terror: at least, I think there is a distinct impression of fear, produced by the notion of infinity ; and certainly there is one of wonder. Immensity of any kind excites the notion of power, and the distant sense of fear. Look at a little green grass-plat before a house ; nothing can be more insignificant : magnify it into a field ; you are not struck with it : let it be a smooth, uniform, boundless plain, stretching on every side further than the eye can reach, and it becomes a sublime object. How vast must be the power that has arranged such a mass of matter ! where does it lead to ? what ends it ? how dreadful it would be to cross it in a storm ! how impossible to procure assistance ! how remote from every human being !—these are the notions which pass rapidly through the mind, and impress it in the awful manner of which we are all conscious on such occasions.

Wonder, in itself, is a pleasing passion ; fear is not ;

and as the sublime inclines more to one or the other, it assumes different shades of character. Sometimes it borders more upon delight, from the *very* faint tinge of fear which is mingled with it; at others, it approaches much nearer to mere terror. There is in this description of the sublime, by Mr. Brydonne, as much delight as is well compatible with it:—

"After contemplating these objects for some time, we set off, and soon after arrived at the foot of the great crater of the mountain. This is of an exact conical figure, and rises equally on all sides. It is composed solely of ashes and other burnt materials, discharged from the mouth of the volcano, which is in its center. This conical mountain is of a very great size; its circumference can not be less than ten miles. Here we took a second rest, as the greatest part of our fatigue remained. We found this mountain excessively steep; and although it had appeared black, yet it was likewise covered with snow, but the surface (luckily for us) was spread over with a pretty thick layer of ashes, thrown out from the crater. Had it not been for this, we never should have been able to get to the top, as the snow was everywhere frozen hard and solid, from the piercing cold of the air.

"In about an hour's climbing, we arrived at a place where there was no snow, and where a warm and comfortable vapor issued from the mountain; which induced us to make another halt. From this spot it was only about 300 yards to the highest summit of the mountain, where we arrived in full time to see the most wonderful and most sublime sight in nature.

"But here description must ever fall short; for no imagination has *dared* to form an idea of so glorious and so magnificent a scene. Neither is there on the surface of this globe, any one point that unites so many awful and sublime objects. The immense elevation from the surface of the earth, drawn as it were to a single point, without any neighboring mountain for the senses and the imagination to rest upon, and recover from their astonishment in their way down to the world; this point or pinnacle, raised on the brink of a bottomless gulf, as old as the world, often discharging rivers of fire, and throwing out burning rocks, with a noise that shakes the whole island: add to this, the unbounded extent of the prospect, comprehending the greatest diversity and the most beautiful scenery in nature; with the rising sun, advancing in the east, to illuminate the wondrous scene.

"The whole atmosphere by degrees kindled up, and showed dimly and faintly the boundless prospect around. Both sea and land looked dark and confused, as if only emerging from their original chaos, and light and darkness seemed still undivided; till the morning by degrees advancing, completed the separation. The stars are extinguished, and the shades disappear. The forests, which but now seemed black and bottomless gulfs, from whence no ray was reflected to show their form or color, appear a new creation rising to the sight; catching life and beauty from every increasing beam. The scene still enlarges, and the horizon seems to widen and expand itself on all sides; till the sun, like the great Creator, appears in the east, and with its plastic ray completes the mighty scene! All appears enchantment; and it is with difficulty we can believe we are still on earth. The senses, unaccustomed to the sublimity of such a scene, are bewildered and confounded; and it is not till after some time, that they are capable of separating and judging of the objects that compose it. The body of the sun is seen rising from the ocean, immense tracts both of sea and land intervening; the islands of Lipari, Panari, Alicudi, Stromboli, and Volcano, with their smoking summits, appear under your feet; and you look down on the whole of Sicily as on a map; and can trace every river through all its windings, from its source to its mouth. The view is absolutely boundless on every side; nor is there any one object, within the circle of vision, to interrupt it; so that the sight is everywhere lost in the immensity: and I am persuaded it is only from the imperfection of our organs, that the coasts of Africa, and of Greece, are not discovered, as they are certainly above the horizon."*

* Brydonne, vol. i. p. 200.

This description, by Sir William Hamilton, of the eruption of Vesuvius, is of a totally opposite character; and the sublimity of it is almost entirely destroyed by the horrors it contains:—

"In an instant," he says, "a fountain of liquid fire began to rise, and, gradually increasing, rose to the amazing height of 10,000 feet, and upward: the blackest smoke accompanied the red-hot, transparent, and liquid lava, interrupting its splendid brightness here and there, by patches of the darkest hue. Within these clouds of smoke, at the very moment they broke out, pale electrical fire was seen playing about in oblique lines. The wind, though gentle, was sufficient to carry these blasts of smoke out of the column of fire, and a collection of them by degrees formed a black and extensive curtain behind it, while other parts of the sky were clear, and the stars entirely bright. All this time, the miserable inhabitants of Ottajano were involved in the utmost distress and danger, by the showers of stones which fell upon them. Many of the inhabitants flew to the churches, and others were preparing to quit the town, when a sudden and violent report was heard, and presently fell a vast shower of stones and large pieces of scoriæ, some of which were of the diameter of seven or eight feet, and must have weighed, before they fell, above one hundred pounds. In an instant, the town, and country about it, was on fire in many places. To add to the horror of the scene, incessant volcanic lightning was rushing about the black cloud that surrounded them, and the sulphureous smell would scarcely allow them to draw their breath. In this dreadful situation they remained about twenty-five minutes, when the volcanic storm ceased at once; and Vesuvius remained sullen and silent."

The sublimity of the first of these descriptions approaches the confines of the beautiful;—in the last, of the horrible. We must take great care, in the selection of sublime objects, not to choose those which are too horrible; or which remind us too intimately of danger; because, as the sublime always implies some mixture of pleasure, strong compassion and violent horror entirely destroy it. "All sounds," says Mr. Alison, "in general are sublime, which are associated with the idea of danger;—the howling of a storm, the murmuring of an earthquake, the report of artillery. All sounds," he adds, "in the same manner, are sublime, which are associated with the idea of deep melancholy,—as the tolling of the passing bell." Now, I confess I do not call either the murmuring of an earthquake, or the howling of a storm, or the report of artillery, or the tolling of a passing bell, *sublime* sounds, but merely *horrible* sounds; they are so devoid of every mixture of pleasure, that they excite nothing but fear or compassion, according as we ourselves, or others, are most nearly affected by them; they are sublime in poetry or in description, but in real nature they are dreadful, and nothing else. In description, almost any thing, however dreadful, may be made sublime by the prodigious mitigation of the real horror, which is always remarkable when the passions are excited at second-hand. As I have before traced a connection between that feeling of the beautiful, excited by the intervention of matter, and that which presents itself to the mind from the contemplation of moral qualities, it is equally easy, in this stronger and more marked feeling of the sublime, to trace a similar resemblance. All those qualities of mind which excite wonder, and any portion of fear,—even that very subdued species of it we call respect,—raise an elevated sentiment in the mind, precisely similar to the sublime of natural objects. Immense courage, whether active or passive, is easily sublime. "In the midst of this dreadful fire and carnage," says Voltaire, speaking of the battle of Fontenoy, "the English officers were seen, with the same coolness they would have displayed on the parade, leveling the muskets of the soldiers with their canes, in order that they might fire with due precision." The death of General Wolfe is *quite* sublime, from the love of life being so entirely swallowed up in the love of glory. "Toward the end of the battle, he received a new wound in the breast; he was immediately conveyed behind the rear rank, and laid upon the ground. Soon after, a shout was heard, and one of the officers who stood by him exclaimed,

'How they run!' The dying hero asked, with some emotion, 'Who run?' 'The enemy,' replied the officer, 'they give way everywhere.' 'Now, God be praised,' says Wolfe, 'I shall die happy!' He then turned on his side, closed his eyes, and expired."

Firmness and constancy of purpose, that withstands all solicitation, and, in spite of all dangers, goes on straightly to its object, is very often sublime. The resolution of St. Paul, in going up to Jerusalem, where he has the firmest conviction that he shall undergo every species of persecution, quite comes within this description of feeling. "What mean ye to weep and to break my heart? I am ready, not to be bound only, but to die, at Jerusalem, for the name of Jesus. I *know* that ye all, before whom I have preached the kingdom of God, shall see my face no more! Wherefore I take you to record this day, that I am pure from the blood of all men. I have coveted no man's silver, or gold, or apparel. Ye yourselves know, that these hands have ministered unto my necessities, and unto them which were with me; and now it is witnessed in every city through which I pass, that bonds and afflictions await me at Jerusalem; but not one of these things move me, neither count I my life dear to myself, so that I might finish my course with joy, and the ministry which I have received, to testify the gospel of the grace of God."

There is something exceedingly majestic in the steadiness with which the Apostle points out the single object of his life, and the unquenchable courage with which he walks toward it. "I know I shall die, but I have a greater object than life,—the zeal of a high duty. Situation allows some men to think of safety; I not only must not consult it, but I must go where I know it will be most exposed. I must hold out my hands for chains, and my body for stripes, and my soul for misery. I am ready to do it all!" These are the feelings by which alone bold truths have been told to the world; by which the bondage of falsehood has been broken, and the chains of slavery snapped asunder! It is in vain to talk of men numerically; if the passions of a man are exalted to a summit like this, he is a *thousand* men! If all the feebleness and fluctuation of his nature are shamed away, you must not pretend to calculate upon his efforts. Under the influence of sublime feelings, sometimes liberty, sometimes religious men, have sprung up from the dust, to shiver the oldest dominions; to toss to the ground the highest despots; to astonish ages to come with the immensity, and power, and grandeur of human feelings. In all desperate situations, these are the feelings which must rescue us: when prudence is mute, when reason is baffled, when all the ordinary resources of discretion are exhausted and dried up,—there is no safety but in heroic passions, no hope but in sublime men. There is no other hope for Europe at this moment, but that high and omnipotent vengeance, which demands years of cruelty and oppression, in order that it may be lighted up in the hearts of a whole people; but which, when it does break out into action, is so rapid and so terrible, that it resembles more the judgments of God than the deeds of men.

Men are very apt to be sublime when they speak of themselves, and give vent to those great passions which the important events of life engender. The speech which Logan, the Indian chief, made to Lord Dunmore, in the year 1775, is full of sublimity. Though he was a great friend to the English, his wife and all his children were murdered by them: this unworthy return excited his vengeance; he took up the hatchet, and signalized himself against the whites. In a decisive battle, however, which was fought upon the great Kanhaway, the Indians were defeated, and sued for peace; and this was the speech made by Logan, which is so fine that its authenticity has been questioned, but it is now established beyond a doubt, by the testimony of Mr. Jefferson. "I appeal to any white man to say, if ever he entered Logan's cabin hungry, and he gave him not meat? if ever he came cold, and naked, and he clothed him not? During the course of the long last bloody war, Logan remained idle in his cabin, an advocate for peace. Such was my love for the whites, that my countrymen pointed as I passed, and said, 'Logan is the friend of white men.' I had even thought to have lived with you, but for the injuries of one man. Colonel Cressop, the last spring, in cold blood, and unprovoked, murdered all the relations of Logan; not sparing even my women and children: there runs not a drop of my blood in the veins of any living creature! This called on me for revenge: I have sought it. I have killed many! I have fully glutted my vengeance. For my country, I rejoice at the beams of peace; but do not harbor a thought that mine is the joy of *fear:* Logan *never* felt fear: he will not turn on his heel to save his life. Who is there to mourn for Logan? not one!"

I am going to say rather an odd thing, but I can not help thinking that the severe and rigid economy of a man in distress, has something in it very sublime, especially if it be endured for any length of time serenely and in silence. I remember a very striking instance of it in a young man, since dead; he was the son of a country curate, who had got him a berth on board a man-of-war, as midshipman. The poor curate made a great effort for his son; fitted him out well with clothes, and gave him £50 in money. The first week, the poor boy lost his chest, clothes, money, and every thing he had in the world. The ship sailed for a foreign station; and his loss was without remedy. He immediately quitted his mess, ceased to associate with the other midshipmen, who were the sons of gentlemen; and for five years, without mentioning it to his parents—who he knew could not assist him,—or without borrowing a farthing from any human being, without a single murmur or complaint, did that poor lad endure the most abject and degrading poverty, at a period of life when the feelings are most alive to ridicule, and the appetites most prone to indulgence. Now, I confess I am a mighty advocate for the sublimity of such long and patient endurance. If you can make the world stare and look on, there, you have vanity, or compassion, to support you; but to bury all your wretchedness in your own mind,—to resolve that you will have no man's pity, while you have one effort left to procure his respect,—to harbor no mean thought in the midst of abject poverty, but, at the very time you are surrounded by circumstances of humility and depression, to found a spirit of modest independence upon the consciousness of having always acted well;—this is a sublime, which, though it is found in the shade and retirement of life, ought to be held up to the praises of men, and to be looked upon as a noble model for imitation.

The confidence which very great men have in themselves, partakes of this feeling. There is something extremely grand and imposing in their firm reliance upon their own genius; and what in *common* men would be the height of presumption, is in them, not only tolerated, but vehemently and justly admired. Such is the answer of Alexander to Parmenio;—Cæsar to the Pilot;—Marius to the man who saw him sitting on the ruins of Carthage. There is a very sublime piece of insolence, which Homer has put into the mouth of Achilles. He has seized upon Lycaon, and is going to put him to death. The young man prays to him, in the most humble and supplicating manner, to spare his life. "Wretch!" says Achilles, "do *you* fear to die? do *you* complain of death? Look at me! how beautiful, how vast, how brave am I!—even *I* must perish! A hero was my father, a goddess produced me, and yet the hour will come, be it morning, or evening, or noon, when even I must fall by the arrow or the spear!" Lucullus, when he marched up to Tigranocerta, had an army of 300,000 men to attack. What was the conduct of Lucullus? He did not go about to his officers and say, "Do you think I had better attack them? or what do you think about it? I have really a great mind to do so." His army and his officers were disconcerted with their numbers. Lucullus, the very moment he glanced at their position, exclaimed, "We have them!" It happened to be on one of those days which the Romans had marked out in their calendar as unfortunate, because it had formerly been memorable by defeats. They requested him to consider this well, and not to hazard a battle on such a day. "*I* will put it among the *fortunate* days," said he, and immediately ordered them to march. A hundred thousand barbarians fell in the battle; with the loss of five Romans killed, and a hundred wounded.

The calm resignation to inevitable fate, equally removed from insolence and fear, and which is so peculiar to great minds, is to be classed among the sublimer feelings of our nature. In this manner Socrates drank the poison; the three hundred perished at the Straits of Greece; so died the Chancellor More on the scaffold, and the great Lord Falkland in the field; and in the same manner, the memorable Lord Strafford pleaded before his enemies: "And now, my lords," he says, "I thank God I have been (by his blessing) sufficiently instructed in the extreme vanity of all temporary enjoyments, compared to the importance of our eternal duration; and so, my lords, even so, with all humility, and all tranquillity of mind, I submit clearly and freely to your judgments; and whether that righteous doom shall be to life or death, I shall repose myself, full of gratitude and confidence, in the arms of the great Author of my existence."

"Certainly," says Whitelock (with his usual candor,) "never any man acted such a part on such a theater, with more wisdom, constancy, and eloquence; with greater reason, judgment, and temper; and with a better grace in all his words and actions,—than did this great and excellent person: and he moved the hearts of all his auditors (some few excepted) to pity and remorse."

All these men, in their different walks of life, as warriors, or as statesmen, seemed, at the approach of their destiny, to have enveloped themselves in their own greatness; and to have been lifted up above us, by a kind of serenity to which we should feel it impossible, in similar situations, to attain.

I have been thus diffuse upon the subject of the sublime in morals, because it is of all things the most inspiring and useful, to contemplate the best models of our own species, and to know what those limits are, to which our nature really does extend; and one of the great advantages of that classical education in which we are trained in this country, is, that it sets before us so many examples of sublimity in action, and of sublimity in thought. It is impossible for us, in the first and most ardent years of life, to read the great actions of the two greatest nations in the world, so beautifully related, without catching, *ourselves*, some taste for greatness, and a love for that glory which is gained by doing greater and better things than other men. And though the state of order and discipline into which the world is brought, does not enable a man frequently to do such things, as every day produced in the fierce and eventful democraties of Greece and Rome, yet, to love that which is great, is the best security for hating that which is little; the best cure for envy; the safest antidote for revenge; the surest pledge for the abhorrence of malice; the noblest incitement to love truth, and manly independence, and honorable labor,—to glory in spotless innocence, and build up the system of life upon the rock of integrity.

It is the greatest and first use of history, to show us the sublime in morals, and to tell us what great men have done in perilous seasons. Such beings, and such actions, dignify our nature, and breathe into us a virtuous pride which is the parent of every good. Wherever you meet with them in the page of history, read them, mark them, and learn from them how to live, and how to die! for the object of *common* men, is only to live. The object of such men as I have spoken of, was to live grandly, and in favor with their own *difficult* spirits: to live, if in war, gloriously; if in peace, usefully, justly, and *freely!!*

LECTURE XVII.

ON THE FACULTIES OF ANIMALS, AS COMPARED WITH THOSE OF MEN.

I CONFESS I treat on this subject with some degree of apprehension and reluctance; because, I should be very sorry to do injustice to the poor brutes, who have no professors to revenge their cause by lecturing on *our* faculties: and at the same time I know there is a very strong anthropical party, who view all eulogiums on the brute creation with a very considerable degree of suspicion; and look upon every compliment which is paid to the ape, as high treason to the dignity of man.

There may, perhaps, be more of rashness and ill-fated security in my opinion, than of magnanimity or liberality; but I confess I feel myself so much at my ease about the superiority of mankind,—I have such a marked and decided contempt for the understanding of every baboon I have yet seen,—I feel so sure that the blue ape without a tail will never rival us in poetry, painting, and music,—that I see no reason whatever, why justice may not be done to the few fragments of soul, and tatters of understanding, which they may really possess. I have sometimes, perhaps, felt a little uneasy at Exeter 'Change, from contrasting the monkeys with the 'prentice-boys who are teasing them; but a few pages of Locke, or a few lines of Milton, have always restored me to tranquillity, and convinced me that the superiority of man had nothing to fear.

Philosophers have been much puzzled about the essential characteristics of brutes, by which they may be distinguished from men. Some define a brute to be an animal that never laughs, or an animal incapable of laughter: some say they are mute animals. The Peripatetics allowed them a sensitive power, but denied them a rational one. The Platonists allowed them reason and understanding; though in a degree less pure, and less refined, than that of men. Lactantius allows them every thing which men have, except a sense of religion: and some skeptics have gone so far as to say they have this also. Descartes maintained that brutes are mere inanimate machines, absolutely destitute, not only of all reason, but of all thought and reflection; and that all their actions are only consequences of the exquisite mechanism of their bodies. This system, however, is much older than Descartes; it was borrowed by him from Gomez Pereira, a Spanish physician, who employed thirty years in composing a treatise on this subject, which he very affectionately called by the name of his father and mother—"Antoniana Margarita." Systems and theories, however, differ very materially in their importance, according to the parent who ushers them into the world, and the obscurity or notoriety of the name to which they happen to be connected. Poor Gomez was so far from having opponents, that he had not even readers: his theory, in the hands of Descartes, excited a controversy which reached from one end of Europe to the other: many, who maintained the opposite hypothesis to Descartes, contended that brutes are endowed with a soul, essentially inferior to that of man; and to this soul some have impiously allowed immortality. But the most curious of all opinions, respecting the understanding of beasts, is that advanced by Père Bougeant, a Jesuit, in a work entitled "Philosophical Amusement on the Language of Beasts." In this book he contends, that each animal is inhabited by a separate and distinct devil; that not only this was the case with respect to cats, which have long been known to be very favorite residences of familiar spirits, but that a peculiar devil swam with every turbot, grazed with every ox, soared with every lark, dived with every duck, and was roasted with every chicken.

The most common notion now prevalent, with respect to animals, is, that they are guided by *instinct;* that the discriminating circumstance between the minds of animals and of men is, that the former do what they do from instinct, the latter from reason. Now, the question is, is there any meaning to the word *instinct?* what is that meaning? and what is the distinction between instinct and reason? If I desire to do a certain thing, adopt certain means to effect it, and have a clear and precise notion that those means are directly subservient to that end,—there I act from reason; but, if I adopt means subservient to the end, and am uniformly found to do so, and am not in the *least* degree conscious that these means *are* subservient to the end,—there I certainly do act from some principle very different from reason; and to which principle, it is *as* convenient to give the name of instinct, as any other name. If I build a house for my family, and lay it out into different apartments, separating it horizontally with floors, and give the obvious principles on which I have done so,—here is plainly an invention of meaning, and an application of previous experience, which any body would call by the name of reason; but if I am detected making folding doors to the drawing-room, putting up snug shelves in the butler's pantry, and making the whole house as convenient as possible, and it is quite plain at the same time that I have no possible motive to alledge *why* I have done these things, that I am quite ignorant folding doors are pleasant at routs, and shelves eminently useful to butlers, for the more orderly and decorous arrangement of glass ware,—there, it is very plain I am not constituted as other men are; that I am not applying previous experience to new cases,—not arguing that what has happened before, *will* happen again; but that I am generically different from all others of my species, and that my mind is not the mind of man. Bees, it is well known, construct their combs with small cells on both sides, fit for holding their store of honey, and for receiving their young. There are only three *possible* figures of the cells, which can make them all equal and similar, without any useless interstices: these are, the equilateral triangle, the square, and the regular hexagon. It is well known to mathematicians, that there is not a *fourth* way *possible*, in which a plane may be cut into little spaces, that shall be equal, similar, and regular, without leaving any interstices. Of the three, the *hexagon* is the most proper both for conveniency and strength; and accordingly, bees—as if they were acquainted with these things—make all their cells regular hexagons. As the combs have cells on both sides, the cells may either be exactly opposite, having partition against partition,—or the bottom of a cell may rest upon the partitions, between the cells, on the other side; which will serve as a buttress to strengthen it. The last way is the best for strength; accordingly, the bottom of each cell rests against the point where three partitions meet on the other side, which gives it all the strength possible. The bottom of a cell may either be one plane perpendicular to the side partitions, or it may be composed of several planes meeting in a solid angle in the middle point. It is only in one of these two ways, that all the cells can be similar without losing room; and, for the same intention, the planes of which the bottom is composed—if there be more than one—must be exactly three in number, and neither more nor less. It has been demonstrated also, that by making the bottom to consist of three planes meeting in a point, there is a saving of materials and labor,—by no means inconsiderable. The bees, as if acquainted with the principles of solid geometry, follow them most accurately: the bottom of each cell being composed of three planes, which make obtuse angles with the side partitions, and with one another, and meet in a point in the middle of the bottom; the three angles of this bottom, being supported by three partitions on the other side of the comb, and the point of it by the common intersection of those three partitions.

One instance more of the mathematical skill displayed in the structure of a honeycomb deserves to be mentioned. It is a curious mathematical problem, at what precise angle the three planes which compose the bottom of a cell ought to meet, in order to make the greatest possible saving, or the least expense of materials and labor. This is one of those problems belonging to the higher parts of mathematics, which are called problems of maxima and minima. It has been resolved by some mathematicians, particularly by Mr. Maclaurin, by a fluxionary calculation, which is to be found in the ninth volume of the "Transactions of the Royal Society of London." He has determined precisely the angle required; and he found by the most exact mensuration the subject could admit, that it is the *very* angle in which the three planes in the bottom of the cell of a honeycomb do actually meet. How is all this to be explained? Imitation it certainly is not; for, after every old bee has been killed, you may take the honeycomb and hatch a new swarm of bees, that can not possibly have had any communication with, or instruction from, the parents. The young of every animal—though they have never seen the dam,—will do exactly as all their species have done before them. A brood of young ducks, hatched under a hen, take to the water in spite of the remonstrances and terrors of their spurious parent. All the great habitudes of every species of animals, have repeatedly been proved to be independent of imitation. I remember Mr. Stewart, in his "Lectures," quotes an experiment of this kind, made by Sir James Hall of Edinburgh, who has distinguished himself so much by his very important experiments upon the chemistry of mineralogy. Sir James hatched some chickens in an oven: within a few minutes after the shell was broken, a spider was turned loose before this very youthful brood;—the destroyer of flies had hardly proceeded a few inches before he was descried by one of these oven-born chickens, and, at one peck of his bill, immediately devoured. This certainly was not imitation. A female goat, very near delivery, died; Galen cut out the young kid, and placed before it a bundle of hay, a bunch of fruit, and a pan of milk; the young kid smelt to them all very attentively, and then began to lap the milk. This was not imitation. And what is commonly and rightly called instinct, can not be explained away, under the notion of its being imitation. Nor can it be mere accident; because, though it is not impossible that one swarm of bees might adopt these figures and measurements, without knowing their importance, it is not to be believed that mere accident can uniformly produce such extraordinary effects. The warmest admirers of honey, and the greatest friends to bees, will never, I presume, contend that the young swarm, who begin making honey three or four months after they are born, and immediately construct these mathematical cells, should have gained their geometrical knowledge as we gain ours, and in three months' time outstrip Mr. Maclaurin in mathematics as much as they did in making honey. It would take a senior wrangler at Cambridge ten hours a day, for three years together, to know enough mathematics for the calculation of these problems, with which not only every queen bee, but every under-graduate grub, is acquainted the moment it is born. A few more instances of a principle of action among animals, which can not be reason,—and I have done upon this part of the subject. If you shake caterpillars off a tree in every direction, they instantly turn round and climb up, though they had never formerly been on the surface of the ground. This is a very striking instance of instinct. The caterpillar finds its food, and is nourished, upon the tree, and not upon the ground; but surely the caterpillar can never tell that such an exertion is necessary to its salvation; and therefore, it acts not from rational motives, but from blind impulse. Ants and beavers lay up magazines. Where do they get their knowledge that it will not be so easy to collect food in rainy weather as it is in the summer? Men and women know these things, because their grandpapas and grandmammas have told them so; ants, hatched from the egg artificially, or birds hatched in this manner, have all this knowledge by intuition, without the smallest communication with any of their relations. Now, observe what the solitary wasp does; she digs several holes in the sand, in each of which she deposits an egg, though she certainly knows not that an animal is deposited in that egg,—and still less that this animal must be nourished with other animals. She collects a few green flies, rolls them up neatly in separate parcels (like Bologna sausages), and stuffs one parcel into each hole where an egg is deposited. When the wasp-worm is hatched, it finds a store of provisions ready made; and what is most curious, the quantity allotted to each is exactly sufficient to support it, till it attains the period of wasphood, and can provide for itself. This instinct of the parent wasp is the more remarkable, as it does not feed upon flesh itself. Here the little creature has never seen its parent; for, by the time it is born, the parent is always eaten by sparrows: and yet, without the slightest education, or previous experience, it does every thing that the parent did before it. Now the objectors to the doctrine of instinct may say what they please, but young tailors have no intuitive mode of making pantaloons;—a new-born mercer can not measure diaper;—Nature teaches a cook's daughter nothing about sippets. All these things require with us seven years' apprenticeship; but insects are like Molière's persons of quality,—they know every thing (as Molière says), without having learned any thing. "Les gens de qualitè savent tout, sans avoir rien appris."

The most strenuous objector to these histories of the singular and untaught instincts of animals, is the Comte de Buffon; and he has been particularly severe upon bees, whose reputation for architecture and civil economy he has attempted entirely to overthrow. Of Maclaurin's discovery of the angle, he takes no notice, and returns no answer to it; neither does he condescend to notice the particular manner in which the comb is placed back to back. His observations upon the hexagonal form of the cell, appears to me, I confess, for so great a man, very singular. "The hexagonal form of the cells of the bee, which have been the subject of so much admiration, furnish an additional proof of the stupidity of these insects. This figure, though extremely regular, is nothing but a mechanical result, which is often exhibited in the rudest productions of nature. Crystals, and several other stones, as well as particular salts, constantly assume this figure. The small scales in the skin of the roussete, or great Ternate bat, are hexagonal, because each scale when growing obstructs the progress of its neighbor, and tends to occupy as much space as possible. We likewise find these hexagons in the second stomachs of some ruminating animals; in certain seeds, capsules, and flowers. If we fill a vessel with cylindrical grain, and, after filling up the interstices with water, shut it close up, and boil the water, all these cylinders will become hexagonal columns. The reason is obvious, and purely mechanical. Each cylindrical grain tends, by its swelling, to occupy as much space as possible in the limited dimensions of the hive: and therefore, as the bodies of the bees are cylindrical, they must necessarily make their cells hexagonal, from the reciprocal obstruction they give to each other."

In the case of the boiled grain, the vessel is close; but the comb, I fancy, in common bee-hives, by no means extends itself through the whole dimensions of the straw hut; therefore, there is *no* pressure on the outside: neither do I see how there is any pressure from within, because the cell is made before the young bee is put in it, and the very first plan and groundwork of each cell is the hexagon, long before the pressure of body in the old bee can effect it. Besides, it really seems quite ludicrous to suppose, that such extraordinary regularity can be produced by the accidental pushing and scrambling of ten thousand insects, working one at one moment at this cell, then flying off to a cowslip, then going to another cell, then appointed to digest wax for the public good. Make the slightest inequality in the pushing, let one bee neglect to scramble for a single instant, or let one be scraping away while the other is adding, and the whole regularity is immediately destroyed, without the possibility of restoring it. And if they did push and scramble with this wonderful meter and rhythm, instead of *destroying* the wonder of the insect, it would be *increasing* it. If there be any necessary connection between the hexagon and this origin of its formation, why do not wasps and ants deposit their nests in hexagons as perfect? or why does not the insect that works the coral? The real fact seems to be, that Nature has originally determined, with scrupulous precision, how every animal shall breed and build; and has confined them to a particular shape, as much as to a particular position. The wasp takes one form, the bee another, the chaffinch another, the robin-redbreast another. Nature has chosen that some animals should be more accurate and fine in their habits; others, more careless, lax, and inattentive. Upon some, she seems to have bestowed vast attention: and to have sketched out others in a moment, and turned them adrift. The house-fly skims about, perches upon a window or a nose, breakfasts and sups with you, lays his eggs upon your white cotton stockings, runs into the first hole in the wall when it is cold, and perishes with as much unconcern as he lives. The bees (as is commonly said of them, and as is strictly true) do live together in a city, with a common object. It has pleased their Maker, that their food should be prepared with considerable labor and art; and their houses constructed with the greatest attention to durability and convenience. What is there in all this, that should make Buffon so angry or skeptical? Can not He who made man, make a miracle one thousand times *less* miraculous than man? If He have implanted in our nature one or two stimuli which are sufficient, in the progress of life, gradually to unfold the soul that lies hidden within us, why may He not have given to another class of animals a great step at first, if He resolved that that should be the only progress they ever were to make in their momentary existence? But there is no use in putting questions why Providence may not have done this, or done that. Providence *has done it!* There are the bees, and there the comb;—there are the rafters, and there is the floor, and there is Colin Maclaurin, with his angle! and get rid of it how you can; and if you are determined to get rid of it, you had better account for the formation of a hive in some more sensible manner, than the pushing and scrambling of Buffon. When I call that principle upon which the bees or any other animals proceed to their labors, the principle of *instinct*, I only mean to say it is not a principle of reason. However the knowledge is gained, it is not gained as *our* knowledge is gained. It is not gained by *experience*, or *imitation*, for I have cited cases of birds and bees that have never seen nest, or cell,—who have made one and the other, as if they were perfectly acquainted with them. It can not be invention, or the adaptation of means to ends; because, as the animal works before he knows what event is going to happen, he can not know what the *end* is, to which he is accommodating the means: and if he be actuated by any other principle than these, the generation of ideas in animals is (contrary to the doctrine of Condillac) very different from the generation of ideas in men.

All the wonderful instincts of animals, which, in my humble opinion, are proved beyond a doubt, and the belief in which has not decreased with the increase of science and investigation,—all these instincts are given them only for the combination or preservation of their species. If they had not these instincts, they would be swept off the earth in an instant. This bee, that understands architecture so well, is as stupid as a pebble-stone, out of his own particular business of making honey; and, with all his talents, he only exists that boys may eat his labors, and poets sing about them. *Ut pueris placeas et declamatio fias.* A peasant girl of ten years old, puts the whole republic to death with a little smoke; their palaces are turned into candles, and every clergyman's wife makes mead-wine of the honey; and there is an end of the glory and wisdom of the bees! Whereas, man has talents that have no sort of reference to his existence; and without which, his species might remain upon earth in the same safety as if they had them not. The bee works at that particular angle which saves most time and labor; and the boasted edifice he is constructing is only for his egg: but Somerset House, and Blenheim, and the Louvre, have nothing to do with breeding. Epic poems, and Apollo Belvideres, and Venus de Medicis, have nothing to do with living and eating. We might have discovered pig-nuts without the Royal Society, and gathered acorns without reasoning about curves of the ninth order. The immense superfluity of talent given to man, which has no bearing upon animal life, which has nothing to do with the mere preservation of existence, is one very distinguishing circumstance in this comparison. There is no other animal but man to whom mind appears to be given for any *other* purpose than the preservation of body.

If I am right in explaining the meaning of instinct, as distinguished from reason, and right in saying that animals are guided by it, a question very naturally arises, how far men are guided by it themselves. It is a question of great difficulty and subtilty, which it would be very tedious to investigate with the attention its intricacy would require. When Locke so successfully attacked the doctrine of innate ideas, and innate principles of speculative truth, he was thought by many to have overturned all innate principles whatever; to have divested the human mind of every passion, affection, and instinct, and to have left in it nothing but the powers of memory, sensation, and intellect. Hence arose many philosophers at home and abroad, who maintained, upon the principles of Locke, that in the human mind there are no instincts, but that every thing which had usually been called by that name is resolvable into association and habit. This doctrine was attacked by Lord Shaftesbury, who introduced into the theory of mind, as faculties derived from nature, a sense of beauty, a sense of honor, and a sense of ridicule; and these he considered as the test of a speculative truth and moral rectitude. His lordship's principles were in part adopted by Professor Hutchinson, of Glasgow, who published a system of moral philosophy, founded upon a sense of instinct, to which he gave the name of the moral sense; and the undoubted merit of his book procured him many followers. It being now supposed that the human mind was endowed with instinctive principles of action, a sect of very lazy philosophers arose, who found it convenient to refer every phenomenon to a separate instinct. Immediately we had the fighting instinct, the loving instinct, the educating instinct, the hoarding instinct, the cheating instinct, and even the sneezing instinct. The most able refuter of these instincts is Dr. Priestley; who maintains, with the earliest disciples of Locke, that we have from nature no innate sense of truth,—that even the action of sucking in new-born infants is to be accounted for upon principles of mechanism. The question is a very difficult one, and I rather decline entering into a long dissertation upon suckling, in this Institution; but I believe Dr. Hartley is in the right, and that it would not be easy to show any clear case of instinct among men; and that children suckle first mechanically, then receive pleasure from it, then associate the action with the pleasure, and then do it from appetite. There is an extremely good article upon the subject of instinct in the Scotch Encyclopædia, in which Dr. Reid is very justly censured for the confusion he has made, in treating of the doctrine of instinct. If a man swallow his food, all the requisite motions of nerves and muscles take place in their proper order, though the man neither knows, nor wills, any thing about them. Breathing, according to the Doctor, depends upon instinct. When a man is tumbling off his horse, and makes an effort to recover himself, he regains his saddle by instinct, according to Dr. Reid. Breathing, with due submission to Dr. Reid, is a mere case of mechanism, with which the mind has nothing to do. If you recover yourself when you fall, your motion depends upon mere habit and association; the muscles that act in swallowing, are, according to the Hartleian theory, and in all probability, moved first mechanically, then by volition. How it comes about, that the *will* can ever move any part of the *body*,—that mind can ever act upon matter,—is another question. That phenomenon is common to almost every description of animate beings; but it is a great abuse of terms to call it by the name of instinct. Actions performed with a view to accomplish a certain end, are rational. Actions performed without the spontaneity of the agent, are automatic. Actions regularly performed without a view to the consequences they produce, are instinctive. Upon these distinctions, every discussion upon human and animal faculties must be grounded.

One of the best attacks made upon the doctrine of instinct, is by Dr. Darwin: but he fights too much against common experience, to combat with much success. One of Dr. Darwin's objections to this doctrine of instinct is, that the instincts of animals bend to circumstances, which, if they were arbitrary admonitions of nature, they would not do. Our domestic birds, that are plentifully supplied through the year with their adapted food, and are covered by houses from the inclemency of the weather, lay their eggs at any season; which evinces that the spring of the year is *not* pointed out to them, says Dr. Darwin, by a necessary instinct. Now I confess, to *me*, this fact points precisely to an opposite inference. What is the instinct? To hatch their young at a season of the year when the weather is mild, and when food is plenty. Nature knows nothing about the Golden Letter; she never looks into the almanac, and is quite ignorant when Easter falls; but she prompts the bird to hatch her young, by those different feelings of body, which copious food, and genial warmth, produce. *They* are the feelings which precede the instinctive action: and if you make perpetual spring to the animal all the year round, similar feelings produce similar instincts; and, instead of refuting the supposition that the animal is under the influence of instinct, powerfully confirm it. Dr. Darwin's mistake proceeds from this: he supposes Nature intended birds to hatch in April or May; whereas, Nature intended they should hatch when they are warm, and well fed; which, in a state of nature, they are in those months; but which, when protected by man, in order that they may be eaten, they are at all times. It would be just as rational to say, that Nature did not intend the production of green peas to depend upon the humid warmth of the spring, because the humid warmth of the spring is counterfeited in hot-houses, and a dish of peas is produced in December, to the astonishment of ordinary understandings, and to the endless glory of the lady at whose table they are displayed.

In the same manner the rabbit digs a burrow in his wild state. In his tame state, he spares himself that trouble. But to this, which delights Dr. Darwin so very highly, I have two answers: a tame rabbit, in all probability, does not burrow in the earth, because he is shut up in a deal box, and kept in a garret; and if he refuse to burrow, though turned out, the explanation of this change in his instincts is accounted for precisely upon the same principles as the last. Nature does not at once put the animal upon making a burrow; but it impels it to do that thing by some previous feeling of body or mind, by hunger, by cold, by fear, or by the change of feelings in the body, when about to produce its young. You change the feelings which by the law of nature precede the action, and then the action is not performed. You may very likely discover some moral affection, or some change in the body, which precedes all instinctive motions; but the difficulty is still as great as it was before. Why does cold make the rabbit dig a burrow? Why does warmth induce the bird to build a nest after that ancient model of nests which it has never seen? Such things do not occur in our species. We must, therefore, find for them some other appellation than that of reason, by which all *our* actions are swayed.

The most curious instance of a change of instinct is mentioned by Darwin. The bees carried over to Barbadoes and the Western Isles, ceased to lay up any honey after the first year; as they found it not useful to them. They found the weather so fine and materials for making honey so plentiful, that they quitted their grave, prudent, and mercantile character, became exceedingly profligate and debauched, eat up their capital, resolved to work no more, and amused themselves by flying about the sugar-houses, and stinging the blacks. The fact is, that by putting animals in different situations, you may change, and even reverse, any of their original propensities. Spallanzani brought up an eagle upon bread and milk, and fed a dove on raw beef. The circumstances by which an animal is surrounded, impel him to do so and so, by the changes they produce in his body and mind. Alter those circumstances, and he no longer does as he did before. This, instead of disproving the existence of an instinct, only points out the *causes* on which it depends. Many actions of animals have been mistaken for instinctive, which are not so; or, rather, the object for which they act has been mistaken. It is supposed that ants lay up their magazines against the winter: "but ants," says Buffon, "are torpid in the winter, and don't eat at all; therefore, what is the use of their magazines?" Why, this is the use of their magazines; that there come often enough, before the season of their torpor, three or four rainy days, when they can not venture out to get any food, and then their magazine is of importance. Besides, the Count should have told us whether they do not revive again before the provisions on which they subsist; if they do, there is *another* reason why they should have a stock in hand. Neither does it disprove the existence of instinct, because the instinct is sometimes not so fine and so minute as might have been expected, or was supposed. "The provisions of the ant, of the field-mouse, and of the bee," says Buffon, "are discovered to be only useless and disproportioned masses, collected without any view to futurity; and the minute and particular laws of their pretended foresight are reduced to the general and real law of feeling." All that this objection amounts to is, that Nature has not impelled these animals to collect a certain quantity *avoirdupois;* that they are taught to collect, and that the impulse only operates within gross limits, but still with sufficient precision for the preservation of the animal. So the instinct of a bird to sit upon eggs exists, though it is given very grossly, for it will sit upon a chalk-stone like an egg. The instinct is to foster, with the heat of its body, that which it produces. In the absence of the bird, you put in that which resembles its production; the bird has no other mode of judging, but by the eye,—the eye is deceived. This only proves that the instinct is gross, *not* that it does not exist. But while I am talking about the instincts of ducks and rabbits, a certain instinct, very valuable in a professor, admonishes me that I am tiring my audience, and that it is time to put an end to my lecture. The enemies of moral philosophy may, perhaps, say this feeling is *experience*, and not instinct; however, be it what it may, I shall obey it, and conclude the subject at our next meeting.

LECTURE XVIII.

ON THE FACULTIES OF BEASTS.

Before I proceed upon the body of this lecture, I wish to state, by anticipation, the doctrines it will contain; and this I shall do very shortly, reserving the proof for its proper place. Animals are not mere machines, like clocks and watches. It is a very dangerous doctrine to assert, that so much apparent choice and deliberation can exist in mere matter. If they are not merely material (like machines of human invention), they must be a composition of mind and matter. There are observable in the minds of brutes, faint traces and rudiments of the human faculties. This position has been maintained by Reid, Locke, Hartley, Stewart, and all the best writers on these subjects. If man were a solitary animal, like a lion or a bear, he would not be so superior to all animals as he is. If he had the hoof of oxen instead of hands, he would not be so superior: neither would he, if he had less perfect organs of speech; nor if his life were confined to a very few years, instead of being extended to seventy. But all these things will not do by any means *alone*, as the degraders of human nature have said; for there are some animals, which very nearly possess all these advantages, and yet are perfectly contemptible, when compared even to the lowest of men. But the great source of man's superiority is, the immense and immeasurable disproportion of those faculties, of which Nature has given the mere rudiments to brutes; that this disproportion has made man a speculative animal, even where his mere existence is not concerned; that it has made him a progressive animal; that it has made him a religious animal; and that upon that mere superiority, and on the very principle that the chain of mind and spirit terminates here with man, the best and the most irrefragable arguments for the immortality of the soul are founded, which natural religion can afford: that, independent of revelation, it would be impossible not to perceive that man is the object of the creation, and that he, and he *alone*, is reserved for another and a better state of existence. These are my principles, in which if any man here present differ from me, I trust at least he will have the kindness and the politeness to hear me.

There is another circumstance, very decisive of the nature of instinct, and which goes strongly to show it is something very different from reason. I mean the uniformity of actions in animals. The bees now build exactly as they built in the time of Homer; the bear is as ignorant of good manners as he was two thousand years past; and the baboon is still as unable to read and write, as persons of honor and quality were in the time of Queen Elizabeth. Of the improvements made by the insect tribe, we can not speak with much certainty; and the advocates for the perfectibility of animals, tell us, it is impossible that ants' nests may be laid out with much greater regularity than they used to be, and that experience may have taught them many methods of draining off water, and preventing the growth of ears of barley. It certainly *may,* but we have no sort of proof that it *does;* and the analogy of all large animals, whose economy we are perfectly acquainted with, and can easily observe, is against the supposition. Neither is it from any lack of inconveniences, nor any extraordinary contentedness with their situation, that any species of animals remains in such a state of sameness. The wolf often kills twenty times as much as he wants; and if he could hit upon any means of preserving his superfluous plunder, he would not perish of hunger so often as he does. To lay traps for the hunters, and to eat them as they were caught, would be far preferable to all those animals who are the cause, and the contents, of traps themselves. Animals, like men, are goaded by wants and sufferings; but, contrary to the nature of men, they do not overcome, but endure them. The flesh of the savage was originally as strong a temptation to the bear, as the flesh of the bear was to the savage. The wants of the one impelled him to invention; the other retained his original stupidity, in spite of his wants. There are some few and inconsiderable instances of tribes of animals making some slight change in their habits, to adapt themselves to any new situation in which they may be placed; but these changes are very little ameliorative of their condition, and by no means go to destroy the supposition of their being directed in many instances by a mere instinct. This sameness of habits in animals does not *demonstrate* that they are not guided by reason, but it renders it in the highest degree improbable that they should be. It is not quite impossible, that animals resolving to build a nest, should for two thousand years build precisely in the same manner, and that this structure should be equally resorted to, by those who have, and who have not, seen the model of the nest;—it is not impossible, but it is so contrary to all former experience, that it certainly gives us no relief from the pain of being forced to believe in instinct. But the Chinese are stationary, and so are the Hindoos;—they are now exactly what they were twenty centuries ago. Certainly they are: but, then, they are so from religious prejudice, transmitted from parent to child; and if it can be proved (which it can not), that bees and ants only gain their habits from old bees and ants, I admit the whole question of instinct is very materially changed: but the fact is the reverse; and if the fact were the reverse also with the Chinese,—if a young Chinese, brought out of his own country very young, were, without ever having seen another Chinese, to begin at the age of five or six to eat rice with two sticks, to clothe himself in blue and nankeen, and adore the great idol Foo, we must call this sameness the sameness of instinct; but as he does these foolish things because he lives with other Chinese, it is the sameness proceeding from imitation, and strengthened, as we happen to know it to be, by religious association. I have thus far attempted to prove that brutes are guided by some principle, which is not the principle of reason. There is another philosophy that degrades them merely to the state of machines. The great Descartes looked upon a brute as a mere machine, that could no more help acting as it does act, and was no more conscious of how it acts, than the Androides, or the chess-playing machine. All that the arguments brought forward by Descartes, go to prove, are, that such a case is possible;—that they *may* be so many machines, not that they *are* so,—that it involves no contradiction to call them machines; which every one who understands any thing of reasoning, would willingly grant: but, observe, when we have no means of subjecting our question to the direct evidence of the senses, or to mathematical demonstration, we must resort to analogy; without which, one conjecture is quite as probable as another. We get from the observation of ourselves, the notion both of voluntary and involuntary motion. We are conscious that when we choose to put one leg before another we can do so. If we tumble out of bed, we are conscious we fall to the ground without the smallest intention of so doing, but that we are overruled by a power we can not resist. Now, having gained the knowledge of these two principles, from what passes within ourselves, we proceed to apply it, with as much attention as possible, to similarity of circumstances. A person sees another man, made to all appearance like himself; he does not think him, perhaps, quite so good looking, but it is the same sort of animal; and when he sees him walk,—presuming that like effects are produced by like causes,—he believes that he is not moved by any principle of mechanism, but that the gentleman walks because he chooses to walk: but the same person puts his foot upon a stone, and falls on a sudden, flat upon his face; that, says the observer, must be involuntary motion, because I have experienced the same myself upon similar occasions. In the same manner, he perceives a horse running after his food, playing with other horses, avoiding pain and seeking pleasure. Upon the same principle, that similar effects are produced by similar causes, he determines that the horse has sensation, and consciousness, and will; still determining the matter by a reference to his own previous experience, which, whether it be a good or a bad guide, is the only one that can possibly be resorted to in such conjectures. By a reference to the same principle, we believe that a stone, let loose from the hand, does not fall to the ground by choice, but by necessity; and between the two clear and extreme points, of motion produced by external agency, and motion produced by will, delicate cases must occur, where the opposite analogies are so equally balanced, that it is impossible to determine whether the subject thinks or not. For instance, does the sensitive plant think, when it contracts its leaves upon being touched? does it *really* feel danger or pain? or is it a mere involuntary contraction, such as takes place in the human body when a nerve is stimulated? When a plant in a dark cellar turns round to drink in a ray of light let in, is this the action of a reasoning being, that knows what is its proper food, and seeks it? or is it a mere case of chemical action, in which there is no interference of the will? Opposite analogies seem to be so balanced in these kinds of questions, that it is very difficult to resolve them: but to comparison alone we can resort for it; and comparison shows us, that animals can not possibly gain some of their knowledge as we gain ours; and it makes it also probable, that they do gain a very considerable part precisely as we do.

Before I proceed to speak of the faculties of animals, I wish to anticipate an objection which has been made to my use of the word *faculty*. Some friends of mine have asked me, whether animals had the religious faculty; and whether I mean to say, in stating they had the rudiments of our faculties, that they had the rudiments of this faculty also. Such sort of questions evince, more than any thing else, the necessity of a little candor and moderation on these topics, and of proceeding to explanation, before we proceed to blame. I never before heard religion called a *faculty:* a knowledge of religion is acquired *by* our faculties, and it is the highest proof of the degree in which we possess them; but if the *power* is to be confounded with the *object* of that power, —if all those things that we acquire by means of our faculties are to be *called* our faculties,—then, navigation, commerce, and agriculture are faculties! Any man is perfectly free to use the word in this sense if he pleases; only let it not be made an objection to me, that I have not followed such an example, and that I have used words as they always hitherto have been used. I shall now proceed to the specification of my authorities.*

Respecting the faculties of animals, I shall translate from "Lettres sur les Animaux," by Bailly, two anecdotes respecting brutes, which Mr. Stewart quotes in his "Elements of the Philosophy of the Human Mind."

"A friend of mine," says Mr. Bailly, "a man of understanding and strict veracity, related to me these two facts, of which he was an eye-witness. He had a very intelligent ape, to whom he amused himself by giving walnuts, of which the animal was extremely fond. One day, he placed them at such a distance from the ape, that the animal, restrained by his chain, could not reach them: after many useless efforts to indulge himself in his favorite delicacy, he happened to see a servant pass by with a napkin under his arm; he immediately seized hold of it, whisked it out beyond his arm, to beat the nuts within his reach, and so obtained possession of them. His mode of breaking the walnut was a fresh proof of his inventive powers; he placed the walnut upon the ground, let a great stone fall upon it, and so got at its contents. One day, the ground on which he had placed the walnut was so much softer than usual, that, instead of breaking the walnut, the ape only drove it into the earth: what does the animal do? he takes up a tile, places the walnut upon it, and *then* lets the stone fall, while the walnut is in this position."

Admitting these facts to be true,—and they appear to be well authenticated,—it is impossible to deny that there passed in the mind of this animal, all that customary process of invention that would take place in our own minds, when we were engaged in similar undertakings. If a man were to drop his hat in the water, and by means of a stick to get it out again, he would

* Locke, pp. 59, 60, 61, 213, 330; Hartley, 247; Reid, 114.

have done much the same sort of thing as this animal did. When Mr. Bramah invents his patent locks, I can tell him what passes in his mind: he first pauses intensely upon the idea of what he wishes to accomplish, —an outside ward or wards, that revolve with the key, or some of the mysteries of locksmithery: after he has paused some time, all the ideas anywise related to this first idea, flock into his mind, and among these, he discovers some relation which one bears to the other, that he did not know before, and which will lead to the end he has in view. Exactly so Condillac's ape: his object was to obtain the walnut; he dwelt upon that idea; a thousand related ideas occurred to his mind; he put out one foot, then another; laid himself down upon his back, to lengthen the extent of his foot as much as possible; and then, when he was dwelling upon these ideas, the relation that subsisted between the napkin and the attainment of the nut, rushed across his mind, and he availed himself of it: and precisely by the same process of understanding he made use of the tile, to lay over the soft earth. When an old greyhound that has been accustomed to follow the hare fairly, begins to run cunning, or when two greyhounds are in pursuit of a hare, and one of them runs to a gap in the hedge, which it had known before, and through which it is probable the hare will pass,—in what does this latter greyhound differ, in his way of acting and reasoning, from an old sportsman, who is too lazy to follow the hounds outright, and cuts across to save time and labor? I have reason to believe that somebody is lost in a snow storm;—I mark the track of his feet, distinguishing it carefully from other footsteps; all of a sudden I lose the track,—what does common sense point out to me to do? I go all round in a circle, at the very spot where the signs were first deficient, to see if I can recover the thread of my pursuit. A little boy, whom I have with me, is perpetually mistaking every mark he sees for the true one, and calling out he has found it; I pay no sort of attention to what he says, for I know that he is young and volatile, and I continue the search myself; but if I hear the voice of a trusty servant at a distance, exclaiming that he has rediscovered the track, I immediately repair to the spot, with a strong belief that it will turn out to be the fact: and it is so. Now, during all this time, have I not been exercising my reasoning? have I not been applying my previous experience to the new cases before me? and could not the reasons upon which I have acted, be drawn out into so many syllogisms? And do not hounds in the pursuit of their game, conduct themselves in a manner similar to this? They go on straightforward as far as the scent lasts; when it fails them, they cast round in a circle to recover it. The old hounds pay not the smallest attention to the yelping of the young ones: they know they are not to be trusted; but the moment an old experienced hound gives tongue, the whole pack resort to him, without the least hesitation, and consider their object as gained. I confess I am quite at a loss to decide what difference there is between the faculties employed on both these occasions. A hunted stag will return again upon the line it has been running, then give three or four strong bounds, scarcely touching the ground, and make off in a lateral direction: sometimes he will run in among other deer and cattle, and endeavor to elude the sagacity of the dogs by these means; at other times he will hide himself up to the nose in reeds and water. All this implies a vast deal of previous observation, a fund of experience, and a ready application of that experience to new cases. The artifices of a gentleman pursued by bailiffs, and the artifices of an animal pursued for his life, are the same thing,—call them by what name you please. Of all animals, the most surprising stories are told of the docility of elephants. The black people, who have the care of them, often go away, leaving them chained to a stake, and place near them their young children, as if under their care: the elephant allows the little creatures to crawl as far as its trunk can reach, and then gently takes the young master up, and places him more within his own control. Every one knows the old story of the tailor and the elephant, which, if it be not true, at least shows the opinion the Orientals, who know the animal well, entertain of his sagacity. An eastern tailor to the court was making a magnificent doublet for a bashaw of nine tails, and covering it, after the manner of eastern doublets with gold, silver, and every species of metallic magnificence.. As he was busying himself on this momentous occasion, there passed by, to the pools of water, one of the royal elephants, about the size of a broad-wheeled wagon, rich in ivory teeth, and shaking with its ponderous tread, the tailor's shop to its remotest thimble. As he passed near the window, the elephant happened to look in; the tailor lifted up his eyes, perceived the proboscis of the elephant near him, and, being seized with a fit of facetiousness, pricked the animal with his needle: the mass of matter immediately retired, stalked away to the pool, filled his trunk full of muddy water, and, returning to the shop, overwhelmed the artisan and his doublet with the dirty effects of his vengeance. Instances of memory in animals, and of the most tenacious memory, are endless. If an animal obey the voice of his master, or love the hand that feeds him, it is association. In what way can a sheep or a dog find his way back thirty or forty miles, over a country he has passed but once, through by-paths and over extensive downs? What is all this but the most acute attention, and the most accurate memory? A dog, to do this, must have paid the most accurate attention to cart-ruts, little hillocks, single shrubs, and the minutest marks which guide him in his course. Almost all animals are very diligent observers of places, and know them by a thousand criteria which we do not observe, and which, from the extent of horizon we comprehend in our view, we have no occasion to observe. It must be from that same habit of observation, common to all animals, and from the same necessity they are under of observing attentively, that American Indians are able to find their way across the woods, in the very surprising manner mentioned by Mr. Weld, in his very sensible, judicious, and *impartial* Travels in America. They will penetrate through a wood of many leagues in extent, which they have not passed for twenty years before, without deviating a single step from their former track: the fact is, they are compelled (like animals), from a consideration of their safety, to observe with the closest attention,—and whatever is observed closely, is remembered tenaciously. Animals profit by experience, as we do,—not so *much*, but in the same manner. All old animals are much more cunning, with much more difficulty caught in traps, and hunted with dogs, than young animals: an old wolf, or an old fox, will walk round a trap twenty times, examining every circumstance with the utmost attention: and those who deceive them, are only enabled to do so by every possible care and circumspection. They have abstract ideas, exactly as we have abstract ideas. When a huntsman whips a hare out of its form, he sees only an individual object; but he knows that this individual animal has qualities and properties common to a whole species; and the greyhound that pursues that particular hare,—be it little or be it big,—knows that it has properties common to all other animals,—that it is quick, cunning, and good to eat: in the same manner, a dog that lives in a town, meets sometimes a man in a yellow coat, sometimes in a green one, sometimes a tall man, sometimes a short man, but he knows they are all men; each man excites in him nearly the same idea from the qualities he possesses, in common with all other men, and in spite of his own individual peculiarities. Locke says that animals have no universal ideas; that they do not abstract: but, then, Locke was mistaken in supposing that men had universal ideas. Bishop Berkeley has demonstrated,—and his demonstration is universally agreed to by every one, —that it is nonsense to talk about universal ideas; that there are no such things as universal ideas; and that what we have called universal ideas are nothing but particular ones, accompanied with the notion that they are common to a species.

Then, again, for the affections of animals. They grieve, rejoice, play, are ennuied, as we are; feel anger, as we do; parental affection, and personal attachment. There are stories in Smellie's "Natural Philosophy," and well authenticated, of a very serious attachment that subsisted between a dunghill-cock and a horse, who happened to be kept in the same paddock together.

Every body has seen the lapdog and the lioness in the Tower; and I believe a lamb also has been kept in the Tower with the lions. In short, every body has innumerable stories to tell of the affections of animals; and the difficulty is, rather to abridge than to multiply them.

Now, if I am right in stating that animals have the same *sort* of faculties as man, the question immediately occurs of the origin of that distinction and superiority which man has gained over all other animated beings. One cause of that superiority I conceive to be, his longevity: without it, that accumulation of experience in action, and of knowledge in speculation, could not have existed; and though man would still have been the first of all animals, the difference between him and others would have been less considerable than it now is. The wisdom of a man is made up of what he observes, and what others observe for him; and of course the sum of what he can acquire must principally depend upon the time in which he can acquire it. All that we add to our knowledge is not an increase, by that exact proportion, of all we possess; because we lose some things, as we gain others; but upon the whole, while the body and mind remain healthy, an active man increases in intelligence, and consequently in power. If we lived seven hundred years instead of seventy, we should write better epic poems, build better houses, and invent more complicated mechanism, than we do now. I should question very much if Mr. Milne could build a bridge so well as a gentleman who had engaged in that occupation for seven centuries: and if I had had only two hundred years' experience in lecturing on moral philosophy, I am well convinced I should do it a little better than I now do. On the contrary, how diminutive and absurd all the efforts of man would have been, if the duration of his life had only been twenty years, and if he had died of old age just at the period when every human being begins to suspect that he is the wisest and most extraordinary person that ever did exist! I think it is Helvetius who says, he is quite certain we only owe our superiority over the ourang-outangs to the greater length of life conceded to us; and that, if our life had been as short as theirs, they would have totally defeated us in the competition for nuts and ripe blackberries. I can hardly agree to this extravagant statement; but I think, in a life of twenty years the efforts of the human mind would have been so considerably lowered, that we might probably have thought Helvetius a good philosopher, and admired his skeptical absurdities as some of the greatest efforts of the human understanding. Sir Richard Blackmore would have been our greatest poet; our wit would have been Dutch; our faith, French; the Hottentots would have given us the model for manners, and the Turks for government; and we might probably have been such miserable reasoners respecting the sacred truths of religion, that we should have thought they wanted the support of a puny and childish jealousy of the poor beasts that perish. His gregarious nature is another cause of man's superiority over all other animals. A lion lies under a hole in a rock; and if any other lion happen to pass by, they fight. Now, whoever gets a habit of lying under a hole in a rock, and fighting with every gentleman who passes near him, can not possibly make any progress. Every man's understanding and acquirements, how great and extensive soever they may appear, are made up from the contributions of his friends and companions. You spend your morning in learning from Hume what happened at particular periods of your own history: you dine where some man tells you what he has observed in the East Indies, and another discourses of brown sugar and Jamaica. It is from these perpetual rills of knowledge, that you refresh yourself, and become strong and healthy as you are. If lions would consort together, and growl out the observations they have made, about killing sheep and shepherds, the most likely places for catching a calf grazing, and so forth, they could not fail to improve; because they would be actuated by such a wide range of observation, and operating by the joint force of so many minds. It may be said, that the gregarious spirit in man, may proceed from his wisdom; and not his wisdom from his gregarious spirit. This I should doubt. It appears to be an original principle in some animals, and not in others;

and is a quality given to some to better their condition, as swiftness or strength is given to others. The tiger lives alone,—bulls and cows do not; yet, a tiger is as wise an animal as a bull. A wild boar lives with the herd till he comes of age, which he does at three years, and then quits the herd and lives alone. There is a solitary species of bee, and there is a gregarious bee. Whether an animal should herd or not, seems to be as much a provision of nature, as whether it should crawl, creep, or fly.

A third method, in which man gains the dominion over other animals, is by the structure of his body, and the mechanism of his hands. Suppose, with all our understanding, it had pleased Providence to make us like lobsters, or to imprison us in shells like crayfish, I very much question if the monkeys would not have converted us into sauce; nor can I conceive any possible method, by which such a fate could have been averted. Suppose man, with the same faculties, the same body, and the hands and feet of an ox,—what then would have been his fate? Anaxagoras is represented by ancient authors as maintaining that man owes all his superiority in wisdom and knowledge to the structure of his hands. That hands will not do every thing, is very plain, because monkeys have hands, and make no use of them for any purpose of ameliorating their condition. All that can be said of the hand is, that it is a very exquisite tool,—but a tool does not make an artist; it is a means by which an artist carries his conceptions into execution,—but his conceptions do not depend upon his tools. There can be no doubt, however, but that the destiny of man, and the extent of his faculties have been very considerably influenced by this mechanism of the hand. The first thing to be done in the progress of civilization, is to mitigate the physical inconveniences by which man is surrounded: this can not be done without smelting the metals, breaking up the surface of the earth, and doing innumerable things, which, without as perfect an organ as the hand, could not be done. Without the hand, man would not have fused metals; without the fusion of metals, he would never have got very far above the pressure of immediate want; and consequently his faculties would not have been what they now are. Neither is it simply by securing to him the free and uninterrupted exercise of his faculties, that the instruments—his hands—have invented, have improved his understanding; but those instruments have opened to his observation new and unlimited fields of knowledge, which have re-excited those faculties by the strongest stimulus of curiosity, and improved them by exercise. Accident, perhaps, first gave the notion of glass: there was some talent in ascertaining the precise circumstances upon which the first observed appearances depended; but to what infinite talent has this discovery contributed! how much curiosity has it excited! what powerful understandings it has called into action! how it has widened the materials of human knowledge, and guided the mind of man to the most abstruse speculations!

Then, again, man owes something to his size and strength. If he had been only two feet high, he could not possibly have subdued the earth, and roasted and boiled animated nature in the way he now does. Something he owes also to the number and perfection of his senses; because, though there may be some one animal which excels him in each particular sense, there are few who enjoy *all* their senses in such perfection.

This is all very well: these (which I have stated) are clearly conspiring causes; but they will not do alone, as the enemies to man have absurdly contended. The ape has hands as good, and stature as great, and is as fond of society, and his senses are as acute as ours; and yet, the ape has certainly hitherto taken no very surprising part in the political revolutions of the earth,—done very little for science,—and seems, with the exception of a few atheists, and metaphysicians, to be held in very little honor by any body. The fact seems to be, that though almost every quality of mind we possess, can be traced in some trifling degree in brutes, yet *that* degree, compared with the extent in which the same quality is observable in man, is very low and inconsiderable. For instance, we can not say that animals are devoid of curiosity, but they have a very slight degree of curiosity:

they imitate, but they imitate very slightly in comparison with men; they can not imitate any thing very difficult; and many of them hardly imitate at all: they abstract, but they can not make such compound abstractions as men do; they have no such compounded abstractions as city, prudence, fortitude, parliament, and justice: they reason, but their reasonings are very short and very obvious: they invent, but their inventions are extremely easy, and not above the reach of a human idiot. The story I quoted from Bailly, about the ape and the walnuts, is one of the *most* extraordinary I ever read; but what a wretched limit of intellect does it imply, to be cited as an instance of extraordinary sagacity!

But all the faculties which every animal possesses, are given him for the mere purposes of existence. When his life is endangered, when his young are to be secured, and his prey entrapped, he develops the limited resources of his nature; for every thing else he has no talents at all; nor has any animal ever betrayed the slightest disposition to knowledge,—except as knowledge gratified immediately his hunger, or as would immediately have secured his life. Whereas, man is so far from being influenced only by the moment which is passing over his head, that he looks back to centuries past for the guide of his actions, and to centuries to come for their motive. In fact, nothing can be more weak, and mistaken than to suppose that the doctrine of the immortality of the soul, depends upon making brutes mere machines, or denying to them the mere outlines of our faculties. To talk of God being the soul of brutes, is the worst and most profane degradation of divine power. To suppose that He who regulates the rolling of the planets, and the return of seasons, by general laws, interferes, by a special act of his power, to make a bird fly, and an insect flutter,—to suppose that a gaudy moth can not expand its wings to the breeze, or a lark unfold its plumage to the sun, without the special mandate of that God who fixes incipient passions in the human heart, and leaves them to produce a Borgia to scourge mankind, or a Newton to instruct them,—is not piety, or science, but a most pernicious substitution of degrading conjectures, from an ignorant apprehension of the consequences of admitting plain facts. In the name of common sense, what have men to fear from allowing to beasts their miserable and contemptible pittance of faculties? What can those men have read of the immortality of the soul? what can they think of the strength of those arguments on which it is founded, if they believe it requires the aid of such contemptible and boyish jealousy of the lower order of beings? what must they feel within themselves, to conceive such arguments? what notion must they communicate to others of the fullness, and sufficiency, and strength of those powers, when they stand quibbling and trembling at every faint semblance of reason, which a beast exhibits in searching for water and flesh, and eluding the spear of the hunter? The enemies of the soul's immortality I do *not* fear; I know how often they have been vanquished before; and I am quite sure that they will be overthrown again with a mighty overthrow, as often as they *do* appear. But I confess I have some considerable dread of the indiscreet friends of religion. I tremble at that respectable imbecility which shuffles away the plainest truths, and thinks the strongest of all causes wants the weakest of all aids. I shudder at the consequences of fixing the great proofs of religion upon any other basis, than that of the widest investigation, and most honest statement of facts. I allow such nervous and timid friends to religion to be the best and most pious of men; but a bad defender of religion is so much the most pernicious person in the whole community, that I most humbly hope such friends will evince their zeal for religion, by ceasing to defend it; and remember that not every man is qualified to be the advocate of a cause in which the mediocrity of his understanding may possibly compromise the dearest and most affecting interests of society. What have the shadow and mockery of faculties, given to beasts, to do with the immortality of the soul? Have beasts any general fear of annihilation? have they any love of fame? do their small degrees of faculties ever give them any feelings of this nature? are their minds perpetually escaping into futurity? have they any love of posthumous fame? have they any knowledge of God? have they ever reached, in their conceptions, the slightest traces of a hereafter? can they form the notion of duty and accountability? is it any violation of any one of the moral attributes of the Deity, to suppose that they go back to their dust, and that we do not? Is it no reason to say, that, because they partake in the slightest degree of our nature, they are entitled to *all* the privileges of our nature;—because, upon that principle, if we partake of the nature of any higher order of spirits, we ought to be them, and not ourselves; and they ought to be some higher order still, and so on. And if it be inconsistent to suppose a difference in duration, then also it is to suppose a difference in degree, of mind; and then every human being has a right to complain that he is not a Newton.

To conclude: Such truths want not such aids. The weakest and the most absurd arguments ever used against religion, have been the attempts to compare brutes with men; and the weakest answer to these arguments have been, the jealousies which men have exhibited of brutes. As facts are fairly stated, and boldly brought forward, the more all investigation goes to establish the ancient opinion of man, before it was confirmed by revealed religion,—that brutes are of this world *only;* that man is imprisoned here only for a season,—to take a better or a worse hereafter, as he deserves it. This old truth is the fountain of all goodness, and justice, and kindness among men: may we all feel it intimately, obey it perpetually, and profit by it eternally!

LECTURE XIX.

ON THE CONDUCT OF THE UNDERSTANDING.—PART II.

I CONCLUDED my last course with a Lecture upon the Conduct of the Understanding* (which I intended, as I do this, merely for the instruction of *young people*); but as such a subject could not, of course, be exhausted in any single discussion, I reserved the conclusion of it for the present period.

As it does not appear to me very material to observe any order with respect to this subject, I shall merely state the observations it suggests, as they occur to my mind, without attempting to arrange them.

It would be a very curious question to agitate, how far understanding is transmitted from parent to child; and within what limits it can be improved by culture: whether all men are born equal, with respect to their understanding; or, whether there is an original diversity antecedent to all imitation and instruction. The analogy of animals is in favor of the transmissibility of mind. Some ill-tempered horses constantly breed ill-tempered colts; and the foal never has seen the sire,—therefore, in this, there can be no imitation. If the eggs of a wild duck are hatched under a tame duck, the young brood will be much wilder than any common brood of poultry; if they are kept all their lives in a farm-yard, and treated kindly, and fed well, their eggs hatched under another bird produce a much tamer race. What is the difference of suspicion and fear observable in the two broods, but a direct transmission of mind, without the possible intervention of any imitation or teaching? However,

* Page 95.

whether mind be transmitted, or whether it be affected afterward by the earliest circumstances of our lives, certainly the fact is, that at the very earliest periods of our existence, the strongest differences are observable between one individual and another; which difference no subsequent art and attention can ever after destroy.

One of the rarest sort of understandings we meet with in the world, among the numerous diversities which are produced, is an understanding fairly and impartially open to the reception of truth, coming in any shape, and from any quarter; and it will be of considerable use, in a discussion on the conduct of the understanding, to consider what those causes are, which render this sort of understanding so very rare. One of these causes, and the first I shall mention, is indolence. Repose is agreeable to the human mind; and decision is repose. A man has made up his opinions; he does not choose to be disturbed; and he is much more thankful to the man who confirms him in his errors, and leaves him alone, than he is to the man who refutes him, or who instructs him at the expense of his tranquillity. Again: our vanity is compromised by our opinions; we have expressed them, and they must be maintained: the object is, not to know the truth, but to avoid the shame of appearing to have been ignorant of it.

Words are an amazing barrier to the reception of truth. It is a most inestimable habit in the conduct of the understanding, before men put their solemn sanction to any opinion,—before war, before peace, before expatriation, and all the great events of life,—that men should ask themselves whether or not the words by which their conduct has been influenced, have really any meaning; and if so, whether they have the meaning, in such instances, intended to be affixed to them. Definition of words has been commonly called a mere exercise of grammarians; but when we come to consider the innumerable murders, proscriptions, massacres, and tortures, which men have inflicted on each other from mistaking the meaning of words, the exercise of definition certainly begins to assume rather a more dignified aspect.

Then comes association as another disturber. A man has heard such opinions very often; or, "I have heard them when I was young; and therefore, they must be ight;"—"I hate all Dissenters," or "all Roman Catholics;"—or, "I can not endure Americans;"—and such other *shocking* opinions, upon which men act all their lives,—and act very badly, and furiously, and very ignorantly, merely because such opinions have been instilled into their earliest infancy, and because they have never had the power of separating two ideas which mere accident first associated together. The cure for this confined and narrow species of understanding, is to see many things and many men; to taste of the sweetness of truth in science, and to cultivate a love of it; to have the words, *liberality*, *candor, knowledge,* often in your mouth, and at length they will get into your heart; to ask the *reason of things*, and find the *meaning of words;* to hear patiently any one who confirms what you thought before, or who refutes it; to propose to yourself in life the same object, as the law proposes in the examination of evidence,—to *get at the truth,* and nothing *but* the truth. Without study, no man can ever do any thing with his understanding. But in spite of all that has been said about the sweets of study, it is a sort of luxury, like the taste for olives and coffee—not natural, very hard to be acquired, and very easily lost. Very few persons begin to study from the love of knowledge, or the desire of doing good; though these are the motives with which they *ought* to begin: but they begin from the shame of inferiority, and better motives come afterward.

One of the best methods of rendering study agreeable is to live with able men, and to suffer all those pangs of inferiority, which the want of knowledge always inflicts. Nothing short of some such powerful motive, can drive a young person, in the full possession of health and bodily activity, to such an unnatural and such an unobvious mode of passing his life as study. But this is the way that intellectual greatness often begins. The trophies of Miltiades drive away sleep. A young man sees the honor in which knowledge is held by his fellow-creatures; and he surrenders every present gratification, that he may gain them. The honor in which living genius is held, the trophies by which it is adorned after life, it receives and enjoys from the feelings of men,—not from their sense of duty: but men never obey this feeling, without discharging the first of all duties; without securing the rise and growth of genius, and increasing the dignity of our nature, by enlarging the dominion of mind. No eminent man was ever yet rewarded in vain; no breath of praise was ever idly lavished upon him; it has never yet been idle and foolish to rear up splendid monuments to his name: the rumor of these things impels young minds to the noblest exertions, creates in them an empire over present passions, inures them to the severest toils, determines them to live only for the use of others, and leave a great and lasting memorial behind them.

Beside the shame of inferiority, and the love of reputation, curiosity is a passion very favorable to the love of study; and a passion very susceptible of increase by cultivation. Sound travels so many feet in a second; and light travels so many feet in a second. Nothing more probable: but you do not care *how* light and sound travel. Very likely: but *make* yourself care; get up, shake yourself well, *pretend* to care, make believe to care, and very soon you *will* care, and care so much, that you will sit for hours thinking about light and sound, and be extremely angry with any one who interrupts you in your pursuits; and tolerate no other conversation but about light and sound; and catch yourself plaguing every body to death who approaches you, with the discussion of these subjects. I am sure that a man ought to read as he would grasp a nettle:—do it lightly, and you get molested; grasp it with all your strength, and you feel none of its asperities. There is nothing so horrible as languid study; when you sit looking at the clock, wishing the time was over, or that somebody would call on you and put you out of your misery. The only way to read with any efficacy, is to read so heartily, that dinner-time comes two hours before you expect it. To sit with your Livy before you, and hear the geese cackling that saved the capitol; and to see with your own eyes the Carthaginian sutlers gathering up the rings of the Roman knights after the battle of Cannæ, and heaping them into bushels; and to be so intimately present at the actions you are reading of, that when anybody knocks at the door, it will take you two or three seconds to determine whether you are in your own study, or in the plains of Lombardy, looking at Hannibal's weather-beaten face, and admiring the splendor of his single eye;—this is the only kind of study which is not tiresome; and almost the only kind which is not useless: this is the knowledge which gets into the system, and which a man carries about and uses like his limbs, without perceiving that it is extraneous, weighty, or inconvenient.

To study successfully, the body must be healthy, the mind at ease, and time managed with great economy. Persons who study many hours in the day, should, perhaps, have two separate pursuits going on at the same time,—one for one part of the day, and the other for the other; and these of as opposite a nature as possible,—as Euclid and Ariosto; Locke and Homer; Hartley on Man, and Voyages round the Globe; that the mind may be refreshed by change, and all the bad effects of lassitude avoided. There is one piece of advice, in a life of study, which I think no one will object to; and that is, every now and then to be completely idle,—to do nothing at all: indeed, this part of a life of study is commonly considered as so decidedly superior to the rest, that it has almost obtained an exclusive preference over those other parts of the system, with which I wish to see it connected.

It has often been asked whether a man should study at stated intervals, or as the fit seizes him, and as he finds himself disposed to study. To this I answer, that where a man can trust himself, rules are superfluous. If his inclinations lead him to a fair share of exertion, he had much better trust to his inclinations alone; where they do not, they must be controlled by rules. It is just the same with sleep; and with every thing else. Sleep as much as you please, if your inclination lead you only to sleep as much as is convenient; if not, make rules. The system in every thing ought to be,—do as you please —so long as you please to do what is right. Upon these principles, every man must see how far he may trust to his inclinations, before he takes away their natural liberty. I confess, however, it has never fallen to my lot to see many persons who *could* be trusted; and the method, I believe, in which most great men have gone to work, is by regular and systematic industry.

A little hard thinking will supply the place of a great deal of reading; and an hour or two spent in this manner sometimes lead you to conclusions, which it would require a volume to establish. The mind advances in its train of thought, as a restive colt proceeds on the road in which you wish to guide him; he is always running to one side or the other, and deviating from the proper path, to which it is your affair to bring him back. I have asked several men what passes in their minds when they are thinking; and I never could find any man who could think for two minutes together. Every body has seemed to admit that it was a perpetual deviation from a particular path, and a perpetual return to it; which, imperfect as the operation is, is the only method in which we can operate with our minds to carry on any process of thought. It takes some time to throw the mind into an attitude of thought, or into any attitude; though the power of doing this, and, in general, of thinking, is amazingly increased by habit. We acquire, at length, a greater command over our associations, and are better enabled to pursue one object, unmoved by all the other thoughts which cross it in every direction.

One of the best modes of improving in the art of thinking, is, to think over some subject, before you read upon it; and then to observe, after what manner it has occurred to the mind of some great master. You will then observe whether you have been too rash or too timid; what you have omitted, and in what you have exceeded; and by this process you will insensibly catch a great manner of viewing a question. It is right in study, not only to think when any extraordinary incident provokes you to think, but from time to time to review what has passed; to dwell upon it, and to see what trains of thought voluntarily present themselves to your mind. It is a most superior habit of some minds, to refer all the particular truths which strike them, to other truths more general: so that their knowledge is beautifully methodized: and the general truth at any time suggests all the particular exemplifications; or any particular exemplification, at once leads to the general truth. This kind of understanding has an immense and decided superiority over those confused heads in which one fact is piled upon another, without the least attempt at classification and arrangement. Some men always read with a pen in their hand, and commit to paper any new thought which strikes them; others trust to chance for its reappearance. Which of these is the best method in the conduct of the understanding, must, I should suppose, depend a great deal upon the particular understanding in question. Some men can do nothing without preparation; others, little with it: some are fountains, some reservoirs. My very humble and limited experience goes to convince me, that it is a very useless practice; that men seldom read again what they have committed to paper, nor remember what they have so committed one iota the better for their additional trouble: on the contrary, I believe it has a direct tendency to destroy the promptitude and tenacity of memory, by diminishing the vigor of present attention, and seducing the mind to depend upon future reference: at least, such is the effect I have uniformly found it to produce upon myself; and the same remark has been frequently made to me by other persons, of their own habits of study. I am by no means contending against the utility and expediency of writing; on the contrary, I am convinced there can be no very great accuracy of mind without it. I am only animadverting upon that *exaggerated* use of it, which disunites the mind from the body; renders the understanding no longer portable, but leaves a man's wit and talents neatly written out in his commonplace book, and safely locked up in the bottom drawer of his bureau. This is the abuse of writing. The use of it, I presume, is, to give perspicuity and accuracy: to fix a habitation for, and to confer a name upon, our ideas, so that they may be considered and reconsidered themselves, and in their arrangement. Every man is extremely liable to be deceived in his reflections till he has habituated himself to putting his thoughts upon paper, and perceived from such a process, how often propositions that appeared before such development to be almost demonstrable, have vanished into nonsense when a clearer light has been thrown upon them. I should presume, also, that much writing must teach a good order and method in the disposition of our reasonings; because the connection of any one part with the whole, will be made so much more evident than it can be before it is put into visible signs. Writing, also, must teach a much more accurate use of language. In conversation, any language almost will do; that is, great indulgence is extended to the language of talkers, because a talker is at hand to explain himself, and his looks and gestures are a sort of comment upon his words, and help to interpret them: but as a writer has no such auxiliary language to communicate his ideas, and no power of re-explaining them when once clothed in language, he has nothing to depend upon but a steady and careful use of terms.

The advantage conversation has over all the other modes of improving the mind, is, that it is more natural and more interesting. A book has no eyes, and ears, and feelings; the best are apt every now and then to become a little languid: whereas a living book walks about, and varies his conversation and manner, and prevents you from going to sleep. There is certainly a great evil in this, as well as a good; for the interest between a man and his living folio, becomes sometimes a little too keen, and in the competition for victory they become a little too animated toward, and sometimes exasperated against, each other: whereas a man and his book generally keep the peace with tolerable success; and if they disagree, the man shuts his book, and tosses it into a corner of the room, which it might not be quite so safe or easy to do with a living folio. It is an inconvenience in a book, that you can not ask questions; there is no explanation: and a man is less guarded in conversation than in a book, and tells you with more honesty the little niceties and exceptions of his opinions; whereas in a book, as his opinions are canvassed where they can not be explained and defended, he often overstates a point for fear of being misunderstood; but then, on the contrary, almost every man talks a great deal better in his books, with more sense, more information, and more reflection, than he can possibly do in his conversation, because he has more time.

There are few good listeners in the world who make all the use that they might make, of the understandings of others, in the conduct of their own. The use made of this great instrument of conversation is the display of superiority, not the gaining of those materials on which superiority may rightfully and justly be founded. Every man takes a different view of a question as he is influenced by constitution, circumstances, age, and a thousand other peculiarities; and no individual ingenuity can sift and examine a subject with as much variety and success, as the minds of many men, put in motion by many causes, and affected by an endless variety of accidents. Nothing, in my humble opinion, would bring an understanding so forward, as this habit of ascertaining and weighing the opinions of others;—a point in which almost all men of abilities are deficient; whose first impulse, if they are young, is too often to contradict; or, if the manners of the world have cured them of that, to listen only with attentive ears, but with most obdurate and unconquerable entrails. I may be very wrong, and probably am so, but, in the whole course of my life, I do not know that I ever saw a man of considerable understanding respect the understandings of others as much as he might have done for his own improvement, and as it was just that he should do.

I touched a little, in my last Lecture, upon that habit of contradicting, into which young men,—and young men of ability in particular,—are apt to fall; and which is a habit extremely injurious to the powers of the understanding. I would recommend to such young men, an intellectual regimen, of which I myself, in an earlier period of life, have felt the advantage: and that is, to assent to the two first propositions that they hear every day; and not only to assent to them, but, if they can, to improve and embellish them; and to make the speaker a little more in love with his own opinion than he was before. When they have a little got over the bitterness of assenting, they may then gradually increase the number of assents, and so go on as their constitution will bear it; and I have little doubt that, in time, this will effect a complete and perfect cure.

It is a great thing toward making right judgments, if a man know what allowance to make for himself; and what discount should habitually be given to his opinions, according as he is old or young, French or English, clergyman or layman, rich or poor, torpid or fiery, healthy or ill, sorrowful or gay. All these various circumstances are perpetually communicating to the objects about them, a color which is not their true color: whereas, wisdom is of no age, nation, profession, or temperament; and is neither sorrowful nor sad. A man must have some particular qualities, and be affected by some particular circumstances; but the object is, to discover what they are, and habitually to allow for them.

There is one circumstance I would preach up, morning, noon, and night, to young persons, for the management of their understanding. Whatever you are from nature, keep to it; never desert your own line of talent. If Providence only intended you to write posies for rings, or mottoes for twelfth-cakes, keep to posies and mottoes: a good motto for a twelfth-cake is more respectable than a villainous epic poem in twelve books. Be what nature intended you for, and you will succeed; be any thing else, and you will be ten thousand times worse than nothing.

If black and white men live together, the consequence is, that, unless great care be taken, they quarrel and fight. There is nearly as strong a disposition in men of opposite *minds* to despise each other. A grave man can not conceive what is the use of a wit in society; a person who takes a strong common-sense view of a subject, is for pushing out by the head and shoulders an ingenious theorist, who catches at the lightest and faintest analogies; and another man, who scents the ridiculous from afar, will hold no commerce with him who tastes exquisitely the fine feelings of the heart, and is alive to nothing else: whereas talent is talent, and mind is mind, in all its branches! Wit gives to life one of its best flavors; common sense leads to immediate action, and gives society its daily motion; large and comprehensive views, its annual rotation; ridicule chastises folly and impudence, and keeps men in their proper sphere; subtilty seizes hold of the fine threads of truth; analogy darts away to the most sublime discoveries; feeling paints all the exquisite passions of man's soul, and rewards him by a thousand inward visitations for the sorrows that come from without. God made it all! It is all good! We must despise no sort of talent: they all have their separate duties and uses; all, the happiness of man for their object: they all improve, exalt, and gladden life.

Caution, though it must be considered as something very different from talent, is no mean aid to every species of talent. As some men are so skillful in economy, that they will do as much with a hundred pounds as another will do with two, so there is a species of men, who have a wonderful management of their understandings, and will make as great a show, and enjoy as much consideration, with a certain quantity of understanding, as others will do with the double of their portion: and this by watching times and persons; by taking strong positions, and never fighting but from the vantage-ground, and with great disparity of numbers; in short, by risking nothing, and by a perpetual and systematic attention to the security of reputation. Such rigid economy,—by laying out every shilling at compound interest,—very often accumulates a large stock of fame, where the original capital has been very inconsiderable; and, of course, may command any degree of opulence, where it sets out from great beginnings, and is united with real genius. For the want of this caution, there is an habitual levity sometimes fixed upon the minds of able men, and a certain manner of viewing and discussing all questions in a frivolous, mocking manner, as if they had looked through all human knowledge, and found in it nothing but what they could easily master, and were entitled to despise. Of all mistakes the greatest, to live and to think life of no consequence; to fritter away the powers of the understanding, merely to make others believe that you possess them in a more eminent degree; and gradually to diminish your interest in human affairs, from an affected air of superiority, to which neither yourself nor any human being can possibly be entitled. It is a beautiful mark of a healthy and right understanding, when a man is serious and attentive to all great questions; when you observe him, with modesty and attention, adding gradually to his conviction and knowledge on such topics; not repulsed by his own previous mistakes, not disgusted by the mistakes of others, but in spite of violence and error, believing that there is, somewhere or other, moderation and truth,—and that to seek that truth with diligence, with seriousness, and with constancy, is one of the highest and best objects for which a man can live.

Some men get early disgusted with the task of improvement, and the cultivation of the mind, from some excesses which they have committed, and mistakes into which they have been betrayed, at the beginning of life. They abuse the whole art of navigation because they have stuck upon a shoal; whereas, the business is, to refit, careen, and set out a second time. The navigation is very difficult; few of us get through it at first, without some rubs and losses,—which the world are always ready enough to forgive, where they are honestly confessed, and diligently repaired. It would, indeed, be a piteous case, if a young man were pinioned down through life to the first nonsense he happens to write or talk; and the world are, to do them justice, sufficiently ready to release them from such obligation: but what they do *not* forgive is, that juvenile enthusiasm and error, which ends in mature profligacy; which begins with mistaking what is right, and ends with denying that there is any thing right at all; which leaps from partial confidence to universal skepticism; which says, "there is no such thing as true religion and rational liberty, because I have been a furious zealot, or a seditious demagogue." Such men should be taught that wickedness is never an atonement for mistake; and they should be held out as a lesson to the young, that unless they are content to form their opinions modestly, they will too often be induced to abandon them entirely.

There is something extremely fascinating in quickness; and most men are desirous of appearing quick. The great rule for becoming so, is, *by not attempting to appear quicker than you really are;* by resolving to understand yourself and others, and to know what *you* mean, and what *they* mean, before you speak or answer. Every man must submit to be slow before he is quick; and insignificant before he is important. The too early struggle against the pain of obscurity, corrupts no small share of understandings. Well and happily has that man conducted his understanding, who has learned to derive from the exercise of it, regular occupation and rational delight; who, after having overcome the first pain of application, and acquired a habit of looking inwardly upon his own mind, perceives that every day is multiplying the relations, confirming the accuracy, and augmenting the number of his ideas; who feels that he is rising in the scale of intellectual beings, gathering new strength with every new difficulty which he subdues, and enjoying to-day as his pleasure, that which yesterday he labored at as his toil. There are many consolations in the mind of such a man, which no common life can ever afford; and many enjoyments which it has not to give! It is not the mere cry of moralists, and the flourish of rhetoricians; but it is *noble* to seek truth, and it is *beautiful* to find it. It is the ancient feeling of the human heart,—that knowledge is better than riches; and it is deeply and *sacredly true!* To mark the course of human passions as they have flowed on in the ages that are past; to see why nations have risen, and why they have fallen; to speak of heat, and light, and winds; to know what man has discovered in the heavens above, and in the earth beneath; to hear the chemist unfold the marvelous properties that the Creator has locked up in a speck of earth; to be told that there are worlds so distant from our sun, that the quickness of light travelling from the world's creation, has never yet reached us, to wander in the creations of poetry, and grow warm again, with that eloquence which swayed the democracies of the old world; to go up with great reasoners to the First Cause of all, and to perceive in the midst of all this dissolution and decay, and cruel separation, that there *is* one thing unchangeable, indestructible, and everlasting; —it is worth while in the days of our youth to strive hard for this great discipline; to pass sleepless nights for it, to give up to it laborious days; to spurn for it present pleasures; to endure for it afflicting poverty; to wade for it through darkness, and sorrow, and contempt, as the great spirits of the world have done in all ages and all times.

I appeal to the experience of any man who is in the habit of exercising his mind vigorously and well, whether there is not a satisfaction in it, which tells him he has been acting up to one of the great objects of his existence? The end of nature has been answered: his faculties have done that, which they were created to do, —not languidly occupied upon trifles,—not enervated by sensual gratification, but exercised in that toil which is so congenial to their nature, and so worthy of their strength. A life of knowledge is not often a life of injury and crime. Whom does such a man oppress? with whose happiness does he interfere? whom does his ambition destroy, and whom does his fraud deceive? In the pursuit of science he injures no man, and in the acquisition he does good to all. A man who dedicates his life to knowledge, becomes habituated to pleasure which carries with it no reproach: and there is one security that he will never love that pleasure which is paid for by anguish of heart,—his pleasures are all cheap, all dignified, and all innocent; and, as far as any human being can expect permanence in this changing scene, he has secured a happiness which no malignity of fortune can ever take away, but which must cleave to him while he lives,—ameliorating every good, and diminishing every evil, of his existence. With these reflections, therefore, upon the conduct of the understanding, I close my Lectures, and with them the Institution, for the present year: but, before I do so, I wish to say a few words respecting this latter subject. Another institution has now risen up in the eastern part of this metropolis; and there appears to be a very strong desire to do all that can be done for the increase of public institutions, by the foundation of libraries, and by lectures given to persons of both sexes. I allow myself to be no very impartial judge in such questions; but still I must take the liberty of expressing my astonishment, that sensible and reflecting men should seriously call in question the value and importance of such sort of establishments. If a man come here with his mind thoroughly stored, and his habits completely formed, and complain that he learns little or nothing; his complaint may be very true, but it applies to all other places of education, as well as to this. Such a man has got beyond what the aid of others can do for him; and must depend upon himself.

Then, again, it is asked what are the great and mighty effects upon the manners of the age, that such institutions are to produce? Great and mighty effects, none; but gradual and gentle effects, effects worth producing, sufficient to justify the expense and trouble bestowed upon institutions. It is, surely, not unfair to suppose that, of the numbers resorting to this Institution, some have felt a zeal for science, which they might not otherwise have felt; that this zeal may, in some instances, have furnished rational amusement to a whole life; in others, be productive of deep knowledge, and important discovery. Is it nothing to inflame young minds? is it nothing to please them with science, and to convey to them the first suspicion, that exquisite pleasure is to be derived from the mere occupations of the mind? Is it nothing to get science generally talked of, though it may not be profoundly discussed; and knowledge widely honored, though it may not be greedily pursued? I can not consider *that* man as a very attentive observer of human nature, who does not believe, that by all the conversation and occupation which this Institution has occasioned, much talent has been awakened, much curiosity for knowledge excited, the dominion of perilous idleness abridged, and the sum of laudable exertions increased. It is the greatest of all mistakes, to do nothing because you can only do little: but there are men who are always clamoring for immediate and stupendous effects, and think that virtue and knowledge are to be increased as a tower or a temple are to be increased, where the growth of its magnitude can be measured from day to day, and you can not approach it without perceiving a fresh pillar, or admiring an added pinnacle. "But, then, such institutions increase the number of smatterers." To be sure they do! And is it not one of the most desirable of all things that they should be increased? If you plant 50,000 oaks in five acres, have you not a better chance of fine trees than when you only plant 10,000 in one acre? Has the production of eggs ever yet been considered as unfavorable to the growth of chickens? or has any reasoner yet contended, that in any country where boys and girls are very numerous, men and women must be very scarce? Every one, in every art and science, is of course, at first, nothing *but* a smatterer. Of these, some can not advance from stupidity, others will not advance from idleness; some get in the wrong road from error, some quit the right from affectation; a few only reach the destined point,—but, of course, the number of these last will be directly and immediately in the proportion of those who started for the race. In short, I have no manner of doubt, if these institutions conduct themselves with as much judgment as they have hitherto done,—if they provide able and upright men to read lectures in this place; and if those men do, without countenancing any narrow and illiberal opinions, and without lending themselves to childish jealousies and groundless alarms, display at all times an honest zeal for sound knowledge, rational freedom, and manly piety,—I see no reason why this Institution may not prosper, and be considered as a valuable addition to the public establishments of this country. That such may be its fate, is my most sincere desire, and ardent prayer: and with these wishes for its prosperity, and with my hearty thanks to this elegant and accomplished audience, for the attention with which I have been heard, I conclude my Lectures; wishing to you all, every possible happiness till we meet again.

LECTURE XX.

ON THE ACTIVE POWERS OF THE MIND.

DIVISIONS OF THE ACTIVE POWERS INTO APPETITES, DESIRES, AND AFFECTIONS.—OF WHAT IS MEANT BY THE TERM "PASSION."—OF THE ORIGIN OF OUR PASSIONS.—THE APPLICATION OF DR. HARTLEY'S THEORY TO THE PASSIONS.—SOME REMARKS ON THE IMPERFECTIONS AND BEAUTIES OF THAT THEORY.

I HAVE had the pleasure of reading here two sets of Lectures,—the one upon the Understanding, the other upon Taste. I come now to the consideration of the Active Powers of the Mind, or those principles of our nature which impel us to action. The distinction between the intellectual and the active powers, or the understanding and the will, is one of very great antiquity; far anterior, I fancy, to the time of Aristotle: and it appears to be one of the most convenient divisions, for arranging the complicated powers of the human mind.

The two popular terms which express this division are *head* and *heart;* it being very natural that men, in their speculations concerning the connection of body and mind, should suppose that particular parts of the mind were more particularly associated with particular parts of the body. I need scarcely say that the notion is quite fanciful;—that it would be quite as philosophical to say of an able man that he had a good liver, or to praise a virtuous man for the soundness of his lungs, as it would be to speak of the head of the one, or the heart of the other. I mention this bodily distinction, not from any idea of the justice of the hypothesis it involves, but merely to show that the common notions of mankind have always gone along with this distinction of the powers of the mind, into those which are *intellectual* and those which are *active.*

This science of mental philosophy has often been represented as vague and unsatisfactory. It certainly is not capable of that precision which many others are; but its most skeptical enemies would not pretend to confound an *idea* with a *feeling*. Nobody would pretend to say that the mind is affected in the same manner by hard, soft, green, or blue, as it is by anger, shame, hatred, and love. Every one feels the necessity of dividing the two classes, and naturally conceives that they are subjected to very different laws. It is not impossible, perhaps, that we might possess every intellectual faculty we now have, without feeling the influence of one single appetite, desire, or affection. Constituted as we now are, there are moments in our existence, when the soul of passion seems to be entirely laid to sleep, and when outward objects are noticed by the understanding without producing the slightest determination of the will: and there are opposite states of tempest and convulsion, when the passions confound the understanding in all its operations, and make it a false and faithless observer of the world without. In old age, in melancholy, and in sickness, the mind appears to be diseased, from the decay of all its active powers. In madness they all exist in excess. The great variety in human character,—that astonishing difference between us, which leaves one man in the little field where he was born, and drives another out to command armies and senates,—this difference principally depends upon the different degrees of curiosity and imitation in each, upon the empire which fear and anger exercise over them; upon how they love, and how they hate; upon the nature and degree of all those active powers, which go to make up the constitution of their minds.

The active principles of our nature are divided by Mr. Stewart and Dr. Reid into appetites, desires, affections, self-love, and the moral faculty. They call those feelings *appetites* which take their rise from the body,—such as hunger and thirst, which operate periodically after certain intervals, and cease only for a time, upon the attainment of a particular object. They mean by *desires*, those feelings which do not take their rise from the body; which do not operate periodically, and do not cease upon the attainment of a particular object. The most remarkable active principles belonging to this class, they consider to be the desire of knowledge, or curiosity, the desire of society, the desire of power, and the desire of superiority, or the principle of emulation. Under the title of affections, they comprehend all those active principles whose direct and ultimate object is the communication of joy or pain to our fellow-creatures. According to this definition, resentment, revenge, hatred, belong to the class of our affections, as well as gratitude or pity. When I explain what they mean by self-love, and the moral faculty, I must do it at full length. This division of the active powers I shall in general adopt, and propose to begin with the affections.

The popular word for affections in their highest degree, is *passion;* and the objection to using it, is, that it only means the *excess* of the feeling: for instance, we could not say that a man experienced the passion of anger who felt a calm indignation at a serious injury he had received; we should only think ourselves justifiable in applying the term *passion* if he were transported beyond all bounds if his reason were almost vanquished, and if the bodily signs of that passion were visible in his appearance. However, if I should hereafter use the common term *passion,* instead of the more accurate term *affection,* I beg to be understood to mean any degree of a feeling, however great or small. Emotion will be found to mean a short and transient fit of passion: however, I shall use it synonymously with the words passion and affection; or, if I do not, I shall say so.

It must be allowed, I suppose, that, in strictness, nothing can be meant by the passion, but the mere feeling of mind. I am under the influence of violent rage from some sudden and serious injury which I have experienced; but the quick respiration, the red cheek, the frowning eyebrow, and the fixed eye, are not the affection of anger,—they are only the *signs* which that affection of anger produces on my body. In the same manner, I have a distinct impression of the person who has injured me; he appears almost to be standing before me: I know also that I have been assassinated in reputation, or ruined in fortune: but all these ideas are not the passion of anger: they are the *causes* of that passion, but not the passion itself. Again, I have the strongest desire to inflict an exemplary punishment upon the person who has done me this injury:—this is the affection or passion of resentment; the *consequence* of anger, but by no means anger itself.

In the same manner, a child loves its mother. The mother is the cause, which excites the affection of love in the mind of the child. The affection may possibly excite the child to do all the good in his power to his mother;—these are its consequences; the affection itself is distinct from either: therefore, in speaking of passions and affections, it should be remembered we are merely speaking of certain feelings of the mind, which it is impossible to define. You may state the *causes* of such feelings, and their *consequences;* but it is as impossible to define them, as it is to define sour, sweet, and savory. Men call the particular feeling annexed to shame, by one name; the particular feeling annexed to anger, by another. They are only believed to be the same in different individuals, because they proceed from the same causes, and produce the same effects. It appears to me of some consequence to remember this; and to separate, in all discussions upon these very difficult subjects, the pure affection of mind, from what gives it birth, and from what it induces men to do when it is produced.

The first question which arises in the consideration of human passions, is their origin. Concerning what passions we do *actually* possess, there can be no dispute; but the question is, respecting their origin. With how many passions and desires are we born? is there any such original principle in our nature as a desire of power, a desire of society, a desire of esteem; or, are all these feelings,—whose existence in the mature man no one doubts,—capable of being resolved into any more simple principles? The same with the passions: are men born with the original capacity of feeling gratitude for good, and resentment for evil? or can it be shown what the history of these feelings is; can their origin be traced, and their progress be clearly shown? The former opinions are entertained at present by the school of Reid, in Scotland; were taught by Hutcheson; and were, I fancy, the commonly received opinions on the subject before the time of Hartley. The disciples of this school may differ a little in their enumeration of the original active principles of our nature,—but they all agree that they are numerous; that no account can be given of their origin; that they are there, because such is the constitution of our nature; that it is an ultimate fact, and can not be reasoned upon. For instance, Dr. Reid would say, that "the passion of resentment is an original passion, implanted by Providence in the breast of all men for the purposes of self-preservation." Dr. Hartley would say, "the passion is there, and Providence intended it for self-preservation; but it was not placed originally in the human mind: provision, and very wise and very curious provision, is made, that it should uniformly spring up there; but it is *not* an original, inexplicable impulse. I can show you the period when it does not exist; I can explain to you by what means it is generated; I can trace it throughout all its gradations, up to the perfect life and entire development of the passion." This is about the state of the question between Reid and Hartley, respecting the origin of the active powers. I shall now give some short account of the progress and nature of Dr. Hartley's opinions.

Every body here present knows what is meant by the association of ideas. When two ideas have, by any accident, been joined together frequently in the understanding, the one idea has, ever after, the strongest tendency to bring back the other: for instance, the celebrated Descartes was very much in love with a lady who squinted; he had so associated that passion with obliquity of vision, that he declares, to the latest hour of his life he could never see a lady with a cast in her eye, without experiencing the most lively emotions. In the same manner, to take the most trite of all instances, the ideas of spirits and of darkness, are so strongly united together in our infancy, that it becomes an exceedingly difficult thing to separate them in mature age. There is no reason upon earth, why twelve o'clock in the middle of the day, or why dinner-time, should not be the proper season for ghosts, instead of the middle of the night. It has pleased anility to make another arrangement; and now, as I have said before, the two ideas of darkness and supernatural agency are so firmly united together, that it is frequently almost impossible to separate them. This is what is meant by the principle of association: and this principle was, I believe, first noticed by Locke; but he had recourse to it only to explain those sympathies and antipathies which he calls unnatural, in distinction from those which he says are born with us; and nothing can be more imperfect than his notions concerning the nature, cause, and effects, of the principle.

Afterward, Mr. Gay, a clergyman in the West of England, endeavored to show the possibility of deducing all our passions and affections from association, in a dissertation prefixed to Bishop Law's translation of King's "Origin of Evil:" but he supposed the love of happiness to be an original and implanted principle; and that the passions and affections were deducible only from supposing sensible and rational creatures dependent upon each other for their happiness. It was upon hearing of Mr. Gay's opinion, that Dr. Hartley turned his thonghts upon the subject; and at length, after giving the closest attention to it, in a course of several years, it appeared to him very probable, not only that all our intellectual pleasures and pains, but that all the phenomena of memory, imagination, volition, reasoning, and every other mental affection and operation, are only different modes or cases of the associations of ideas; so that nothing is necessary to make any man whatever he is, than a capacity of feeling pleasure and pain, and the principle of association. These are the simple rudiments and beginnings of our nature; these are the fountains of sorrow and of joy; from hence come all the passions which gladden, and all which embitter life. Hence come

> "The radiant smiles of Joy, the applauding hand
> Of Admiration; hence the bitter shower

That sorrow sheds upon a brother's grave;
Hence the dumb palsy of nocturnal Fear,
And those consuming fires that gnaw the heart
Of panting Indignation."

Such is the celebrated theory of Dr. Hartley; in which I have totally passed over his doctrine of vibrations, because, as every body knows, it is very foolish, and no way connected with the valuable part of his system.

I shall now give two or three specimens of the manner in which the various active powers are traced up to simple pleasure and pain, guided by association; and I will begin with one of the passions,—the passion of fear. Ask any one, whence comes the passion of fear? and he will tell you it is an original passion of our nature: at the same time it is evident to observation, that a child is wholly unacquainted with fear till he has received some hurt. If fear were coeval with birth; or a capacity of being afraid, implanted in us independently of all experience, a child of four months old would be afraid of the flame of a candle, the first moment he saw it,—he would shrink from a viper, and be frightened into fits at the sight of a loaded pistol. Try a child of that age with a lighted candle; he is so far from having any notion of fear, that his first effort is to grasp it: when he has been once burned, and suffered pain, the passion of fear—which is nothing more, in its early state, than the *expectation* of pain—is immediately formed. Put the candle to him again: he has now associated two ideas,—the light of the flame, and the pain of his body; the appearance of the flame, therefore, immediately gives him the notion that he is going to suffer,—and this feeling is what we call fear. In the same manner, a child learns to be afraid of sharp weapons, of animals that bite and scratch, and of all the common objects of juvenile terror; and, perceiving into how many inconveniences he is betrayed by his ignorance, falls into a *general* apprehension of all striking and *unknown* objects, because he can not appreciate the degree of mischief to be expected from them. This, I confess, appears to me a plain and true history of the passion of fear. If it were an original passion, the sight of a dagger would as immediately produce fear in a young child, as the touch of ice would produce cold in him: but before he can experience this passion, it is necessary he should suffer pain; and it is necessary that the object which has inflicted the pain should again be presented to him, in order to recall the feeling which has been associated to it.

I observe, what those persons stand out for the most, who are the most conversant with children, is the fear of falling which they express, even though they have never fallen. But does it not seem rather capricious and singular, that, among all the innumerable perils by which children are surrounded, the fear of falling should be the *only* one against which they have any instinctive warning? A child will eat poison if it be sweet; set himself on fire, play with gunpowder, swallow needles, run into any kind of mischief, from which he has suffered no previous pain; and amid these ten thousand avenues to destruction, we believe that the only one he is warned not to approach, is that which would break his arm or his leg, or give him a great blow on the head. So that the child may be burned, poisoned, stabbed, cut, mangled, or any thing else, provided he is not bruised. But what is the meaning of a child being afraid instinctively? If he is afraid of an object, he must, I suppose, have an idea of that object. Is he, then, born with the ideas of fire, of boiling water, of sharp-pointed weapons, of medical gentlemen, and all other objects which can do him harm;—or, if Locke has driven us out of these antiquated notions, shall we suppose, that he has no previous acquaintance with them; but that when they are perceived for the first time, the passion of fear immediately takes place? Is a child, then, startled by a brass blunderbuss the first time he sees it? "But this is not a natural object:" true; but is he, then, startled by arsenic, any more than with powdered sugar? To what do these instinctive terrors extend? It appears to me, I confess, quite impossible to make common sense of any supposition but that of Hartley, which says, that pain is the teacher of fear. Before pain there is *no* fear; and when that passion exists, however great the distance, and however circuitous the course, *there* is the fountain-head from which it sprang.

I will now consider two of the most important principles of our nature,—the desire of doing harm to others, and the desire of doing good;—resentment and benevolence. It will be curious to observe how far they fall into this doctrine of association. A young child, soon after his birth, has not the least desire to do good or harm to any one; he has no such passions: and it is our business to explain how he gets them. The food he eats or drinks gives him pleasure; but observing, in process of time, that the nurse is always present when he receives his food, the sight of the nurse gives him pleasure, because it reminds him of his food; yet in process of time the idea of the food is obliterated, and the sight of the nurse gives him pleasure, and, without the intervening idea that she is useful to him, he loves her immediately *after* his appetite of hunger is satisfied, as well as before: his passion for her, which first proceeded from an interested motive, becomes quite disinterested; and he loves her without the slightest reference to the advantages she procures him. This is the origin of his love for his nurse: and then, as all kindred ideas are very easily associated together, he proceeds from loving her to desiring her good; for, perceiving that other people like what he likes, it is very natural, that the idea of his own gratification in eating, should suggest the idea of the nurse's gratification; and that he should offer her a little morsel of his apple or his cake, or any puerile luxury which he happens to be enjoying. The association is easy to be comprehended, and seems perfectly natural. Besides, a child begins very early to associate his own advantage with benevolence. Cake, and commendation, the parent of cake, are lavished upon the child who shows a disposition to please others. Cuffs, and frowns, and hard words, are the portion of a selfish and a malevolent child: he begins with loving benevolence for the advantage it affords him, and ends with loving it for itself: he is not born with love of any thing, but merely with the *capacity* of feeling pleasure; which he first feels for the milk, then for the mother, because she gives him the milk, then for her own sake: then, as she makes him happy, association gives him the idea of making *her* happy; and he gains so much by benevolence, that he loves it first for the advantages it affords, then for itself. Reverse all this, and you will have the history and progress of the malevolent passions. A young child hates nobody. If you were to pinch or scratch him, he would feel pain; if you did it often, he would associate the idea of you with the idea of pain, and would hate you, first, on account of the ideas you suggested, then hate you plainly and simply without any cause. After he had learned by observation, that you were similarly constituted with himself, he would be led to associate your painful feelings with his own; and thus a foundation of malevolence toward you would be laid. Again: a child is deterred from doing any thing by threats and by pain; and he perceives that other persons are deterred by similar means; he therefore associates these ideas with prevention; threatens and beats whoever contradicts him; and cherishes resentment as a means of gratifying his will, and effecting whatever object he has in view. It is quite impossible that a child can be born with any feeling of resentment. He can never tell that the way to prevent another child from beating him, is to beat that child again; it would be an enormous thing that he who does not yet know black from scarlet, should be acquainted with the dominion which pain has over the mind, and make use of it to accomplish his purposes; and yet, such is the opinion that they adopt, who consider this passion as innate, and coeval with our existence.

I have said that the child first associates with his mother the idea of food, and loves her in consequence of this association; then loves her from disinterested motives, without any association at all: and I have said that he hates his tormentor, first, from associating painful ideas with his appearance; and then hates him without any association at all. This leads me to the mention of a very general, and very important law of association: and that is this;—the medium idea by which two others are associated, is always at length destroyed, and the two others coalesce, and make the association: for instance, whatever we love for its uses, we love for itself. A man begins to love his horse because he carries him well out hunting: he ends with loving the horse without the slightest reference to his utility; and keeps him when he is blind and lame, with as much attention as in the vigor of his youth. Here, the middle term (if I may use the expression), which united together the two ideas of horse and affection, was utility: that middle term was effaced; and the affection remains for the horse, when all notion of utility is completely at an end. The middle term here is like a cramp or a screw put upon two pieces of wood, just glued together,—it serves to keep them together at first, but can be removed with perfect safety, when the cement is solid, and the union complete.

I remember once seeing an advertisement in the papers, with which I was much struck; and which I will take the liberty of reading:—"Lost, in the Temple Coffee House, and supposed to be taken away by mistake, an oaken stick, which has supported its master not only over the greatest part of Europe, but has been his companion in his journeys over the inhospitable deserts of Africa; whoever will restore it to the waiter, will confer a very serious obligation on the advertiser; or, if that be any object, shall receive a recompense very much above the value of the article restored." Now, here is a man who buys a sixpenny stick, because it is useful; and totally forgetting the trifling causes which first made his stick of any consequence, speaks of it with warmth and affection; calls it his companion; and would hardly have changed it, perhaps, for the gold stick which is carried before the king. But the best and strongest example of this, and of the customary progress of association, is in the passion of avarice. A child only loves a guinea because it shines; and, as it is equally splendid, he loves a gilt button as well. In after-life, he begins to love wealth, because it affords him the comforts of existence; and then loves it so well, that he denies himself the common comforts of life to increase it. The uniting idea is so totally forgotten, that it is completely sacrificed to the ideas which it unites. Two friends unite against the person to whose introduction they are indebted for their knowledge of each other; exclude him their society, and ruin him by their combination.

I might, upon the same principle, proceed to explain a vast variety of passions and desires, which are all commonly spoken of as original principles of our nature. For instance: nothing appears to me more decided and indisputable, than that men are not born with any love of power, any love of society, or any love of esteem; all these feelings,—which we all experience so strongly,—have all sprung from pleasure, pain, and association; and are entirely explicable upon that system. But, if I were to go through with them, I should merely be treading over the same ground I have passed already: the principle once understood, there is no great difficulty in making the application to particular cases.

I beg leave again to observe,—and I request the particular attention of my hearers to it,—that the only difference between the friends of this doctrine of association, and their antagonists, is, respecting the *origin* of all these feelings and passions. Respecting their *existence*, there is none. Every one agrees that there is a love of parents, a love of country, a desire of esteem, and a desire of knowledge: the only question is, respecting their origin. Are they primitive? Can no account be given of their causes? or from what are they derived? They say, in tracing up a river to its source, we find it bursting out from innumerable streams. We say, this is very true; but you stop short too soon, you don't look far enough; we can show you your numerous fountains distinctly terminating in one,—the plain, ancient, and undoubted source of the stream. The admirable simplicity of this doctrine ought certainly to recommend it to universal attention; as, independent of other considerations, it wears the face of that simplicity in causes, and variety in effects, which we discover in every other part of nature

"In human works, though labor'd on with pain,
A thousand movements scarce one purpose gain:

> In God's, one single can its end produce;
> Yet serves to second, too, some other use."

Nor let any man imagine that the power and goodness of Providence is diminished in the estimation of man, by that philosophy which teaches that we come into the world void of all passions, and acquire them by these simple means. Is it wiser and greater to move every planet by a fresh power, or to guide them all in their spheres by the simple principle of gravity? Did Newton *degrade* our notions of Providence when he discovered one great law presiding over heaven and earth? Did Locke diminish our admiration of the human mind, and of Him who made it, when he showed us how all its infinite variety of ideas grow out of mere sensation and reflection? To show us that a variety of movements in a machine all proceed from one and the same original power, is to show us that that machine has been conceived clearly and grandly; for imbecility, and want of resources, are shown by calling in a vast variety of powers to produce one plain effect. But opulence of thought, and immensity of mind, are shown by producing an infinite variety of effects, from one simple cause. Providence did not originally implant in men a love of esteem, or a love of knowledge; but Providence implanted that *capacity* of feeling pleasure and pain, and that *facility* of association, which as infallibly produce the love of esteem and knowledge, as if they had been original feelings of the mind.

But what says Dr. Reid and his school?—That Providence, which moves all the heavenly bodies by one simple cause;—that Providence, which darts the blood of man through a million vessels by the contraction of one single organ;—that Providence, always so simple and so grand, is in the fabrication of the mind, *alone* complicated and confused, arranging without order, and planning without art. What was the first command? Not "let there be colors?" not "let the herb be green, and the heavens be blue:" but, "let there be *light!*" and forthwith there was every variety of color! So with us; the first mandate was not, "let man be affected with anger and gratitude," but "let man feel;" and then, matter let loose upon him, with all its malignities, and all its pleasures, roused up in him his good and his bad passions, and made him as he is,—the best and the worst of created beings.

I have heard it said, as an objection against this theory, that there is a neatness in it, an *arrondissement*, which gives it a great appearance of quackery and imposture. This is very likely; but I am not contending that the theory *looks* as if it were true, but merely that it *is* true. At the same time, there is a great deal of merit in the observation; for discoveries in general, especially upon such very intricate subjects, are more ragged, uneven, and incomplete; there is here a little light, and there a great deal of darkness; in one place you make a great inroad, and then you are stopped by impenetrable barriers: but here is one master-key which opens every bolt and barrier; a philosophy which explains every thing, and leaves the whole subject at rest forever. All these are certainly presumptive evidences against the theory; but if it perform all that it promise, those presumptive evidences are, of course, honorably repelled.

I beg leave, however, before I conclude this lecture, to repeat again and again, that I by no means undertake to burthen myself with the *whole* of Dr. Hartley's theory. The vibrations, every one laughs at. The doctrines of necessity, which he has chosen to add on to it, I have nothing to do with: the subject is improper for this place; and the whole question, rightly considered, more a question of words, than of any thing else.

The great principle of Hartley, which I am exclusively endeavoring to maintain, is this,—that all the passions are derived from pleasure and pain, guided by association. For that opinion I am responsible, and for no other. I now take leave of it with saying, that, in my very confined and inconsiderable attention to such sort of subjects, I have felt a security and a satisfaction in this system, which I never did in any other: every day convinces me more and more, that it *is* a discovery of vast importance; fresh facts arrange themselves under it; it solves new difficulties; and as it remains longer in the mind, it increases in durability and improves in strength.

"Love, Hope, and Joy,—fair Pleasure's smiling train;
Hate, Fear, and Grief,—the family of Pain:
These, mix'd with art, and to due bounds confin'd,
Make and maintain the pleasures of the mind;
The lights and shades, whose well-accorded strife
Gives all its strength and color to our life."

LECTURE XXI.

ON THE EVIL AFFECTIONS.

OF THE MALEVOLENT AND UNPLEASANT PASSIONS: THEY ARE ALL DERIVED FROM PAIN, GUIDED BY ASSOCIATION.—OF THE GENERATION OF RESENTMENT, AND THE RESTRAINTS IMPOSED UPON IT BY EDUCATION.—OF MALICE, FEAR, SHAME, AND THE PAIN OF INACTIVITY.

THERE have been almost as many different arrangements of the passions, as there have been writers who have treated on the subject. Some writers have placed them in centrast to each other, as Hope and Fear, Joy and Sorrow. Some have considered them as they are personal, relative, or social; some according to their influence at different periods of life; others, as they relate to past, present, or future time. The academicians advanced, that the principal passions were Fear, Hope, Joy, and Grief. They included Aversion and Despair under the passion of Grief; Hope, Fortitude, and Anger under Desire. Dr. Hartley has arranged the passions under five grateful and five ungrateful ones: the grateful ones are, Love, Desire, Hope, Joy, and Pleasing Recollection; the ungrateful ones, Hatred, Aversion, Fear, Grief, and Displeasing Recollection. Dr. Watts and Mr. Grove have both followed different arrangements, which I will not detain you by stating: whoever is desirous of seeing them at length, may consult Dr. Cogan's book on the Passions, who has also proposed and followed an arrangement of his own.

Conceiving that we are born merely with a capacity of feeling pleasure and pain, and that from this capacity, directed by association, all the affections of our nature spring, it appears to me that the plainest and most natural arrangement will be, to divide the affections according to their origin, as they are derived from the one or the other of these great principles of our nature, and as they belong to the family of pleasure or of pain.

I shall begin with those affections of the mind which are formed by painful associations; premising, that I by no means intend to pursue this subject as far as it would lead me, or to enter into very minute and accurate distinctions, because such an analysis would be excessively tedious, and would better become a professed treatise on the passions, than a course of Lectures on Moral Philosophy.

All ungrateful passions are the sensation of evil: but it may be evil long passed (for the remembrance of which we have no name); or it may be present evil, either of body or mind, and from different causes, as pain, grief, and fear; or it may be the apprehension of evil to come, which is fear. From the sensations of evil, comes the desire of inflicting it, or malevolence. Hence anger, jealousy, malice, envy, and all the train of bad passions, which are all compounded of the same principles,—displeasure, and a desire of displeasing; or, in more common words, hatred and revenge. So that all the vices of our nature come from remembering evil, feeling it, anticipating it, and inflicting it (the consequence of these three preceding states).

The difference between grief and pain is, that we apply the expression of *grief* to those uneasy sensations which have not the body for their immediate cause; *pain*, to those which have. The loss of reputation occasions grief; the loss of a limb, pain.

Grief is that uneasy state of mind which proceeds from the loss of some good, or the presence of some evil. A singular circumstance respecting grief, is, that there is not always, in the suffering person, a very ready disposition to get rid of his sorrow: he clings to the remembrance of it; gathers round about him every thing which can recall the idea of what he has lost; and appears to derive his principal consolation from those trains of ideas which an indifferent person would consider as best calculated to exasperate his affliction. The reason of this, I take to be, that it is pleasant to be pitied, pleasant even to think how we *should* be pitied, if the world were well acquainted with all the minute circumstances of our loss,—with all the fine ties and endearments which bound us to the object of our affections. We are fond of representing ourselves to our own fancies as objects of the most profound and universal sympathy. Death never took away such a father, such a husband, or such a son; we dwell upon our misfortunes, and magnify them, till we derive a sort of consolation from reflecting on that exquisite pity to which we are entitled, and which we should receive if the whole extent of our calamity were as well known to others as to ourselves. We dwell upon our affliction, however, not merely from the sympathy to which it appears to entitle us, but because in that train of ideas there are many that give an immediate relief of pleasure, which, though purchased dearly by the subsequent pain to which they expose us, are still resorted to for that immediate pleasure. For instance, a man reduced to sudden poverty, may take some pleasure in thinking a moment on the luxuries which he has been accustomed to enjoy: he pays dearly enough for such reflections, when he is forced to perceive what his present state is; but still the train of thought has been pleasant for the moment,—it has given him some immediate relief, and therefore he has indulged it. "Grief," says Constance,—

> "Grief fills the room up of my absent child,
> Lies in his bed, walks up and down with me;
> Puts on his pretty looks, repeats his words,
> Remembers me of all his gracious parts,
> Stuffs out his vacant garments with his form."

These two causes appear to me to explain the singular phenomenon, that sorrow should ever be pleasant, and justify the usual poetical expression of *the luxury of grief*.

Grief, it should be observed, seems to be a general term for all sensations of evil, when that sensation has not a specific name.

That sensation of evil which proceeds from the loss of esteem, has a specific name; it is called shame. Most of the other sensations of evil,—as that which proceeds from the loss of friends, or the loss of fortune, or from frustrated ambition,—pass under the common and inclusive name of grief; though there is no reason that I know of, why that uneasiness which proceeds from the loss of power, should not have a specific name as well as that which proceeds from the loss of esteem.

Grief produces resentment or not, according as it is accompanied with the notion of its being occasioned by a voluntary and rational agent. For instance, a young boy walks under an old, ruinous building; a stone falls on his head, and he is killed: in this case you feel nothing but pure affliction:—but you learn immediately after, that some wicked and malicious person has pushed down this stone upon the child's head, and killed him: here grief is immediately followed by resentment; and you are actuated by the strongest and most irresistible motives to do all possible harm to the murderer of your son. So that resentment is always preceded by uneasy sensations of the body, that we call pain; or of the mind, which we call grief; though grief and pain do not always produce resentment. It will be curious to investigate the origin and progress of this difference, and to decide how it is, that precisely the same degree of grief does sometimes produce violent resentment, sometimes not.

As I stated in the last Lecture, it is quite impossible to suppose that a child is born with all those compound notions which enter into the word *resentment;* for, observe all the knowledge which this implies: first, you suppose the child of a month old, or a day old, to know that my hand guided the pin with which I pricked him; next, that I can guide my hand where I please; next, that I feel pain as he does, and that he has a right to inflict the same pain as I have inflicted upon him. There is not the slightest evidence that the child has any one of all these ideas; and I would just as soon believe that a child just born could say the three first books of Ariosto by heart, as that he is born with any such wisdom. He learns by experience, that other human creatures feel pleasure and pain as well as himself; that they are allured by pleasure to do him good, and by pain intimidated from doing him harm. Hence the origin of his benevolence and his resentment; of his desire to do harm, or to do good, to his fellow-creatures. A young child of seven or eight months old, if you take him away from any object that attracts his attention, will cry, express great grief, and all that agitation of body, and impatience of mind, which is frequently occasioned by grief; but there is not the slightest appearance of resentment. It never appears to occur to a child of that age, that you are the cause of this privation; that you can feel pain, and that therefore he will inflict it. It is long *after* this period, that he acquires this very compound idea; and he acquires it, as he acquires the power of knowing black from white, and tall from short,—by observation.

It may appear very extraordinary that there should be such a prodigious tendency in after-life to connect grief with resentment, when they were not originally connected together by nature. But I think the doctrine of acquired perceptions, must convince any man how much the work of association is like an original impression of nature; and how impossible it is to distinguish the laminæ put together by association, from those which were originally solid and continuous. Besides, too, all similar passions naturally generate each other, as we shall see hereafter; and there is a very strong resemblance in the effects of grief, pain, and resentment; and, having once been joined together, the one has the strongest possible disposition to produce the other. I am not speaking of the highest-refined London grief,—the grief of civilization and softness; but the grief of a savage and a child. The grief of nature in its first stage is a violent, impatient, irritating passion, very much resembling anger. The natural effect of grief and pain is, to cry out as loud as possible, and to kick and sprawl in all possible directions; and I believe, if people would do so much more than they do, they would be all the better for it. The sitting on monuments smiling, and the green and yellow melancholy, is quite a subsequent business, entirely the result of education.

Having acquired the feeling of resentment, the child is, of course, very unlearned at first in the application of it; he has not yet learned what objects have life and feeling, what not; and at the age of two years, when thrown into a violent rage, it is not impossible but that he will beat the chair upon which he has knocked his head, or the table that has thrown him down, as vehemently as if they were capable of suffering from his malevolence. In a very little time he learns the folly of this; distinguishes between objects that feel, and objects that do not; and is more learned and skillful in directing the effusions of his wrath. After he has learned to direct his resentment only against objects that have life and feeling, education limits the confines of his resentment still more, by infusing in his mind the idea of justice; by instructing him that he must not resent unless the injury has been done intentionally,—unless he who has been guilty of it, has done it without any fair and lawful pretext; and that after all, where it can not be forgiven with propriety, it must be punished with moderation. So that education teaches us at last to support a large class of griefs without gratifying the propensity to resentment; and confines the gratification of that passion to where the injury has been inflicted by a rational being, intentionally and unjustly. There still exists, however, through life, the strongest disposition to connect together grief, pain, and resentment; and it requires the strongest and steadiest appeal to the principles of justice to keep it down. We often kick a stock or a stone, over which we have stumbled, from the mere habit we have acquired of associating resentment with pain. We feel a sort of resentment against the person who brings us bad news. Zinzis Khan cut off the head of one of his favorites for venturing to inform him of a partial defeat his troops had sustained. The raising up of the passion of resentment, causes an immediate diversion of the passion of grief; and therefore, the feeling of resentment in cases of grief, seems to be sought after, in some badly constituted minds, as a sort of relief. Suppose any person were to purchase a piece of painted glass for three or four hundred pounds; it is discovered to have fallen down, and is broken to pieces;—the disposition of resentment to follow displeasure is so great, that I am afraid it would be some relief to find that this had been knocked down by a careless servant; and that the master would not be very well pleased with his servant, who could give him such an account of the business as precluded the master from all possibility of scolding. A child is rarely deformed, or rarely dies, by the hand of nature; but, according to the parent, the nurse has mismanaged it, or the physician destroyed it by his ignorance. Men in violent pain are excessively irascible, very strongly disposed to quarrel and find fault. A gamester, who has lost a thousand pounds, comes home, and relieves his uneasiness by quarreling with his wife and children, and abusing his servants. All these are instances of the strong disposition of mankind to associate together grief and resentment; in these instances, the disposition is so strongly evinced that it entirely overpowers all sense of justice.

Contempt is that painful emotion which a human being excites in you, by his degrading qualities or conduct. Contempt only diminishes resentment, in those injuries which depend upon the character of the person who inflicts them. A libel may be written by a man so infamous, that all the severe things he has said are rendered harmless by the name which is subscribed to them; here, my resentment is less, because the grief I feel, is so much less, from having been traduced by such a man: but if the same man were to set my house on fire, or assault me with a large stick, the general contemptibility of his character would certainly have very little effect in diminishing my resentment. Contempt diminishes resentment by diminishing danger—the cause of resentment.

Peevishment is resentment, excited by trifles. Envy is resentment, excited by superiority,—not by *all* superiority, but by that to which you think you are fairly entitled: for a plowman does not envy a king; but he envies another plowman who has a shilling a week more than he has. Malice is pure malevolence; a desire to inflict injury without a cause; an abstract love of doing mischief;—at least, so it is commonly said to be: but there can hardly be any such passion; it must be a desire of doing mischief for some very slight and foolish cause. I don't like the cut of a man's coat, or the make of his face; or, he talks too quick, or too slow, or some other such absurd and childish reason,—which makes me his enemy, and inclines me to do him harm.

Sulkiness, is anger half subdued by fear. Jealousy, is another modification of anger;—the causes of which, I believe, there is no occasion I should explain. Cruelty, is rather a habit than a passion: it will easily appear, however, that it is the genuine and necessary offspring of anger, often indulged and gratified. It is most apt to arise in proud, selfish, and timorous persons, who conceive highly of their own merits, and of the consequent injustice of all offenses committed against them; and who have an exquisite feeling and apprehension in respect of private gratification and uneasiness. Montesquieu has made this remark: he says, that all persons accustomed to the implicit gratification of the will, are very apt to be cruel.

Fear, is the apprehension of future evil. Habit diminishes fear, when it raises up contrary associations; and increases it, when it confirms the first associations. A soldier, who has often escaped, begins to disunite the two ideas of dying and fighting; he connects also with fighting, a sense of duty, and a love of glory. Habit, I should think, would increase the sensation of fear, in a person who had undergone two or three painful operations, and was about to submit to another. A man works in a gunpowder-mill every day of his life, with the utmost *sang froid*, which you would not be very much pleased to enter for half an hour: you have associated with the manufactory, nothing but the accidents you have heard it is exposed to; he has associated with it, the numberless days he has passed there in perfect security. For the same reason, a sailor-boy stands unconcerned upon the mast; a mason upon a ladder; and a miner descends by his single rope. Their associations are altered by experience; therefore, in estimating the degree in which human creatures are under the influence of this passion, we must always remember their previous habits. A woman conceives, early in life, such dreadful notions of war, and all the instruments of war, that no degree of maternal tenderness, probably, would induce her to take a sword and pistol, and go and fight; but in the time of a public plague, she would despise her own life, nurse her sick husband, or her children, and expose herself to death, as boldly as any grenadier. In the late attack upon Egypt, our soldiers behaved with the most distinguished courage; but a physician did what, I suppose, no soldier in the whole army would have dared to have done;—he slept for three nights in the sheets of a patient who had died of the plague! If the question had been to encounter noisy, riotous death, he probably could not have done it; but where pus and miasma were concerned, he appears to have been a perfect hero. Fear, is the most contagious of all the passions; and the reason is obvious enough why it becomes so: it is much more likely that the cause of your fear should concern me, more than the cause of any other of your passions. If I see you very angry, it is not probable, unless we happen to be intimately connected, that the cause of your anger would prove to be a cause of mine; but if I see you dreadfully frightened, it immediately occurs to me, that I am implicated in the same cause of fear:—you have discovered that the play-house in which we are both sitting, is on fire; you have seen an enraged bull, running in the streets: I am not easy for an instant, till I have discovered the cause of your terror, and satisfied myself, that it does not concern us both.

The passion of fear, in its ordinary state, is a vibration of the mind, between the expectation of good, and the expectation of evil; in which contest, however, the expectation of evil preponderates. The moment all hope is banished, and nothing remains but despair (the expectation of certain evil), the passion assumes a new form;—very often that of the most furious resentment. A rat is a very timid animal, with respect to men; but get a rat into a corner, where all possibility of escape is precluded, and a rat will fly at you like a tiger. The instances are innumerable of the heroic exploits performed by small bodies of troops, whose fears, despair has converted into resentment. In cases where there is no room for resentment,—as in shipwreck,—despair produces various species of insanity, stupor, and delirium, while the sailors are only afraid; that is, while there is a mixture of two passions, they work, and do all they can for their safety. The moment there is no more hope,—so impossible is it for the ordinary mass of human beings to look steadily at great and certain evil, that many jump overboard and drown themselves; some are quite stupefied; others completely raving mad.

A great propensity to fear is, I should imagine, capable of some degree of cure. The living with brave men, would certainly go a great way to diminish this passion of fear;—as all our qualities of mind, whether good or bad, are highly contagious. To put ourselves in situations where we must act before many witnesses, operates as a check upon fear, by raising up contrary passions, of the dread of shame. It very often happens, in cases of danger, that some one present, is more under the influence of this passion than ourselves, and that this example, instead of increasing our fear, produces the contrary effect,—of diminishing it: we become ashamed of our companion's weakness; then of our own. Vanity induces us, also, to make a display of our superiority; and, by this effort, the fear is diminished. Fear is repeatedly overcome by affection, and compassion. A mother would run away from a dog, if her child was not with her; but she faces him very boldly when her fears are excited for another. A sudden cry of distress will induce a man, very often, to do what no regard for his own safety could possibly impel him to perform.

Suspicion, clearly belongs to the family of fear: it is that passion applied to the motives and intentions of human creatures. For instance, we should not call a man suspicious who was extremely careful of his health; and who was always believing, when he walked out, that it was going to thunder, or rain; but we should call that person suspicious, who believed that every person with whom he lived, was laying plots to defraud and deceive him. Fear, is certainly a strong predisposing cause to suspicion. It is highly probable that a suspicious man is naturally a timid man; though the converse is not equally probable,—that a timid person should be suspicious. Women are timid, but not suspicious;—much the contrary.

The particular kind of grief we feel for the loss of reputation, is called shame; the aversion occasioned by which feeling,—the desire to escape it,—is, perhaps, the most powerful of all the passions. The most curious offspring of shame, is shyness;—a word always used, I fancy, in a bad sense, to signify misplaced shame; for a person who felt only diffident, exactly in proportion as he ought, would never be called shy. But a shy person feels more shame, than it is graceful, or proper, he should feel; generally, either from ignorance or pride. A young man, in making his first entrance into society, is so ignorant as to imagine he is the object of universal attention; and that every thing he does is subject to the most rigid criticism. Of course, under such a supposition, he is shy and embarrassed: he regains his ease, as he becomes aware of his insignificance. An excessive jealousy of reputation, is the very frequent parent of shyness, and makes us all afraid of saying and doing, what we might say and do, with the utmost propriety and grace. We are afraid of hazarding any thing; and the game stands still, because no man will venture any stake: whereas, the object of living together, is not security only, but enjoyment. Both objects are promoted by a moderate dread of shame; both destroyed by that passion, when it amounts to shyness;—for a shy person not only *feels* pain, and *gives* pain; but, what is worse, he incurs blame, for a want of that rational and manly confidence, which is so useful to those who possess it, and so pleasant to those who witness it. I am severe against shyness, because it looks like a virtue without *being* a virtue; and because it gives us false notions of what the *real* virtue is. I admit that it is sometimes an affair of body, rather than of mind; that where a person wishes to say what he knows will be received with favor, he can not command himself enough to do it. But this is merely the effect of habit, where the cause that created the habit has for a moment ceased. When the feelings respecting shame are disciplined by good sense, and commerce with the world, to a fair medium, the body will soon learn to obey the decisions of the understanding.

Nor let any young man imagine (however it may flatter the vanity of those who perceive it), that there can be any thing worthy of a man, in faltering, and tripping, and stammering, and looking like a fool, and acting like a clown. A silly college pedant believes that this highest of all the virtues, consists in the shame of the body; in losing the ease and possession of a gentleman; in turning red; and tumbling down; in saying this thing, when you mean that; in overturning every body within your reach, out of pure bashfulness; and in a general stupidity and ungainliness, and confusion of limb, and thought, and motion. But that dread of shame, which virtue and wisdom teach, is, to act so, from the cradle to the tomb, that no man can cast upon you the shadow of reproach; not to swerve on this side for wealth, or on that side for favor; but to go on speaking truly, and acting justly: no man's oppressor, and no man's sycophant and slave. This is the shame of the soul; and these are the blushes of the inward man; which are worth all the distortions of the body, and all the crimson of the face.

I come now to the pain of inactivity, or *ennui*. All young animals have a great pleasure in motion; and when they have moved for a long time, they have a great pleasure in remaining at rest. In the one feeling, nature secures the activity of animals, and distinguishes them from the vegetable and the mineral kingdom; by the other, prevents that activity from destroying them. When the mind entertains no desire nor aversion strong enough to induce us to act, either with the body, or by thinking, we are *ennuied*, and in a state bordering upon the greatest misery. The solitary imprisonment recommended by Howard, has, I fancy, been given up, from its having driven several persons to insanity. The absence of desire and aversion, or which includes them both, *motive*, destroyed their reason. A man much given to speculation might have supported himself, per haps, in such a situation; or a mind fertile in inventing occupations; but it is such a strain upon human nature, that none but its choicest and strongest materials can support it Baron Trenck, in his dreadful imprisonment, took to engraving pewter pots, which, I believe, was his sole occupation before he began to contrive his escape. Count Saxe, in his solitary cell, formed a strict friendship with a large spider, provided it with flies and gnats, and every dainty that was on the wing; and had so far familiarized the creature to him, that it would crawl upon his hand with the most perfect security, and come out of its hiding-place upon a noise which the count was accustomed to make. It is added, that the jailer, when he perceived the amusement which the count derived from the spider, *killed it!*

Count Rumford availed himself, in a very ingenious manner, of the pain of *ennui*. He compelled all the new-comers in his school to sit quite idle, and do nothing. The misery they felt from remaining entirely without occupation, operated as the strongest stimulus in them, to desire work; and they received his permission to labor in the manufactory, as a liberation from the most painful feelings they had ever experienced. "I have already mentioned," says the Count, "that those children who were too young to work, were placed upon seats, built round the hall, where other children worked. This was done in order to inspire them with a desire to do that, which other children, apparently more favored, more caressed, and more praised than themselves, were permitted to do; and of which, they were obliged to be idle spectators: and this had the desired effect. As nothing is so tedious to a child as being obliged to sit still in the same place for a considerable time; and as the work which the other more favored children were engaged in was light and easy, and appeared rather amusing than otherwise (being the spinning of hemp and flax, with small light wheels, turned with the foot), these children who were obliged to be spectators of this busy and entertaining scene, became so very uneasy in their situations, and so jealous of those who were permitted to be more active, that they frequently solicited, with the greatest importunity, to be allowed to work; and often cried most heartily, if this favor was not instantly granted them. How sweet these tears were to me, can easily be imagined; and I always found that the joy they showed upon being permitted to descend from their benches, and mix with the working children below, was equal to the solicitude with which they had demanded that favor."

It is remarkable, when the body requires rest, the mind is very easily amused: after severe toil in hunting, or war, savages will remain whole days in a state of inactivity. Any thing which occupies the mind agreeably, or disagreeably, is an antidote to *ennui:* severe pain is not compatible with it. There is a story of a very respectable tradesman, who had retired from business, and who confessed to a friend of his, that the happiest month in the year to him, was the month in which his fit of the gout came on. He was so totally unable to fill up his time, that even the occupation afforded by pain was a relief to him.

There is no word in our language to signify the remembrance of evil that is past, as there is to signify the anticipation of the evil which is to come; no word contrasted to this meaning of fear: probably because the *recollection* of pain, is not very painful, as being contrasted with present ease; and because such recollection produces no events, and leads to nothing; whereas, fear—the anticipation of evil—is a very remarkable passion, and immediately leads to a state of activity. Remorse is not the recollection of any past grief, but the sensation of *present* grief, for *past* faults now irremediable.

It appears, then, from this enumeration of the ungrateful passions, which lead men to act from feelings of aversion, that they are all referable to the memory of evil, the actual sensation, the future anticipation of it, or the resentment which any one of these notions is apt to excite. The remembrance of past evils, produces melancholy: the sensation of present evils, if they be referred to the body, pain; if to the mind, grief. Envy, hatred, and malice, are all modifications of resentment, differing in the causes which have excited that resentment, as well as in the degree in which it is entertained. Shame is that particular species of grief, which proceeds from losing the esteem of our fellow-creatures; fear, the anticipation of future evils. This is the catalogue of human miseries and pains; and it is plain why they have been added to our nature. By the miseries of the body, man is controlled within his proper sphere, and learns what manner of life it was intended he should lead: fear and suspicion are given to guard him from harm: resentment, to punish those who inflict it; and by punishment, to deter them. By the pain of inactivity, we are driven to exertion;—by the dread of shame, to labor for esteem. But all these pregnant and productive feelings are poured into the heart of man, not with any thing that has the air of human moderation,—not with a measure that looks like precision and adjustment,—but wildly, lavishly, and in excess. Providence only impels: it makes us start up from the earth, and do something; but whether that something shall be good or evil, is the arduous decision which that Providence has left to us. You can not sit quietly till the torch is held up to your cottage, and the dagger to your throat: if you could, this scene of things would not long be what it now is. The solemn feeling which rises up in you at such times, is as much the work of God, as the splendor of the lightning is His work; but that feeling may degenerate into the fury of a savage, or be disciplined into the rational opposition of a wise and a good man. You *must* be affected by the distinctions of your fellow-creatures,—you can not help it; but you may envy those distinctions, or you may emulate them. The dread of shame may enervate you for every manly exertion, or be the vigilant guardian of purity and innocence. In a strong mind, fear grows up into cautious sagacity; grief, into amiable tenderness. Without the noble toil of moral education, the one is abject cowardice, the other eternal gloom; therefore, there is the good, and there is the evil! Every man's destiny is in his own hands. Nature has given us those beginnings, which are the elements of the foulest vices, and the seeds of every sweet and immortal virtue: but though Nature has given you the liberty to choose, she has terrified you by her punishments, and lured you by her rewards, to choose aright; for she has not only taken care that envy, and cowardice, and melancholy, and revenge, shall carry with them their own curse,—but she has rewarded emulation, courage, patience, cheerfulness, and dignity, with that feeling of calm pleasure, which makes it the highest act of human wisdom to labor for their attainment.

LECTURE XXII.

ON THE BENEVOLENT AFFECTIONS.

OF THE AGREEABLE AND BENEVOLENT AFFECTIONS, AND THEIR ORIGIN.—OF THE NATURAL SIGNS OF THE PASSIONS.—OF THE AFFINITY BETWEEN THE PASSIONS. — OF THE EFFECT OF CONTRARY PASSIONS ON EACH OTHER.

In my last Lecture, I treated on such of the active powers as had the evil of others for their object; or were characterized by the pain which they inflicted on him, in whose mind they were observed. I come now to an opposite set of agents,—those which have the good of others for their object, or are characterized by the pleasure which they impart to that person, in whom they are observable. I am aware this division of the principles of our nature, which lead us to action, is not perfectly accurate; but it is accurate enough for that very *general* view which I propose to take of them, and which I believe is all that *could* be tolerated in a Lecture of this nature.

The origin of these benevolent affections, I should explain exactly after the same manner as their opposite,—the malevolent feelings: the one proceed from pain, guided by association; the other, from pleasure, guided by association. To trace them up to this orgin, would be merely to repeat my last Lecture over again, with the alteration of a single word—*pleasure* for *pain;* and therefore I shall pass it over, presuming that I have sufficiently explained myself on that subject.

The pleasing and benevolent affections of our nature, may be divided into the memory of past good; the enjoyment of present good; the anticipation of future good; and benevolence, or a desire to do good to others.

The memory of past good, and the memory of past evil, are both without a specific name in our language; though it should seem, that they require one, as much as hope or fear,—to which, in point of time, they are contrasted. We all know that present happiness is very materially affected by happiness in prospect: but, perhaps, it is not enough urged as a motive for benevolence.

Mankind are always happier for having been happy; so that if you make them happy now, you make them happy twenty years hence by the memory of it. A childhood passed with a due mixture of rational indulgence, under fond and wise parents, diffuses over the whole of life, a feeling of calm pleasure; and, in extreme old age, is the very last remembrance which time can erase from the mind of man. No enjoyment, however inconsiderable, is confined to the present moment. A man is the happier for life, from having made once an agreeable tour, or lived for any length of time with pleasant people, or enjoyed any considerable interval of innocent pleasure: and it is most probably the recollection of their past pleasures, which contributes to render old men so inattentive to the scenes before them; and carries them back to a world that is past, and to scenes never to be renewed again.

The recollection of pleasures that are past, is tinged with a certain degree of melancholy,—as every survey we take of distant periods of time always is. This gives it its peculiar characteristic, and distinguishes it from the animated sensations of present enjoyment: but still, such recollections is always one of the favorite occupations of the human mind; and, to many dispositions, the most fruitful source of happiness.

In the passion of fear there is always a mixed expectation of good and evil; but the evil preponderates. When all expectation of good ceases, the feeling which takes place is that of despair. In hope, the expectation of good preponderates. But there is no name for that feeling, when all expectation of evil ceases, and the good appears certain;—this is the opposite of despair. Upon this tendency to look forward to future happiness, or back upon happiness past, is founded a very obvious distinction in human character:—contemplative men, of a poetical cast, who are always looking with a kind of fond enthusiasm upon the past, and contrasting it with the prospect which lies open before them; and bustling active men of the world, whose face is always turned the way they are going,—in whose mind the memory of the past has very little share, but who look keenly forward in the game of life, with all the eagerness of the most sanguine hope. For my part, I must confess myself rather an admirer of the active school, and no great friend to that pleasant but disqualifying melancholy, which makes a man believe he has extracted all the pleasure and enjoyment from human life, before he has passed half through it,—that no grass is green, except the grass where he played when he was a boy,—and that all the pleasures of which a man of genuine feeling and taste partakes, ought, like the wine he drinks, to be fifteen or twenty years old. So far as the contemplation of the past does not go to put us out of conceit with the future, it is wise: when it *does*, it is the idleness of genius and feeling; but it *is* idleness, and is a corruption which comes from those imperfect moralists, the poets, who are ever disposed to chant mankind out of the vigorous cheerfulness of hope, and to infuse, in its stead, a feeling of past happiness; which, however calm and beautiful it may appear, is injurious when it softens and unstrings the mind, and renders it useless for the struggles of life.

The different degrees of present enjoyment are signified by a vast variety of expressions; from complacency and satisfaction, to the most exalted rapture. The general term for the desire to do good to others, is—benevolence. The most common causes of benevolence are love, gratitude, and compassion: these are very ancient subjects, and it is not very easy to say any thing new upon them; but there is another source of benevolence, which is not so commonly adverted to, nor so frequently discussed,—I mean the benevolence excited by power, and by wealth; not proceeding from any idea of profiting by the power or wealth of others, but a disinterested, impartial admiration of power and wealth, and a high degree of benevolence excited toward the rich, the great, and the fortunate. The operations of envy are very limited; we merely envy those immediately above us,—whose advantages might possibly have been ours: but the splendor placed entirely out of our reach, we admire with the fondest enthusiasm.

"When," says Adam Smith, "we consider the condition of the great, in those delusive colors in which the imagination is apt to paint it, it seems to be almost the abstract idea of a perfect and happy state. It is the very state which, in all our waking dreams, and idle reveries, we had sketched out to ourselves, as the final object of all our desires. We feel, therefore, a peculiar sympathy with the satisfaction of those that are in it: we favor all their inclinations, and forward all their wishes. What pity, we think, that any thing should spoil and corrupt so agreeable a situation! We could even wish them immortal: and it seems hard to us, that death should, at last, put an end to such perfect enjoyment. It is cruel, we think, in Nature to compel them, from their exalted station, to that humble, but hospitable home which she has provided for all her children. Great King, live forever! is the compliment, which, after the manner of Eastern adulation, we should readily make them, if experience did not teach us its absurdity. Every calamity that befalls them, every injury that is done them, excites in the breast of the spectator, ten times more compassion and resentment than he would have felt, had the same things happened to other men. It is the misfortunes of kings only, which afford the proper subject for tragedy. They resemble, in this respect, the misfortunes of lovers. Those two situations are the chief that interest us upon the theater; because, in spite of all that reason and experience can tell us to the contrary, the prejudices of the imagination attach to these two states, a happiness superior to any other. To disturb, or put an end to, such perfect enjoyment, seems to be the most atrocious of all injuries."

Every man's experience, I should think, must have furnished him with sufficient examples of this kind of feeling;—of the examples of men who have nothing to wish, or to want; who are utterly incapable of forming a base or ungenerous sentiment; but who, with the most honest and disinterested views, are quite *enslaved* by the admiration of greatness. Their benefits can extend to a few; but their fortunes interest almost every body. We are eager to assist them in completing a system of happiness, that approaches so near to perfection; and we desire to serve them, for their own sake, without any recompense, but the honor or the vanity of obliging them.

Upon this disposition, however, to go along with the passions of the rich and powerful, is founded the distinction of ranks, and the order of society. Watched over, and kept within due bounds, it is a sentiment which leads to the most valuable and important consequences. But I hope I shall be pardoned for observing, it is a terrible corrupter of moral sentiments, when it destroys that feeling of modest independence, which is quite as necessary to the *real* welfare of society, as a wise subordination, and difference of rank.

As every thing which excites pain, is apt to excite resentment, so, every thing which excites pleasure, is apt to excite benevolence. A good countenance, or a good figure, always conciliates a considerable degree of favor;—certainly, very unjustly; because, no man makes his own figure, or his own face; and the distresses of others, or their merits, are the only legitimate objects of benevolence. The messenger of good news, is always an object of benevolence. Every one knows, that an officer who brings home the news of a victory, receives a donation in money, and is commonly knighted, or promoted. Strictly speaking, it would be just as equitable to mulct him of half a year's pay, for bringing home the news of a defeat, as it would be to present him with £500, for bringing home the news of a victory: but, if they be not *too* great, all men sympathize with the excesses of the generous and benevolent passions; while they restrain the malevolent principles within the most rigid bounds of justice. That the messenger of disastrous news should be punished, would appear to the impartial spectator, the most horrible injustice; but no one envies his reward to him who brings good intelligence, though no one pretends to say that he has deserved it. A thousand instances may be observed, where the tendency of pleasure to excite benevolence, gets the better of justice; but, because it is an excess of the right side, it is less noticed, and less blamed. A witty, agreeable man, with a good address, may be guilty, I am afraid, of innumerable faults, which a dull and awkward offender would never be able to get over. The question always is, "what he is to *us;*" not, what he *is*, in his general relations to society. If he succeed in giving pleasure, he is almost certain of exciting benevolence. For this reason it is, that the little excellences so very often beat the great; and that a person who has the dining and supping virtues, so often plays a more conspicuous part in society, than the greatest and most august of human beings. "Those amiable passions," says Adam Smith, "even when they are acknowledged to be excessive, are never regarded with aversion. There is something agreeable, even in the weakness of friendship and humanity. The too tender mother and the too indulgent father, the too generous and affectionate friend, may sometimes, perhaps, on account of the softness of their natures, be looked upon with a species of pity, in which, however, there is a mixture of love; but can never be regarded with hatred and aversion, nor even with contempt, unless by the most brutal and worthless of mankind. It is always with concern, with sympathy, and kindness, that we blame them for the extravagance of their attachment. There is a helplessness in the character of extreme humanity, which more than any thing interests our pity. There is nothing in itself, which renders it either ungraceful or disagreeable: we only regret that it is unfit for the world, because the world is unworthy of it; and because it must expose the person who is endowed with it, as a prey to the perfidy and ingratitude of insinuating falsehood, and to a thousand pains and uneasinesses which, of all men, he the least deserves to feel; and which generally, too, he is, of all men, the least capable of supporting. It is quite otherwise with hatred and resentment. Too violent a propensity to these detestable passions, renders a person the object of universal dread and abhorrence, who, like a wild beast, ought, we think, to be hunted out of all civil society."

There is a species of benevolence, which ought to have an appropriate name; because names are of immense importance in teaching virtue, and in securing it: A *love of excellence*,—a benevolence excited by all superiority in good, as envy is the *hatred* excited by that superiority;—an honest and zealous admiration of talent, and of virtue, in whatever corner and nook of the world they are to be found,—an admiration which no disparity of situation, no spirit of party, none of the hateful and disuniting feelings can extinguish. In all ages of the world, the ablest men have been the first to express their admiration of excellence; and, while they themselves were extending the triumphs of the human understanding, they have worshiped its powers in other minds, with veneration bordering upon idolatry. The best cure for envy, is, to inspire the Young, at a very early period of their lives, with the deepest respect for virtue and talent; to kindle this feeling up into a passion; to make their acknowledgment of merit a gratification of pride; the homage they pay to it, an irresistible impulse,—like that which is felt at the image of sublime beauty, or the spectacle of matchless strength.

Respect and esteem are low degrees of benevolence, excited by the severer part of the social virtues;—as, justice and integrity; or, by the prudent virtues:—as, temperance and caution. Affection is always more permanent when it happens to be mingled with respect and esteem; because the absence of respect and esteem implies disapprobation, which in time might destroy benevolence. A certain mixture of fear, is not unfavorable to affection; it must be very small; but, whether it be that we get tired with one attitude, and like to be affected in a different manner, a sprinkling of fear or resentment, upon the sweeter passions, seems to be very well relished, and perhaps serves to keep them from corrupting so soon as they otherwise would do. These are the principal observations which I have to offer on the benevolent affections, in particular. We see by them, and by what I have said on the malevolent passions, that Nature allures us to a particular system of actions, by the pleasure she has annexed to them; and deters us from the opposite system, by the pains of which it is productive. She *might* have punished alone; but she punishes and rewards *also.* As it is true that there is a grateful flavor in ripe fruit, and an enticing smell to draw us toward it, it is *as* true, and *as* notorious, that there is a real pleasure in benevolence, a charm in compassion, in candor, and every species of goodness.

We are guided in our physical aversion by nauseous and irritating tastes; and are taught as plainly to love, and to forgive, by those bitter pangs which hatred and resentment never fail to leave behind them, when they are indulged without the restraints of justice. Nothing which it is important we should do, or should avoid, is left to the determination of reason *alone*, but the object is always secured by aversion or by desire. We do not eat or drink when reason points out to us to do so, but when the feelings of nature admonish us: we are urged by an impetuous feeling to be compassionate, to resist atrocious injustice, and to do every thing which it is necessary for the well-being of society that we should do.

I shall now proceed to make some general observations on the passions and affections, whether benevolent or malevolent.

It has been supposed by some writers, that nature has appropriated some particular signs of the countenance, or gesticulations of the body, to denote some passions, and other signs for other passions: and that we are born with a knowledge of these signs; that is, that, previous to all experience, the child knows the first smile to be the sign of pleasure; and the first frown the sign of pain. This appears to me to be quite a preposterous notion. Where the acquisition of any knowledge can be explained by the usual method of experience, it is very useless, as well as pernicious, to invent new first principles to account for it. The child sees the nurse smile when she is good humored, and therefore connects together the ideas of smiling and kindness: previous to that, there is no evidence that the child connects any idea with any particular change of the countenance. And if we can suppose a child to have been so educated, that while he was corrected, the person who punished him took care to smile; and while he was praised, it was always accompanied with frowns; to such a child a frown would be the indication of benevolence,—and a smile, of resentment. But has nature made the signs of the passions steady and uniform, so that though they are not known at the birth, they are easily learned and remembered afterward? The signs of *some* passions, certainly *not*. Blushing, which we call the natural sign of shame, certainly can not exist in a negro: besides, it is a sign of *anger*, as well as shame; and of innocent bashfulness, as well as guilty shame; and of ill health, and fainting away, and a thousand other affections of mind and body: so that if you choose to say nature has given us this, as an indication to others, of what passes in our minds, it is an extremely dangerous and deceitful guide, —and as likely to put us out of the way as in it. There is some fallacy also in this, that whenever we see what we call the signs of the passions, they are accompanied with such a plain context, that their interpretation is wonderfully facilitated. The face of an angry fishwoman would indicate, I suppose, the signs of the passions; but these signs certainly borrow something of their perspicuity, from the oaths which accompany them; and something from the blows she might bestow on the object of her indignation. However, it can not be denied that nature has given some very *general* indications of the passions; and the doctrine is only ridiculous, when pushed to such extremes as some writers have carried it. If the whole body be taken in, as well as the countenance, the violent agitation of the limbs in great anger, and the perfect state of rest under the feeling of complacency and satisfaction, are, no doubt, phenomena which always follow those affections of mind: nor do I suppose there is any nation on the face of the earth, which expresses content as we express anger,—or, *vice versâ*, anger as we do content: at least, no nation, the inhabitants of which express sudden indignation by assuming a more tranquil position than before; or perfect content by every extravagance of gesture and motion. In these respects, probably, all nations are alike: but the finer signs may differ; for in grief, one muscle, or set of muscles, contracts; in displeasure, another. But it is not simply the contraction of this muscle, which is our sign of the passion; but generally, the effect which this contraction produces upon all the other features of the face: for instance, the first mark of dejection is, that it makes the eyebrows rise toward the middle of the forehead, more than toward the cheek; but the effect of this, can not possibly be the same with a fine Italian face, and with the physiognomy of a Chinese. The general effect upon the countenance, produced by the contraction of the same muscle, must be so different, that the smile of complacency of one race of men, may exactly correspond to the smile of contempt in another. Therefore, if nature has made such a language of looks, it is only vernacular in each particular country;—it is not the language of the whole world.

The doctrine of natural signs, taken thus grossly, is true; carried to any greater degree of minuteness, will be found to involve its advocates in a thousand absurdities.

There is a great affinity between all the good affections; and the same affinity between all the malevolent and painful ones. It is a common thing to become very fond of those whom we pity; approbation, long exercised toward any particular person, generates, at last, affection. So does esteem; and still more, admiration. Every body is in love with great heroes.

The pleasures of the body are favorable to all the benevolent virtues,—and its pains unfavorable. No one is so inclined to good nature, courtesy, and generosity, when cold, wet, and dirty, as after pleasant feeding, and during genial warmth. A courtier, who had a favor to ask of his master, would never choose a moment of ear-ache, or a fit of the gout, as the happiest opportunity of preferring his request. Count Rumford has been accused of being too fanciful, because he has advanced that there is a great connection between cleanliness and virtue. It is a position, certainly, very capable of being turned into ridicule; but if it be seriously examined, and if the affinity between our feelings be properly attended to, there can surely be no absurdity in conceiving that all the filth and pains of body, and little privations, to which the poor are subjected, must produce an irritation of mind, infinitely more favorable to the malevolent than to the good passions.

The inference from these facts is, that one very successful method of making people good is to make them happy; and that the most effectual preventive of punishment, and the most powerful auxiliary to moral advice, is to diffuse over their lives those feelings of comfort and ease, which have an almost mechanical influence in cherishing the social and benevolent virtues.

That virtue gives happiness, we all know; but if it be true, that happiness contributes to virtue, the principle furnishes us with some sort of excuse for the errors and excesses of able young men, at the bottom of life, fretting with impatience under their obscurity, and hatching a thousand chimeras of being neglected and overlooked by the world. The natural cure for these errors is, the sunshine of prosperity: as they get happier, they get better; and learn, from the respect which they receive from others, to respect themselves. "Whenever," says Mr. Lancaster (in his book just published), "I met with a boy particularly mischievous, I made him a monitor: I never knew this fail." The *cause* for the promotion, and the kind of encouragement it must occasion, I confess appear rather singular; but of the *effect* I have no sort of doubt.

In the same manner, the bad passions herd together; and where one exists in any strength, the others are much more likely to find an easy reception. Pain, as I have said before, produces anger; fear gives birth to cruelty; displacency is the parent of revenge: so that by gaining one good habit, we have the chance of gaining many others similar to it; and by contracting one bad one, of adding very rapidly to the stock of our imperfections.

Sometimes it happens that passions, originally different from each other, give force to each other. When we would affect any one very much by a matter of fact, of which we intend to inform him, it is a common artifice to excite his curiosity,—delay as long as possible to satisfy it,—and, by that means, raise his anxiety and impatience to the utmost, before we give him a full insight into the business. We know this curiosity will precipitate him into the passion which we propose to raise, and assist its influence upon the mind. Hope is, in itself, an agreeable passion, and allied to friendship and benevolence; yet it is able, sometimes, to increase anger, when that is the predominant passion. Nothing communicates more force to our emotions, than an opposition of contrary passions,—love and revenge; hatred and admiration; gratitude and envy.

> "Horror and doubt distract
> His troubled thoughts, and from the bottom stir
> The hell within him; for within him hell
> He brings, and round about him, nor from hell
> One step, no more than from himself, can fly
> By change of place: Now conscience wakes despair
> That slumber'd; wakes the bitter memory
> Of what he was, what is, and what must be
> Worse; of worse deeds worse sufferings must ensue,
> Sometimes toward Eden, which now in his view
> Lay pleasant, his griev'd look he fixed sad;
> Sometimes toward heaven, and the full-blazing sun,
> Which now sat high in his meridian tower:
> Then, much revolving, thus in sighs began."

In all this altercation of passions, those of an opposite nature, instead of destroying each other, appear to communicate to each other additional force; they all add to the quantity of the excitement, all violate the state of rest, and raise the mind into a state of unnatural agitation; and of such importance in our mental constitution does it seem, to overcome the state of tranquil apathy, and such is the proneness of all strong feelings, whether good or bad, that the progress from any one passion to another, seems to be quite as easy and natural, as the progress from tranquillity to passion at all. It cost

Timotheus, I dare say, a great deal of fine playing, to throw the soul of Alexander into a tumult of feeling; but that once accomplished, the bard harped him into any passion he pleased. However this be true of Timotheus and Alexander, it is certainly true of music in general. If we are stupid or indolent, we resist its powers for some time; but when the twangings, and the beatings, and the breathings once reach the heart, and set it moving with all its streams of life, the mind bounds from grief to joy, from joy to grief, without effort or pang, but seems rather to derive its keenest pleasure from the quick vicissitude of passion to which it is exposed. It is the same with acting. It is difficult to rouse the mind from an ordinary state, to a dramatic state; but that once done, we glide with ease from any passion, to one the most opposite.

All objects of sense,—every thing that we hear and see,—excite the passions in an infinitely greater degree than the same thing conceived by the description of others. This was the defense always made by the Roman Catholics, for the worship of images,—that it was difficult to keep up any fervor of devotion by a mere speculative notion. It required the forcible impression of an object of sense, to invigorate the passion, and keep it alive. This is the use of colors, in the day of battle: when the carnage becomes very dreadful, the words *duty* and *country*, and every other speculative notion that can be gathered together, are often of very cold operation;—but the actual sight of their colors in danger, will do more in an instant, than all the stimulating ideas which the whole resources of language can present to men. An appeal is made to the passions through the senses, and such appeals are always the most irresistible, particularly with the lowest class, who have fewer ideas of reflection, in comparison with their ideas of sense.

A thing, I am very sorry to say, is sometimes more pleasant because it is forbidden. This is because the love of power is excited by the prohibition;—and any one excitement always increases any other excitement. The efforts made to surmount the obstacle, rouse the spirits and enliven the passions. I forget what comedy it is in, where a lady, who is about to be married with the consent of her parents, refuses to give her hand to the husband in the usual manner, but insists upon the apparatus being provided, and that she should be stolen away, according to the strictest etiquette of clandestine marriages.

Uncertainty, has the same effect as opposition. The agitation of the thought; the quick turn which it makes, from one view to another; the variety of passions which succeed each other, according to the different views: all these produce an emotion in the mind; and this emotion transfuses itself into the predominant passion. Security, on the contrary, diminishes the passions; the mind, when left to itself, immediately languishes; and, in order to preserve its ardor, must be every moment supported by a new flow of passion.

Nothing more powerfully excites any affection, than to conceal some part of its object, by throwing it into shade; which, at the same time that it shows us enough to prepossess us in favor of the object, leaves still some work for the imagination. Besides, that obscurity is always attended with a kind of uncertainty, the effort which the fancy makes to complete the idea rouses the spirits, and gives an additional force to the passion.

> "The other shape,
> If shape it might be call'd that shape had none
> Distinguishable in member, joint, or limb,—
> Or substance might be call'd that shadow seem'd,
> For each seem'd either,—black it stood as night,
> Fierce as ten Furies, terrible as Hell,
> And shook a dreadful dart: what seem'd his head,
> The likeness of a kingly crown had on.
> . . . .
> The undaunted fiend what this might be admired;
> Admired, not fear'd: God and his Son except,
> Created thing naught valued he, nor shunn'd."

As despair and security, though contrary, produce tne same effects; so, absence is observed to have contrary effects, and, in different circumstances, either increases or diminishes our affections. Rochefoucault has remarked, that "absence destroys weak passions, but increases strong; as the wind extinguishes a candle, and blows up a fire." Long absence naturally weakens our idea, and diminishes the passion; but where the affection is so strong and lively as to support itself, the uneasiness arising from absence increases the passion, and gives it fresh force and influence. The imagination and affections have together a close union; the vivacity of the former, gives force to the latter: hence, the prospect of any pleasure with which we are acquainted, affects us more than any other pleasure which we may own to be superior, but of the nature of which we are wholly ignorant: of the one we can form a particular and determinate idea, the other we conceive under the general notion of pleasure.

When we apply ourselves to the performance of any action, or the conception of any object, to which we are not accustomed, there is a certain unpliableness in the faculties, and a difficulty in the spirits, to move in the new direction; hence, every thing that is new is most affecting, and gives us either more pleasure, or pain, than what, strictly speaking, should naturally follow from it. When it often returns upon us, the novelty wears off; the passion subsides, the hurry of the spirits is over, and we survey the object with tranquillity and ease.

Any satisfaction we have recently enjoyed, and of which the memory is fresh and perfect, operates on the will with more violence than another, of which the traces are decayed and obliterated. Contiguity in time and place, has an amazing effect upon the passions. An enormous globe of fire, which fell at Pekin, would not excite half the interest which the most trifling phenomenon could give birth to nearer home. I am persuaded many men might be picked out of the streets, who, for 1000 guineas paid down, would consent to submit to a very cruel death, in fifteen years from the time of receiving the money. This, for the main, is a wise provision of nature; for the progress of life, generally speaking, and the order of the world, depend upon an attention to present objects: but this, like every other moral provision, is given without any limit or adjustment; and it becomes the great object of wisdom and of virtue to restrain it within proper limits. By all that we can look upon an object of sense, and (admitting its capacity of affording present pleasure) steadily reckon up its influence upon future happiness; by all *that*, are we advanced in power of thought, and rectitude of action. The great labor is, to subdue the tyranny of present impression; to hold down desire and aversion, with a firm grasp, till we have time to see where they would drive us. The men who can do this, are the men who do all the praiseworthy actions that are done in the world;—who write lasting books, make treaties, lead armies, and govern kingdoms; or, if their life be private, live pleasantly and safely. Those men, on the contrary, who can acquire *no* knowledge, enjoy *no* praise, and feel *no* peaceful happiness, seem only to have lived to destroy the moral order of the world, and dishonor the works of God.

LECTURE XXIII.

ON THE PASSIONS.

EFFECTS OF PASSIONS ON THE BODY, AND OF SURPRISE ON THE PASSIONS.—OF WHAT IS SAID ABOUT RULING PASSIONS.—OF TEMPER; HUMOR; NATURE.—THE DIFFERENT DEGREES OF THE PASSIONS, AND PARTICULARLY OF THE PASSIONS IN THEIR LOW DEGREES.—HOW FAR A STATE OF PASSION IS AGREEABLE TO THE MIND.—THE EFFECTS OF PASSIONS AND TALENTS ON EACH OTHER.

THE powerful part which the passions were intended to act in our constitution, is clearly evinced by those rapid and dreadful effects which they frequently commit upon the body. Instances are very numerous of persons who have been driven mad by joy,—who have dropped down dead from anger or grief. Great numbers of people die every year, pining away from deranged circumstances, or from disgrace, or disappointed affection, in a state which we call broken-hearted. The passions kill like acute diseases, and like chronic ones too. Every physician who knows any thing of the science, has seen innumerable cases of all the disorders of the body, originating from disturbed emotion, and totally inaccessible to all the remedies by which mere animal infirmities are removed. Dr. Gregory, of Edinburgh, in his "Lectures on the Practice of Medicine," mentions so singular an instance of the effects of joy, that, but for such highly respectable authority, I should hardly think it credible. He was sent for in the course of his medical practice, to a family in the country, consisting of a mother and two daughters. They had recently come to a very large, and a very sudden accession of fortune. Upon his arrival at the house, he was met by the eldest daughter, who, with a great appearance of agitation, cautioned him against her mother and sister; and informed him they were both mad. He very soon perceived that this lady was so herself; and upon visiting the other two, perceived they were not a jot better. The truth turned out to be, that their astonishment and joy was so great, upon being raised from poverty to extreme opulence,—they had so many plans of equipage; and so many disputes whether they should go to Bath before they went to London, or London before they visited Bath,—that the small share of reason they ever could have possessed, fell a sacrifice to the agitation. Independent of the mere magnitude of the passion, a distinct effect is produced by the suddenness of it; or rather, perhaps, it would be clearer to say, that all the passions are considerably increased by surprise, and diminished by expectation. To be thoroughly informed of the nature and extent of any danger, to which we are about to be exposed,—to have leisure to summon up resolution, and invent resources,—diminishes very materially the feeling of that danger: a sudden exposure to it, might completely overset the mind. In the same manner with grief. A long struggle with death, and a finely-graduated decay, familiarize us to the loss of our friends: the countenance which grows paler day by day, and the form which every hour emaciates, inure us so to the pang of separation, that we meet with calm resignation a misfortune, which, suddenly communicated, would bear down all authority of reason, and leave, perhaps, the mind itself a mere ruin beneath its pressure. In this respect, there is a great analogy between body and mind. It is not difficult, by gradations, to accustom the body to any thing; while it receives the most violent injuries from changes that are sudden. This dread of sudden vicissitude, admits of no explanation; it is one of the means by which the powers of man are limited, and he is controlled within the sphere in which he at present moves. It is curious to observe the very little time necessary to the mind for its changes; and how short a preparation obviates the worst and most dangerous effects of the passions. To come into a room suddenly, and say such a person is dead, might very likely kill the person to whom it was addressed: but "he is not quite so well as could be wished; there is some little danger; he was getting worse," and so on;—by the presentation of a mournful idea, which the mind can bear, and by the gradual increase of it up to the point which you wish to establish, though you can never prevent the feelings of nature, you blunt them, and deter their excesses from acting so tremendously upon the infirmities of the body.

Any one passion may act upon the mind, when it is in one of these three states:—first, when it is under the influence of a similar passion; next, when it is under the influence of an opposite passion; next, when it is in a state of rest, and under the influence of no passion at all. For instance, I may receive such news as would overwhelm me with grief, and, at the moment previous to my receiving it, I may be in a state of joy, or sorrow, or in a state of indifference; the question is, in which of these three states will the new passion produce its greatest effects? Is the grief greater for being added to grief, or being contrasted to previous joy? or from its falling on the mind when it was in a passionless state? If the two states of grief and joy can not cöexist, so that they neutralize each other, then the grief is always more intense from the contrast. If a father were to learn that his son had distinguished himself very much in battle, and were then to be told, in the midst of his joy, that his son had died of his wounds, the joy and the grief stand so opposed to each other, that the one would go rather to inflame, than to diminish the other. "Dead at the very moment that I expected to see him return with the highest reputation! in the midst of all the congratulations I was making to myself for his safety!"—these are the ideas with which a parent would naturally exasperate his misfortune. But if the joy and the grief were in no wise related together, then the joyful passion would neutralize the sad one. To hear that my fortune was materially diminished, would affect me less, if I had just recovered my health, or had just gained a distinguished reputation. I should set off the good against the evil, and bring my mind to a kind of equilibrium of feeling and passion.

Some men possess a much stronger tendency to particular passions than to others,—and passions, like talents, are transmitted by birth from parent to child: some say, *acquired* by early imitation; but the analogy of animals rather leads us to suppose that birth influences the qualities of the mind, as well as the limbs and general figure. All the foals of an ill-tempered horse are very often as vicious as the sire, whom they have never seen. Cock-fighters are extremely attentive to the breed of their fowls: a valiant cock has his eggs sent about as presents, that they may be hatched into heroes; and these heroes have certainly had no communication with their parents, and no opportunity of forming their manners upon such models of valor.

It is very often (not *always*) true, that there is a ruling passion which obscures or absorbs all the rest. In some minds, two or three of the great passions appear to hold a divided empire. In others, there is such a want of prominence in the active principles, that it is extremely difficult to say which governs,—which obeys. It is, however, an extremely important circumstance in the investigation of character, to ascertain what are the paramount motives, by which any human being is habitually impelled; and the most complicated phenomena, after such a key to their interpretation is once obtained, become clear and comprehensible. We speak of a man's disposition according to the predominance of good or bad passions in his nature.

There are three expressions in our language, which, because they refer to the kind and degree of the passions, require some explanation in this place;—Temper, Humor, and Nature. When used with adjectives of blame and praise, temper and humor mean nearly the same thing. A good-humored person, or a good-tempered person, is one in whom the intentions and actions of others do not easily excite bad passions,—who does not mistake the motives by which the rest of the world are actuated toward him. A good-natured person is a man of active benevolence; who seeks to give pleasure to others in little things. Good-temper measures how a man is acted upon by others: good-nature measures how he acts for others. The presumption is, that the two excellences would be found uniformly conjoined together; that a man who was passively benevolent, would be actively so too: but the reverse is often the case in practice. There many men of inviolable temper, who never exert themselves to do a good-natured thing, from one end of the year to the other; and many in the highest degree irritable, who are perpetually employed in little acts of good-nature. It must be observed, that all the three words refer only to the little vices and virtues. Repeated fits of peevishness, constitute ill-temper. Violent hatred, and deadly revenge, require and receive a much graver name. To do little favors to others, and contrive small gratifications and amusements for them, is the province of a good-natured man. A more exalted and difficult benevolence immediately assumes a more dignified appellation, and ceases to be called good-nature. To bring a large twelfth-cake to a child, is good-nature; to give him education, support, and protection, though he have no natural claim upon you, is compassion, and the summit of good feeling.

Of all the affections, there are various degrees. There is that degree in which it is scarcely perceptible; there is that calm state of the affection, where it leaves the reason unbiased; and there is that last, and most violent degree of it, which assumes the name of passion. This is quite as true of the malevolent, as of the benevolent affections. Resentment may be calm, or it may be furious. There is a silent apprehension, and a fear exhibiting itself in the most acute paroxysms. Now, it seems evident that *reason*, in a strict sense (meaning by that term the judgment of truth and falsehood), can never be any motive to the will, and can have no influence, but so far as it touches some passion or affection. What is commonly, and in a popular sense, called *reason*, and is so much recommended in moral discourses, is nothing but a general and calm passion, which takes a comprehensive and distant view of its object, and actuates the will, without exciting any sensible emotion. A man, we say, is diligent from reason; that is, from a calm desire of riches and fortune. A man adheres to justice from *reason;* that is, from a calm regard to public good, and to a character with himself and others. For observe all that reason can do; reason only enables us to judge of propositions. This man is miserable; this man is going on in a way which will terminate in his complete ruin; by a prudent set of measures, I will save and convert him. By your reason you prognosticate his future good; but the *motive* which induces you to plan his extrication, has nothing to do with reason. If God have not planted the benevolent passions in your heart, you may go on reasoning and anticipating to all eternity, without the slightest disposition to *act.* All motives come from the passions; all means and instruments, from reason.

The same objects which recommend themselves to reason, in this sense of the word, are also the objects of passion when they are nearer to us; and acquire some other advantage, either of external situation, or congruity to our internal temper. Evil near at hand produces aversion, and is the object of passion; at a great distance, we say it is avoided from reason. The common error of metaphysicians has been in ascribing the direction of the will entirely to one of those principles, and supposing the other to have no influence. In general, we may observe that both these principles operate on the will; and what we call strength of mind, implies the prevalence of the calm passions above the violent; though we may easily observe that there is no person so constantly possessed of this virtue, as never on any occasion to yield to the solicitations of violent desire and affection: and from these variations of temper, proceed the great difficulty of deciding with regard to the future actions and resolutions of men, where there is any contrariety of motives and passions.

Without some calm passion,—some degree of some species of desire,—the mind could not long endure. Such a state is probably the state of fatuity, or idiotism. A man in such a condition, would stop in the middle of a street, and remain there all his life. Some degree of passion, therefore, is not only pleasing, but necessary. Whenever this stimulus of passion does not exist in due proportion, we feel *ennui:* when there is a just degree of passion, and that passion directs us to objects easily attainable, we feel contented,—for content is not the absence of calm passion, but the constant facility of *gratifying* it without too much difficulty, and without subsequent inconvenience. Not only is a state of calm passion pleasant, but a state of violent emotion appears to have its allurements. Young persons love danger for danger's sake. School-boys climb walls and trees because it is agreeable to them to be afraid of tumbling;—and this explains the pleasure of mischief. A school-boy flings a stone into a window, and, running to some distance, stops to enjoy the violent rage of the person whose window has been broken: the moderate risk he runs, is a very pleasant excitement to him. Nay, he will tie a rope across a place where he knows people are to pass, even where he can not wait to see them tumble: the mere imagination of so much terror and confusion, fills him with pleasant feelings, and he is convulsed with laughter at the very thoughts of it.

Young men turn soldiers and sailors from the love of being agitated; and for the same reason, country gentlemen leap over stone walls. This—and not avarice—is the explanation of gaming. Men who game, are, in general, very little addicted to avarice; but they court the conflict of passions which gaming produces, and which guards them from the dullness and *ennui* to which they would otherwise feel themselves exposed. The love of emotion is the foundation of tragedy; and so pleasant is it to be moved, that we set off for the express purpose of looking excessively dismal for two hours and a half, interspersed with long intervals of positive sobbing. The taste for emotion may, however, become a dangerous taste; and we should be very cautious how we attempt to squeeze out of human life, more ecstasy and paroxysm than it can well afford. It throws an air of insipidity over the greater part of our being, and lavishes on a few favored moments the joy which was given to season our whole existence. It is to act like school-boys,—to pick the plums and sweetmeats out of the cake, and quarrel with the insipidity of the batter:

whereas the business is, to infuse a certain share of flavor throughout the whole of the mass; and not so to habituate ourselves to strong impulse and extraordinary feeling, that the common tenor of human affairs should appear to us incapable of amusement, and devoid of interest. The only safe method of indulging this taste for emotion, is by seeking for its gratification, not in passion, but in science, and all the pleasures of the understanding; by mastering some new difficulty; by seeing some new field of speculation open itself before us; by learning the creations, the divisions, the connections, the designs, and contrivances of nature. If we seek relief from the lassitude of common thoughts and common things, these are the only emotions which at once are innocent, inexhaustible, and sublime.

It is impossible not to suppose that there is a considerable degree of connection between the intellectual, and active powers; that talents must produce a striking influence upon affections, and affections upon talents. The extremes are very easily perceived; there is a degree of energy in the active powers, utterly incompatible with any exercise of the understanding at all. In paroxysms of rage and grief, not only the arrangement of ideas, but even the utterance of *words*, becomes quite impossible: and on the opposite side, it can not be conceived how the understanding comes to act at *all;* how it does any thing more than merely perceive, without the influence of some desire or affection; however low and however calm that degree may be. The influence of passion upon the understanding, will, of course, be very different, according to the different parts of the understanding to which it is applied. To all efforts of the imagination, a certain degree of passion appears highly favorable;—anger quickens wit, multiplies images and words, and gives a flow and a fecundity, of which the mind is utterly destitute in its ordinary state. Every man is eloquent in speaking of himself, from the direct influence which his passions have upon his imagination. The finest and most affecting parts of Cicero, are always about himself; every passion of his great mind, seems to be at work, in that noble conclusion of the second philippic, which afterward cost him his life. "But do you, Antony," he says, "look to yourself; and I will confess what are my principles: I have defended the republic when I was young, I will not desert it now I am old: I have despised the sword of Catiline, and the sword of Antony shall not alarm me. Most willingly would I sacrifice this body, if, by my death, the liberty of Rome could be established. Did not I say twenty years ago, in this very senate, that when a man perished who had reached the dignity of consul, he could not be said to have perished prematurely? And do you think, now that old age is come upon me, I will retract or deny this doctrine? Conscript fathers, I wish for death; I have gained all that the republic can bestow; I have performed all that it can require! Let death come when it will, I am prepared to meet it. I have only two things to implore: first, that my country may deal out to all her children the punishment or the reward they merit; next, that when I do die, I may leave the Romans free. If the Gods grant me this, there is nothing else which they can bestow."

No one could say of Mr. Burke, that he did not write with passion; and whenever his passions are awakened, his imagination appears to be fecundated: he is metaphorical at all times; but when he feels strongly, every thing is simile, allusion, and metaphor; and these are poured out, in a manner quite natural; as if the habitual effect of passion in him, were, to conjure up all this splendid imagery, and to give unusual promptitude to the current of his ideas.

But, though passion always comes in aid of a fine imagination, it very often happens that we meet with imagination without passion or feeling,—and feeling and passion without imagination.

There is a beautiful passage in the book of Ruth, which, though full of feeling, has no imagination. "And Ruth said to her mother, Naomi, Entreat me not to leave thee: for whither thou goest, I will go; and where thou lodgest, I will lodge; thy people shall be my people, and thy God shall be my God: where thou diest I will die, and there will I be buried: the Lord do so to me, and more also, if aught but death part thee and me!" Nothing can be more beautiful, but there is no imagination in it. If Cowley, or any of the poets of Cowley's school, had had to express the same degree of affection, he would most probably have found several reasons why the affection of Ruth for Naomi resembled lightning, smoke, air, fire, water, and clouds; what properties it had in common with the shooting of a meteor; and in what way it might be compared both to morning and evening, and the middle of the day: in short, he would have displayed a great deal of imagination totally barren of all passion.

To inventive reasoning, the passions are very favorable. The resources which men exhibit in shipwrecks, and on desert islands, are perfectly astonishing. In the attempt to escape from prison, as much has been done with a rusty nail, as the best artisan could hardly have effected with the best tools, in any ordinary state of excitement of mind. In short, the process of invention in reasoning, is exactly the same as the process of invention in poetry. In passion, the mind dwells intensely on one object; all the ideas related to it, occur from association; and we seize upon the epithet, the argument, or the mechanical invention, which we judge the best. Passion aids the understanding, by multiplying the associations. It was precisely the same effect which passion produced, that aided Cicero when he attacked Antony; Archimedes, when he defended Syracuse; and Baron Trenck, when he broke out of prison. It may be doubted, whether quick and strong passions are not inimical to those circumspect habits of mind, which are necessary to a good taste; for I should conceive that, in the acquirement of a fine taste, first emotions must be very often checked, and the mind kept in a state of suspense, till the relation of each part to the whole has been examined, and the effect of surprise properly allowed for.

There is a state of mind, however, in which it is as important to keep a crowd of ideas out of the mind, as it is at others to excite them; and, at such periods, the presence of any lively passion must be detrimental. When we wish to fix the attention upon one object, to ascertain all its properties, and the relations it bears to some other object, nothing can be more unfavorable to such habits of accurate observation, than that crowd of slightly related ideas, with which the passions are apt to people the understanding.

With respect to the general connection between passions and talents, no rule can be laid down, by which the existence of the one is with any certainty inferred from the existence of the other. Great passions may coexist with a very low state of talent; and great talents with a very low state of passion. Nor does it by any means appear, that the cold-blooded race of men, are intended to act a less conspicuous part on the theater of the world, than those whose passions are the most acute, and the most irritable. The liberty of Europe, is at present threatened by a man of the most impetuous passions; the independence of America, was established by a man who certainly had his passions in the most perfect command. Alexander was a madman; Augustus, calm and artful. When we compare together the retarding, and the impelling part of the machinery, it would be crude and hasty language, to give one any preference over the other. If there be any man, who has great passions which he can command, and obey, according to circumstances, such a man must in the end be greater than all others of equal talents.

The passions, I have before stated to be affected by every circumstance which affects the body; as age, health, climate, and race: they are affected by government, by rank, by sex, by education, by the degree of refinement of the age, by solitude, by society, and by habit. In fact, the passions are acted upon by every outward and inward circumstance; but these are the principal. It is very easy to conceive, that governments absolutely under the control of the people, and absolutely under the control of one person, must have a strong tendency to encourage different passions: that the same circumstance must be true of commercial, and of military nations; that where the youth of any country hear nothing spoken of, at their first coming into life, but the acquisition of property, and perceive that every one increases in estimation as he advances in opulence, it is highly probable that the active principles by which he will be controlled, will be of a very different nature from what they would have been, if he had been nursed in the tumult and glory of arms. Civilization must have a prodigious effect upon the passions; it must supersede the necessity of revenge, by strengthening the power of law; whereas, in barbarous times, a man has only his own malevolent passions to trust to for protection. Courtesy, and the appearance of benevolence, are fashionable; reputation becomes valuable, and a certain degree of good faith is more generally diffused.

The most considerable difference between the active powers of the sexes, is, that women are more generally under the influence of fear; and they rather avoid shame, than seek glory. They are probably, also, more under the influence of the benevolent feelings than men, because, in the distribution of duties, a great number of benevolent offices devolve upon them; and because they are exempted from all those which require an immediate exertion of the malevolent passions, or at least a *suppression* of the benevolent ones. It is the duty of men to cut off limbs, hang criminals, and massacre the enemies of their country, whenever they are able: they are soldiers, judges, and physicians:—women are carefully protected from every situation which requires the sacrifice of a single instant of benevolence. Speaking very generally and grossly, the effect of solitude is to cherish great virtues, and to destroy little ones. "Society," says Adam Smith, "is the best preservative of that equal and happy temper, which is so necessary to self-satisfaction and enjoyment: men of retirement and speculation, who are apt to sit brooding at home over either grief or resentment, though they may often have more humanity, more generosity, and a nicer sense of honor, yet seldom possess that equality of temper which is so common among men of the world."

The difference of the passions, and the different proportions in which the same passions are measured out to different individuals, form the leading and most prominent diversities in human character. Men differ from each other very materially, as their desires are negative or positive ;—as they wish to obtain praise, or to avoid blame. In the first class are the vain, the ambitious, and the active part of the human race: the last contains men of reserve, of humility, and of caution; who, provided they do not incur ridicule and disgrace, are well contented to leave to others the contest for distinction.

Men differ, as their desires are vehement or weak. Some can hardly be said to have any desires at all; others would overturn kingdoms, and mingle heaven with earth, to effect the least of all their desires.

Another variety in human character is, the length or continuation of desire, which, united with vehemence of desire, makes, I believe, what we call strength of character; for we could not deny to any man that attribute, who wished any thing vehemently, and continued in the pursuit of it steadily; at least, if it was his *habit* to feel and act after this manner. Then again, we may observe a striking dissimilarity among men, as they are governed by near or distant motives; or, in other words, as they are under the influence of calm, or strong passions. We distinguish, also, between warm and cold dispositions, that is, between different *degrees* of the benevolent feelings,—as we do between different degrees of irascibility, in the epithets *irritable* and *patient.* Some men are extremely benevolent in little things, and distinguish themselves by their politeness; others have the great virtues, and not the lesser ones.

A disposition to fear, or to hope, makes two different classes of men; so does the place, or degree, in which a man puts himself, with regard to his fellow-creatures. It has often been said, that, where the passions are the most difficult to be roused, they are the most terrible when they *are* roused. It is most probable that this opinion is not quite *so* true as it is supposed to be, from the deception which, in this case, must necessarily be exercised upon the imagination by the contrast. Whoever were to see a beautiful young lady in a violent rage, would be apt to think it much more excessive and violent, from the mere novelty and surprise of the thing, than if he had beheld a captain of a man-of-war in a similar situation of mind. Again, it must be remembered, that the causes which throw a person of a mild disposition into a fit of rage, must be very strong, to commit such an outrage upon the customary habits of his nature; whereas, an equal degree of indignation may easily be produced in a more irritable disposition, by a cause less grave and important. But, the degree of provocation being given, and the effects of novelty allowed for, it is not easy to see, why the passions of a phlegmatic man, once roused, should be stronger and more difficult to be allayed than those of one more accustomed to passion. One solution, indeed, there is, which has some appearance of plausibility. Men accustomed, for instance, to anger, may often have suffered from anger; though unable to check the passion entirely, they have learned a certain degree of control over its wildest excesses, and are not, at those moments, quite so unable to govern themselves as they appear to be: but, where passion is new, it is unsuspected, unaccustomed to any check, and much more likely to hurry on to excesses, because its excesses are not feared, and hardly known. There is a certain analogy to this in drunkenness. Professed regular drunkards preserve a certain glimmering of reason, and are seldom very extravagant in their behavior: drunkenness in a person unaccustomed to it is often perfect madness.

Such are a few of the most striking phenomena of the passions, which move the world, and make up the secret life and inward existence of man; for what we do see and know with certainty of any human creature, is, whether he is lodged in marble or in clay,—whether down or straw is his bed,—whether he is clothed in the purple of the world, or molders in rags. The inward world, the man within the breast, the dominion of thought, the region of passion,—all this we can not penetrate: we can never tell how a kind and benevolent heart can cheer a desperate fortune; the comfort which the lowest man may feel in a spotless mind,—the firmness which a man derives from loving justice,—the glory with which he rebukes the bad emotion, and bids his passions be still. Therefore, not to the accidents of life, but to the fountains of thought, and to the springs of pleasure and pain, should the efforts of man be directed to rear up such sentiments as shall guard us from the pangs of envy; to make us rejoice in the happiness of every sentient being; to feel too happy ourselves for hatred and resentment; to forget the body, or to enslave it forever; seeking to purify, to exalt, and to refine our nature. This is the rigid discipline of moral philosophy, which, rigid as it is, is so beautiful and so good, that without it no condition of life is tolerable; with it, none wretched, sordid, or mean.

LECTURE XXIV.

ON THE DESIRES.

Dr. Reid, in his essay upon the Active Powers, remarks of our desires, that they have, all of them, things, *not* persons, for their object. They neither imply any good nor ill affection towards any person, nor even toward ourselves. They can not, therefore, with propriety be called either selfish or social. But there are various principles of actions in men, which have persons for their immediate objects, and imply, in their very nature, our being well or ill affected to some person, or at least to some animated being. "Such principles," says Dr. Reid, "I call by the general name of affections; whether they dispose us to do good or hurt to others." This method, by which passions are referred to persons, and desires to things, has been also adopted by Mr. Dugald Stewart, in his "Outlines of Moral Philosophy," without any alteration. But if desire concern only things, why is the love of esteem classed among the desires? for that, surely, respects persons; and why are joy and grief classed among the passions without any limitation? for grief may be occasioned by the loss of £20,000., as by the loss of an aunt or a cousin. There is a grief occasioned by persons, and a grief occasioned by things; but both Dr. Reid and Mr. Stewart would not scruple to call grief—let its cause be what it would—by the name of passion. The first object, surely, in all investigations of this nature, is to ascertain in what sense such words are actually used: and then, after showing that such uses are unsatisfactory or vague, to propose that deviation from the established meaning, which, being the most useful, is the least violent. In chemistry, mineralogy, or any science remote from common life, the popular language which respects them, is commonly not only useless, but it conduces to error; and is better kept out of view: but in the language of feeling, words are of great importance, because every man feels they are the repositories of human judgments, upon a subject on which all men are, more or less, calculated to judge. It will appear, I believe, that, in all this business of feeling, there are three things which have particularly attracted our notice:—the violent perturbation or derangement the mind suffers; the wish to do something, or obtain something, with which that perturbation is accompanied; and the cause from which that perturbation is derived.

> "Achilles heard: with grief and rage opprest,
> His heart swell'd high, and labor'd in his breast;
> Distracting thoughts by turns his bosom ruled,
> Now fired by wrath, and now by reason cool'd:
> That prompts his hand to draw the deadly sword,
> Force through the Greeks, and pierce their haughty lord;
> This whispers soft, his vengeance to control,
> And calm the rising tempest of the soul."

In this, and in every other picture of extreme passion, it is to the perturbation itself, its causes, and its consequences, that we direct our inquiry. Whenever the emotion proceeds from a bodily cause, and is accompanied with a wish to act, or to obtain, we give to that emotion the name of appetite;—as in the instance of hunger and thirst. Here the mind is thrown into a state of emotion,—the body is the cause of that emotion; and it is accompanied by a wish to obtain, and to act. No one would now call hunger and thirst, passions; or imagine that the celebrated authoress of the Plays on the Passions, is bound, in the prosecution of her task, to bring forward a hero who has not eaten any thing for forty-eight hours, and to conclude such a play with the catastrophe of a dinner or a supper.

We say a *desire* for food, as well as an *appetite* for food; but in speaking of *the desires*, and *the appetites*, we should hardly class together the desire of knowledge, and the desire of drink. It seems generally agreed, where any kind of precision is required, to call the bodily emotions by the name of appetites; and the mental ones, by those of passion or desire.

When the cause, then, of the emotion is the body,—and when it is accompanied with an active tendency, it is called appetite; when it is *not*, it receives simply the name of bodily pain or pleasure. We may say metaphorically, that gout, rheumatism, and lumbago, are the unpleasant passions of the body; that warmth and repletion are its agreeable passions.

Whenever we see any emotion of the mind which has not the body for its cause, we call it desire, if it lead to action;—passion, if it do not. No one calls grief and joy, hope and fear, by the name of desire. To suffer from the desire of grief, is nonsense; to suffer from the passion of grief, is the customary phrase. They are not called desires, because they are not the immediate causes of action. We say the desire of knowledge, the desire of esteem, the desire of power, because they are emotions leading immediately to action. Some emotions we call indiscriminately by the name of passion or desire: but this exactly confirms what I say; for when we speak of the passion of revenge, we are more particularly thinking of the perturbation the mind endures; when we speak of revenge as a desire, we have in mind the tendency to action which it occasions: therefore, if I am right, the idea of referring desires to things, and passions to persons, is quite unfounded; and this will turn out to be somewhere near their meaning.

Appetites are emotions of mind, proceeding from a bodily cause, and leading immediately to action: there are also animal pains and pleasures, which are emotions of the mind proceeding from a bodily cause, and not leading immediately to action.—Passions are emotions of the mind, not proceeding from a bodily cause, and not leading immediately to action.—Desires are emotions of the mind not proceeding from a bodily cause, and leading to action.—And lastly, whenever we use the two words, *desire* and *passion*, for the same affection of mind, it is because in the one, we consider what the mind endures from the emotion; in the other, how it is impelled to *act* by the emotion.

I am aware it would be very curious, as well as very useful, here to consider how far the same divisions and distinctions obtain in other languages, which are adopted in our own: it would not be very difficult to do it, but it would necessarily lead to long verbal discussions, which might be very agreeable to two or three persons, and very tiresome to every one beside.

I have already classed those emotions of the neutral class, which are called either desires or passions, among the latter; because I found them so classed, and because it did not then occur to me, what was the distinguishing circumstance between the passions and desires. The desires, of which I shall treat at present, are, the desire of knowledge, the desire of esteem, the desire of power, the desire of possession, and the desire of activity: not that these are the only desires which possess the mind, but that almost all the lesser motives are immediately resolvable into them. Let every man consider the innumerable principles of action by which he is every day impelled, and he will very soon discover that these desires are the origin of them all. You take a walk; that is, you are under the influence of that principle of nature, which makes continued rest painful to you; or you go to call upon some one, who will make you more rich, or more powerful; or you go to a tailor, who will make you more respectable in your appearance. These great operating principles are broken down into innumerable divisions and subdivisions; but there are very few of our actions which can not be traced to their source. The ten thousand minute things which we all perform every day, all proceed, directly or indirectly, from the great principles which I have enumerated. Look at the bustle of Bond street; drive from thence to the Royal Exchange; observe the infinite variety of occupations, movements, and agitations, as you go along: nothing can appear more intricate,—more impossible to be reduced to any thing like rule or system; and yet a very few elements put all this mass of human beings into action. If a messenger from heaven were on a sudden to annihilate the love of power, the love of wealth, and the love of esteem, in the human heart; in half an hour's time the streets would be as empty, and as silent, as they are in the middle of the night. I take it to be a consequence of civilization, that all the feelings of mind which proceed from the body excite little sympathy, in comparison with those which have not a bodily origin. The loss of a leg and an arm is a dreadful misfortune; but the slightest disgrace would be considered as a much greater. To be laid up seven months in the gout every year is a piteous state of existence; to lose a brother or a sister is a state of existence, in common estimation, still more miserable. The slightest pang of jealousy, or wounded pride, may be brought upon the stage; but the most intense pain of body, introduced into a play, would excite laughter rather than compassion. Who would endure a tragedy, where the whole distress turned upon a fit of the palsy, or a smart rheumatic fever? Nothing could be more exquisitely ridiculous! The fact is, as a nation advances in the useful arts, all bodily evils are so much mitigated, and guarded against, that they cease to excite that sympathy which they formerly did, because they are less generally felt.

How ridiculous, as I before remarked, a play would be, of which a hungry man were the hero! Why?—because we never suffer from extreme hunger, and have very little sympathy for it; there is hardly any such thing known in civilized society: the author himself would, probably, be the only man in the whole playhouse, who had ever seriously felt the want of a dinner. But if a nation of savages were to see such a drama acted, they would see no ridicule in it at all; because starving to death is, among them, no uncommon thing: they are advanced such a little way in civilization, that to fill their stomachs, is the great and important object of life: and I have no doubt, that to an Indian audience, the loss of a piece of venison might be the basis of a tragedy which would fill every eye with tears; but, on the contrary, they might be very likely to laugh, to hear a man complain of his wounded honor, if it turned out that he had ten days' provision beforehand in his cabin. In the same manner, the loss of a leg is the consummation of all evil, where there is nothing but body; but it becomes an evil of the lowest order, where there remain behind the pleasures of imagination, of elegant learning, of the fine arts, of all the luxuries and glories of civilization,—the tendency of which is always to put down and vilify every thing which belongs to the body, and to exalt all the feelings in which the mind alone is concerned. In some of the Greek tragedies, there is an attempt to excite compassion by the representation of the agonies of bodily pain. Philoctetes cries out and faints from the extremity of his suffering, exclaiming upon the stage, "Oh, Jupiter! my leg, my leg!" Hyppolitus and Hercules are both introduced as expiring under the severest torments. These attempts to excite compassion by the representation of bodily pain, are certainly among the greatest breaches of decorum, of which the Greek theater has set the example; and afford a strong suspicion that their audience was less elegant and refined than that which presides over our modern theaters. And the reason why such sort of appeals to the passions would not now be tolerated, is, not so much on account of the pain they would excite (because, the sufferings of the mind excite pain), but because *bodily* pain is a dull, stupid, unvarying, uninteresting spectacle, in comparison with all those critical and delicate emotions of mind, which are universally felt in a state of civilization,—and in that state alone. Dr. Adam Smith seems to imagine that our disregard of the bodily appetites and passions, can be accounted for on general principles. "Such is our aversion," he says, "for all the appetites which take their origin from the body: all strong expressions of them are lothsome and disagreeable. According to some ancient philosophers, these are the passions which we share in common with the brutes, and which, having no connection with the characteristical qualities of human nature, are upon that account beneath its dignity. But there are many other passions which we share in common with the brutes, such as resentment, natural affection, even gratitude, which do not, upon that account, appear to be so brutal. The true cause of the peculiar disgust which we conceive for the appetites of the body, when we see them in other men, is, that we can not enter into them. To the person himself who feels them, as soon as they are gratified, the object that excited them ceases to be agreeable : even its presence often becomes offensive to him; he looks round to no purpose for the charm which transported him the moment before; and he can now as little enter into his own passion as another person."*

I can not think this explanation to be just; but it seems to me, that all the pains and pleasures of the body are degraded, and put down, by the greater pains and pleasures of the mind introduced by civilization.

Having premised these observations, I proceed to consider the desire of knowledge itself.

A child loves novelty, because the excitement which it occasions is agreeable: he does not consider whether the novelties which attract his attention are useful or not; but he merely loves them because they *are* new. It is from this passion that he becomes so rapidly acquainted with the properties of matter. In what we call his idlest moments, he is making himself acquainted with the qualities of objects, and the powers of his own body;—is wax soft? is iron hard? is wood fit to eat? how high can I jump? what can I carry? and such like questions, which may be called the grammar of existence, a child is perpetually resolving, under the influence of novelty. The desire of knowledge is this same principle, guided by utility; for no person, I believe, is said to acquire knowledge, who merely acquires new truths, but only he who acquires new useful truths. It would not be impossible to ascertain how many persons there are in Great Britain whose names begin with an S. A person who ascertained this, would acquire new truths; but we should hardly say he was influenced by a desire of knowledge.

The love of knowledge is, perhaps, very seldom genuine: it is not loved for the direct pleasure it affords, but to avoid disgrace; or to obtain money, or fame, or

* Dr. Adam Smith's "Moral Sentiments," part i. p. 46.

power; or for the pleasure of communicating it. There are, I fancy, very few of those who love knowledge the best, that would pursue it with any great degree of ardor, if they were so completely excluded from society, as to render it impossible that they should communicate with mankind, either in person, or by their works. The fact is, that to seek for those novelties which are hidden in history, or in science,—to wait for our gratifications so long, and to withstand so many present impulses of sense, as every lover of knowledge must do,—is no very easy thing. It requires all these auxiliary passions to help it out. It rewards so much, that it ought to be rewarded; it confers so much honor, that it ought to be honored; it communicates so much pleasure, that it ought to be pleased; it is so immensely valuable to mankind, that no motive which gives it birth can be a bad one. The best, however, of all motives is (as Lord Bacon has told us), that we may employ the gift of reason, given us by God, to the use and advantage of man. The love of knowledge, merely for its own sake, and without any reference to its utility, is a passion quite similar to that which is felt by a child;—a desire to procure excitement from novelty and surprise. The immediate and instant pleasure derived from reading an ingenious problem in Euclid, is not different from that which a child would feel at the sight of a new toy; but a man before he sets about gratifying this passion for novelty, satisfies himself that the novelties which he is seeking, are useful. So that the love of knowledge is very often a mere secondary passion; and it proceeds from the love of that fortune and fame, which is the consequence of knowledge; or, when it seems more original, it may be resolved into the love of emotion or novelty.

But though, in common, the love of knowledge is solvable into some other passion at its origin, and before it is formed by association, yet there are some very remarkable instances of the pure love of knowledge, where it is not easy to ascribe its existence to any other cause. Such appears to have been the case with James Ferguson, the philosopher and the mechanic. He was born in Scotland, of the poorest parents; and his love of knowledge began to exert itself at the earliest age. He learned to read from hearing his father teach his brother: and had made that acquisition before any one suspected it in the slightest degree. He made a prodigious advance in mechanics while he was a farmer's boy, without any instructor, or the help of any one book. Of an evening after he had brought home the sheep, he employed himself in contemplating the stars; and began the study of astronomy, by laying down, from his own observation only, a celestial globe: in these observations and occupations he was discovered, and introduced to public notice.

The famous Buxton had not the slightest recollection when his passion for numbers began. His attention was, from the earliest times of his life, so constantly fixed upon arithmetic, that he frequently, when a child, took no cognizance of external objects; and when he did, it was only of their numbers. If any space of time was mentioned, he immediately reduced it to seconds; if any person mentioned that he had been traveling so many miles, Buxton told him the number of hair's-breadths he had been over. At church, he found it quite impossible to attend to the meaning of what the clergyman said, but he knew exactly of how many words, syllables, and letters, the sermon consisted. It is very difficult to ascribe such instances as these to any other cause than the mere love of knowledge itself; but in general, it is the instrument of some other desire at first, —till at last, by the customary process of association, it becomes to be loved on its own account. The desire of knowledge in any people begins from the love of novelty, is cherished by the love of utility, and then principally encouraged by the fame and distinction to which it leads. Curiosity would be the first motive in a savage, to examine the arms and instruments of Europeans; a consciousness of their utility would increase this desire; and, in process of time, the distinctions obtained by inventors and improvers of these things, would be the most customary incitement to the cultivation of knowledge. Nothing can be more important to the welfare of a community, than the wide extension of rational curiosity in the desire of knowledge; it not only increases the comforts, enlivens the feelings, and improves the faculties of man, but it forms the firmest barrier against the love of pleasure, and stops the progress of corruption. Every nation has its chances for happiness increased, in proportion as it honors and rewards a spirit which, above all things, honors and rewards it.

The strongest of all our desires, seems to be the desire of esteem. It is the cause of innumerable other desires: it is the frequent cause (as I have before said) of the love of knowledge: it is the cause, very often, of the love of wealth; for no man, I presume, who lived in a desert, and moved about without a single soul to look at him, would care what sort of a coat he wore, provided he was kept from the cold; or whether he eat out of earthenware, or silver, provided his meat was kept out of the dirt. In the same way, the love of power may be traced to it; not but that there exists a love of power, quite independent of it,—but that men very often love power, only for the additional esteem they gain from it among their fellow-creatures. The love of life perpetually gives way to the love of esteem; men are shot, and hacked to pieces, from the hope of gaining esteem, or the fear of losing it. Upon this subject of the desire of esteem, there are two opinions which require consideration; the one of Dr. Adam Smith, the other of Mr. Hume. "We are not content," says the former of these writers, "with praise, unless we deserve it; nor are we content with deserving it, unless we obtain it." It is probable, therefore, that there are two original principles in the human mind: the one, the love of praise; the other, the love of praiseworthiness. In the same manner, we are not easy when we are blamed, even though we deserve it; nor are we easy to deserve it, even though we are not blamed: therefore, here the double principle is observable,—first, the dread of blame; next, the dread of blameworthiness. The opinion of Mr. Hume is, that there is no love of the esteem of others, except as that esteem enables us to esteem ourselves; that the thing wanted is self-approbation; and the praise of others is only important as it is a means of gratifying this feeling.

In the first place, what, in a mere *moral* point of view, is meant by self-approbation? (Put religion out of the question for a moment.) Examine, in a mere *human* point of view, what passes in your own mind when you approve yourself. It is really nothing more than that pleasure which results from the esteem of all honest and reflecting men. When you are universally blamed, though you know you have done right, you always comfort yourself that the world would have determined otherwise, had they been acquainted with all the circumstances, and informed of the real motives. You refer the matter to a more enlightened tribunal, or to posterity: you do not pretend to set up your own self-approbation, against the judgment of others; but you approve yourself, merely because you say, better men, more enlightened men, and more impartial men, would have decided in a very different manner. Therefore, I can not see how self-esteem, and the desire of the esteem of others, can be compared together: for, called upon to define self-esteem, I could say nothing else of it than that it was that agreeable feeling which proceeds from the belief that we possess, or that we *ought* to possess, the esteem of others. Then again, it is very true, that we love praise, and we love to *deserve* praise; but the love of praiseworthiness is merely a consequence of the love of praise,—not an original principle. To make my meaning the more clear, I will put this case:—A great battle is gained, the plan and dispositions of which are admirable; the general who conducted the army is considered as a consummate master of the military art, and arrives at the very summit of reputation as an accomplished officer; but this plan of the battle was drawn out for him the evening before, by one of his aides-de-camp, whose original conception it was, and to whom all the merit is really due. Which is the most enviable situation? His, who is praised without being praiseworthy; or his, who is praiseworthy without being praised? Nobody here could entertain a moment's doubt about the matter, that the praiseworthiness is preferable to the praise. But why? Merely *from* the love of praise; merely because it, in the end, procures more praise. A miser may refuse a sum of money, because, by so doing, in the end he may gain a greater: his reputation is worth more to him than the sum which he is offered for it; he does not love reputation better than money, but he loves reputation merely because he loves money. Just so with praiseworthiness: it grows out of the love of praise, and is only preferred to it at any particular time, because, by that temporary preference, it is probable more praise, in the end, will be obtained; at last, like every other preference, it grows into a habit.

The desire of power, I can not better describe than in the words of Mr. Dugald Stewart. I quote from his "Outlines of Moral Philosophy;" and his views upon this subject appear to be so truly excellent, that I shall quote them at some length:—

"Whenever we are led to consider ourselves as the authors of any effect, we feel a sensible pride or exultation in the consciousness of power; and the pleasure is, in general, proportioned to the greatness of the effect, compared to the smallness of the exertion.

"The infant, while still on the breast, delights in exerting its little strength upon every object it meets with; and is mortified, when any accident convinces it of its imbecility. The pastimes of the boy are, almost without exception, such as suggest to him the idea of his power:—and the same remark may be extended to the active sports, and the athletic exercises, of youth and of manhood.

"As we advance in years, and as our animal powers lose their activity and vigor, we gradually aim at extending our influence over others, by the superiority of fortune and of situation, or by the still more flattering superiority of intellectual endowment: by the force of our understanding, by the extent of our information, by the arts of persuasion, or the accomplishments of address. What but the idea of power, pleases the orator, in the consciousness of his eloquence; when he silences the reasons of others by superior ingenuity; bends to his purposes their desires and passions; and, without the aid of force or the splendor of rank, becomes the arbiter of the fate of nations?

"To the same principle we may trace, in part, the pleasure arising from the discovery of general theorems. Every such discovery puts us in possession of innumerable particular truths, or particular facts; and gives us a ready command of a great stock of knowledge, to which we had not access before. The desire of power, therefore, comes, in the progress of reason and experience, to act as an auxiliary to our instinctive desire of knowledge.

"The idea of power is, partly at least, the foundation of our attachment to property. It is not enough for us to have the use of an object. We desire to have it completely at our own disposal; without being responsible to any person whatever.

"Avarice is a particular modification of the desire of power; arising from the various functions of money in a commercial country. Its influence as an active principle is much strengthened by habit and association.

"The love of liberty proceeds, in part, from the same source; from a desire of being able to do whatever is agreeable to our own inclination. Slavery mortifies us, because it limits our power.

"Even the love of tranquillity and retirement has been resolved by Cicero, into the same principle.

"The desire of power is also, in some degree, the foundation of the pleasure of virtue. We love to be at liberty to follow our own inclinations, without being subject to the control of a superior; but this alone is not sufficient to our happiness. When we are led, by vicious habits, or by the force of passion, to do what reason disapproves, we are sensible of a mortifying subjection to the inferior principles of our nature, and feel our own littleness and weakness. A sense of freedom and independence, elevation of mind, and the pride of virtue, are the natural sentiments of the man, who is conscious of being able, at all times, to calm the tumults of passion, and to obey the cool suggestions of duty and honor."

LECTURE XXV.

ON SURPRISE, NOVELTY, AND VARIETY.

STATEMENT OF DIFFERENCE BETWEEN SURPRISE, NOVELTY, AND VARIETY.—EFFECTS OF SURPRISE.—OF CONTRAST.—OF THE TWO KINDS OF NOVELTY.—OF VARIETY.—EFFECTS OF CHANGE.—AND THE EXPLANATION OF THOSE EFFECTS.—HOW FAR NOVELTY IS AGREEABLE.—EXPLANATION OF THE PLEASURE OF NOVELTY.

Wonder, surprise, and admiration,—words often confounded,—denote, in our language, sentiments, which though allied, are also in some respects distinct from one another. What is new and *singular*, excites the sentiment which, in strict propriety, is called wonder; what is *unexpected*, surprise; and what is great or beautiful, admiration.

We wonder at all the rare phenomena of nature;—at meteors, comets, and eclipses; at singular plants and animals; and at every thing, in short, with which we have before been, either little, or not at all acquainted; and we still wonder, though forewarned of what we shall see.

We are surprised with those things which we have seen very often, but which we little expected to meet with in the place where we find them. We are surprised at the sudden appearance of a friend, whom we have seen a thousand times, but whom we did not imagine we were to see then. We admire the beauty of a plain, or the vastness of a mountain, though we have seen both often before; and though nothing appears to us in either, but what we had expected with certainty to see. Or, to take it by illustration, and to exemplify the usages of the three words in one object:—The first time I see St. Paul's, I wonder at it; the hundredth time, I only admire it. If I wake in a coach, and find myself in

St. Paul's Churchyard, when I thought I was in Pall Mall, I am surprised by the appearance of the building. For the first time of seeing such a building, surprise, admiration, and wonder might *all* be excited at the same moment; afterward, surprise and admiration, or admiration alone.

When an object of any kind, which has been for some time expected and foreseen, presents itself, whatever be the emotion which it is by nature fitted to excite, the mind must have been prepared for it, and must even in some measure have conceived it before, because the *idea* of the object having been so long present to it, must have excited some degree of the same emotion which the object *itself* would excite. The change, therefore, is less considerable, and the passion which it excites glides gradually, and easily, into the heart without violence, pain, or difficulty. But the contrary of all this happens when the passion is unexpected. If it be a strong passion, the heart is thrown by it into a violent and convulsive emotion, such as sometimes occasions immediate death: sometimes the suddenness of the ecstasy so entirely disjoints the frame of the imagination, that it never after returns to its former tone and composure, but falls either into a frenzy, or habitual lunacy; or such as almost always occasions a momentary loss of reason, or of that attention to other things which our situation or our duty requires. From the apprehension of these consequences, we are very cautious of communicating bad news on a sudden. The panic terrors which sometimes seize upon whole armies in the field, or great cities, when an enemy is in the neighborhood, and which deprive, for a time, the most determined of all deliberate judgment, are never excited but by the sudden apprehension of danger.

Fear, though naturally a very strong passion, never rises to such excesses, unless exasperated by wonder, from the uncertain nature of the danger, and by surprise, from the suddenness of the apprehension. There are some very interesting observations on this subject in the tracts of Dr. Adam Smith; one passage from which I shall take this opportunity of quoting. "Surprise, is not to be regarded as an original emotion, of a species distinct from all others. Violent and sudden change produced upon the mind, when an emotion of any kind is brought suddenly upon it, constitutes the whole nature of surprise. But when not only a passion, and a great passion, comes all at once upon the mind, but when it comes upon it while the mind is in the mood most unfit for conceiving it, the surprise is then the greatest. Surprises of joy when the mind is sunk into grief, or of grief when it is elated with joy, are therefore the most insupportable. The change is, in this case, the greatest possible. Not only a strong passion is conceived all at once; but a strong passion, the direct opposite of that which was before in possession of the soul. When a load of sorrow comes down upon the heart that is expanded and elated with gayety and joy, it seems not only to damp and oppress it, but almost to crush and bruise it, as a real weight would crush and bruise the body. On the contrary, when, from an unexpected change of fortune, a tide of gladness seems, if I may say so, to spring all at once within it, when depressed and contracted with grief and sorrow, it feels as if it suddenly extended and heaved up with violent, irresistible force, and is torn with pangs, of all others the most exquisite, and which almost always occasion faintings, deliriums, and sometimes instant death. For it may be worth while to observe, that though grief be a more violent passion than joy,—as, indeed, all uneasy sensations seem naturally more pungent than the opposite agreeable ones,—yet, of the two, surprises of joy are still more insupportable than surprises of grief."*

These observations are very true, and very interesting; but they would have been introduced, perhaps, with greater accuracy, if the phenomena to which they refer, had been classed under the head of *contrast* rather than *surprise;* for contrast and surprise, though feelings which very much resemble each other, are unquestionably very separable and distinct. This is a case which will set the distinction between contrast and surprise in

* Dr. Adam Smith's "History of Astronomy," p. 8.

a strong light:—If I have long been suffering from abject poverty, and suddenly receive the intelligence of coming into possession of a large fortune, the unexpectedness of the news excites in me the feeling of surprise; but another distinct feeling is excited in me, by the contrast which I draw between my present fortune, and my past: which last feeling, I should have had even though I had expected my riches every day for a twelvemonth past.

Not only grief and joy, but all the passions, are more violent when opposite extremes succeed each other. No resentment is so keen as that which follows the quarrels of lovers;—no love so passionate, as that which attends their reconciliation: when near relations quarrel, they are generally ten times more vindictive than ordinary disputants. Contrast, produces just the same effects in the body. Moderate warmth, appears to be intolerable heat, if felt after extreme cold. What is bitter of itself, will seem more bitter, when tasted after what is very sweet. A dirty white, looks bright and pure, when placed by a jet black. In short, the vivacity of every sentiment, and of every sensation, seems to be greater or less, in proportion to the change made by either, upon the situation of the mind or organ; which change must, of course, be the greatest when opposite sensations or sentiments are contrasted, and succeed immediately to each other. Contrast is extremely favorable to ugliness, or any natural disadvantages, where there are other recommendations to overcome them. The first impression, from appearance, is so disagreeable, that it animates all the pleasing impressions from merit, by the mere effect of contrast; and therefore, it matters not what it is,—whether it be the loss of an eye, or an ill-contrived set of features, or a rustic gait,—it is merely an obstacle in the beginning. If you have merit of any kind to get over it, you will afterward derive good from it, rather than harm; and be extolled as much above your true standard, as you were first of all depreciated below it. A great deal of the propriety of common behavior is regulated by contrast. No one could endure to see a judge dance, or a bishop vault into his saddle. A very regulated and subdued pleasantry and relaxation, is all that can be allowed to men habitually and officially dignified. Contrast in trifling objects, which can excite no high emotion, is the source of humor.

There are two kinds of novelty;—novelty in detached objects, and novelty in their succession. It was a novelty to the Romans to behold the elephants of King Pyrrhus: and it is a novelty to us to see men made drunk and mad by breathing a certain air; it is an order of events, to which we have never been accustomed. We have not connected together the phenomena of drunkenness, and the reception of an aërial fluid into the lungs. There are also different *degrees* of novelty. An extensive building, or a complicated machine, may be new, after I have seen them three or four times; because, it is impossible to remember all the parts and relations, where they are so extensive and intricate.

Another degree of novelty exists in objects, of which we have some information at second-hand; for description, though it contribute to familiarity, can not do away entirely with the effect of novelty, when the object is presented. The first sight of a lion occasions wonder, after a thorough acquaintance with the best pictures and statues of that animal; and no man could see the great wall of Tartary without shuddering, even if he had read a whole circulating library full of embassies to, and travels in China.

We have the greatest disposition to find resemblances, and to class objects together which affect the mind in a similar manner; and so strong is this propensity in our nature, that it is hardly possible we can see any thing, without likening it to something we have seen or conceived before. The inhabitants of Owhyhee had no animals larger than hogs, and when they saw a goat on board Captain Cook's ship they called it a bird. Some white travelers, seized by the natives in the interior of Africa, were immediately pronounced to be a species of the monkey; and as the Indian corn had been lately very much plundered by that animal, they well nigh escaped being stoned to death. It is, in fact, hardly possible that we should see any thing without finding a resemblance for it; and therefore, *strictly* speaking, nothing is absolutely new: but things differ in the degree in which they resemble our previous ideas. The love of variety seems to be a low degree of the love of novelty; for in running from the town to the country, and the country to the town, I seek for a succession of objects, some of the properties and qualities of which I have forgotten, and the revival of which produces in my mind a low degree of the same sort of excitement which is always consequent upon novelty. A person has been absent a whole winter, in London: the parlor, the drawing-room, and the lawn, in the country, can not be said to be absolutely new, but still, in a certain degree, they are faded away from the memory; the little traces are gone, the great work of oblivion is clearly begun, and the pleasure we experience at revisiting the haunts of our childhood, is derived from the treachery and infirmity of our faculties. In the same manner, we are apt to tire of our companions. When we have seen them some time, we fly to others for relief, whose style and conversation has become slightly obliterated in our minds, and by the comparative freshness of which, we are more excited.

All these phenomena of which I have been speaking, the effects of contrast, variety, and novelty, are all referable to one fact,—the effects of change upon the mind; for the mind is in a state of rest, when the ideas which pass through it are not very different from each other, nor very sudden in their approach, nor very new: but these three sorts of change,—novelty, suddenness, and contrast,—rouse it in a moment from its slumbers, and let loose all the storms of passion.

"I was sitting," says the author of some Letters upon the Earthquake at Lisbon, "I was sitting playing with my kitten, and just going to breakfast. I had one slipper on, and the other was in pussy's mouth; when my attention was roused by the sudden sound of thunder; the floor heaved under me, and I saw the spire of the church of the Holy Virgin come tumbling to the ground, like a plaything overturned by a child. I rushed into the street, unknowing what I did, and where I went; and beheld *such* a scene, as made it come into my mind, that the end of all things was at hand, and that this was the judgment-day appointed by God! By this time the air was filled with the screams of the mangled and the dying. The dwellings of men, the trophies of conquest, the temples of God, were falling all around me, and my escape appeared quite impossible. I made up my mind for death."

There is in this picture, I think, suddenness, contrast, and novelty, in abundance! Nor is it inappositely contrasted with the calm and familiar state of his ideas, previous to the commencement of the earthquake.

It is commonly said and thought that no account can be given of these effects of change upon our minds,—that we are pleased with novelty, and affected by surprise and contrast, because such is the law of nature; and that no *other* reason can be given. But surely the explanation of it is, that all the changes of matter are so apt to affect us with pleasure and pain, that, on this account, we watch its changes. If no object that you could present to a child, could give that child either pleasure or pain, I submit to every body here present, whether it seems very probable that the child would care one farthing about the changes of objects: but some objects are sweet, and some are disgusting,—like physic; and some smooth, and some prick him; and therefore, as every object presented to him affects his interests, he gains rapidly those habits of attending to the changes of objects, which, because the origin of it lies hidden in the remotest infancy, we indolently pronounce to be an ultimate fact, and incapable of explanation. A child is originally excited by new objects, and by objects suddenly presented to his notice, from the hope of the pleasures, or fear of the pains, it may produce. For the very same reason, he is struck by contrast. He has an interest in studying the qualities of every thing with the greatest quickness. The mind travels with more difficulty from a sheep to an elephant, than from a sheep to a lamb. The difficulty of mastering and arranging the new ideas, from their great dissimilarity with those which preceded them, is that excitement of mind which contrast produces; and variety is the same thing, in a less degree. If matter could do us neither good nor harm, we should see Gorgons, Chimæras, and Minotaurs, starting up under our feet, with as much indifference as we think about them; and the only reason why surprise, novelty, and contrast, in our conceptions, are not as strong as in our perceptions, is, that they have little to do with pleasure or pain. No man had more new, surprising, and contrasted ideas, than Ariosto; but nobody ever heard of his surprising himself into swoons by his own conceptions: a mouse running across the room has probably startled him much more than all his own beautiful extravagances have ever been able to do.

We have, in the same manner, a pleasure in contemplating the resemblances of objects, and their differences: hence, method and classification in science; the mode of arguing by analogy; and the rules laid down for the regulation of common life. It seems to be most probable that all this comes from the strong motive which pain and pleasure communicate to us, for observing the resemblances of matter; for a child that loves sugar, observes the appearances of sugar, and every thing white is a resemblance, which is apt to excite his appetite: perhaps he takes up a piece of salt, and the pain which this mistake inflicts, excites him to fresh observation, and makes him more attentive in his classifications. If he got nothing by observing whether objects were alike or unlike, he would never observe or classify at all. I beg leave to observe, that I am only speaking of the *origin* of contrast, novelty, discernment, and variety; for after the mind has once got the notion, that new things are to be watched, on account of their consequences, the middle term, according to the usual process of association, is soon omitted, and novelty is remarked on account of itself; just as, at last, money is loved for itself. And this is another reason why the *cause* of the feeling is forgotten, and it is supposed to be original.

If this be the history of our attention to change, the next question is, how far is change agreeable? In the first place, we must remember that novelty excites the mind, and that when the mind is in a state of excitement, any passion which falls upon it becomes stronger than it otherwise would be. Whoever was frightened by a storm at sea, would be more frightened if he were at sea for the first time, because the novelty exciting his mind, would come to the aid of the passion of fear. Whoever saw a beautiful spectacle on the stage, would feel the pleasure rendered much greater by the excitement of novelty. There is also a pleasure in the excitement of *mere* novelty, though perhaps not a very great one. No one would go out of his way to see a rat, but we should have some pleasure in seeing a white rat: the novelty of the color would in some measure overcome the disgust which that animal occasions. A Spaniard dressed as an Englishman would excite no curiosity;—if he passed the streets in the dress of his native country, we should turn aside to look upon him. It is not easy to find instances, where we receive much pleasure from mere novelty. What we call the pleasures of novelty, are generally the pleasures of something else. A new cap, or a new gown, is the pleasure of figure, and the pleasure of color, or the pleasure of fashion, the association with elegance and gayety: the pleasure of *novelty* forms but a very small part of it.

In contemplating the falls of Niagara, it would be the sublimity and the terror of the scene that we should call by the general name of novelty: innumerable objects, quite as new, would be infinitely less striking, from their inferior sublimity. In the rage for traveling, the object is not so much to gratify the love of novelty as the love of excellence; not merely to see new things, but new grand things, new beautiful things, new excellence, in which the grand and beautiful will, I should think, upon reflection, be found to have a much greater effect, than the new.

This appears very much against the power of novelty; that whenever its effects seem to be very great, it is always found in conjunction with other principles; whenever it is found alone, its influence is very inconsiderable.

Nearly the same observations may be made of surprise. Surprise increases pleasure and pain; and in itself is slightly agreeable. If any one were to tell me that in taking a walk in the country, I should find a little seal, or a silver thimble, lying in a pathway where it had been left, nothing could be more indifferent to me than to look upon it; but if I were to light upon such objects all of a sudden, I might derive a faint gleam of satisfaction from the mere surprise. It is only in such little objects that the question can be tried; for when surprise comes to be mingled with great passions, it is very difficult to know what to give to surprise, what to the feelings with which it is conjoined. A man thinks, and hears, that his son is killed in battle, and all of a sudden his son enters into the room where he is sitting, and the father drops down in a swoon; but if a maid-servant, whom he believed to have been dead three years before, had entered his room, no such violent symptoms would have taken place, though the mere surprise, the unexpectedness of the vision, would have been quite as great: therefore, it seems fair to say, that the effect is to be attributed in a greater measure to the conflicting passions within, than to the mere surprise; for, all surprise out of the question, and the father prepared, months before, to meet the son whom he had supposed to be dead, and aware of the very hour and moment of the meeting, yet still the trial would be very dreadful and severe. But, all-important affection out of the question, the mere surprise would not be of much consequence; for if a pointer-dog were to enter the room, whose death had been considered as certain, the effect produced would be quite inconsiderable; and yet in this case the mere *unexpectedness* is quite as great as in any of the others. But this is curious, that suddenness and admiration, or novelty and admiration in their combined state, produce effects infinitely more powerful than their separate effects, added together, could ever be supposed to produce. It is impossible to look upon York Minster for the first time, without feeling a degree of transport; but these transports are certainly not felt by the mayor or aldermen of York, who see it every week,—though even their callousness must be sometimes excited by it.

The only circumstance in which they differ from a stranger is, in wanting the feeling of novelty; which feeling by itself I have before shown to be very insignificant; but, add it to admiration, and the whole effect is very striking. Mere surprise, by itself, produces no very stupendous consequences; the separate power of novelty is not very strong; mere contrast can very well be endured. Admiration, devoid of all these, is comparatively weak; but when a new object is suddenly presented to our view, contrasted with all other objects, and in *itself* a subject of admiration, it is then that the strongest sensations which the mind is capable of feeling are always produced.

The same, or nearly the same, observations might be gone over respecting contrast and variety: and the result of the inquiry is, that, in all these considerable changes of our ideas, there is a pleasure, arising from the excitement which they produce; and that the desire of occasioning that excitement, is very often a stimulus to action. It is notorious, however, in the instance of novelty, that it is more a stimulus with the young, than with the old. It will be curious to ascertain what are the causes of this remarkable difference between the different periods of life. Experience has taught to old men the danger of change, and the difficulty of foreseeing its effects. They become lazy in the exertion of their faculties, and dislike that strain and excitement of mind, which new things occasion: whereas, excitement is agreeable to the young; they have quite a passion for it. Whatever men have done long, it is painful for them not to do; to whatever they have done long, or seen long, they attach the very agreeable notion of self: "I have been accustomed to do so;"—"this was the case in my time;"—"I have always seen this, or that,"—and such-like references to self; which always establish a pleasing connection of ideas. So that fear, indolence, reason, and habit, are constantly at work to destroy the power of novelty; and the love of what is customary, becomes as much the characteristic of one age, as the love of what is new is that of another: and the reason why the balance is commonly against novelty, is, that so much more power is lodged in the hands of the old, than of the young. Let thirty-five be a middle period, dividing mankind into two classes. The elder of these two classes has infinitely a greater share of power and authorty than the other: in the youngest even of this upper class, novelty has lost a great deal of its power, and habit has begun to fix its empire. The young object and complain, and think they can improve; but they are compelled to wait so long before the power comes to them, that they are familiarized by habit, though not, perhaps, convinced by reason. So it happens, and happens, perhaps, very fortunately *upon the whole*, that the power is lodged in the hands of those who have constitutionally an aversion to innovation;—more fortunately, certainly, than if it were lodged in the hands of those who had a love of it.: but the best of all would be, that we should know the bias of every period of life, guard against it, and decide upon questions, not as they are new or old, but as they are good or bad. The pleasure occasioned by the excitement of these emotions, produces, as may be easily seen, the most important effects upon human happiness. Novelty is the foundation of the love of knowledge; which is nothing but the desire of *useful* novelty. The love of surprise and wonder, have been the parents of poetical fiction, and of all those errors which held such deep hold upon the mind of man;—witchcraft, demonology, astrology, and the manifold instances of superstition, which depended upon the supposed agency of invisible spirit. Whoever tells any thing wonderful, contributes to the pleasure of those who hear him, and therefore enjoys a temporary pre-eminence; but, as the imagination is soon warmed up to this pitch, the next stage of narration must bring with it a new stage of astonishment: and in this way evidence is handed down to succeeding ages, till it requires the greatest efforts of labor, and force of acuteness, to gain a glimpse at the real truth. Mr. Knight has some very sensible remarks on the bad effects which the love of novelty produces upon taste, which to me are new, though very probably they may not be so to my hearers:—"The style of Virgil and Horace in poetry, and that of Cæsar and Cicero in prose, continued to be admired and applauded through all the succeeding ages of Roman eloquence, as the true standards of taste and eloquence in writing; yet no one ever attempted to imitate them, though there is no reason to believe but that the praises bestowed upon them were perfectly sincere; but all writers seek for applause,—and applause is only to be gained by novelty. The style of Cicero and Virgil was new in the Latin language when they wrote; but in the age of Seneca and Lucan it was no longer so; and though it still imposed by the stamp of authority, it could not even please without it; so that living writers whose names depended upon their works, and not their works upon their names, were obliged to seek for other means of exciting public attention, and acquiring public approbation. In the succeeding age, these writers became cold and insipid; and the refinements of Statius and Tacitus were successfully employed to gratify the restless pruriency of innovation. In all other ages and countries, where letters have been successfully cultivated, the progress has been nearly the same; and in none more distinctly than in our own: from Swift and Addison, to Johnson, Burke, and Gibbon, is a transition precisely similar to that from Cæsar and Cicero, to Seneca and Tacitus. In the imitative arts, from the effects of novelty, the progress of corruption has been nearly the same."* Mr. Knight adds afterward,—and with perfect justice,—that though the passion for novelty has been the principal means of corrupting taste, it has also been a principal means of polishing and perfecting it.

I have said a great deal upon the subject of novelty, and I do not know how I can better conclude than with the termination of an Essay on the same subject, which Dr. Johnson has pronounced to be one of the best-written pieces in the English language. "To add no more," says the writer, "is not this fondness for novelty, which makes us out of conceit with all we already have, a convincing proof of a future state? Either man was made in vain, or this is not the only world he was made for:

* Knight, on Taste.

for there can not be a greater instance of vanity than that, to which a man is liable to be deluded, from the cradle to the grave, with fleeting shadows of happiness; his pleasures die in the possession, and fresh enjoyments do not rise fast enough to fill his mind with satisfaction. When I see persons sick of themselves any longer than they are called away by something that is of force enough to chain down the present thought; when I see them hurry from one place to another, and then back again; continually shifting postures, and placing life in all the different lights they can think of,—surely, say I to myself, life is vain, and the man beyond expression stupid or prejudiced, who, from the vanity of life can not gather, that he is designed for immortality."

LECTURE XXVI.

ON HABIT.

It appears to be the law of our nature, that our past thoughts and actions should exercise a very material influence upon those which are to come. Whatever ideas and whatever actions have been joined together, have, ever after, a disposition to unite, exactly in proportion to the frequency of their previous union; till at last, the adhesion becomes so strong, that it frequently overcomes the earliest and the most powerful passions of our nature. This power of habit extends to the brute creation; and appears to have some effect upon organized matter, as I shall hereafter endeavor to show. Why we should be thus affected by habit, I presume can not be explained. We might have been so constituted as not to have had the smallest disposition to do again, what we had been constantly doing for ten years before; we might have found it as difficult to pursue a track of thought to which we had been accustomed, as it is to strike into one entirely new: the fact is the reverse,—and that is all we can say; when we get there, we arrive at the end of all human reasoning. Every one must be familiar with the effects of habit. A walk upon the quarter-deck, though intolerably confined, becomes so agreeable by custom, that a sailor, in his walk on shore, very often confines himself within the same bounds. "I knew a man," says Lord Kames, "who had relinquished the sea, for a country life: in the corner of his garden he reared an artificial mount, with a level summit, resembling most accurately a quarter-deck, not only in shape, but in size; and here he generally walked. In Minorca, Governor Kane made an excellent road, the whole length of the island, and yet the inhabitants adhered to the old road, though not only longer, but extremely bad. The merchants of Bristol have an excellent and commodious Exchange, but they always meet in the street. There is hardly any convenience of life, or any notion of utility or beauty, which may not be entirely changed by habit; it is needless to multiply the instances."

When ideas are united together in consequence of their having been previously joined by some accident, we call it association. There are various kinds of associations; and it may, perhaps, render what I am going to say more clear, if I recapitulate a few of the different kinds of association. One idea may be associated to another idea; the lowing of a cow may, in my mind, be constantly united with the idea of a green field. 2dly. An idea and a feeling may be constantly associated together. Peter, the Wild Boy, as Lord Monboddo informs us, could never bear the sight of an apothecary; it threw him into the most violent fits of rage: a practitioner had once given him so very nauseous a draught, that he never afterward forgot it, and could with the utmost difficulty be restrained from flying at any of the faculty that came within his reach.

In the like manner, joy, or any other passion, may suggest ideas. A good father, when he is visiting any beautiful country, or partaking of any amusement, may wish that his wife and children were there to participate in his satisfaction. Here the feeling of joy, introduces the idea of his family; and this, in a benevolent mind, may grow into an association.

A state of body may be associated with an idea. A man who had been very often to the high northern latitudes, might very possibly associate the idea of whales and bears with the feeling of cold; or an East Indian might associate a state of heat with the idea of his white cotton dress, or any of the peculiar habits or objects of his country.

A state of body might be associated with a passion; cold might always produce joy in a Norwegian, if it reminded him of the scenes where he had passed a happy infancy; or heat would produce unhappiness in a man who had been confined three or four years in the prisons of Seringapatam, and who had suffered dreadfully in such a situation from the ardor of the climate. Now, when all these conjunctions of ideas, feelings, and states of body, are confined merely to the intellect, they pass under the name of association: but whenever we begin to *act* in a customary manner, whenever any outward observable *action* becomes a member of the series, there, we begin to use the word *habit*.

If a person, by accident, had lived with a great number of snuff-takers, and had been accustomed to perceive that in any little pause of conversation, they all took out their snuff-boxes, the silence would immediately produce the idea of snuff,—and this we should call association of ideas; but if he were a snuff-taker himself, the silence would probably animate him to a pinch,—and this we should call habit. Whatever passes in the mind, only in consequence of custom or repetition, is association: where there is outward action, it is habit. There is no use whatever in the two names: they are, on the contrary, an evil; because they multiply names without multiplying ideas; but the reason is, that the effects of habit have long been observed, because every one notices actions. It is not above a century since association has been thought of, or much attended to, because it is very difficult to trace and to describe the operations of the mind.

Habits may be divided into active and passive;—those things which we do by an act of the will, and those things which we suffer by the agency of some external power. I begin with the active habits; and, after stating a few of the most familiar of them, I will shortly analyze the examples, in order to show that they are merely referable to association. It may be as well, perhaps, to give a specimen of the life of a man whose existence was, at last, entirely dependent upon the habits he had contracted: it is a fair picture of the dominion which habit establishes over us, at the close of life. "The professed rule of Mr. Hobbes," says Dr. White Kennet, in his Memoirs of the Cavendish Family, "was to dedicate the morning to exercise, and the evening to study. At his first rising, he walked out, and climbed up a hill: if the weather was not dry, he made a point of fatiguing himself within doors, so as to perspire; remarking constantly, that an old man had more moisture than heat; and by such motion, heat was to be acquired, and moisture expelled. After this, the philosopher took a very comfortable breakfast, and then went round the lodgings to wait upon the earl, the countess, the children, and any considerable strangers; paying some short addresses to all of them. He kept these rounds till about twelve o'clock, when he had a little dinner provided for him, which he eat always by himself, without ceremony. Soon after dinner, he retired to his study, and had his candle, with ten or twelve pipes of tobacco, laid by him; then, shutting the door, he fell to smoking, thinking, and writing, for several hours. He could never endure to be left in an empty house; whenever the earl removed, he would go along with him, even to his last stage, from Chatsworth to Hardwick. This was the constant tenor of his life, from which he never varied, no, not a moment, nor an atom."

This is the picture of a man whose life appears to have been entirely regulated by the past; who did a thing because he *had* done it; who, so far as bodily actions were concerned, could hardly be said to have any fresh motives; but was impelled by one regular set of volitions, constantly recurring at fixed periods. Now, take any one of his habits, and examine its progress; it will afford a natural history of this law of the mind, and will show what circumstances in that law are most worthy of observation.

He smoked: how did this begin? It might have begun any how. He was staying, perhaps, at some house where smoking was in fashion, and began to smoke out of compliance with the humors of other persons. At first, he thought it unpleasant; and as all the expirations and inspirations were new, and difficult, it required considerable attention; and at the close of the evening he could have distinctly recollected, if he had tried to do so, that his mind had been employed in thinking how he was to manage and manœuver the pipe. The practice goes on; the disgust vanishes; much less attention is necessary to smoke well: in a few days the association is formed; the moment the cloth is taken away after supper, the idea of smoking occurs: if any accident happen to prevent it, a slight pain is felt in consequence; it seems as if things did not go on in their regular track, and some confusion had crept into the arrangements of the evening. As the association goes on, it gathers strength from the circumstances connected with it; from the mirth and conversation with which it is joined: at last, after a lapse of years, we see the philosopher of Malmsbury advanced from one, to one dozen of pipes; so perfect in all the tactics of a smoker, so dexterous in all the manual of his dirty recreation, that he would fill, light, and smoke out his pipe, without the slightest remembrance of what he had been doing, or the most minute interruption to any immoral, irreligious, or unmathematical track of thought, in which he happened to be engaged: but we must not forget, that though his amusement occupied him so little, and was passed over with such a small share of his attention, the *want* of it would have occupied him so much, that he could have done nothing without it; all his speculations would have been at an end, and without his twelve pipes he might have been a friend to devotion, to freedom, or any thing else which, in the customary tenor of his thoughts, he certainly was not. The phenomena observable here are, that the physical taste lost its effect; that which was nauseous, ceased to be so. Next, the habit began with a considerable difficulty of bodily action, and with a full attention of the mind to what was passing. It was not easy to smoke, and the philosopher was compelled to be careful, in order to do it properly; but as the habit increased, he indulged in it with such little attention of mind or exertion of body, that he did it without knowing he did it. Lastly, any interruption of the habit would have occasioned to him the greatest uneasiness. As these are the circumstances observable in all habits, they will each require and deserve some consideration. 1st. It appears to be a general law, that habit diminishes physical sensibility: whatever affects any organ of the body, affects it less by repetition. Brandy is begun in tea-spoons; but the effect is so soon lost, that a more generous and expanded vehicle is very soon had recourse to: the same heat to the stomach, and the same intoxication to the head, can not be produced by the same quantity of the liquor. So with perfumes; wear scented powder, and in a month you will cease to perceive it. Habituate yourself to cold or to heat, and they cease to affect you. Eat Cayenne pepper, and you will find it perpetually necessary to increase the quantity, in order to produce the effect. "My perfumed doublet," says Montaigne, "gratifies my own smelling at first, as well as that of others; but after I have worn it three or four days together, I no more perceive it: but it is yet more strange, that custom, notwithstanding the long intermissions, and intervals, should yet have the power to unite and establish the effect of its impressions upon our senses, as is manifest in those who live near to steeples and the frequent noise of bells. I myself lie at home in a tower, where every morning and evening a very great bell rings out the *Ave Maria*, the noise of which shakes my very tower, and at first seemed insupportable to me; but having now a good while kept that lodging, I am so used to it, that I hear it without any manner of offense, and often without awaking at it. Plato reprehends a boy for playing at some childish game: 'Thou reprovest me,' says the boy, 'for a very little thing.' 'Custom,' replied Plato, 'is *no* little thing.' And he was in the right; for I find that our greatest vices derive their first propensity from our most tender infancy, and that our principal education depends upon the nurse."*

In all these cases, the sensibility of the different parts of the body is diminished by repetition; and the same substances applied to them, can not produce the same effects. The habit, it should be observed, does not act by individual substances, but often by classes: if you have accustomed yourself to opium, all soporific drugs have less effect upon you; if to one species of wine, you

* Montaigne, vol. i. p. 131.

are capable of bearing a greater quantity of any other: the sensibility of the body is not only diminished toward that object, but toward many others similar to it; chiefly, however, toward the object upon which the habit was founded. There are some facts, which do not, at the first view, appear to fall in with this doctrine. A taster of wines increases in his power of discrimination. A man accustomed to judge of the fineness of cloths by feeling them, feels them with more accuracy from practice. A blind man, from mere habit, improves so astonishingly in the power of touch, that his nicety, in this respect, is hardly to be credited by a person endowed with sight. Whence comes it, if habit lessens bodily sensibility, that habit increases it in these instances? My answer is, that it is not *habit* which increases the sensibility in these instances; that the sensibility is actually diminished; and better judgments made, with impaired sensibility, and increased *attention*, than others make with more sensibility and less attention. The man who has been rubbing cloths all his lifetime between his finger and thumb, has most probably not such an acute feeling as I have, who have made no such use of my finger and thumb; but he has a fixed and lively attention to what feeling he has, and he knows the quality of cloth, of which that feeling is the indication. In all feeling, where attention is not concerned, he is just like every one else: heat affects him less if he has been exposed to it frequently; so does cold: in his own particular art he does not deviate from the general law of diminished sensibility; but counteracts that law, by his great increase of attention. This rule of the diminution of sensibility by habit, includes, of course, pleasure as well as pain: nothing which we eat or drink constantly, can remain either pleasant or painful; repetition infallibly diminishes both the pleasure and the pain. If the common part of our diet is not originally insipid,—as bread or water,—it becomes uninteresting, and no notice is taken of the flavor,—as is the case with salt. Tastes that are luscious, repetition not only destroys, but converts into disgusts. The habits of mankind are not so frequently formed upon these tastes, as they are upon others, slightly disagreeable at their origin; as coffee, olives, port wine, and tobacco: none of these are agreeable in their origin. The reason of this is, perhaps, rather moral than physical. In the luscious taste you set off from a pleasure, which becomes every day less and less, and at last terminates in a disgust. This is a good reason why you should stop. In the case of the olives and the coffee, you set off with a slight disgust, and go on to a negative state, or slight pleasure: and the reason why you encounter the first disgust, is fashion, or health; or some use which you propose to derive from the disgustful object: thus, coffee clears the head, olives provoke to the use of wine, and so on. Hitherto I have endeavored to show the effect of habit on those pleasures and pains which have the body for their cause; and that effect appears to be, a diminution of every kind of sensibility. The next subject for consideration will be, whether habit weakens our passive impressions, where the body is not concerned; that is, whether because we have felt a passion, we are less likely to feel it again; that there is a less proneness to that kind of sensibility, than there was before? The general rule is in the affirmative,—that habit strengthens our active determinations, while it weakens our passive impressions: this, I say, is the general rule; I *suppose* it is the true one; but as I can not reconcile innumerable cases to that rule, I shall very frankly, but at the same time in all humility, avow my dissent. If this rule were true, it would follow that a man is less liable to feel the passion of anger again, in proportion as he has felt it often before. This man is a very irritable man; why so? because we have never seen him in a passion;—but here is another man, whom you may trust with the utmost impunity; we have beheld him in such violent and such frequent fits of anger, that we are convinced he is the most peaceable man in the world. Habit weakens passive impressions, and previous irritation must therefore be the best security for the absence of all irritable feeling. If this rule were true, the best method of teaching a child good-temper, would be to irritate him as much as possible. He might be cured of avarice by being taught to hoard; rendered benevolent by being indulged in malice; and cured of every vice, to the practice of which he had been diligently trained.

Take fear; there is a certain degree, at least, of that passion, which does not diminish the passive impression; he who has been once heartily frightened by a great dog flying at him, is not likely, for any thing I can see, to be the less alarmed if he is attacked by a bull the following day,—but rather the more. To have slept in a house which caught fire,—to have run a narrow risk for life by the fall of a horse,—would not improve the confidence of a horseman, nor add to the soundness of sleep. Fear seems to increase the liability to fear, rather than to diminish it. What has led to a contrary opinion, seems to be this,—that we become less afraid of the same object, or same class of objects. The first time I make a voyage to the West Indies, I am afraid; the tenth time, I am not;—why? not because my sensibility is blunted, but because my reason is instructed: I perceive there are much greater resources in skill and science, than I imagined; that the ship can ride with safety over those monstrous waves which at first bid fair to destroy; that an unctuous and weather-beaten personage, by turning a wheel near him, can guide the prodigious animal, in whose inside I am sailing, with the most unerring precision. It is not that I meet the same danger better, but that I have found out it is a much less danger. In almost all the instances where men encounter those perils to which they are accustomed, with greater resolution than at first, it is because they have found out new resources and methods, by which they may be opposed; or, because experience convinces them, the danger itself, independently of all methods of obviating it, was not so great as they had begun with supposing. Compassion is in favor of the rule; for it is always worn out where it is frequently exercised. It is quite impossible that a surgeon can feel much at an operation,—that a bookseller can have any very strong compassion for authors,—or that an overseer of the poor, who lives in the midst of misery, can care for it in a very lively manner. This is true in such extreme cases; but then, again, a certain degree of exercise rather increases the passion than diminishes it; for a man who had carefully stifled every emotion of compassion for half his life, would be ten times more unfeeling than he who had been over-stimulated by the too frequent contemplation of wretchedness. So that this fact, respecting compassion, contradicts the rule, as much as the other confirms it. Envy is perpetually and uniformly increased by habit; so is jealousy: by all that we have indulged in these two feelings, exactly in the same proportion are we likely to be affected by them again. So that I really can not comprehend how the rule can be true, stated in so very general a manner. Some passions are increased by habit, others are decreased by habit; others increased up to a certain point, then decreased. So that, in fact, there is no *general* rule about the matter; and the effect of habit must be learned in each particular passion. It seems as if the rule had been taken from the organs of the body, and applied to the passions of the mind. Mr. Stewart's principal inferences are all taken from the body; nor does he seem to doubt, but that they both follow the same law:—

"I shall have occasion afterward to show, in treating of our moral powers, that experience diminishes the influence of passive impressions on the mind, but strengthens our active principles. A course of debauchery deadens the sense of pleasure, but increases the desire of gratification. An immoderate use of strong liquors destroys the sensibility of the palate, but strengthens the habit of intemperance. The enjoyments we derive from any favorite pursuit, gradually decay as we advance in years: and yet we continue to prosecute our favorite pursuits with increasing steadiness and vigor.

"On these two laws of our nature is founded our capacity of moral improvement. In proportion as we are accustomed to obey our sense of duty, the influence of the temptation to vice is diminished; while at the same time, our habit of virtuous conduct is confirmed. How many passive impressions, for instance, must be overcome, before the virtue of beneficence can exert itself uniformly and habitually! How many circumstances are there in the distresses of others, which have a tendency to alienate our hearts from them, and which prompt us to withdraw from the sight of the miserable! The impressions we receive from these, are unfavorable to virtue: their force, however, every day diminishes; and it may, perhaps, by perseverance, be wholly destroyed. It is thus that the character of the beneficent man is formed. The passive impressions which he felt originally, and which counteracted his sense of duty, have lost their influence, and a habit of beneficence is become a part of his nature."*

It is clear from this passage, that Mr. Stewart conceives the same rule to obtain respecting the feelings of the body, and the feelings of the mind. The doctrine itself, he avows himself to have taken from Butler: it may be found in the 121st page of his "Analogy.' It may very likely be true; and in dissenting from such truly great authorities, I am only stating the nature and extent of my own ignorance: but it is better to do this candidly at once, than to subscribe to opinions, which, after all the attention I am capable of giving to them, appear to me to be wrong.

I remarked in my picture of Hobbes and his smoking, the pain the philosopher would have experienced if any circumstance had interrupted his habit. A very curious part of habit,—that though we feel *no pleasure* in doing the thing, we feel a great pain from *not* doing it: and the pain is not infrequently felt, before the cause is ascertained; you don't feel as you have been accustomed to feel; and, after some time, perceive that somebody is missing, whom you have been accustomed to see, or somebody or something present, which you have not been accustomed to see,—that you have left some insignificant thing behind you, which you always carried with you: the habitual current of your thoughts and actions has been interrupted, and you are awakened by the pain of that interruption, to examine into the cause.

Habit uniformly and constantly strengthens all our active exertions: whatever we do often, we become

* Stewart's Elements, p. 525.

more and more apt to do. A snuff-taker begins with a pinch of snuff per day, and ends with a pound or two every month. Swearing begins in anger; it ends by mingling itself with ordinary conversation. Such-like instances are of too common notoriety to need that they be adduced; but, as I before observed, at the very time that the tendency to do the thing is every day increasing, the pleasure resulting from it is, by the blunted sensibility of the bodily organ, diminished; and the desire is irresistible, though the gratification is nothing. There is rather an entertaining example of this in Fielding's "Life of Jonathan Wild," in that scene where he is represented as playing at cards with the Count, a professed gambler. "Such," says Mr. Fielding, "was the power of habit over the minds of these illustrious persons, that Mr. Wild could not keep his hands out of the Count's pockets, though he knew they were empty; nor could the Count abstain from palming a card, though he was well aware Mr. Wild had no money to pay him."

No reason that I know of, can be given, why the habit of having done a thing, should increase the tendency to do it: all reason stops at this point,—it is not possible to explain it. The pain annexed to the interruption of the habit is the means by which obedience to the law is secured. Nature is too good a legislator to pass any act without annexing a smart penalty to the violation of it.

There remains to notice the very little attention of mind, and the very little bodily exertion, with which all habitual actions are performed. A boy, at his first beginning to learn arithmetic, adds together a column of figures with the greatest difficulty, and with the greatest uncertainty: an expert arithmetician adds up the longest sum with the most unerring precision, and with as much rapidity almost as is required to advance his hand from the bottom to the top of the page.

Montaigne says, in his chapter on "Custom and Law," "I saw the other day, at my own house, a little fellow who came to show himself for money, a native of Nantes, born without arms, who has so well taught his feet to perform the services his hands should have done him, that indeed they have half forgot their natural office, and the use for which they were designed; the fellow, too, calls them his hands, and we may allow him to do so, for with them he cuts any thing, charges and discharges a pistol, threads a needle, sews, writes, and puts off his hat, combs his head, plays at cards and dice, and all this with as much dexterity as any other could do who had more and more proper limbs to assist him; and the money I gave him, he carried away in his foot, as we do in our hand. I have seen another, who, being yet a boy, flourished a two-handed sword, and (if I may so say) handled a halberd, with the mere motions and writhings of his neck and shoulders, for want of hands; tossed them into the air, and caught them again; darted a dagger; and cracked a whip, as well as any coachman in France."*

Every one, except Dr. Crotch, must remember the difficulty with which they first learned music. The correspondence between the note on the piano-forte and the note in the book was the first thing to be ascertained; then, that note is to be struck with a particular finger, with a particular degree of velocity; and if she should sing at the same time, all these are to be accompanied with certain inflections of the voice. The difficulty with which all this is done, the blunders which are made, and the slowness of the progress that is made at first, there can be no occasion I should describe, as there are so many here who must have felt it. At last, such is the astonishing facility acquired by habit, that there are many persons who will sit down to a glee which they have never seen before, play the bass with one hand, the treble with the other, and sing the third part; that is, read three different languages, and perform three different sets of actions at the same time: and this, with such little effort of faculty or of finger, that they shall have plenty of leisure to observe who comes in and goes out; who is dressed ill, who well; and to pursue the usual train of thought, which passes in our minds on such occasions: and though it be absolutely necessary that each musical note, and each key of the piano-

* Montaigne, vol. i. p. 133.

forte, must have been thought of by such a musician during the performance, they have passed through the mind with so much ease and rapidity, that it is impossible, or at least exceedingly difficult, to recall any of them. The reason of this astonishing facility, is partly to be explained by bodily, partly by mental causes. It proceeds from the strengthened association between the sign, and the thing signified: we read music with greater ease, and, the very instant we look at the note, and the musical line on which it is placed, know immediately to what part of the piano-forte the finger is to be carried. The other cause is merely a bodily cause: the actions of the fingers become associated together; and one finger having followed the other in a certain direction, follows it ever after with much more ease. To shake on the piano-forte is extremely difficult to beginners. However desirous any one may be of moving these two fingers rapidly, the muscles obey the decision of the will will with extreme difficulty; but when the respective motions of the two fingers are completely associated, so slight a determination of the will produces the desired effect, that it becomes difficult to recollect, the very moment after, that we have thought any thing about the matter. Just so in learning to walk, or in grown-up persons learning to skate; it requires a specific resolution to put one leg before another. A skater stands tottering and trembling in his slippery career; and when he has resolved which leg he will move the next, is obeyed by that leg in a very awkward, reluctant, and mutinous manner,—the very leg which, when it has acquired a great number of associated strains and postures, is to gain its master deathless reputation as a flying Mercury, and render him the envy and glory of the Serpentine.

It is impossible not to perceive in this analysis, which I have gone through, of the nature of habit, that powerful effect which it must exercise upon human happiness, by connecting the future with the present, and exposing us to do again that which we have already done. If we wish to know who is the most degraded, and the most wretched, of human beings;—if it be any object of curiosity in moral science, to gage the dimensions of wretchedness, and to see how deep the miseries of man can reach;—if this be any object of curiosity, look for a man who has practiced a vice so long, that he curses it and clings to it; that he pursues it, because he feels a great law of his nature driving him on toward it; but, reaching it, knows that it will gnaw his heart, and tear his vitals, and make him roll himself in the dust with anguish. Say every thing for vice which you can say,—magnify any pleasure as much as you please, but don't believe you can keep it; don't believe you have any secret for sending on quicker the sluggish blood, and for refreshing the faded nerve. Nero and Caligula, and all those who have had the vices and the riches of the world at their command, have never been able to do this. Yet you will not quit what you do not love; and you will linger on over the putrid fragments, and the nauseous carrion, after the blood, and the taste, and the sweetness are vanished away. But the wise toil, and the true glory of life, is, to turn all these provisions of nature—all these great laws of the mind—to good; and to seize hold of the power of habit, for fixing and securing virtue; for if the difficulties with which we begin, were always to continue, we might all cry out with Brutus,—"I have followed thee, O Virtue! as a real thing, and thou art but a name!" But the state which repays us, is that habitual virtue, which makes it as natural to a man to act right, as to breathe; which so incorporates goodness with the system, that pure thoughts are conceived without study, and just actions performed without effort: as it is the perfection of health, when every bodily organ acts without exciting attention; when the heart beats, and the lungs play, and the pulses flow, without reminding us that the mechanism of life is at work. So is it with the beauty of moral life! when man is just, and generous, and good, without knowing that he is practicing any virtue, or overcoming any difficulty: and the truly happy man, is he, who, at the close of a long life, has so changed his original nature, that he feels it an effort to do wrong; and a mere compliance with habit, to perform every great and sacred duty of life.

LECTURE XXVII.

ON HABIT.—PART II.

Before I proceed upon my present Lecture, I beg leave, in a very few words, to bring to your recollection the topics which I have dwelt upon in my last.

My first object was to show that habit was to action, what association is to thought; or, in other words, that it is *associated action*. I then divided habits into active, and passive: those things which we are prone to do, because we have done them; and those things which we are prone to suffer, because we have suffered them. In those passive impressions, produced upon the mind through the body, I endeavored to show that the sensibility of the bodily organ was materially impaired by repetition, but that this rule was by no means to be extended to the affections; that it was not generally true that *they* were weakened by habit. I noticed the pain consequent upon the interruption of habit; the uniform increase of active habits; and lastly, the diminished attention of mind; which latter circumstance I attributed, partly to the strengthened association of ideas, partly to the improved association of actions. This was the substance of my last Lecture; and I now go on to make those additional observations on habit, which I had not then time to comprehend in the discussion.

It has very often been asked when a habit begins to exist. There must be a period in its formation, when custom can have little or no influence, and when we have nothing but a temporary and casual motive for the performance of the action. When is the action habitual?—when not? What is the delicate and discriminating circumstance which decides you to call that mode of acting a *habit?* Nothing, for instance, is more common than to see persons beating the ground with their feet in any moment of vacancy of mind; and it easily degenerates into a habit: the first or second time after it is done, it can not be called a habit; is it so the tenth time? or when can the habit be fairly said to have established itself? It does not, I confess, appear to me to be by any means very difficult to answer this question. An active habit for any thing may be said to be formed, when we feel either a difficulty in not doing it, or a pain from its not being done; and when the principal cause for this pain, or difficulty, is, that we have done the thing often before. For instance, to recur to the previous example, you tap the floor with your foot; some one, who happens to be nervous, or indisposed, requests you to abstain: you very readily comply; and in five minutes, when the prohibition is out of your mind, begin again; and so on, perhaps, for three or four times. The proneness to do the thing, and the difficulty of *not* doing it, are here clear indications that the connection between the beating of the foot, and the vacant good-humored feeling of mind, is not in you merely casual and momentary, but that the one has the strongest disposition to produce the other; and the only cause that can be alledged *why* they should be connected, is, that they have been connected before. You see a person drinking out of a particular mug or tumbler:—put another in its place; if they both do equally well, of course there is no habit; but if the tumbler be missed, and the other complained of, it is clear that a habit is formed: there is a connection between the act of drinking, and the idea of that tumbler, which can not be separated without giving pain. Who could drink tea out of a wine-glass, or beer out of a tea-cup, or take up wine with a spoon? The displeasure that would ensue from separating the liquid and the particular kind of vessel in which it had been customarily conveyed, is a plain proof that the habit, in each particular case, is formed. In the same manner with passive habits. A passive habit may be said to be formed when the passive impression can not be separated without pain, or difficulty, from that which preceded it;

and when the principal cause of this pain or difficulty, is the mere circumstance of their having been connected. A man is habitually peevish,—that is, in his mind; the little crosses and accidents of life are not overlooked, but strongly associated with resentment: let him attempt to separate them,—let him endeavor to take a good-natured and forgiving view of human life; it costs him the greatest efforts, exposes him to the most mortifying failures, and is only to be acquired, at last, by very magnanimous resolution. The fish is not dressed to his liking, or a turkey comes to table when he had set his affections upon a goose. You immediately perceive a great deal of ill-temper; and whatever reasons there may be for hiding it, or whatever efforts may be made to hide it, it is still very visible. You say this man is *habitually* peevish, from the great difficulty he finds in separating the accidents of life from the acute malevolent feelings with which he has connected them; and for which difficulty,—as it is felt in a much less degree by the average of men,—no other reason can be given, than the previous indulgence of such sort of feelings. Every one might feel a little peevish at the accidents of life; and a slight difficulty might be universally experienced in attempting to check it; but the degree of that difficulty appears to be so much greater in such instances as I have mentioned, that we determine without scruple that they are to be referred to something more than the mere original tendency of nature; and that that *something more*, is *habit*.

The period of time in which a habit renews its action, or (if I may be allowed the expression) the orbit of a habit, is of very different dimensions. We may have a habit of shrugging up the shoulders every half-hour; or, of eating three eggs every morning; or, of dining at a club once a month; or, of going down to see a relation once a year: but it is difficult to conceive any habit forming itself for a period greater than a year. I can easily conceive that a person who set off on every 1st of June, to pay a visit, might have the force of habit added to his other inducements, and go, partly because he loved the persons, partly because he had done it before;

but is it easy to believe that there is a habit of doing any thing every other year? or, how very ridiculous it would sound for two persons to say, "We agreed a long time ago to dine together every Bissextile, or leap-year, and it is now grown into a perfect habit!" This limitation of habits to the period of a year,—which I by no means lay any great stress upon, but which has some degree of truth in it,—depends somewhat upon the revolution of names and appearances. To do any thing the first day of a month, or on one particular day every year, is to strengthen a habit by the recurrence of names or seasons; but if an action be performed every third or fourth year, the same name and the same appearances have occurred, without being connected with the same deed, and therefore the habit is impaired.

The strength of habit depends partly upon the length of its duration, partly upon the violence of the cause which gave it birth. Whoever had seen any person burned to death by accident, might probably acquire an habitual dread of fire, and would certainly acquire it very rapidly; because the deep impression of the original cause would multiply the number and increase the strength of the associations. The famous Isaac Barrow, the mathematician and divine, had an habitual dislike of dogs, and it proceeded from the following cause:—He was a very early riser; and one morning, as he was walking in the garden of a friend's house, with whom he was staying, a fierce mastiff, that used to be chained all day, and let loose all night, for the security of the house, set upon him with the greatest fury. The doctor caught him by the throat, threw him, and lay upon him; and, while he kept him down, considered what he should do in that exigence. The account the Doctor gave of it to his friends was, that he had once a mind to have killed the dog; but he altered his resolution upon recollecting that it would be unjust, since the dog only did his duty, and he himself was to blame for rambling out so early. At length he called out so loud, that he was heard by some in the house, who came out and speedily separated the mastiff and the mathematician. However, it is added, that the adventure gave the doctor a strong habitual aversion for dogs: and I dare say, if the truth were known, fixed in the dog's mind a still stronger aversion to doctors. It may be questioned whether any habits formed by the gradual accumulation of repeated facts, ever equal in power these deep marks left in the mind, by the rude and rapid inroads of passion.

No habit formed (if I may use the expression) against the stream, can ever be so strong as one that goes with it. It is natural to mankind to resent injuries; I don't say *commendable*, but *natural:* therefore, no habit of commanding resentment is so secure of remaining, as a habit of gratifying it. A habit of intemperance, is stronger than a habit of temperance; and whatever may be the time for which habits are laid aside, they are always more liable to be resumed, than any other train of actions: the road may be stopped up, and overgrown with brambles; and another road of much greater convenience opened in a contrary direction; but, in spite of all this, there is a prodigious tendency to move in the old track; and we are very frequently never satisfied till we get back to it.

Those persons are most liable to contract habits, either good or bad, whose lives are the most monotonous, and move on with the most complete uniformity. He who has lived in various countries, will have no national habits; in various parts of the same country, no provincial habits. If he have never been compelled to a particular line of occupation, he will have no professional habits; and if he have not voluntarily sunk into a sameness of existence, if he have seen many different circumstances, and done many different things, it is probable he will have no individual habits. Uniformity of occupation, is the cause both of bodily, moral and intellectual habits. It is very often easy enough to discover a military man by the general air and style of his behavior: he has put on one look, and done one thing, so often, that the habit sticks to him. There is a clerical air as well as a military air, from the same causes. Exactly in the same way, is there a style of understanding, a love of contention, and a perpetual affectation of wit, in lawyers, who have contracted the bad habits of their profession; and unrivaled vigor, quickness, and temper, in those who have availed themselves of the good. With equal diversities of occupation, those persons are, perhaps, the most likely to contract objectionable habits, who are prevented, by any cause, from reviewing and considering themselves; as absent men, very profound men, very busy men, very proud men. As bad habit implies associated action not common to the world at large, it will probably be most visible in those who are not accustomed to compare themselves much with others.

Men aware of the power of habit, escape its influence; and therefore, it is among the most trite principles of education to discover the particular habits to which we are exposed by situation and profession; and, when they are discovered, to resist them. Without any intentional efforts to resist professional habits, they are unconsciously resisted by the magnitude and variety of some men's minds; and by the liberal pursuits which they contrive to connect with their professions. There is an effect of custom and habit to which we are all extremely indebted, and that is, that it regulates every thing which nothing else regulates, where there is no propriety, and no duty, to be consulted. The reference is always to habit,—in dress, in ceremony, in equipage, in all the circumstances of life where almost any conduct would be virtuous, a compliance with custom is the only conduct that is wise, and a man of sense is rather pleased that the public legislate for him on points where choice would neither be easy nor useful. It is a strong mark of a good understanding, to allow custom an easy empire on these occasions. It is a much surer mark of talent, that men should rise above the influence of habit, and be better and greater than that to which the circumstances of their lives, or the character of their age, would appear to doom them. This is the reason why we admire men, who, born in poverty, and accustomed to objects of sense, have been able to conceive the dignity, the value, and the pleasure of intellectual gratification; who, deviating from every model they had seen, and guided only by their inward light, have steadily, and successfully, pursued the path of virtuous fame. By this subjugation of habitual thoughts, and escape from habitual objects, Bacon the friar, Czar Peter, Lord Verulam, and all great men, in law and in arts, have preceded the ages in which they lived, and become the beacons of future times. The mass of men, say whatever is said, do whatever is done, think whatever is thought, and can not easily conceive any thing greater and better than what is already created. But, in the grossest period of monastic ignorance, Bacon saw that the whole art of war might be changed by the invention of gunpowder; the Czar pulled down a nation habitually victorious, roused and elevated a people habitually stupid and depressed: Lord Verulam looked upon his own times with the same cool estrangement from the influence of habit, as if he were contemplating a nation of the ancient world; and was so little imposed upon by the imperfect philosophy which then prevailed, that he effected that entire revolution in physical reasoning, by which we are all benefited to the present hour. Such victories over present objects,—such power of reflecting, where attention is not stimulated by novelties,—are generally great triumphs of the human understanding, and decisive proofs of its vigor and excellence, in every individual instance where they are found. Whoever is learned in an ignorant age; whoever is liberal in a bigoted age; whoever is temperate and respectable in a licentious age; whoever is elegant and enlarged in his views, where his profession chains him down to technical rules and narrow limits; whoever has gained any good which habit opposes, or avoided any evil which habit might induce,—that man has vindicated the dignity and the power of his mind, by the fairest of all tests—by doing what the mass of mankind can not do.

There is no degree of disguise, or distortion, which human nature may not be made to assume from habit; it grows in every direction in which it is trained, and accommodates itself to every circumstance which caprice or design places in its way. It is a plant with such various aptitudes, and such opposite propensities, that it flourishes in a hot-house, or the open air; is terrestrial, or aquatic; parasitical, or independent; looks well in exposed situations, thrives in protected ones; can bear its own luxuriance, admits of amputation; succeeds in perfect liberty, and can submit to be bent down into any of the forms of art: it is so flexible and ductile, so accommodating and vivacious, that of two methods of managing it—completely opposite—neither the one nor the other need to be considered as mistaken and bad. Not that habit can give any new principle; but of those numerous principles which *do* exist in our nature, it entirely determines the order and the force. The horror of bodily pain is a very strong principle; but an American chief invites it. At the very moment that his body is burning, and his sinews snapping asunder in the flames, he tells his murderers that they are quite ignorant of the science of tormenting; that if they were bound to the stake instead of him, he would torment them with much more ingenious and exquisite cruelty than they have employed against him: he never for an instant bewails his fate, or seems to look upon it as extraordinary; it is the end that he has looked to habitually, and he has from his earliest infancy reared up a fabric of magnanimous courage to endure it. What feeling more powerful than the love of life! A Spartan soldier, however, combed his hair, set up a song, and in a very few minutes was no more. An Indian widow burns herself to death, from etiquette. Who could imagine that men and women would shut themselves up in monasteries, and nunneries, living the absurd life which they do, in such sort of places?—yet, the greater part of nuns and friars, who came over here, immediately shut out the daylight of common sense, and fell to forming nunneries and monasteries again.

The Indian settlement in Paraguay, formed by the Jesuits, is among the most curious victories of habit over the ordinary propensities of nature. It presents the curious spectacle of several millions of human creatures leading the life of school-boys; all desire of power, all love of property, swallowed up in a blind and habitual obedience to the Jesuits. One village was exactly a model for the manners and customs of another. At a certain hour, all the nation was put to work; in the middle of the day, they dined by ring of bell; and in the same way, were sent to bed by the curfew. It is an instance quite equal, in point of singularity, to any thing that is told of the power of habit among the Spartans. In like manner, there is not a single principle of our nature, which may not be cherished to the complete exclusion and subjugation of the rest.

Such deeply-rooted habits have so much the air and appearance of nature, that many men have doubted whether it is not absurd to speak at all of the moral nature of man; whether what we call the trammels of the Chinese and the Hindoo, are not as natural a state of existence as the comparative liberty of thinking and acting enjoyed in Europe. What is the fact with respect to these former nations? One or two of the principles of our nature, has, by the help of education and religion, gained an ascendency over all the rest. The Turk does not cultivate letters, and acquire knowledge. Why? Not because he does not feel that same principle of novelty which has impelled us, but because other principles of his nature have been unduly strengthened, to the destruction of that principle: his pride, as applied to the Mohammedan religion; his contempt, as applied to Europeans: which makes him imagine that every thing worth knowing is to be found in the Koran; and which makes him averse to receive instruction from those whom he looks upon to be so far beneath him. A Hindoo is of the same trade as his father: and so it has gone on for centuries. Why? Not because the son of a Hindoo tradesman may not have talents and feelings to rouse him to something better; but because the whole force of law and religion have been directed to cherish the principles of imitation and obedience, to the exclusion of all others. In the same manner, a sincere Quaker does not fight;—not because he wants the element of resentment from nature, but because he has taken care to choke and overlay it. Therefore, as all men acquire very early the same active powers, and impelling principles, it is fair to say that that people is in the most natural state, where all those principles are developed; and where one or two leading principles do not operate to the complete exclusion and subjugation of the rest. A Spartan, who cared nothing about his wife, or his children, and merely thought of the more extended relation of country, was not in a natural state of mind. The principle was natural, but not natural in that *degree*. A head is natural, but a disproportionate head is not. Wherever any one of the few great principles of our nature is missing, or wherever any one of them operates in a whole people, to the exclusion of the rest, it is an abuse of terms to speak of that as a state of nature. Outward nature is an upright body, endowed with life and strength, and capable of motion: there must be the hand for grasping, and the leg for moving, and the foot for support. Inward nature is grief, joy, resentment, the love of power, the love of esteem, the love of possession, and all the great feelings which I have been so long endeavoring to describe: if the greater part of these are exhausted and destroyed, the remnant may be nature, but it is nature abridged in principle, and mutilated in form.

The mere body itself, independent of any influence of mind, is acted on by habit. Opium, and every kind of medicine, loses its effects by habit. The body of a Russian is not injured by rolling in the snow, after he comes out of a warm bath. So very much is the body the creature of habit, that it not only must have all the feelings it has been accustomed to, but have them precisely in the same order of time. Wine is drunk at dinner, and tea at breakfast: they both agree perfectly well with the body, taken in this order of time; but many delicate constitutions would be seriously indisposed by attempting to change the order of these habits: for it is not enough to say, nature is accustomed to these things; Nature is so punctilious, that she has settled, one thing must be done at one hour, and another at another; and you can not at first violate it with impunity. There is no doubt but that, by degrees, a person would accustom himself to walk for an hour in the open air without either coat or waistcoat; but if he had done that for many years at a particular hour, he could not change that hour with impunity: he might do so between nine and ten with safety, if that was his hour; but it does not at all follow, that he could do the same thing between two and three. The body might have prepared itself, and would have prepared itself, for an exposure to unusual cold at the first hour, but by no means be ready for it at the second. The degree to which the power of habit may be carried in the body, has hardly been ascertained. There are some very remarkable instances of it, however, in birds. The eagle and the hawk have been brought to live upon bread and milk; and the dove upon raw flesh: this, I believe, was done by Spallanzani. In the same manner, we may observe individuals of the vegetable tribe accommodate themselves to different situations; to soil, climate, and the state of cultivation. These variations may be daily seen, by examining the plant as it grows on the mountains, in the valleys, in the garden, or the field; or by bringing it from a rude, uncultivated state, when it sometimes lays aside its prickles, and changes the color and structure of its flowers. The apple-trees which are sent from England to New England, blossom at first too early for the climate, and bear no fruit; and it is only after some years, that they conform themselves to their new situation. The design of this accommodating principle, is to fit both the plant and the animal for a more extensive and varied range of existence. Habit has the same effect in the history of man. It is by habit that he is enabled to support himself in every diversity of situation, in which he is thrown by the ever-changing scene of human life: he is neither surfeited by abundance, nor exhausted by penury; but contracts with a cottage, and expands with his palace; preserving, in either extreme, that calm level of feeling to which habit at length reduces every human passion. The grief which convulses, and threatens to destroy,—the wildest tumults of joy,—are brought down to the common standard; the fiercest enemies embrace, the bitterest contentions cease; every deficiency supplied, every irregularity brought to order, every elevation laid low, by the silent and unnoticed operation of this great principle. It is, in fact, *habit,* which alone neutralizes the passions, and deadens their stupendous powers.

> "Ni faciat, maria ac terras cœlumque profundum
> Quippe ferant rapidi secum verrantque per auras."

Without it, we should sink under the first emotion of sorrow or of joy; and it is only from the protecting influence of habit that we are safely intrusted with such tremendous agents.

A beautiful effect of habit is, that it endows with preternatural strength every quality of the mind or heart which it calls into more than ordinary action. If protection is wanted, men are ready, long *habituated* to the fear of death. If gentleness and benevolence are wanted to lessen the miseries of life, women are *habitually* gentle and benevolent. If patient industry, you have it in the laborer, and the mechanic. What but the power of habit, has given to us the advantage of those fine legal understandings, that have gradually formed the system of law in this country? How are our naval victories gained, but by *habitual* character, skill, and courage? Whence the effusions of eloquence every day to be witnessed in the senate, but by that intrepidity, self-possession, and command of words and images, which habit only can confer? Fresh, youthful, untaught nature can *never* do such things as these. It is nature in its *manhood,* instructed by failure, fortified by precedent, confirmed by success, *riveted by habit,* and carried to a pitch of glory, by intense adhesion to one object, which, with all the primary efforts of its rude vigor, it never could have reached; diminishing the pleasure of vice, and strengthening the *habit* of virtue.

These are the principal observations which I have to make on the nature of habit; and with them I conclude my Lectures on the Passions.

I am conscious how very imperfectly I have treated the subject: but it is of great difficulty; one, in which very little assistance is to be gained from books, and to which, if ever I repeat these Lectures again—(as some years hence it may most probably be my lot to do)—I may, perhaps, do more justice, than I have been able to do at present. One principal object in my Lectures has been perpetually to refer to the very simple and beautiful origin of the passions, and to show, that however mixed and disguised, they all take their rise from pleasure and from pain. We are born with sensibility alone; and to that cause is every feeling of our nature to be traced. The moment that Providence ordained man to feel pleasure and pain from the objects which surrounded him, and connected the impressions of his mind by association, at that moment the passions were created, and the mind subjected to that variety of active principles, by which it is at present impelled. That I have not been doing a useless thing, and that it is important to examine those active principles, and to throw all the light which we can upon the theory of the passions, no man of reflection will, I presume, be inclined to deny. The passions are in morals, what motion is in physics: they create, preserve, and animate; and without them, all would be silence and death. Avarice guides men across the deserts of the ocean; pride covers the earth with trophies, and mausoleums, and pyramids; love turns men from their savage rudeness; ambition shakes the very foundations of kingdoms. By the love of glory, weak nations swell into magnitude and strength. Whatever there is of terrible, whatever there is of beautiful in human events, all that shakes the soul to and fro, and is remembered while thought and flesh cling together,—all these have their origin from the passions. As it is only in storms, and when their coming waters are driven up into the air, that we catch a sight of the depths of the sea, it is only in the season of perturbation that we have a glimpse of the real internal nature of man. It is then only, that the might of these eruptions shaking his frame, dissipate all the feeble coverings of opinion, and rend in pieces that cobweb veil, with which fashion hides the feelings of the heart. It is then only that Nature speaks her genuine feelings; and, as at the last night of Troy, when Venus illumined the darkness, Æneas saw the gods themselves at work,—so may we, when the blaze of passion is flung upon man's nature, mark in him the signs of a celestial origin, and tremble at the invisible agents of God!

Look at great men in critical and perilous moments, when every cold and little spirit is extinguished: their passions always bring them out harmless; and at the very moment when they *seem* to perish, they emerge into greater glory. Alexander, in the midst of his mutinous soldiers; Frederick of Prussia, combating against the armies of three kingdoms; Cortes, breaking in pieces the Mexican empire:—their passions led all these great men to fix their attention strongly upon the objects of their desires; they saw them under aspects unknown to, and unseen by common men, and which enabled them to conceive and execute those hardy enterprises, deemed rash and foolish, till their wisdom was established by their success. It is in fact the great passions alone which enable men to distinguish between what is difficult and what is impossible: a distinction always confounded by merely *sensible* men; who do not even *suspect* the existence of those means, which men of genius employ to effect their object. It is only passion which gives a man that high enthusiasm for his country, and makes him regard it as the only object worthy of human attention;—an enthusiasm, which to common eyes appears madness and extravagance; but which always creates fresh powers of mind, and commonly insures their ultimate success. In fact, it is only the great passions, which, tearing us away from the seductions of indolence, endow us with that continuity of attention, to which alone superiority of mind is attached. It is to their passions, alone, under the providence of God, that nations must trust, when perils gather thick about them, and their last moments seem to be at hand. The history of the world shows us that men are not to be counted by their numbers, but by the fire and vigor of their passions; by their deep sense of injury; by their memory of past glory; by their eagerness for fresh fame; by their clear and steady resolution of ceasing to live, or of achieving a particular object, which, when it is *once* formed, strikes off a load of manacles and chains, and gives free space to all heavenly and heroic feelings. All great and extraordinary actions come from the heart. There are seasons in human affairs, when qualities fit enough to conduct the common business of life, are feeble and useless; and when men must trust to emotion, for that safety which reason at such times can never give. These are the feelings which led the ten thousand over the Carduchian mountains; these are the feelings by which a handful of Greeks broke in pieces the power of Persia: they have, by turns, humbled Austria, reduced Spain; and in the fens of the Dutch, and on the mountains of the Swiss, defended the happiness, and revenged the oppressions, of man! God calls all the passions out in their keenness and vigor, for the present safety of mankind. Anger, and revenge, and the heroic mind, and a readiness to suffer:—all the secret strength, all the invisible array, of the feelings,—all that nature has reserved for the great scenes of the world. For the usual hopes, and the common aids of man, are all gone! Kings have perished, armies are subdued, nations moldered away! Nothing remains, under God, but those passions which have often proved the best ministers of His vengeance, and the surest protectors of the world.

THE END.

www.ingramcontent.com/pod-product-compliance
Lightning Source LLC
LaVergne TN
LVHW020118110826
845151LV00001B/192

* 9 7 8 1 4 2 5 5 4 2 7 6 4 *